Anne
of Austria

Queen of France

ANNE D'AUTRICHE REINE DE FRANCE 1622

Anne of Austria, by Daniel Dumoustier, 1622. Cabinet des Estampes, Bibliothèque Nationale, Paris. By courtesy of the Bibliothèque Nationale.

Anne
of Austria

Queen of France

Ruth
Kleinman

Ohio State
University Press
Columbus

B
An74k

Library of Congress Cataloguing in Publication Data

Kleinman, Ruth, 1929–
    Anne of Austria, Queen of France, 1601–1666
    Bibliography: p.
    Includes index.
    1. Anne, Queen, consort of Louis XIII, King of France,
1601–1666. 2. France—History—Louis XIII, 1610–1643.
3. France—History—Louis XIV, 1643–1715. 4. France—
Queens—Biography. I. Title.
DC124.K55   1985   944′.032′0924 [B]   85-15453
ISBN 0-8142-0389-2

For my loved ones

CONTENTS

Preface

WIFE OF LOUIS XIII, MOTHER OF LOUIS XIV AND REGENT FOR HIM during his youth, she deserves to be called Anne of France rather than Anne of Austria. Her mother had come from Austria to marry Philip III of Spain, but Anne herself had never seen that land. Why the French named her as they did is not clear. The appellation, however, underlines the fact that she never quite lost her alien status in the eyes of many of her subjects and, indeed, in the eyes of most French historians since.

From historians Anne has had mixed notice, much of it less revealing about her than about their own political preoccupations and historical tastes, or about the changing fashions in historiography. Before the French Revolution, she was taken for granted as an ancestress of the royal family, and little attention was paid to her. She hardly figured in accounts of the reign of Louis XIV, and even Father Griffet, in his detailed history of the reign of Louis XIII, treated her marginally.[1] It is true that memoirs by her contemporaries were gradually being published in the eighteenth century, but she occupied a central role in only one work, the memoirs of her attendant and friend Madame de Motteville.[2] Madame de Motteville's memoirs were almost a biography of Anne, consisting largely of Motteville's observations and recollections of the queen's actions from 1643 to the queen's death in January 1666. The lady had a tendency to moralize, and also nourished some solid prejudices, most notably against Anne's first minister, Cardinal Mazarin. On the other hand, she worshiped Anne and, with the queen's permission, kept notes on the queen's remarks. Despite her prejudices and preferences, therefore, Madame de Motteville can be reasonably trusted to have reported accurately whatever Anne actually said to her. Although Madame de Motteville thus had produced at least the raw material for a biography, for the time being none appeared: Anne's life held no appeal for Enlightenment writers.

It was different after the French Revolution, when royalists as well as republicans began to mine history for justification; when history itself was being discovered as a tool at once for expressing and for molding nationality. Then the raw materials came to be valued, and early in the nineteenth century, editors began great series to publish or republish historical memoirs, including Madame de Motteville's.

But the past had to be not only made available, it had to be reevaluated. In the first half of the nineteenth century, no one did that on a grander scale, or more colorfully and persuasively, than Jules Michelet.[3] He took it as his mission to show the history of the French people: the people, not their kings. About kings—particularly the Bourbon kings, who had constructed royal absolutism—he had little good to say. When he came to Anne of Austria, however, "our Spanish queen," vituperation knew no bounds. He depicted her as weak, narrow-minded, ignorant, fat, lazy, and vain; accused her of adultery and claimed Cardinal Mazarin was the father of her second son, on no evidence except that the boy was "Italian" in his mind and morals.[4] Worst of all, according to Michelet, after Louis XIII's death Anne became "the female king" who mismanaged everything and precipitated civil war because she gave herself and the state into the hands of Mazarin, "that Italian clown."[5] As far as Michelet could see, her only merit had been to bring some vigorous blood into the royal house.[6] The clue to Michelet's passion lay in his comment on the civil war, the Fronde, that Anne and Mazarin not only weathered but put down: "The *Fronde*, on the whole, was the war of the honest people against the rogues."[7] He took the Fronde as a preview of the Revolution, and could not forgive the "rogues," that is, the supporters of royal absolutism, for having won.

Michelet's negative assessment of Anne's and Mazarin's work did not go unchallenged. National pride became more important than revolutionary fervor, and among the next generation of historians, Adolphe Chéruel cast a new light on the period of Anne's regency, the Fronde, and the ministry of Mazarin.[8] Chéruel combed the archives for documents and correspondence, particularly Mazarin's diplomatic and political correspondence, that he was editing. He concluded that it had been the *frondeurs* who were the rogues, that Anne and Mazarin between them had saved the monarchy and national unity, and that Mazarin's continuation of Richelieu's foreign policy assured French dominance in Europe and prepared a glorious future for the kingdom.

By and large, this view of Mazarin's contribution became the standard one. Mazarin's and Anne's reputations were therefore rehabilitated to some extent, with the reservation that they had done very well considering they were foreigners, and that Anne, being a woman, had played a mostly passive part. Consequently there seemed to be little need for a serious biography of her, and in fact only one book appeared that could remotely fit the category: Capefigue's *Anne d'Au-*

triche, reine-régente, et la minorité de Louis XIV,[9] in essence an addendum to his earlier *Richelieu, Mazarin, la Fronde et le règne de Louis XIV*.[10] *Anne d'Autriche* was a short work, and, like its predecessor, its chief claim to distinction was that the author had taken the trouble to include some documents from the Spanish archives, though in a very unsystematic way. Capefigue's effort may have inspired an Englishwoman, Martha Walker Freer, to bring out *The Regency of Anne of Austria*,[11] an undistinguished book based apparently on secondary materials.

What caught the imagination of the reading public about Anne was not politics but romance, thanks to the historical novel by Alexandre Dumas, *Les Trois Mousquetaires*.[12] Although she was not the heroine, her troubles—an unhappy marriage, a frustrated love affair with the English duke of Buckingham, persecution by her husband's minister Cardinal Richelieu—furnished the occasion for the plot. Dumas had discovered the mainspring of his action in a dubious incident reported in La Rochefoucauld's memoirs,[13] but readers did not worry over its historical accuracy. The image of the beautiful and unfortunate young queen proved so appealing that it received a new incarnation as late as 1937 in Meriel Buchanan's semifictional *Anne of Austria, the Infanta-Queen*.[14]

In France, meanwhile, the recipe for successful books about Anne of Austria was set: a combination of Dumas's romantic vision and the scandals spread by Michelet. In succession there appeared Robiquet's *Le Coeur d'une reine: Anne d'Autriche, Louis XIII et Mazarin*,[15] La Varende's *Anne d'Autriche, femme de Louis XIII, 1601–1666*,[16] Herbillon's *Anne d'Autriche, reine, mère, régente*,[17] Saint-Félix's *La Reine stérile*,[18]—all anecdotal and more or less insubstantial. The latest in the series is Madame Claude Dulong's *Anne d'Autriche, mère de Louis XIV*,[19] a retelling of all the familiar stories and innuendoes.

The one thing missing from the literature is a picture of Anne as she was: a woman who had faults but who also had the strength to survive difficult circumstances, to go beyond what she had been taught, and to adopt a new allegiance. That is the woman this book will attempt to present. It is true that she did not usually act directly or independently in politics, or spend her time reading dispatches—she was not trained for it. Her upbringing had fitted her to be a royal wife and mother, not a queen ruling in her own right; and when she had to act in political matters, she was content to act through men. But biology itself can become a political matter, and in her love for her firstborn son, she learned to take advice, overcome old prejudices, and give up old loyalties, all for the sake of handing on to him intact the state his father had left him.

Admittedly it is not easy to study a person who rarely committed her thoughts or feelings to paper, but it is not impossible. A political biography is out of the question for lack of direct evidence. Until her husband's death, she was kept in the background; and although she seems to have been a more or less aware participant in various conspiracies, we have little more than speculations about the extent of her involvement. When Anne became regent in 1643, she did have an overt political role, but then she entrusted business to Mazarin and moreover kept no record of her daily conferences with him. Like many, if not most, women of her time, Anne lived by the spoken, not the written, word. The masses of official letters sent out over her signature tell us nothing about her, since she probably did not read most of them and had the secretary of her hand sign them. That leaves a few notes to various people, including Richelieu, transcripts of some of her secret letters to her friends and to her brother Ferdinand during the 1630s, and a dozen of her confidential letters to Mazarin as survivors of a personal correspondence that was not large to begin with. However, although none of this material is unknown, except for the letters to Mazarin it has not been fully exploited. Moreover, in France the Archives Nationales, the manuscript collection of the Bibliothèque Nationale, the Archives du Ministère des Relations Extérieures, and in Spain the Archivo General de Simancas contain documents that have been used superficially or not at all: her father's instructions when she was about to leave Spain for France, deliberations of the Spanish royal council, intelligence reports, sets of household accounts, to mention a few. Cardinal Mazarin's memoranda books, though they do not record the decision-making process, do offer insights into Anne's political education, and have not been consulted for that purpose in well over a century. The testimony of memoirs continues to be important, especially the memoirs of Madame de Motteville, if sifted judiciously. And lastly there is one source that has been completely neglected with respect to Anne of Austria, namely, the *Gazette de France*. The *Gazette*, from its inception in 1631 to Anne's death in 1666, published increasingly detailed reports of the queen's occupations, pastimes, and travels. During the Fronde these reports thinned out at times, and in general it is necessary to use the *Gazette* with caution because it was a semiofficial organ, took an adulatory stance, and left much unsaid. As a simple chronicle of events, however, it is invaluable. The pamphlet literature of the Fronde on the other hand—the so-called *Mazarinades*, directed against Anne as well as against Mazarin—is a source only for the issues of the Fronde and the techniques of the *frondeurs*. Contrary to what Michelet believed, the pamphlets did not reveal valid truths about either the queen or Mazarin.

The work of other historians has been of great help to me, and my debt to particular authors is acknowledged both in the footnotes and the bibliography. Special acknowledgement, however, is in order for permission to use the resources, and for the generous assistance of the staff, of the Archives Nationales, the Archives du Ministère des Relations Extérieures, the Bibliothèque Nationale, the Bibliothèque Mazarine, and the Archivo General de Simancas. Thanks also go to the Columbia University Libraries, which functioned as home base, to the New York Public Library and the Boston Public Library, to the interlibrary loan services of Brooklyn College and of Princeton University. In addition I am indebted to M. Daniel Alcouffe, of the Musée du Louvre, for having shown me Anne's summer apartments at a time when they were not open to the public because remodeling was in progress.

It would have been impossible to write this book without stretches of free time made available by an individual research grant from the National Endowment for the Humanities, as well as a fellowship leave and a special leave of absence from Brooklyn College. I express my gratitude to these institutions, and also to the Research Foundation of the City University of New York for an emergency grant of funds for the processing of microfilm.

Colleagues have been extremely generous with their time and with helpful comments, notably: Elizabeth W. Marvick, who read a sizeable portion of the manuscript; Georges Dethan, chief librarian of the Ministère des Relations Extérieures, who shared with me some of his insights into the period and into Mazarin's career, as well as several letters I had not located in the archives of the ministry, and also read a chapter; Madeleine Laurain-Portemer, who talked to me about her work on Mazarin; A. Lloyd Moote, who read several chapters; and John H. Elliott, who drew my attention to references of which I had been unaware. Any shortcomings in the book are, of course, my own.

Warm thanks are also due Florine C. Ferns, who patiently typed and retyped the manuscript. And it is with special gratitude that I thank René C. Mastrovito, and particularly Paula S. Fichtner, for having seen me through the rough spots, of which there were many.

Anne
of Austria

Queen of France

Chapter One

The Infanta Doña Ana

ON A CHILLY DAY IN NOVEMBER 1615, a young bride stood on the left bank of the Bidassoa, waiting to step into a gaily decorated boat. The lace ruff around her throat set off the rounded oval of her face and her closely curled blond hair, and her golden gown caught the light as the trailing sleeves and wide skirts moved in the breeze. Her father had chosen the dress, cloth of gold striped with blue, because blue was the favorite color of her husband, the most Christian king Louis XIII of France, whose realm she would enter on the other side of the river. The bride was the infanta Doña Ana Maria Mauricia of Spain.[1]

Philip III, her father, had given her his farewell blessing in Fuenterrabía that morning. He had been moved to tears at parting from his favorite daughter, and she also had wept, both knowing that they were not likely to meet again in life. But now on the riverbank, Doña Ana was composed, as a queen should be, while around her a thousand people milled in the confusion of impending embarkation and leave-taking. She had been looking forward to this moment for three years. In preparation for her new life, she had learned a little French, though in most other respects her training had been concentrated on what was desirable for any girl: a religious upbringing to make her a good Christian, a dutiful wife, and a conscientious mother. As a king's daughter, moreover, she had early learned all the social arts of royalty: gracious greeting according to rank, presiding in company, and maintaining dignity and self-possession. More specific education for her future career she had none, and she knew nothing of practical politics. From her mother's power struggle with her father's favorite friend and minister, the duke of Lerma, she might have observed that the path of a queen did not always lie smoothly. Her mother's example may not have been in her mind, however, as she waited to cross into France, no longer to be the infanta Doña Ana but Queen Anne. To onlookers she seemed confident, even eager. Having been much loved and feeling assured of her importance as a princess of Spain, the greatest monarchy in the world, it was natural for her to expect to meet affection and deference in France as at home. She was fourteen years of age and had much to learn.

Anne had been born on 22 September 1601, the anxiously awaited first child of Philip III and Margaret of Austria. Court chroniclers reported that from her first days she was as well formed and pretty as a year-old,[2] perhaps an exaggerated compliment. If Anne's parents felt any disappointment at having a daughter instead of a son, no one recorded it. Princesses were eligible for the Spanish royal succession; besides, other children would follow by the grace of God, and meanwhile there was much joy in Spain over the birth of this first one.

Five days later, on 27 September, it was the turn of France to rejoice: after half a century of barrenness in the royal house when the crown had to pass from brother to brother to cousin, Henri IV's queen Marie de Medici was delivered of a son and heir to the throne. Guns saluted, the *Te Deum* was chanted in churches, and citizens set up fountains of wine and decorated their houses to welcome the dauphin, the future Louis XIII. At last there would be an end to problems of succession and threats of civil war between princes related to the royal house. Henri IV's elation knew no bounds, and for months letters and embassies of congratulation arrived from all the courts of Europe. Between Paris and Madrid, of course, the congratulations were mutual, as were speculations about the infants' destinies.

Contemporaries found the proximity of Anne's and Louis's birth dates striking. Within a few years, astrologers claimed the children were sure to be bound by a special tie, if not marriage then at least extraordinary affection.[3] The astrologers lagged behind the diplomats, however. Before Louis was a year old, the Spanish ambassador in Paris, Hieronimo de Taxis, spoke unofficially of a double wedding: Louis would be married to Anne, and the children the queens of France and Spain were currently expecting would marry each other. Taxis was sure the queen of Spain would have a son this time, and the queen of France a daughter.[4] Louis's attendants for their part joked with him regularly about his bride-to-be, the infanta, as though the matter was quite settled; indeed, they never joked in that way about any other princess. The matter was far from settled though. Royal children often had their marriages arranged in their cradles, but marriage projects, like all diplomatic negotiations, were subject to changes brought by time, circumstance, and shifting calculations of advantage. In the case of Louis and Anne, Taxis proved to have been a true prophet, although his prophecy took a decade to be realized. Meanwhile the children grew up, each in its own world of family, courtiers, and customs.

We do not know whether Anne's household talked to her about the French match. Her maids may well have dangled this or another splendid destiny before her eyes, but it is not likely that her mother permitted the liberty of speech in which Louis's people indulged. It was not considered fitting for a girl child to fix her imagination on any young man unless her marriage contract had been signed and the man was her promised husband. Such was the modesty prescribed by religion as well as by manners, and Anne's mother, Margaret of Austria, was a very religious woman. Margaret herself came from a household noted for its piety. She was a daughter of Archduke Charles of Styria and his wife Maria of Bavaria.[5] At home in Graz, Archduchess Maria had personally supervised all her children's religious education, taken them to the chapel to pray before hearing mass, encouraged them to carry food to the poor and to visit hospitals, and concluded each day with family prayers. All clergy and monastic orders were honored at the archducal court, but the Jesuits enjoyed special influence and consideration, and it was the spirituality they adapted to lay life that made itself felt in the children's religious training. Altogether the family in Graz was a model of post-Tridentine piety.

When Margaret at fifteen went to Spain to marry Philip III, she took a Jesuit confessor with her, Father Richard Haller. According to Spanish custom, the Franciscans had the privilege of providing the queen's confessor. Although Margaret was docile in every other way, and anxious to conform to what was expected of her in her new home, she steadfastly refused to accept a Franciscan friar. She lied: she said she did not know the language well enough to confess herself in Spanish, and kept Father Haller to direct her conscience and advise her for the rest of her short life. She favored the Jesuit order in Spain, as her parents had done in Styria, and took great interest in the canonization of the society's founder, Ignatius Loyola. That was not the limit of her spiritual inclinations, however. She showed an extraordinary veneration for relics and saints, whether Austrian, Italian, or Spanish; and her library included works of Saint Teresa of Avila, Saint Luis of Granada, and Saint John of God, among others. She was charitable, especially in her concern for wounded veterans, and spent much time visiting convents and counted nuns her closest friends.

Other trustworthy friends she had none, for as soon as she arrived at court, she found herself isolated by her husband's favorite, the duke of Lerma, who did not intend to share his influence with any rival, not even a wife. Margaret wrote home to Graz that Philip was good to her and treated her lovingly; nevertheless, he took a long time to trust her

and respect her judgment. Lerma fomented misunderstandings between husband and wife and, when that failed, carried Philip off on
long hunting parties and trips to country palaces. Lerma's enemies
were the queen's supporters; to one of them, Margaret cried out, "Pity
me, for I do not possess my husband's heart."[6] Neither did she possess
any power over court appointments, whether in her own household or
the households of her children. Such offices went to the duke's relatives or clients, and Lerma put his own sister, the countess of Altamira,
in charge of the nursery establishment set up for the Infanta Doña Ana
and her future brothers and sisters.

It was normal for royal children to have a separate household, with
governesses, governors, doctors, clergy, nurses, maids, valets, cooks,
and lesser attendants. Princes and princesses at any court saw their
parents on ceremonial occasions and on daily formal visits if they
happened to be staying in the same palace. If the children spent most
of their time away from court, for the sake of better air and tranquillity,
the visits to mother and father were correspondingly rarer. Parents'
preferences could change the protocol, however. Lerma's watchful-
ness notwithstanding, Margaret followed the example her own
mother had set and personally supervised her children's prayers and
religious training. Philip could have prevented this if he had wished
to, but he had great reverence for religion himself, and respected his
wife's devotion to maternal duty. Besides, he too enjoyed the society
of his children. As each year brought the birth of another prince or
princess, family feeling gradually lessened Philip's attachment to
Lerma and increased his confidence in Margaret. Anne consequently
saw more of her parents, and particularly of her mother, than might
have been expected by ordinary custom. Two things at least she must
have learned at her mother's knee: reliance on the pillar of religion,
and resistance to royal favorites. For Margaret resisted Lerma, not only
in her quiet pursuit of religion and family life, but by open confrontation in the Council of Castile. Had Margaret lived longer, she might
well have induced her husband to take on more personal responsibility for government and curtail Lerma's power. Spaniards, at any rate,
credited her with the ability to accomplish these things, and mourned
her sincerely when she died in October 1611, from complications
after childbirth.

Anne and her brother, the crown prince, were old enough to grieve
for their mother. It was reported that they both felt extreme sorrow,
though their sorrow was no more extreme than their father's. Philip III
almost a decade later still reminded his daughter of the anniversary of

her mother's death, when he wrote to her saying she would note what day this was and that he was well aware of it also.[7] For the rest of Anne's life during her early years, there is very little evidence. Neither her governess nor anyone belonging to the royal household kept any diary or record of her daily activities. Indeed, Spanish princesses were seldom seen, at least by the public or by foreigners, and they were rarely talked about.

At one point, when Anne was just turning seven, the Venetian ambassador reported to his superiors that Anne had a remarkable charm and wit and that she said and did such apt things that she was the admiration of her governess and the joy of her parents.[8] He did not receive this information from firsthand observation however. Even the French ambassadors who were negotiating her marriage saw Anne only on rare occasions. Whenever she was permitted to receive them in audience, they would report home how she looked and what pretty and charming things she said.[9] Since it was, however, a question of impressing the French court, it must be supposed that at least some of the pretty things she said had been rehearsed and did not necessarily afford true insight into her mind or character.

The accounts of her appearance as a child are not very adequate either. The ambassadors were most anxious, of course, to confirm that she was in good health, sound of limb, and growing satisfactorily. For the rest their remarks were unspecific. They thought she surpassed the portrait of her that had been sent to Paris; that in fact the portrait did not do her justice although it had been greatly admired when it had been received. That portrait has disappeared, but the Instituto Valencia de Don Juan in Madrid has a picture of her standing with her brother, the future Philip IV, both children formally dressed like miniature adults. It is difficult to judge her age. Since she is shown wearing a coronet, however, the picture probably dates from a time after her betrothal in 1612 when she was already being addressed and treated as a queen. She would have been about eleven or twelve, thirteen at most. If the painting can be taken as true to life, Anne was a very self-possessed girl, dark blond, with green eyes set well apart under level brows and her lower lip slightly prominent. It is a charming face in its way, though in this particular picture also exceedingly solemn.

Undeniably Anne was a pretty princess, and it is easy to understand the dismay that was felt both in Madrid and in Paris when at the end of 1613 she caught smallpox. Bulletins sped from Spain to France about the course of her disease and the progress she was making, and it was with a universal sigh of relief that her attendants noted at the beginning of the New Year that she would have no pockmarks on her face because she had been careful not to scratch herself or even touch her skin. Vaucelas, the French resident ambassador, tried to make sure of this by requesting an audience with her as soon as she was sufficiently recovered, though in the end his wife saw the princess before he did.[10] The eyewitness report was satisfactory, however. This seems to have been the only major illness of Anne's childhood, except for having some teeth pulled.[11] Indeed, her robust good health was to be characteristic of her throughout most of her life.

Her routine in the years before and after her betrothal may be inferred from the occupations her father described in his letters to her after her marriage.[12] He faithfully reported the amusements and the travels of the royal family, trying to make her feel a part of all this activity, which obviously she herself had shared while she was still living in Spain. The children, sometimes accompanied by their father, often paid visits to convents on holy days and other occasions. During the carnival season, the ladies of the court would put on plays, and at any time there would be outings to country palaces, an occasional bullfight, or an auto-da-fé. Anne also enjoyed hunting, and if Vaucelas can be believed, she had enough skill to bring down deer and boar with the crossbow.[13]

On the whole, Anne apparently led a calm, well-regulated life, and the family seems to have enjoyed much companionship. Until 1608 Philip and Margaret and their children had resided in the royal palace in Valledolid because it was convenient to Lerma's estates nearby. After 1608, however, Philip was prevailed upon to return to Madrid. In the following years, therefore, the court resumed a more normal course of movement from the Escorial to the palaces in Madrid and to the country palaces at Aranjuez or Valledolid or even further afield. Anne thus saw at least a variety of royal residences and had some picture of Castile, if only through her travels in the royal train. She did not really emerge into public view though, or into general report, until her marriage and her entry into France.

Although we know relatively little of Anne's early life, the contrary is true of Louis XIII. For his childhood there is almost too much information to permit fair assessment. As soon as Louis was born, he had been handed over to the man who would remain his personal physician for more than two decades, Jean Héroard. Colleagues described Héroard as somewhat eccentric. One form his eccentricity took was to keep a daily journal of the dauphin's activities and, in particular, of what he ate and drank and what he eliminated.[14] Héroard also included notations of the dauphin's behavior, his actions, his sayings, his outbursts of temper, his relations with other members of the household, and his relations with his royal parents and siblings. This journal was maintained even into Louis's adulthood. It gives such a detailed picture of Louis's life that it has been used as source material by historians interested in Louis's psychological development. The journal, however, is so one-sided, in its emphasis of Héroard's preoccupations, that the picture it gives of Louis as a child may not be the most accurate. Nevertheless, the journal is the most complete, if not the only, source available, and may be used with caution.

Louis, as well as his eventual brothers and sisters, was quartered in the old castle of Saint-Germain some distance outside Paris. It overlooks the Seine at a slight elevation, in a spot that was considered particularly healthful for its good air and good drinking water. The nursery establishment came to include Louis's illegitimate half-brothers and half-sisters, children of Henry IV's mistresses. The queen, Marie de Medici, did not relish this arrangement; neither did young Louis. He seems to have learned at a very early age the distinction between the legitimate royal blood and royal blood derived from the left side. Very early he lorded it over his younger brothers and sisters and even more so over his illegitimate siblings. He also very early displayed remarkable stubbornness, outbursts of temper when ordered to do anything against his will, and in general a hunger for stable affection. He saw his parents rarely. Henry and Marie occasionally visited Saint-Germain, and sometimes Louis and the other children would be brought to visit the king and queen in Paris or at one of the other royal residences nearby. Consequently no actual family life existed between the parents and the children.

It might have been thought that infrequent contact would at least have reduced friction, but this was not the case. Henry, jovial though he could be with his children, was anxious to have his eldest son properly obedient and submissive, and more than once Louis's stubbornness enraged him. Indeed, Henry is reported to have said to the queen that, considering her own obstinacy, her son's stubbornness foretold that she would have difficulties with him in the future. With his mother Louis appears to have had a distant but nevertheless intense relationship. She was not affectionate with any of her children but least so with her eldest. Louis had substitute mothers: his governess, Madame de Montglat, and his nursery maids. He remained attached to Madame de Montglat all his life, or, more properly, all her life. His mother, however, though she was distant, seemed to be an object of longing for him, and the relationship between them never developed into anything more satisfying.

Whether Louis could have come close to his father, if his father had lived, is not possible to know. He repudiated several aspects of his father's life, exhibiting a conscious primness with regard to sexual laxity and making it plain that he wished to differentiate himself from his father's conduct in such matters and, indeed, even from too loose speech. However, he also respected him enormously, and he was desolate when his father was assassinated on 14 May 1610.

From that day on, Louis was king, with his mother acting as regent for him until the ceremonies that marked his coming of age in October 1614 when he entered upon his fourteenth year and his majority. Even after that date, Marie de Medici continued to control the affairs of the kingdom, and she did not give up this control when Louis reached an age to take a more active interest in political matters. On one occasion when, conscious of his office and his duty, he tried to take part in the royal council, Marie reportedly took him by the arm and ushered him out, saying "go play elsewhere."[15] His relationship with his mother obviously had not improved with time or tragedy.

Marie has been described as a timid woman with all the obstinacy of timid persons.[16] Moreover, she had no intellectual scope and did not form her political attachments on the basis of reason but rather of inclination. The persons in whom she confided most at that time were her mistress of the wardrobe, Leonora Galigaï, and Leonora's husband, Concini, who was soon promoted to be marshall d'Ancre. Between them Leonora and Concini dictated all Marie's appointments, benefited hugely from the royal treasury, and eventually changed the personnel of the royal council. Louis was excluded from all this. He seemed so insignificant, so inapt to assert himself—particularly since he had suffered for years from a stammer—that Concini on more than one occasion publicly showed him contempt. Marie, meanwhile, not only indulged her taste for power but also her taste for extravagance. She had accumulated large debts in the lifetime of Henry IV; not only did she fail to pay these but she went on to incur vastly greater expenses. Some of them, such as gifts or pensions to rebellious princes, had a political justification, but many were purely personal and involved the purchase of jewelry and gifts to friends. Marie had a passion for diamonds in particular. To keep herself in funds, she was not above extorting private payments for appointments; in other words, she was not above abusing her position. She also exceeded her powers, in the view of at least some officials, by forcing the treasurers to surrender to her Henry IV's great cash reserve that had been stored in the Arsenal. Considerable amounts of these monies found their way abroad, invested by her with banking houses in Italy as well as Germany and the Netherlands as though she were foreseeing a time when she would no longer be welcome in her son's kingdom.[17] In short, Marie de Medici acted like a cold, grasping woman and showed neither warmth nor understanding for the young king. Such warmth and understanding as she possessed went to his younger brother Gaston, the future duke of Orléans.

Louis had resources for coping with his isolated situation, though some of his favorite occupations seemed unkingly to contemporaries. His formal education was undistinguished; he did not fancy book-learning. He had lessons in drawing, painting, and sculpture, and these he liked better and grew to be very proficient in painting especially.[18] He also showed talent and enthusiasm for music. For the rest he preferred practical studies such as cartography, and especially the mechanical and military arts. He had a little forge in his private quarters and became adept at making working models of cannon as well as other arms and devices, including clocks. However satisfying, it was not an activity to prepare him for leadership among men. He did enjoy at least one traditionally royal pastime, hunting, and on horseback was a credit to his riding master, the famous Pluvinel. Of all the forms of hunting, he was most fond of falconry, and took the keenest interest in his falcons' care and training. He liked keeping other birds, too, sometimes letting the falcons use them as prey, which does not show his personality in an attractive light.

Louis's passion for falconry brought him the acquaintance of a young man, Charles de Luynes, who held an office under the grand falconer of the crown. Luynes soon received exclusive charge of Louis's personal hunting birds and became his closest friend. Luynes seemed too insignificant to worry either Marie de Medici or Concini, so that they left Louis to enjoy this attachment undisturbed. He did not have many.

It has been represented that Louis's notable inability as a child and as an adult to form satisfying relationships may have been the result of the upbringing to which he was subjected—more particularly the result of the supervision of his physician Héroard.[19] Héroard's insistence on controlling every aspect of his patient's life—indeed, his insistence on treating his charge as a patient and his continual interference with the child's bowel habits—may have produced in Louis a chronic lack of self-confidence and a distrust of others as well as of himself. His stammer, aside from any physical causes, could have been a sign of inner conflicts. Héroard's influence may not have been wholly responsible for this; Louis, after all, had the experience also of a rejecting mother.

Whatever the reasons, the effects of his early life were unfortunate. It is worthy of note that Louis disliked dealing with people face to face; when he had to communicate something unpleasant, he would try to do it through intermediaries. Although he seemed, especially in his youth, to give his confidence quite fully to at least a few persons such as Héroard or Luynes, it eventually became apparent that even there he could not give it without reserve.[20] Besides, he never gave his confidence to women, with the possible exception of his nurse. Although he took a protective interest in his sisters, he did not treat them as equals. As for his mother, we can hardly say that she enjoyed his confidence: he never had the opportunity to give it to her, since she did not reciprocate his longing for a greater closeness or even for approval. A taciturn, somewhat withdrawn boy, distrustful of people, most content when by himself or engaged in activities that he could control completely, Louis presented a great contrast to the Spanish princess who was growing up in Madrid loved by her parents and, whatever her private difficulties may have been, generally reputed a serene and happy girl.

Congruence of personalities, however, was not a prime criterion for royal marriages. What mattered was equality of rank, as well as diplomatic advantage. Situated as they were, the one the heir to a venerable throne, the other the eldest daughter of a house that considered itself only just below the emperor's, Louis and Anne did not have a wide range of possible partners. The choice was further limited by the fact that numerous royal and princely houses were Protestant and therefore ineligible under normal circumstances. The French, it is true, permitted themselves a little more freedom than the Spaniards in matrimonial connections. For the Spanish Habsburgs, especially for the oldest children, the most frequent recourse was marriage into the Austrian Habsburg branch. But France could also be an attractive prospect, and it was natural for Philip III to consider it when thinking of the future of his eldest daughter.

The first approaches for a marriage between Anne and the French crown prince came from the Spanish side in the lifetime of Henry IV.[21] The suggestion was, as the Spanish ambassador had correctly foretold in 1602, that the dauphin marry Anne and that the prince of the Asturias, the Spanish crown prince, marry Louis's oldest sister, Elizabeth.

There was a diplomatic motive in this, namely, the hope of stabilizing relations with France and keeping Henry IV from making war against the Habsburgs in the empire or in Italy or the Netherlands. At least, this was the duke of Lerma's thinking.

It was possible to regard the matter also in a religious light, and this was the way in which queen Margaret and her Jesuit confessor Father Haller saw the marriage project. Father Haller feared that if Henry IV went to war in the empire, as he seemed to show intentions of doing, French hostilities against Spain would follow. In that case Father Haller expected the Spanish government to encourage French malcontents to rebel against Henry, a tactic used not long before by Philip II in the last days of the French wars of religion. Furthermore, Haller thought Spain might even urge the pope to declare Henry a relapsed heretic and annul his second marriage, that is to say, his marriage to Marie de Medici—a move that certainly would widen the gulf between France and Spain and possibly lead to a renewal of the Italian wars and the wars of religion combined. According to Father Haller, therefore, the salvation of Christendom depended on the preservation of peace between France and Spain, and the best way to accomplish that would be to marry the infanta to the dauphin and the prince of the Asturias to Louis's sister Elizabeth. Whether Haller based his thinking on actual knowledge of the intentions of Lerma and the Spanish government, or whether he spoke purely from personal speculation, he convinced Queen Margaret.

Because Lerma found the marriage project useful from a secular, diplomatic point of view and had already opened tactful discussions about it, Queen Margaret for once got her way. In 1609, at Father Haller's suggestion, she asked the Florentine ambassador in Madrid to return to Florence by way of Paris and to pay a call on his master's niece, Marie de Medici, and her husband, Henry IV, to sound them out regarding the marriage proposal. For discretion's sake the Florentine ambassador, the marquis of Campiglia, was to leave Margaret's name out of the talks, but she did request portraits of the dauphin and his sister. Campiglia with the consent of the grand duke of Tuscany, his master, carried out Margaret's instructions. Henry IV for his part did not show himself eager to commit either himself or the dauphin; he was toying with the thought of an English marriage, and was also considering the daughter of the duke of Lorraine as a possible wife for Louis, a choice that would strengthen French connections with the empire and might in time also strengthen French claims to the duchy of Lorraine.[22] Meanwhile, Henry proceeded with preparations to intervene militarily in the empire on behalf of the Protestant elector of Brandenburg over the question of the Cleves-Jülich succession.

The situation changed in May 1610. After Henry's death Marie de Medici had no inclination to pursue warlike projects. Louis was only nine years old, and, as in any period of regency, the weakness of the crown encouraged overmighty subjects to demand personal favors and concessions under threat of rebellion. The Protestant and the Catholic great nobles were alike unreliable. In these circumstances Marie proved amenable to the Spanish marriage project.

Historians have criticized her for having sacrificed French interests to Spanish policy, for having attached France to the coattails of Spain.[23] However, from her point of view, a treaty of friendship and a double marriage with Spain would secure external peace and might enhance royal authority at home. To be sure, by taking that direction she was abandoning Henry's anti-Habsburg orientation, and she was also abandoning Henry's tactic of balancing the Huguenot and the devout Catholic factions against each other. Instead she and her council subscribed largely to the demands of the devout for peace and understanding between Catholic princes. The pope supported them and through the nuncios in Paris and Madrid did his best to further the French-Spanish marriages.[24]

Huguenot leaders were alarmed at what seemed like a pronouncedly Catholic foreign policy. As a concession to their feelings, Marie entered into negotiations for the marriage of her second daughter, Christine, to the Prince of Wales, Prince Henry of England.[25] But these negotiations were conducted with some hesitancy by her, and they ended in any case with the death of Prince Henry in 1612. Opposition to the Spanish marriages came not only from such Huguenot leaders as Henry IV's old friend Marshall Lesdiguières and the dukes of Rohan and Bouillon, but also from the Catholic prince of Condé, who as a member of the Bourbon family stood closest to the throne and feared that his importance in the kingdom would be diminished. There was foreign interference too. Duke Charles-Emmanuel I of Savoy, disappointed that his own negotiations for the marriage of his heir, the prince of Piedmont, to Louis's sister Elizabeth were being broken off, did his best to fan distrust of the Spanish proposals. In view of all this opposition, Marie kept her preliminary exchanges with Spain secret even from her own council until matters had advanced so far that preparation for the marriage contracts became necessary.

There was much backing and filling in the process of bargaining. Each side wanted the eldest daughter of the other while proffering a younger daughter of its own. Unlikely though it was to influence decisions, the French ambassador was allowed to hear that Anne had exclaimed that if her younger sister Maria were chosen as Louis XIII's bride, she herself would enter a convent and never marry at all.[26] The battle for prestige was finally given over, however, and the news that agreements had been reached for the marriage of Louis XIII and the infanta Doña Ana and of the prince of the Asturias to Madame Elizabeth was made public in Spain in January 1612 and in France in February. The happy prospects were celebrated especially lavishly in Paris as soon as the weather permitted, in the month of April, with several days of allegorical pageantry, mock combats, and fireworks in the Place Royale.[27] Meanwhile the French ambassador in Madrid, Monsieur de Vaucelas, began to address Anne as "Her Majesty," and an extraordinary embassy came from France to sign the marriage contracts at the Prado Palace in Madrid on 22 August 1612. Anne, dressed in embroidered cloth of silver, received the French and Spanish gentlemen who came to pay their respects to her and to kiss the hem of her dress.[28] A reciprocal Spanish embassy in Paris signed the French copies of the contracts with Louis and Marie de Medici on 25 August.

By the terms of the contracts, each princess was to receive a dowry of 500,000 gold écus, although no money was actually to be paid by either side unless one or the other marriage should not be concluded.[29] In addition, each princess was to bring with her jewelry worth 50,000 gold écus and to renounce her rights of inheritance. This meant more on the Spanish side than the French, since French royal lawyers for centuries had maintained that the crown of France could not be transmitted by a woman whereas in Spain there was no barrier to a princess succeeding to her father's crown if she had no surviving brothers. On the part of the respective bridegrooms, Louis and Marie promised Anne an endowment paying 20,000 gold écus annually, and Philip III and his son undertook to provide similarly for Madame Elizabeth. Each party also promised to maintain the new bride in a state suitable to her condition and the customs of her husband's court.

The amounts of money mentioned were not extraordinary. Henry II's daughter Elizabeth of Valois had brought as large a dowry to Philip II, and more recently Marie de Medici's own dowry when she married Henry IV had been much larger. But what mattered in the present case was the even exchange between partners of equal rank and not financial advantage.

More important for Anne's future, however, than the material goods she would carry was the intangible baggage of her father's expectations. Philip III counted on her to influence her husband's policies in favor of Spanish interests. As it turned out, the charge Philip thus put on his daughter could not have been better calculated to cause her trouble and unhappiness in her new home. Only after decades was she able to free herself of her old loyalties and burdens and fully take the part of the kingdom into which she had married.

Chapter Two

The Road to France

THE LARGER PURPOSE OF THE Spanish-French marriages, according to the texts of the contracts, was to maintain friendship between the two kingdoms and preserve peace in Christendom: a conventional formula but one that was still significant for its underlying meaning. For centuries royal marriages had been arranged to seal alliances and crown peace treaties. More often than not, the marriages had not prevented renewed hostilities or diplomatic realignments. Erasmus, the pacific humanist, had long ago pointed out this incongruity and had advised kings and princes to avoid useless foreign entanglements and to marry one of their own subjects.[1] Moreover, he thought it hard on young princesses to be sent far from home to live among strangers whose customs and language were alike unfamiliar.

Nevertheless, royalty continued to send its daughters to far-off courts. A king's marriage to a subject was apt to produce jealousies and dangerous disaffection in the noble houses whose daughters had not been chosen—a problem Erasmus conveniently ignored though it had been sufficiently demonstrated. Besides, however different language and customs might be from one court to another, royal families still assumed a basic community of interest between themselves and their counterparts in other states. Although the Protestant Reformation had impaired the unity of Christendom, the concept of Europe as an extended family of kingdoms persisted within the new religious institutions. International royal marriages, however ineffective as instruments for perpetual peace, embodied the deep-seated belief in a common basis for at least potential cooperation. The contracts drawn up on such occasions expressed this assumption by the reciprocity of gifts and settlements, and time-worn though the references to the peace and friendship secured by the marriage might have been, the contracting parties took them seriously.[2]

Beyond that, of course, there often existed hopes that were not explicitly voiced—hopes for the possibility of eventual dynastic inheritance, for example. Sometimes too the bride's family hoped to use the marriage to control what it considered a weaker partner; the bride's mission in that case was to attach her husband's kingdom as a satellite to her family's orbit. Such an assignment was apt to contradict the principle of mutuality and to place the young woman in a false position with respect to her husband and to her new people. It was bound to turn out badly unless the husband chose to accept the dominance of his in-laws, and that did not often happen. Philip III evidently expected that Louis XIII would be one of those exceptions, judging by the memorandum of secret instructions he gave Anne when she was on the point of departure from Spain.[3]

The first part of Philip's instructions was harmless, concerning her personal conduct. He enjoined his daughter to observe her religious duties so as to honor her obligation to God and set a good example to her subjects; to remember what she had been taught in her family; and especially to be mindful of her mother's piety as a model.[4] But then Philip went on to what were plainly political counsels. First of all he urged Anne to give care and energy to the opposition of heresy. She should bring Louis to be of the same mind, although she would need great prudence for that because, as Philip put it, God permitted heresy to exist in France and she would find many obstacles in her way.[5]

Further Philip reminded Anne of one of the reasons for her marriage, namely, to ensure that no war would arise in future between the Catholic princes of Europe without great cause. To this end Anne should maintain close relations with her brothers in Spain, with her aunt who governed the Low Countries, with the emperor and empress, and with her maternal aunts and uncles in Austria. Anne would actually be doing her husband a favor, since in Philip's opinion friendship between France and the Spanish Low Countries in particular would be of great advantage to Louis. Lastly Philip urged Anne to do what she could so that the French would not give assistance to any rebellions that might arise against Spain.[6]

There is no indication that Louis's sister Elizabeth received anything like such instructions when she left France, or that Philip would have permitted her to exercise any political role. In attempting to assign such a role to Anne, Philip no doubt underestimated his son-in-law: an understandable mistake because all that the world at large knew about Louis as yet was that he seemed young for his age and appeared to submit to his mother's authority in all things with great docility. Small wonder if Philip believed that Louis might be led by a wife as effectively as by a mother.

By the time Anne left Spain with her instructions, she was fourteen, presumably old enough to have some sense of their importance. Originally it had been anticipated that the princesses would be exchanged and the marriages performed by the end of 1613. That term was not kept. Marie de Medici found herself faced with protests from the notables of the kingdom, such as the prince of Condé and the duke of Bouillon. In the ensuing pamphlet war, the opponents of the marriage argued that these agreements were a reversal of Henry IV's foreign policy, which had been directed against Spanish tyranny, and that Spanish tyranny was as odious as ever. They also pointed out that France and Spain were inveterate enemies and that connections between them in the past had brought nothing but trouble. Furthermore, the opponents argued, the children were too young; and in any event, the best match for Louis would be a Bourbon princess, specifically the duchess of Montpensier. He would be wise altogether to lean on the prince of Condé and put his trust in Frenchmen instead of Spaniards.[7]

Clearly this advice proceeded from the circle surrounding the prince of Condé. Marie de Medici's supporters countered with the argument that Henry IV himself had entered on the marriage negotiations; that France would in no way lose any advantages by the marriage treaty; and as for the question of age, the pope had full power to grant any dispensations necessary. Marie's apologists also pointed out that the marriages would benefit the Catholic religion by uniting so closely two staunchly Catholic houses. To anyone who might still harbor doubts, it was explained that the power of the crown included the right to make foreign alliances and that royal authority was not subject to conditions imposed by rebels.[8]

Condé and some of his Protestant friends had indeed become rebels. They issued a manifesto against the regent's policies in February 1614, raised troops, and hoped, although in vain, for popular support. The duke of Bouillon went so far as to ask the king of Spain for subsidies, offering to dismember the French kingdom, just as the duke of Guise had made similar offers to Philip II during the wars of religion. Philip III, warned by his ambassador in France that this was a harebrained scheme, did not allow himself to be distracted by it.[9] Under these pressures, however, Marie de Medici yielded to Condé's demand that the marriages at least be postponed until Louis had come of age and until the Estates-General had met. Relations with Spain were not as cordial as they might have been either, for there were continuing disputes over the Navarre frontier.

By the spring of 1615, at last all obstacles seemed on the way to being overcome. Louis had entered on his majority in September 1614 and the subsequent Estates-General had not been as troublesome as the princes may have hoped, so that Marie's fears began to subside. In March 1615 the first bridal gift arrived in Madrid: Louis sent Anne his portrait set in a costly diamond bracelet.[10] Arrangements were made for the marriages by proxy that would precede the exchange of the princesses in September. Because it would have been beneath the dignity of either a Spanish infanta or a daughter of France to leave her native kingdom unmarried, Anne was to marry Louis by proxy in the Cathedral of Burgos and Elizabeth would marry the prince of the Asturias in the same fashion in the Cathedral of Bordeaux. Preparations for Anne's wedding trip had started as early as 1614. The men of her household received new liveries—green, her mother's color—and Philip's and the prince's households were also outfitted in color for the first time since the death of Queen Margaret. Anne's trousseau was being gathered too. In France, Louis expressed concern over whether the Spaniards would bring as much as his sister was taking out of the kingdom,[11] but he need not have worried. Spanish chroniclers reported that Anne had enough silver for twelve royal houses.[12] This was an exaggeration, though certainly her equipment was rich, ranging from a complete set of altar vessels in silver gilt for her chapel to all manner of utensils for her personal needs: fourteen great silver serving pieces as well as numbers of silver braziers, basins, kettles, pans, pails, baskets, salvers, porringers, bowls, ladles, candlesticks, not to mention forks, spoons, and incidentals such as salt cellars, a measuring cup and apothecary's tools, and twenty-four silver plates with forty-eight crystal cups. She also brought two items new to France, square silver tables, presumably to be used as sideboards. Although silver balustrades and fireplace fittings existed in the Louvre in Paris, silver furniture as such was unknown before Anne brought her tables.

The rest of her trousseau was on an equally lavish scale. She had bed linens of batiste by the dozens, dressing gowns, night caps, shifts, handkerchiefs, and ruffs, all of batiste trimmed with Flemish lace and most of them embroidered. Her wardrobe too was extensive. Fortunately for her, Spanish and French styles resembled each other more closely than they would later in the century. She had dresses in all colors: silver, red, green, blue, yellow, black; of satin or watered silk or velvet; all lined in taffeta. Neither the colors nor the designs were particularly youthful by modern standards, but special fashions for young people were still unknown in Anne's time. Nor is it to be supposed that she herself chose her dresses. Presumably the selection was made by her governess, the Countess Altamira, perhaps with the aid of Philip III or even the duke of Lerma.

Three of Anne's gowns were especially sumptuous: two red ones were embroidered in pearls and silver, and a green one was covered with pearls. Another nine dresses were richly embroidered in gold and silver and decorated with gold and silver spangles or beads. Dresses for less gala occasions were more simply trimmed with gold and silver lace or with rows of satin braid and flounces. The outfits were coordinated. Some included a skirt, a bodice, and sleeves, all separate and to be laced together. Often there were two pairs of sleeves, one pair narrow and one pair long and full to be worn as an oversleeve. Other gowns consisted of a long robe, with an underskirt, a bodice, and sleeves. Not only was each gown a matching set but for variety Anne had twelve pairs of sleeves embroidered in gold and silver and twenty-four pairs of plainer ones in assorted colors. In addition, there were underskirts, some of cloth of gold, some of brocade; hoopskirts; cloaks both long and short; coats, jackets, and hats; silk stockings in mother-of-pearl color; and twenty-four pairs of shoes in assorted colors of cordovan leather. She was provided with everything a lady might need down to velvet purses, belts, rolls of ribbons, silk lacing cord in quantity, and reels of sewing silk. To hold all this, twelve great trunks were bought and twenty-two smaller cases of various sizes, not counting her special toilet case. She also carried with her twelve portable writing desks, so that we may assume her father expected her to write to him often.

To go with her elaborate wardrobe, Anne had a considerable quantity of personal jewelry in addition to the amount stipulated in the marriage contract: two hundred pearls, assorted chains, rings, earrings, bracelets, and belts of gold set with diamonds, emeralds, and aquamarines. There were also one hundred fifty gold and enamel buttons. The dowry jewels were another matter. They were of greater value and included a long chain and a necklace of wrought gold, enameled in white, red, green, and gray and set with diamonds; a hundred-one buttons, a belt, bracelets and a headdress, all in wrought gold set with rubies and diamonds; a large diamond and ruby pendant; diamond bracelets, headdress, chain and belt; and lastly a square table diamond intended for her wedding ring.

None of these pieces are to be found in the inventory of Anne's jewels that was made after her death. Evidently, over the decades, the precious stones had been reset, exchanged, or sold, and the gold melted down. But Anne may not have felt much sentimental attachment to her dowry jewels. Their chief function after all was an official and financial one, and the jewelry her sister-in-law Elizabeth brought was carefully calculated to the same value as Anne's.[13] What it lacked in bulk it made up in the number of pearls and diamonds, and for Elizabeth's wedding ring Louis provided a large diamond cut in the shape of a heart.

Preserving equality was more difficult in the enumeration of the ladies and household servants each princess would bring with her. The negotiations over this matter lasted until the final moment before the exchange of the princesses themselves. It was customary for a royal bride to bring with her attendants from her parents' court, persons with whom she was familiar and whose presence would serve to ease the shock of transplantation. Such foreign households settled within the bride's new court often created problems, however, and both Marie de Medici and Philip III intended to keep the foreign personnel brought by their respective daughters-in-law to a minimum while at the same time making the suite of their own daughters as large as possible. Names were stricken from proposed lists time after time until by final agreement Anne was permitted to bring with her four chaplains with their servants, three ladies of honor, three ladies in waiting, twelve ladies of the chamber, and a number of cooks, wine butlers, and squires. The other personnel, all those who might have expected to accompany Anne to her new home in Paris, were to return to Spain.[14] The number of that suite was large indeed. The household that traveled with Anne from Madrid included more than two hundred fifty persons, not counting their dependents and lesser servants.[15] In the end, despite the efforts to limit the size of the Spanish contingent upon Anne's arrival in France, the French still complained that she had brought with her a hundred people instead of the stipulated fifty-three. It was the first of many discords that were to complicate Anne's life in her new home.

In the early summer of 1615, the Spanish royal family left Madrid and moved closer to the frontier. They spent July in Valledolid at the residence of the duke of Lerma, with the intention of reaching Burgos for Anne's marriage by proxy in September. On the French side, however, Madame Elizabeth fell ill on the way from Paris to Bordeaux, which occasioned a month's delay. By mid-October both parties had reached their appointed places. In Burgos, Philip and Anne had a novena held in the famous convent of Saint Augustine to pray for the success of the impending marriages. Thereafter Anne formally renounced her rights of succession to the Spanish throne, and on 18 October in the Cathedral of Saint Augustine at Burgos, she married Louis XIII, for whom the duke of Lerma was standing proxy. All observers reported happily that she pronounced her "yes" firmly and gaily.[16] They also agreed that she was full of grace and beauty in one of her magnificent trousseau gowns of deep red satin embroidered with pearls and silver. A banquet and ball followed the ceremonies in the cathedral, and the festivities continued the next day with a great feast in the palace of the duke of Lerma.

Also on 18 October, Madame Elizabeth had married the prince of the Asturias in the Cathedral of Saint Andrew in Bordeaux, with the duke of Guise standing proxy for the prince. It was significant that the duke of Guise should have been chosen for this honor. No one had yet forgotten that the Guise family had led the ultra-Catholic faction in the French wars of religion, and the duke of Guise's position as proxy for the Spanish prince, as well as his assignment to receive Anne at the frontier and escort her to Bordeaux, signified to all that here was a triumph of Catholic foreign policy.[17]

On 21 October, Elizabeth left Bordeaux for the frontier by easy stages, and the Spaniards likewise began their progress to the Bidassoa River. There were reports that Philip III was finding it hard to part from his daughter and was delaying the journey.[18] It is true the royal party lingered in San Sebastian and indulged in visits to convents, picnics, and water parties. Delays were also caused by weather and assorted mishaps. The worst of these occurred when the baggage mules and a number of coaches were stuck in an arroyo on the way to Fuenterrabía. It was no easy matter for such a large company to proceed to its destination on schedule. The escort and households for King Philip, for his son the prince of the Asturias, for the duke of Lerma's son the duke of Uceda, and Anne herself comprised more than one thousand persons. The quantity of horses, coaches, and sumpter mules for the baggage and for Anne's trousseau was commensurate. It was a small army on the move equipped with all necessities for camping out should lodgings fail in the small towns through which the cavalcade passed. Even the magnificent blankets that covered the mules, crimson velvet trimmed with gold, served a double purpose, for these blankets became hangings in the tents put up for the notables when better lodgings could not be found.

At last on 9 November, the day of leave-taking came. Philip gave Anne his blessing as she was preparing to depart from Fuenterrabía for the last stage of her journey on Spanish soil. It was reported that both father and daughter were much moved, but Anne at least seems to have regained her composure on the short trip to the Bidassoa, where the crossing into France had been arranged.

For months court officials on both sides had been busy with plans and preparations.[19] In the middle of the river, a pavilion had been constructed on four boats serving as pontoons, and in the exact center of this pavilion the border between France and Spain was marked. On each side of the river, a smaller pavilion had been set up and provided with refreshment tables in case the princess and the queen should wish to have a light meal. In the event, neither stopped for the collation.

The Spaniards were the first to arrive in sight of the river and consequently held back until it was seen that Elizabeth on her side was also descending to the bank. Then exact timing was observed so that neither Anne's nor Elizabeth's boat should leave first. The princesses duly arrived at their respective sides of the river pavilion simultaneously and proceeded to the center line where they greeted each other, embraced, and exchanged compliments. Anne, in gold and blue, and Elizabeth, in silver, were observed to be gracious and composed, although it was noted that Elizabeth seemed a trifle too eager to enter her new realm.[20] The suites were presented to each other, and finally the duke of Uceda, acting for his father, the duke of Lerma, handed over Anne to the duke of Guise while the duke of Guise passed on Elizabeth to Uceda. Thereafter the two ladies proceeded in the reverse order in which they had come, Elizabeth to the Spanish side of the river and to Fuenterrabía to meet Philip III and her husband, Anne to the French side and to Saint-Jean-de-Luz, where she would spend the night and the next day resting.

At Saint-Jean-de-Luz the reality of emigration came home to Anne. At supper on her first night in France, she greatly missed Spanish bread, and she also missed the snow with which beverages at the royal table were cooled in Spain.[21] Her accustomed food was important to her; she was so fond of certain Spanish dishes, in particular of the vegetable stew known as *olla,* that she ordered it served every day at her table; and when it became clear that her French household did not like to see this reminder of Spain, she had the stew brought secretly to the rooms of her chamberwoman, where she could enjoy it in private.[22]

Presumably she became accustomed to French bread and to the lack of snow for cooling drinks. At any rate, she traveled to Bordeaux, keeping to the same stopping places that her sister-in-law had used, though taking twelve days for the journey. Bad weather hampered the progress of the train. The coaches and baggage bogged down in mud between Bayonne and Dax, and on another occasion, Anne was left without either her maid or her dressing case. On the last day out from Bordeaux, Louis XIII came to meet her incognito, hiding himself behind the window of a house in a small village through which she had to pass. He was pointed out to her; she stole a glance. He looked at her with more leisure, but neither was permitted by etiquette to speak. Later on, in open country, they greeted one another: he doffed his hat, while she saluted prettily by taking off her gloves, joining her hands, and bowing her head.[23] Formal notes of greeting had been exchanged between them since she had first set foot on French soil, but these stolen glimpses had spontaneity and at least some friendly warmth.

Later on that day, 21 November, Anne arrived in Bordeaux. In her honor the guns on the city walls and in the city castle saluted as did the ships in the port. Since it was already evening, paper lanterns in all colors illuminated the streets. The city magistrates met her outside the gates, and twelve pages had been sent to light her coach to the archbishop's palace, where Marie de Medici awaited her. Marie was an imposing sight as she greeted her young daughter-in-law, dressed in her usual black, relieved only by her favorite pearl necklace and a diamond cross. She showed every cordiality that could have been expected, embracing Anne and kissing her. She told Anne as she did so, "I'm doing French fashion," because she knew Anne was not accustomed to that form of greeting. They talked a little, using the Spanish ambassador, Cardenas, as interpreter, and then went to the king's room, Marie leading Anne by the right hand. As the king met them near the door of his room, his mother announced, "Here is the queen your wife whom I am bringing to you." He took off his hat and bowed, kissed Anne, and told her that it was the greatest happiness for him to see her in this place where she was all powerful.[24] It was a gallant fashion of making her welcome. Thereafter Anne was left to rest.

On the following day, 22 November, Anne visited Marie after having received a visit from Louis. Louis had gone to the kitchens personally to order his queen's breakfast and called on her while she was still dressing. She needed a feather for her headdress, and Louis offered her one from the plumes on his hat but asked for one of her ribbons in exchange. All the onlookers were delighted by what seemed such promising signs of mutual pleasure and dawning affection.[25]

The wedding itself took place on 25 November, Saint Catherine's day. The cathedral was decorated as it had been for the marriage by proxy of Madame Elizabeth, and the crowd filling the church was as great, if not greater, than it had been on the earlier occasion. Only the most prominent persons had reserved seats. The rest arrived as early as four in the morning in order to be sure of a place, even though the ceremonies were not to begin until late afternoon. When Louis and Anne appeared, they were met with a great outcry of admiration and benedictions. Everyone noted how handsome Louis looked with his chestnut curls and healthy coloring, set off by a suit of silver brocade covered with gold embroidery and precious stones. The charm of novelty, of course, belonged to Anne, whom one of the Spaniards described as more beautiful than an angel.[26] She wore the French royal robes of purple velvet embroidered with gold fleur-de-lis, lined and bordered with ermine, and had on her head a heavy closed crown. The crown was so unwieldy that one of the great ladies who bore Anne's train had to repair the young queen's hairdo and secure the crown better. Even so, Anne was observed to put up her hand to the crown frequently during the ceremony in order to ease the weight of it. No one seems to have remarked that this might have been an unfortunate omen, though at the very least it showed a lack of foresight to provide an object so heavy for a young girl to wear. What did strike observers was a remarkable resemblance between Anne and Louis; one reporter exclaimed they might have been brother and sister.[27] Everyone also noted with satisfaction that the king often looked smiling at his queen and that she could not keep from smiling back even though she was blushing. It all seemed a most encouraging and auspicious beginning to the royal marriage and the fulfillment of both Spanish and French hopes.

As soon as the mass was over, Anne retired and was relieved of her heavy robes to rest. She and Louis had their supper separately, and then Marie de Medici staged the bedding of the bride. In order to encourage Louis, his gentlemen entertained him at supper with racy stories; then Marie came to fetch him and brought him to Anne with instructions to the royal nurses to leave the young couple together for an hour or two. About eleven o'clock, Louis returned to his room and Anne to hers, and it was reported by the nurses that the marriage had been consummated.[28]

Some historians have refused to believe the official account of this event, holding that it had been drafted purely for propaganda purposes in order to make it impossible for Condé and other opponents of the king's Spanish marriage to suggest an annulment.[29] Others believe the fact but deplore it because of the young age of Louis and Anne, contending that this experience at fourteen must have been a harmful, psychological shock.[30] What they forget is that fourteen was not an abnormal age for marriage in the seventeenth century, particularly in royal families, although regular cohabitation in such cases was usually discouraged. Furthermore Anne and Louis were not doing something shameful and forbidden: on the contrary, they were doing what both church and parents had sanctioned and what their peoples expected. At least, it should have been that way if both had reached a normal stage of psychological development. It is true that in Spain, Elizabeth, now known as Isabella, and the prince of the Asturias did not consummate their marriage until 1621, but Philip III had no need to hurry matters for the sake of circumventing internal opposition.

The fact that Louis and Anne slept together was confirmed by Louis's physician, Héroard, who noted in his journal that Louis told him he had intercourse twice, and Héroard confirmed that Louis's sexual organs looked as though this was true.[31] Louis may have exaggerated his report of his performance, however. He still seemed very young, especially to the Spaniards, one of whom wrote to the duke of Lerma regretfully that it seemed likely that after this initial meeting, Louis and Anne would keep apart for the next six months.[32] In the event, they did not sleep together again for more than three years, to the despair of Philip III and of every well-wisher to the Spanish cause. It would seem that the experience of his wedding night had not after all been a happy one for Louis, despite the clinical observations of Doctor Héroard. As for Anne's feelings in the matter, the only person who thought to inquire after them was Héroard, who asked Louis whether she had liked it. Louis replied "She liked it; I did it twice."[33]

Chapter Three

The Neglected Bride

WHATEVER MAY HAVE OCCURred between Anne and Louis, pamphleteers celebrated the wedding in the most lyrical terms:

> "Rejoice, France, for after this happy night, so much desired by these two lovers and all their people, heaven and this princess promise you a succession of kings and princes and you shall see her as fertile as a vine, bearing fruit in abundance and in all seasons."[1]

That was indeed the hope of all, though it was understood it would not happen immediately because of the youth of the two parties. Pictures of the time showing the entry of the royal pair into this or that city depicted them as children—that is to say, as miniature adults—much smaller than Marie de Medici, who accompanied them.[2]

Awaiting time and maturity, the little queen seemed to be settling in as well as could be expected. On her way to Bordeaux, one of the Spaniards in her suite had reported that she sorrowed and wept in private for her father, although in public she had been firm and encouraged everyone around her.[3] Whether she still grieved for her home after the wedding we do not know. To all observers she appeared contented and pleased. Marie de Medici and Louis were also pleased; at least they wrote Philip III to that effect.[4] One of the French ladies who saw Anne in those days left a charming picture of her. She described the queen as sitting on a cushion on the floor in the Spanish manner, dressed in green with her long slashed oversleeves caught at elbow and wrist with diamond buttons, wearing a green bonnet to match her dress, with a black heron feather that emphasized her blondness.[5]

It was a season for exchanging gifts. Louis presented Anne with jewelry that had been crafted by the court jeweler, Corneille Roger: a pair of earrings of enameled gold set with diamonds from the crown jewels, and a necklace of thirty large round pearls, also from the crown jewels. In addition she received a chiming watch on a long chain with diamonds and enameled gold, a round cross of black enamel set with diamonds, and from Marie as well as Louis, eight ornaments of flow-ers, enameled in various colors and set with diamonds.[6] Meanwhile gifts from Spain arrived for Louis: twenty magnificent horses capari-soned in brocade that were much esteemed. Marie de Medici ex-pressed herself as very content with the chests full of presents sent by the duke of Lerma, and the duke of Guise was so overjoyed by the quality of the horses he received that he kissed the animals.[7]

Four days after the wedding, on 29 November, Anne and Louis held their solemn entry into Bordeaux, Anne dressed in dark red embroi-dered with pearls, under the royal mantle she had worn at the mar-riage services.[8] A round of festivities followed. But everyone was be-ginning to have enough of travel in strange places. The universal plaint of the courtiers was, "The Bordelais is all very well but there is only one Paris; when are we going to return there?"[9] Besides, rebel troops under the prince of Condé were in nearby Saintonge confront-ing a royal army, and the outbreak of open hostilities was feared. In December, therefore, the court began its slow journey northward, passing through Poitiers, Tours, and Blois in easy stages that took four months.

Entry into the capital was an important and elaborate affair. The city council of Paris had asked the king for instructions betimes, apologiz-ing in advance that the preparations for the queen's reception in Paris would not be as sumptuous as the city fathers could wish, in view of the burden that great expenditure would impose on the people. Louis graciously replied that he did not want the city to go to extraordinary expense and that the council should observe the same order for the queen's reception as for his own when he had returned from Brittany the previous year.[10] From the end of April to the middle of May, there-fore, the Paris city council was busy about its preparations, ranging from the composition of a suitable armed escort for the queen to the commission of a large picture showing Their Majesties on one side and the city officials on the other—a picture that was to be affixed over the Porte Saint-Jacques, by which the queen would enter Paris. For months a complicated allegory was being organized and rehearsed. The city would come to meet Anne symbolically in a procession rep-resenting the four parts of the world, each headed by a classical deity, and this procession was to be led by Jupiter himself. Then there were to be military drills and a great float representing a ship, bearing a nymph as Paris who embraced Peace with one arm and Victory with the other. From the mast of the ship would hang a large globe that was to open, showing Cupid and Hymen treading Discord under foot. The prettiest children had been picked from all the quarters of Paris to take part in these representations.

Louis had announced the queen's entry for 16 May. When Anne arrived at the gate, the provost of the merchants—that is to say, the first in rank among the city magistrates—harangued her on his knees: "May we thus, Madame, see the lilies of France flower in the golden fleece of Spain in a happy lineage, for which we implore Heaven."[11] Thereafter Anne and Louis proceeded to Notre-Dame and then home to the Louvre, where two days later delegations from the sovereign courts as well as the city council waited on Louis, Anne, and the queen mother with further speeches of welcome.

The Louvre, in which Anne now took up residence, was nothing as magnificent as her father's palaces of the Escorial or the Prado. It was a complex of buildings that was still partly medieval.[12] The royal apartments were located in the angle between the west wing and the south wing and in the south wing itself, in the more modern parts of the palace. A small gallery, the gallery of Apollo, which ran from the angle of the west and south wings down to the Seine, was also complete, as was Henry IV's great gallery connecting the end of the south wing with the Tuileries, parallel to the river. On the east side, the tower of Charles V, a fourteenth-century construction, housed the royal chapel; on the north side, there were still medieval structures that resembled a fortification more than a palace. The courtyard itself was considerably smaller than it is today, and the space between the Louvre and the Tuileries was filled with a huddle of kitchens and outbuildings as well as town houses and lesser dwellings. The main entrance to the Louvre, on the east side, was extremely narrow and led from the rue d'Autriche, also narrow and very inconvenient, especially for carriages. For recreation and open air, there were the gardens of the Tuileries and Marie de Medici's new river garden between the south wing of the Louvre and the Seine. That garden afforded some privacy since, unlike the Tuileries, it was not open to the public.

What impression the Louvre made on Anne in 1616 we do not know, nor do we know what she thought of her own quarters in it. At least she cannot have had any expectation of shared family living because among royalty and great nobles in Spain as well as in France, and indeed everywhere, spouses and other family members occupied separate rooms and maintained separate households. In the Louvre tradition dictated the arrangement of the royal apartments, an arrangement that remained basically the same from 1585 until the time of Louis XIV.[13] The king's quarters were in the royal pavilion at the junction of the south and west wings. The ground floor contained the council chamber and the king's antechamber, and on the first floor were his chamber of state, his cabinet, and a smaller cabinet. The second floor could be used to house princes and favorites, and the fourth floor, with a magnificent view, contained the king's collections and was also the workroom in which he pursued his hobbies. The queen's apartments connected with the king's on the first floor, the floor of honor; they occupied the south wing of the palace overlooking the courtyard on one side and the garden of Marie de Medici and the river on the other. The queen's chamber could be entered from the king's small cabinet and, in turn, led into her salon, antechamber, and guardroom. Marie de Medici had occupied these rooms until Louis's marriage. Now she vacated them and moved into similar apartments on the ground floor. Very little is known about the decorations or furnishings of the Louvre at this time, except that Marie had her own and Anne's apartments refurbished. In the style of the day, the rooms probably gave a somber impression, with a great deal of wood paneling and high beamed ceilings.

The isolating effect of separate living quarters was reinforced by the presence of a multitude of service personnel and by the demands of ceremony. Anne was accustomed to this; ceremonial at the Spanish court was, if anything, more rigid than in France. But it is unfamiliar to us nowadays, so that we need to be reminded of the practical circumstances that influenced Anne's life and marriage.

Counting the households of the king, the queen, and the queen mother, well over 2,000 persons assured the service and the safety of the royal family, if not their comfort. Many of these household officers were on rotating duty, serving by trimesters, which the French called "quarters," so that on any given day there were only some five hundred persons in evidence. That did not include noble visitors, petitioners, tradesmen, not to mention the personal retinue of all the great and lesser courtiers. In order to govern such a potentially disorderly multitude and to ensure the respect and reverence due the king and the members of the royal family, regulations had been established long before for the proper order to be observed in every detail of life.[14]

Admittedly some of these regulations were more honored in the breach than in the observance. The court of France was famous for crowd scenes on great occasions, when even the king or queen could hardly get through the press of courtiers who had forgotten all rules of precedence. In the normal way, there was a routine, however, and it began early. At four A.M. in the summer and at five in the winter, porters were to begin cleaning the courtyards, staircases, and hallways so that no filth or rubbish might offend the king. It must be remembered that, in the absence of public lavatories, such daily cleaning was an absolute necessity. Also at five A.M., porters were to begin cleaning the guardrooms and antechambers, and the royal ushers started their duty, though the gentlemen-in-waiting started their day at seven. The kitchens had to have the king's two main meals ready at fixed times every day. It is to be assumed that the dishes were robust and did not spoil with waiting, for the king did not always choose to order his meals served precisely when they were announced to be ready. Similar order was taken for the meals of the queen and of the queen mother, and the various members of the royal households all ate at tables assigned to them according to their rank, that is to say, gentlemen of honor ate in one place, gentlemen-in-waiting in another, and so on down the line.

Access to royal persons was strictly regulated. Thus it was set forth in detail who had the duty and who had the right to wait in the royal antechamber for the king's awakening and who, by contrast, had to wait in the audience chamber. As soon as the king let it be announced that he was awake, those in attendance in the audience and antechamber were permitted to enter, not all at once, but in stages. Four valets of the chamber ordered drinking water fetched from the cellarer's service (the "service of the goblet" as it was called), and the two gentlemen butlers in attendance had the soup, broth, bread, and napkin brought by the gentlemen of the kitchens and the pantry. At that point the king's officers might enter, and when he had asked for the wine and had been served, other gentlemen and all those who were waiting in the antechamber could enter also. The highest-ranking prince handed the napkin and the bread to the king or, if no princes were present, a cardinal or, failing that, the first in rank among those attending. After this breakfast the king asked for his hat and sword, the formal sign that he was ready to dress and leave his chamber, and again there was a definite duty roster and order of precedence to establish who had the right and the duty of escorting the king to mass or anywhere else he chose to go until dinnertime, and again after dinner until supper and the king's formal retiring. Normally, all great nobles and officials at court were expected to form this escort unless they were otherwise employed by the king or had a legitimate excuse.

When the king commanded his dinner to be brought, usually to his chamber of state or audience chamber, he customarily ate alone. His grand almoner or one of the other almoners gave the benediction, and thereafter none of those who had the right to watch the king eat could speak to him unless he spoke to them first. While the king was out of his private chamber, the valets cleaned it and set it to rights, and no unauthorized person was permitted to enter it. The order for supper was similar as for dinner except that the king might take it in the queen mother's apartments or elsewhere. At eight P.M. the king retired formally, took off his hat and sword, and accepted his nightshirt from the grand chamberlain or his first gentleman-in-waiting, or from the highest-ranking noble if there were nobles present. Then he withdrew into his cabinet, where he was followed only by those whom he had ordered to appear on business or otherwise invited. Two gentlemen-in-waiting brought a collation of bread and wine, and this concluded the public day of the king. The general mass of courtiers had to leave the palace by eleven; after that the gates were closed and the night watch set.

The queen's protocol was much the same as the king's except that normally she did not have to set aside time for council meetings and had fewer public duties, such as audiences with ambassadors or royal officials. Of course the queen was attended personally more by ladies than by gentlemen, and the appointment of these ladies as well as of the rest of Anne's household had been placed in the hands of Leonora Galigaï, Marie de Medici's favorite. A memorandum for this first household of 1616 exists; the various offices are described in it, but the only person specifically named was Armand de Richelieu, the bishop of Luçon, who was to be Anne's grand almoner.[15] Richelieu at this time was not only the protégé of Marie de Medici and Leonora but also counted as a member in good standing of the devout pro-Spanish party. From a later cumulative listing of Anne's personnel, however, we can reconstitute her first household.[16]

The most important office in it was that of the lady of honor, who had in her charge all matters pertaining to the person and the chamber of the queen. The lady of honor administered the oath of loyalty to all the ladies and women of the chamber, controlled the budget, authorized extraordinary expenditures, countersigned orders for goods, and certified service. As it happened, Anne had two ladies of honor, for the French one, the widow of Constable Montmorency, had to share the office with the Spanish countess de la Torre. This shared responsibility created difficulties and constant friction. The second most important post was that of lady-in-waiting. The lady-in-waiting had sole responsibility for the queen's wardrobe and jewels and disposed of a staff of servants and valets of the wardrobe. Furthermore, by the nature of her duties, she had the important privilege of approaching the queen at any hour. This position was occupied by Louisa de Osorio, another Spanish lady who had accompanied Anne from Madrid. For ordinary attendance Anne had seven ladies, four French ones and three Spanish. In addition, she had a number of maids-of-honor, young ladies of good birth who lived under the supervision of a governess and appeared in public only to accompany the queen on special ceremonial occasions. For the service of Anne's chamber, the first chamber woman supervised four French women and twelve Spanish ones, also wellborn though not of high rank, not counting the serving women and laundresses who took care of the ladies.

Anne's religious needs were to be served by her grand almoner, Richelieu, assisted by her first almoner, an almoner-in-ordinary, and four lesser almoners. The queen had her own confessor; two other confessors were provided for the household and also eight chaplains, with four clerks of the chapel and two servants assigned to them. According to protocol, the queen had a gentleman of honor who was expected to be in her antechamber at eight in the morning to await her rising and whose duty it was to accompany her whenever she left her apartments. This position was held by the duke of Uzès, who served her until his death decades later. The first maître d'hôtel, with his assistants, supervised a number of gentlemen servants and squires, ushers and porters, the kitchen staff from master cook to scullery boys, the pantry, the cellar, and the fruit store. The medical department of physicians, surgeons, apothecaries, and their assistants, four upholsterers, two cabinetmakers, a tailor, two spinet players, and a number of musicians completed the ordinary list of services. Artisans such as jewelers, watchmakers, shoemakers, lacemakers, florists, wigmakers, hoopmakers, were commissioned as required. Last but not least came the service of the stables, which included attendants and grooms, horses, mules, carriages, and litters.

To deal with any legal questions that might arise from her dower lands and revenues, Anne had a council that comprised a chancellor and attorney-general, twenty-six masters-of-requests, a secretary, a secretary-interpreter, twenty-six ordinary secretaries, as well as ushers and valets. An intendant of the household and director of finances supervised the treasurer-general, who paid out the quarterly salaries from monies he received from the treasurer of the *épargne*, the royal funds. A controller-general was responsible for all the accounting and met all expenses other than salaries.

The queen's household, therefore, was a sizable apparatus, about half as large as the king's though not quite as large as Marie de Medici's.[17] It not only served the queen but also isolated her from ordinary cares of life as well as from her husband. King and queen moved in their separate households as in small worlds that intersected only according to protocol. It was entirely normal that neither should have direct knowledge of what went on in the other's world except by hearsay or formal inquiry. Under these circumstances opportunities abounded for intrigue and misrepresentation by courtiers for their own advantage. A strong-willed monarch could overcome this network of ceremonious protocol. Henry IV had managed to ignore ceremonial when it suited him, so that he and Marie de Medici had shared at least some domestic life in the intervals between their quarrels. Louis, however, felt more comfortable with the formality dictated by court custom. Normally he and the queen dined separately, and he called on her twice a day in mid-morning and mid-afternoon visits, during which both were surrounded by their attendants and made polite conversation.[18]

In this way Anne spent her first years in France surrounded by her French and Spanish ladies and maids, disposing around her the possessions she had brought from home, and displaying the dresses of her trousseau. We do not know whether she had formal lessons or tutoring of any kind. Her father complimented her on the knowledge of French she showed in a note to her sister-in-law, the crown princess of Spain,[19] but she never wrote French perfectly, and we may assume that her training had not been very demanding. In his instructions to her when she left Spain, Philip had urged her always to have some work such as embroidery to occupy her hands.[20] Nothing indicates, however, that either in her youth or at any later time she did such handiwork. Her father had also urged her not to seek acquaintances but to converse only with her husband, the queen mother, and her own ladies and maids.[21] She probably followed this last advice for lack of opportunity to do otherwise.

Such a routine might have become boring, but the court did have its amusements. Aside from the celebration of religious holidays, there were other festive occasions. In June 1616, shortly after Anne's arrival in the Louvre, the city council of Paris received permission from Louis to invite Anne to the traditional celebration of Saint John's Eve.[22] She thanked them for their invitation and said she would do as the king commanded her. Since the records of the city council do not refer further to this event, perhaps she was prevented from attending. Two years later, however, the city of Paris invited her again, and this time she graced the festivities with her presence, Louis having given her leave to go although he excused himself.[23] On 23 June 1618, she arrived at the city hall accompanied by her sisters-in-law Christine and Henrietta-Maria, was met by the governor of the city of Paris and by all the dignitaries of the city council in their robes of office, and then watched the dancing at the ball, enjoyed a collation of preserves, fruits, and jams, and played cards. At eight in the evening, she ordered the Saint John's bonfire lit; and all the dignitaries, garlanded with carnations and accompanied by music, marched three times around the woodpile that had been prepared in the square outside the city hall and then lit the fire. As soon as it grew dark enough, fireworks crowned the celebration. When Anne left, she thanked the gentlemen of the city heartily and expressed herself as being very pleased with them.

On other occasions the family made excursions to country palaces. Already in July 1616, Louis introduced Anne to Saint-Germain, his favorite place of sojourn in which he had spent most of his time as a young child. The attraction of country palaces lay in their game parks. Louis loved to hunt, and Anne eventually loved to keep up with him. Four years later her father, having heard that she had lately spent twelve hours in the saddle, commended her for wishing to follow her husband but cautioned her not to overtire herself.[24]

Whether the court followed the schedule of evening entertainments established by protocol, that is to say, the weekly balls and concerts, it is difficult to tell. In any event, Marie de Medici had plays put on, particularly Italian comedies;[25] and in the carnival season, there were always elaborate court ballets produced by the king.[26] They called for many rehearsals and involved complicated stage sets and machinery. The subject was most often allegorical and had to provide opportunity for numerous *entrées*—appearances by the king, his friends, the chief noblemen of the court, their friends, and, of course, the queen and her ladies as well as the princesses and ladies of rank in the kingdom. The ballets were usually performed on a stage set up in the great hall of the Louvre, the half of the west wing that had been completed in the sixteenth century, or else in the palace of the Petit-Bourbon across the rue d'Autriche. Anne wrote her father all about these entertainments, which were unknown at the Spanish court. Philip replied with reports of the Spanish court festivities, such as masked balls, bullfights, and, according to the Spanish carnival tradition, plays.

It seems to have been a family habit of the Habsburgs to keep in as close touch as possible with daughters who had been sent far away to marry. The Austrian Habsburgs sometimes sent the girl's brothers to visit her.[27] No one suggested that Anne should receive a visit from her brothers, but the correspondence between her and her father, as well as other members of her family, was a steady one.[28] Philip's letters to her are not matched in any way by Louis's rather formal notes to his sisters, Elizabeth in Spain or, later, Christine in Savoy and Henrietta Maria in England. On the whole, Philip appears to have been a better correspondent than his daughter. He was always impatient for letters from her although when, by chance, the courier delivered several at once, he was apt to be concerned lest she strain her eyes by too much writing. He sent her news of his own health, of the health of her brothers and sisters, and their trips and amusements. Sometimes the news was bad, as in March 1617, when he had to write of the death of her youngest sister, Margaret. At all times he rejoiced over Anne's progress. He had heard that she was filling out and becoming a pretty young woman, and when she asked him to have clog shoes sent to her with lower soles, he happily deduced she must be growing. He wrote her that he would love to see her and wanted more portraits of her. He had had one painted while she was at Burgos before her departure for France, but he wanted to see her as she was now. He also sent presents of pocket money and presumably obliged when Anne asked for a gift of Spanish melons. He was not the only member of the family to send Anne presents: her aunt who administered the Spanish Netherlands, the infanta Clara Isabella Eugenia, sent a parrot to amuse her.

But Philip was an anxious as well as an indulgent father. He worried over his daughter whenever he heard that she was ill, as for example when she suffered from fever in the fall of 1617 and from measles in 1618. At such times he incessantly asked for reports until he was assured of her recovery. Above all, however, he worried over the success of her marriage. To ensure smooth relations in her new family, he had admonished her from the beginning to be polite and soft-spoken with her mother-in-law, and also to treat Marie's favorite, Leonora Galigaï, with all consideration. Instead Anne had been heard being a trifle short with Marie, and this was a failing Philip thought Anne should correct for her own good.[29] While Anne's marriage was still being negotiated, Marie had expressed fears that, although they were cousins on the maternal side, Anne would look down on her once she came to France because the Medici lineage was not as illustrious as her own. The Spaniards had taken great pains to reassure Marie concerning Anne's respect for her,[30] but evidently Marie's fears had not been altogether groundless. Nevertheless, whatever pride Anne may have shown, there were sufficient other reasons for the lack of cordiality between her and her mother-in-law even though Philip did not seem to appreciate them.

Marie may have given up her apartment in the Louvre to Anne, but she had not surrendered her power over Louis or her dominance in affairs of state. This was true to such an extent that when officials referred to the queen, they usually meant Marie de Medici, whom, according to etiquette, they should have called the queen mother. Anne's position in this respect did not improve even after Marie lost her power temporarily. Leonora Galigaï's husband, Concini, marshall d'Ancre, who had been governing the royal council and abusing the royal finances through the influence of his wife, was assassinated in April 1617 by Louis's friends, and Leonora herself was arrested and put on trial. It is not clear whether Louis had actually approved the killing; but he did not disavow the deed, and it became in fact his declaration of active kingship, if not of independence. He followed up his victory over his mother's favorites by exiling Marie herself from court and sending her to Blois in May.

This did not mean that he now turned to his wife as a partner in his confidences. The new dominant figure in Louis's life was Albert de Luynes, who had encouraged his opposition to the former favorites and now reaped the reward of his services. It was he who controlled the appointment of ministers, and, although he came of relatively modest origins, Louis authorized his marriage to a young woman of the bluest blood, Marie de Rohan, daughter of the duke of Montbazon. In a few years, Marie de Rohan was to become Anne's closest friend, but meanwhile the attention Louis paid Marie because she was Luynes's wife caused in Anne noticeable jealousy. Indeed, for Anne the effects of the palace revolution seemed to be anything but promising. She had written her father about it, and Philip, who also had been officially informed by Louis, reassured her that if her husband had arranged Concini's death, he must have had good reason and would, no doubt, proceed with all necessary prudence; as a good wife, she must take his side.[31] What that meant most immediately for Anne, however, was the loss of some of her Spanish household. Louis disliked Spain and Spaniards. He had been encouraged in this feeling as a child and had used to repeat that he did not care for Spaniards except, of course, for the infanta.[32] Consequently he did not like to see the Spanish ladies and maids surrounding his wife, nor did he like the fact that Monteléon, the Spanish ambassador, held the office of majordomo of Anne's Spanish household. That office gave Monteléon access to the queen or her women without the necessity of asking for formal audience like other ambassadors. Now that Louis felt he was his own master, he had Monteléon forbidden his free access to the palace, and in the course of the same year, 1617, the first of Anne's Spanish attendants were sent home: two ladies and seven chamber women, the first almoner, and Anne's two Spanish physicians.[33] That left Anne with her Spanish confessor, four Spanish chamber women, one of the Spanish ladies, and, of course, Louisa de Osorio, her lady-in-waiting, and the countess de la Torre, the lady of honor. The days of their stay in France, however, were numbered.

Louis's dislike of Anne's Spanish attendants may not have been wholly irrational. The younger ones among them apparently adapted themselves readily enough to French fashions and court customs, but they along with their Spanish speech reminded Anne of her original home and continued to attach her to it. Philip particularly depended on the countess de la Torre to watch over his daughter and keep her mindful of his instructions in such matters as not staying up too late or injuring her health by overindulgence in amusements. He also relied on the countess for a constant stream of information about his daughter's doings. The countess, a cousin of the duke of Lerma, used her interest with Philip to promote the affairs of her sons and daughters in Spain. Philip took this in good part and repeatedly exhorted Anne to show the countess the esteem he thought she deserved.[34] Considering the frequency of his admonitions, it seems clear that Anne did not share her father's enthusiasm for the lady, and indeed a neutral observer, the papal nuncio at the French court, noted that the countess was abusing her position by defrauding the young queen of monies allocated for the household and putting her in debt.[35] Anne herself seems to have liked Louisa de Osorio better than the countess. They were companions in the court pastimes, and Anne wrote to her father that she and her lady-in-waiting were becoming very French in their appearance. Philip replied that he was sure, however French they might be in externals, they were still good Spaniards at heart.[36] That probably was just what Louis feared. At least it was what he alleged when he was pressed to explain why, as the years went by, he was still not living with Anne as a husband should be with his wife.

Louis's neglect of his marital duties caused Philip the greatest worry of all, and not him alone. The Roman curia shared his concern as it had shared his hopes for the diplomatic fruit of the French marriages. Both courts, Rome and Madrid, entertained a vision of the Catholic world beleaguered by the forces of heresy—a vision that admittedly had its counterpart in contemporary Protestant fears of a Catholic crusade. But though anchoring France to the Catholic cause was important to the Vatican, Philip III had additional and more specific goals such as keeping the French from interfering with the Spanish hegemony in Italy.[37] France had a long tradition of supporting Italian princes who chafed under Spanish dominance, and the Spaniards hoped Louis XIII could be prevented from following the example of his predecessors in this respect. Things were not turning out that way, however. By 1617, instead of seeing the French court taking its lead from Spain in foreign affairs, Philip found that Spanish influence in Paris was being threatened by arguments from the most troublesome of the Italian princes, Charles Emmanuel I of Savoy.

Charles Emmanuel, his duchy caught between the two great powers of France and Spain, was at this point preaching the necessity of a league against overweening Habsburg might. In the hope of drawing France into the league, he proposed marriage between his heir prince Victor Amadeus and Louis's sister Christine. Spain found it difficult to counter this challenge since Anne, who should have been Spain's most effective advocate, was languishing on the sidelines. Philip still counted on her to adhere to the instructions he had given her, for in his letters he mentioned French political matters, both foreign and domestic, as though he expected her to be fully involved.[38] His ministers also attached great importance to whatever Anne might contribute; Philip's secretary had orders to send her letters on to the royal council as quickly as possible if they contained reference to Italian affairs.[39] Undeniably, however, Anne's usefulness was compromised by the ambiguity of her status as a wife in name only.

Spanish anxiety about Anne's marriage grew increasingly acute in 1617 and 1618. For a while the Spaniards suspected the Savoyard ambassador in Paris of trying to undermine Anne's position, and at one point the Spanish ambassador and the papal nuncio Cardinal Bentivoglio surmised that Savoy had enlisted the help of Louis's favorite, Luynes, in an effort to keep Anne and Louis apart.[40] The ambassador and the nuncio eventually convinced themselves that Luynes was not hostile to Anne, though he was certainly encouraging the marriage negotiations with Savoy. If Luynes was not the culprit, it must be Louis himself; Anne's backers began to concentrate pressure on him through all possible avenues. The Spanish ambassador Monteléon besieged Luynes; Cardinal Bentivoglio worked on Father Arnoux, Louis's confessor; and both men appealed to the king himself in order to persuade him, as they said, to consummate his marriage. Evidently they discounted whatever had happened on Louis and Anne's wedding night, or at least they did not regard it as a true beginning of married life. In January 1618 they were led to believe that Louis would finally sleep with the queen during their stay at Saint-Germain; but the trip to Saint-Germain passed, and nothing happened.

Some courtiers thought that perhaps Louis should be initiated by an experienced woman, a counsel of despair that Father Arnoux urged Louis to ignore. Cardinal Bentivoglio noted the consoling thought proffered by others that Louis's father Henry IV had also begun late and yet had never been shy with the ladies afterward.[41] No one could really understand why Louis was so reluctant to become a lover and a husband. People assumed that he distrusted his powers and somehow had found his wedding night humiliating,[42] although his physician had not noticed any despondency in the young king on the morning after. Indeed, he had reported Louis to be cheerful and hungry for his breakfast.[43] Louis himself, when pressed by his confessor, protested that he was still too young for sexual intercourse and said he feared he might suffer physical harm from it. Héroard, the physician, officially pronounced the king would not be too young once he had turned seventeen, but not even Héroard's sanction seemed to be effective. Perhaps Louis's resistance was the result of Héroard's relentless monitoring of his bodily functions during his childhood. It would seem that now Louis stubbornly guarded whatever remained to him of his autonomy; neither his confessor's exhortations nor Héroard's permission sufficed to overcome his resistance.

By the spring of 1618, Cardinal Bentivoglio began to fear the worst. As he wrote to the papal secretary of state, if current conflicts of interest between France and Spain and Italy should lead to fighting, Louis and Anne's marriage would break up and as a result a great storm, the most disastrous ever seen, would descend on Christendom.[44] If Louis had indeed repudiated Anne, it would certainly have meant a rupture of the Spanish alliance, and the insult to the court of Madrid would have been an enormous one. There is no evidence, however, that Louis thought of doing any such thing. Instead he merely wanted to get rid of the remaining Spanish attendants in Anne's household.

Luynes intimated to the Spanish ambassador and thus to Philip that as soon as the Spaniards had left the court, on the very evening, Louis would begin to live with Anne as a husband should.[45] So anxious was Philip to secure his daughter's future that he eventually agreed to let the rest of her Spanish household come home. He wrote Anne that everything concerning this matter would be arranged for her contentment.[46] The French court made the Spanish ladies generous allowances for transport and travel expenses in accordance with each one's rank.[47] In December 1618, therefore, the only Spaniards left in Anne's service were her confessor and one chamber woman.

This exodus did not produce any change in Anne's relations with Louis. The king still made no move toward his wife, and communication between them remained on the formal level of protocol. She sent her people to attend his morning *lever* to inquire after his health; he did the same for her. He visited her in her apartments twice a day, surrounded by courtiers and attendants. Aside from these official meetings, Anne could neither see the king nor speak to him without a special request having been made and permission granted.

What were Anne's feelings during these long years of uncertainty and rejection? She herself never said; we can only guess at them. Her father cannot have made the waiting easier for her, with his constant refrain that he dearly wanted to hear news of a grandchild on the way. As early as 1616, he had started to bombard her with coy questions, wishing to know whether Louis did not sometimes spend the night with her. But when it came to help, all Philip could do was to offer encouragement: she should be attentive to Louis and Marie de Medici, put her trust in God, and in the end all would be well. Evidently Anne did have recourse to divine aid because Philip praised her for her new devotions—rising early in order to hear two masses on the day she took communion and saying the Rosary and the Office of the Virgin.[48]

She did not wear her heart on her sleeve, however. The French courtiers thought her cold and haughty. They were pleasantly surprised when she showed jealousy over Louis's markedly courteous attentions to Luynes's new wife, Marie de Rohan: jealousy seemed to prove that Anne had a heart after all. By the spring of 1618, that heart became more apparent. She was making herself as pretty as she could whenever Louis came to visit, and it seemed obvious that she would have liked to make advances if modesty had not held her back.[49] Louis did not respond though, and a king could not be forced. Anne's Spanish ladies found that out when on one occasion they tried to prevent Louis from leaving: he became very angry, which made matters worse. Malherbe, the court poet, reminded Louis in vain that he should act like the youth he was and keep placid repose for old age when the blood runs colder. The papal nuncio was more direct. Louis had settled that the marriage between his sister Christine and Victor Amadeus should take place in February 1619. In January, Cardinal Bentivoglio took the opportunity of a royal audience to ask Louis if he wanted to see his sister bear an heir to Savoy before he himself had a dauphin.[50] Louis blushed and said "no," but there still seemed no immediate prospect that he would change his manner of living.

Shortly thereafter, however, the Venetian ambassador reported a remarkable occurrence to his government. On 20 January, Louis's half-sister, Mademoiselle de Vendôme, wedded the duke of Elboeuf. According to the ambassador's report, Louis watched the newlyweds consummate their marriage, whereupon Mademoiselle de Vendôme laughingly told him he would do well to go and do likewise with the queen.[51] Whether the story was true is uncertain. Héroard noted in his journal only that Louis went with other persons to tease the bridal pair as was customary.[52] Perhaps Louis did watch. No one thought it amiss that nurses or maids stayed in the room when married persons retired for the night, so perhaps on this occasion Louis was indeed invited to be present in the good cause of giving him encouragement. In the end, however, it took direct intervention by Luynes to set Louis on the path of love. Late in the evening of 25 January 1619, as the king was once again preparing to sleep alone, Luynes took him firmly by the arm and led him, despite his troubled protests, to the queen's chamber and closed the door on him. The next day Héroard reported in his journal that Louis had had intercourse with Anne; the *Mercure Français* announced the consummation of the king's marriage to the mutual satisfaction of both Louis and Anne; and the news was given out officially to all foreign ambassadors in Paris.[53] The Spanish ambassador triumphantly wrote to Philip that now Anne would probably have more influence and could serve as a useful intermediary in diplomatic negotiations between France and Spain.[54] Cardinal Bentivoglio was in even greater rapture over the fortunate turn of events. Writing a few weeks later to Rome, he reported that the king and queen had been together almost every night, so that now the marriage could be taken as secure. He considered this a success of the greatest importance because, as he said, the good that had always been hoped for from the union would now be realized—that is to say, the Huguenots and other malcontents would be silenced and the party of Catholicism strengthened. He praised Anne for her patience and submission during the years past, and, like the Spanish ambassador, he believed that she would surely gain the will and heart of Louis.[55] At his next audience with the couple, Cardinal Bentivoglio duly congratulated Louis and Anne and assured them that the pope was rejoicing in their happiness.

The marriage between Marie Christine and Victor Amadeus on 10 February almost took on the character of a double wedding. The high point of the festivities came on 12 February with a court ballet on the theme of Godefroi de Bouillon's siege of Jerusalem. The ballet was presented with the most magnificent changes of scenery, a pantheon of gods and goddesses of antiquity, crowds of shepherds and shepherdesses, and a host of crusaders. Louis was attentive to a radiant Anne while a chorus of angels sang a paean of praise to her beauty "which shone more brightly than either they or the sun and had captured the thoughts and the power of the greatest king in the universe."[56]

Chapter Four

Louis's Amaryllis

THE ROYAL HONEYMOON seemed destined to last forever. It was apparently true what Louis had sworn to Anne the morning after their first night together: that he loved her, that he would love only her and would always be faithful.[1] Also he informed the Spanish ambassador that he, Louis, adored his wife above anything in the world and that everyone was aware he was proving it to her to the best of his ability.

At that time, according to Héroard's journal,[2] the couple slept together two or three times a week, and everyone at court and in the country in general expected an announcement of fortunate hopes at any time. It was even taken as a sign of Louis's great affection for Anne that he did not go directly to her with any complaints or slight disagreements but rather charged Luynes to relay such matters to the Spanish ambassador, who passed them on to Anne. This apparent delicacy might better have been taken as an ominous sign for the marriage. It meant that even in their first tenderness, Louis and Anne did not deal face-to-face with each other. Louis evidently had not outgrown his childhood avoidance of direct personal confrontation. In crises with persons important to him, he continued to favor the use of intermediaries and even of the written word. It was a habit that did nothing to improve his personal relationships, least of all his marriage.

For the time being, however, no one looked for evil portents. Instead everyone looked for a dauphin. Ambassadors, courtiers, the papal nuncio, all asked the queen when she would give the kingdom a crown prince. Anne developed a standard response to such questions: she would blush, smile, and reply that that must await the will of God. There are references in memoirs to repeated unsuccessful pregnancies, although Héroard's journal corroborates only one of these at a later time. However, she was believed to have suffered a disappointment of that kind in the spring of 1619; and in December of the same year, rumor had it that an heir might again be expected. If so, she was having a hard time of it: the Venetian ambassador, who saw her dining in public, reported that she looked pale and thin and seemed languishing to such an extent that had he not seen her eating, he would not have been able to tell whether she was alive or dead.[3] By the end of January, her condition was clearer: it was not a case of pregnancy but of illness. She suffered intense fever, and for some days the royal physicians feared for her life. Precisely what this illness may have been we do not know; the contemporary diagnosis of double tertian fever is not very illuminating.

Louis for the only time in his life suspended court protocol and ceremonial and stayed near his wife both day and night. He ordered public prayers and religious processions. He had relics brought to the sickroom. He made a vow of pilgrimage, as Anne did herself. He persuaded her to take the doctors' remedies, exhorting her to be brave and assuring her there was nothing in the world he would not do for her even if it cost him half of his kingdom. And above all, Louis wept while he believed her to be in danger. After eleven days the doctors announced that there was improvement, and several days after that they declared her recovery was certain. Anne responded to Louis's solicitude gratefully, saying she could see he loved her with all his heart. When she was beginning to feel better and Louis was still at her bedside, she looked at him affectionately, took his hand, and kissed it. In his relief Louis himself announced Anne's impending recovery to Philip III, "God having accepted my vows at the urgent prayers of my people."[4]

During that spring of 1620, love seemed to blossom more than ever. Louis wrote a song to Amaryllis, a poem that was set to music, in which he told the sun that it turned pale near Amaryllis; told the lilies that they were insignificant near Amaryllis; and concluded that the beauty of spring flowers mattered nothing to him when he saw tears in the eyes of Amaryllis.[5] It is not a poem marked by great originality or depth, but it was the tribute of a man in love. The general public had a rare chance to convince itself of the king's sentiments on a Sunday in May when Louis, with some thirty noblemen, ran and won a series of races for the ring in the Place Royale in Paris. In this equestrian exhibition, the contestants tried to spear a ring suspended from a post while riding full gallop. Louis in white satin on a white horse was one of the three finalists and emerged as the victor after two runoff rounds. Anne, seated in the tribune erected for the royal ladies and noblewomen, had a diamond ring to present to the victor. When Louis came to the tribune to claim his prize, he saw that her eyes were filled with tears of emotion and was himself so touched that he leaped up the steps, took her in his arms and kissed her to the immense delight of all the spectators.[6]

The mood of celebration continued. As they did every year, the Paris city officials invited Their Majesties to celebrate Saint John's eve by attending the lighting of the official bonfire. This time both Louis and Anne accepted. The provost of merchants and the city council accordingly made extraordinary preparations. Public rooms in the Hôtel de Ville were decorated with tapestries and oriental rugs; throne chairs covered with cloth of gold were set up in the main hall under a canopy of gold-brocaded velvet; a dance floor was prepared for the ball. The best preserves were chosen from the stock of the grocers Dupont and Racyne for Their Majesties and the courtiers' collation, and the city's official cook, Dame Coiffier, picked out the best fruit from the market. On the day itself, 23 June, Anne opened the ball with the count of Soissons, and Louis, who arrived later, watched the dancing. Then they did justice to the collation that had been set out for them and condescended to share the special delicacies with their immediate attendants. The collation for the rest of the court, as the city's official record noted, was over very quickly: the courtiers in their rush overturned the buffet tables and broke the faience dishes—a spectacle that gave the king particularly great amusement. Thereafter, Louis, wearing the customary sash and bonnet of white carnations, went in procession with the provost of merchants, the governor of Paris, and the city council to light the Saint John's Eve fire. Magnificent fireworks concluded the evening, and Their Majesties left to return to the Louvre at about 10 P.M..

Anne had enjoyed herself thoroughly. When next day the city fathers waited upon the king and queen to thank them for the honor they had done the city by attending the celebration, Anne received the company in her bedroom even though she was not yet dressed, a condescension that the city fathers took as a very great favor. She also assured them that if she ever had an occasion to do something to please the city, she would very gladly use it.[7]

In that golden time, Louis trusted Anne enough to leave her in charge of the government while he went on military campaign. That had not been necessary the year before when he spent the summer trying to pacify his mother, who had raised a revolt against him. On that occasion he and Anne had traveled together on a leisurely progress through the Loire country, enjoying pleasurable side trips or hunting. With a renewal of the queen mother's revolt in 1620, a fresh campaign became necessary, and this time Louis left alone early in July. In his absence Anne was not expected to make major decisions on her own; she had the chancellor of France and part of the royal council to guide her. But Louis's declaration on departing for Normandy made it clear that her authority was to be honored as though it were the king's own and that orders coming from her should be obeyed without question.[8] She probably did not have much to do with the royal edicts that were issued in her name, such as the act of 14 July prohibiting unlicensed levies of armed men in the Paris area. On the other hand, she did fulfill representative functions, swearing in the newly installed officers of the Paris militia, administering the oath to the recently elected provost of merchants and other city officials, and ordering Te Deum to be sung at Notre-Dame in Thanksgiving for the reconciliation of Louis with his mother and the apparent end of civil war.[9] That happened in the middle of August, and now that the military campaign was over, Louis asked Anne to meet him at Tours, writing, "Come as gaily as you will be awaited by me who wishes passionately to see you."[10] Presumably Louis was well content with the public role his wife had played.

We have a drawing by the court artist Daniel Dumoustier to show us how Anne looked at that time.[11] She had evidently discarded the Spanish fashions she had brought with her and had adopted a newer style, for she is depicted wearing a wide lace collar that rises from a V-neck to frame her head and her hair is no longer curled tightly around her face but drawn back and slightly puffed over the ears. She wore what had evidently become her favorite jewelry, her choker of large matched pearls and her tear-drop pearl earrings. In almost all her portraits to the end of her life, she was to wear these pieces regardless of what other jewels she might have on.

Her forehead was well proportioned and shows to good advantage in her new hairstyle; her cheeks and nose seem a bit fleshly and her lower lip is slightly prominent, but her mouth could be called a rosebud tucked in at the corners. Although her eyes are heavy lidded, they are large and glowing. In short, the portrait shows the face of a young woman, somewhat wary but curious and eager, not to say greedy, for life. That life, however, was beginning to show its shadow side.

No matter how much Louis may have loved and trusted Anne, in all matters of importance his confidence went to the duke of Luynes. On the whole, he even spent more time with Luynes than with Anne, since Luynes had political as well as court duties to perform and, after he became constable of France, assumed supreme military command under the king's authority as well. Anne had always resented Luynes and yielded only to the pleas of her father and perhaps also to necessity in finally reconciling herself to his constant presence and the degree of his influence. At least she reconciled herself in appearance, was gracious to him, and when the king went on campaign without her, addressed her inquiries for news more often to Luynes than to

Louis himself. Still it was not really a cordial relationship. Luynes indeed had induced Louis finally to consummate his and Anne's marriage, but that fact may not have endeared Luynes to her. Nor had she liked it that Luynes's young wife had been imposed on her as superintendent of her household and head of her council in 1618.[12] Marie de Rohan, duchess of Luynes, was an extremely pretty, lively, and witty brunette, merely a year older than the queen. From her youth on, men seemed to be irresistibly attracted to her. Louis himself appeared to be fascinated to the point that Anne showed signs of jealousy. The Spaniards came to think there was a serious problem. In May 1620 the Spanish resident wrote Philip in alarm:

> . . . After the many demonstrations of love that her husband gave during [the queen's] illness, a great chill is apparent and every day sees an increase in the king's . . . conversations and visits with the duchess of Luynes. Although the queen feels it acutely, she dissembles with much prudence and gives the duchess and her husband all manners of favors and caresses.[13]

Fortunately this report proved to be exaggerated. Marie took care to dissipate any resentment Anne may have felt and set herself to win Anne's good will. As superintendent of the queen's household, Marie used every opportunity to please her with delicate attentions and small services. Moreover she amused the queen, as indeed she amused everyone. Marie had an infectious gaiety that chased away boredom and endeared her wherever she went throughout most of her life. Within a year or so, Anne and Marie were fast friends.

As Anne's circumstances improved in one direction, however, they worsened in another. When Louis made peace with his mother and Marie de Medici began to regain something of her former influence, her relations with her daughter-in-law produced conflict. During the two years Anne had lived at court before Marie left in 1617, she had been in the shadow of the older woman; but in those days she had been younger, the king's wife in name only, and therefore without real credit at court. It would seem that now Anne expected things to be different. Already when Louis and Marie had celebrated their first reconciliation at Tours in 1619, a thorny question of precedence had been raised. The queen mother claimed the right to precede her daughter-in-law even though the daughter-in-law was actually the queen regnant. Opinions were divided on this matter. Some observers believed it was proper for the younger woman to show deference to the older one by yielding her precedence on private occasions but that in state appearances, where the queen's majesty was, as it were, a reflection of the king's own authority, the reigning queen should take precedence over the queen mother.[14] Marie nevertheless insisted, and Louis, thus torn between his mother's and his wife's entreaties, grew irritated, decided in favor of his mother, and turned on his wife. Report had it that on one occasion he shouted at Anne because she was not, as he claimed, treating his mother properly.[15] There is no doubt that Louis had violated precedent by his decision, and that cannot have been any comfort to Anne. She had no wish to consider Marie de Medici in the place of a mother and yield to her, remembering the distance of birth between them.

After Marie's second reconciliation with her son in 1620, these frictions became more acute because the occasion for them was more frequent. By 1622 Marie de Medici once more sat in on royal council meetings, a privilege never accorded to Anne herself. Anne's later friend and biographer, Madame de Motteville, claimed that Marie deliberately fostered misunderstandings between her son and daughter-in-law in order to lesson Anne's influence on Louis and possess his mind more surely.[16] Madame de Motteville, however, did not give any examples of this strategy, if indeed it existed. What is certain is that once again Marie completely eclipsed the reigning queen in all serious matters. This disregard, the knowledge that her husband did not give her first place in his esteem, must have been sufficiently painful for Anne, even without deliberate ill services from her mother-in-law.

Natural events meanwhile brought their own sadness. Philip III died on 31 March 1621. When the news reached Paris on 8 April, Louis visited Anne, flanked by her confessor and by Mirabel, the Spanish ambassador, and announced without much preamble that he had just received dispatches that left no doubt her father was dead. Anne took it very hard. She wept uncontrollably, and Louis wept with her. He did what he could to console her, ordered the court into mourning for his late father-in-law, and commanded funeral services at Notre-Dame cathedral.[17] But there could be no question that her father's death was a heavy blow for Anne, all the heavier because she still had no children to create a family of her own around her.

According to the Spanish camp, Anne's continued childlessness was Louis's fault, and for a strange reason. The same resident who had raised the alarm over Marie de Rohan, had gone on in his report to Philip:

> . . . The king comes seldom or never to sleep with the queen since her illness, and it is believed [he thinks] if he has sons, however young

they are, they will be the cause of civil war in his kingdom. Whenever
the queen is thought to be pregnant he shows much regret. It is to be
feared that the interests of the queen are in danger from this disposition
of the king. . . .[18]

Philip's correspondent did not give the sources of his information,
though he implied that it was common knowledge. If so, it contradicts
all the traditional French accounts of Louis's life, every one of which
stresses his desire to have children. It is possible, of course, that
Louis's feelings in the matter were mixed, just as they had been about
the consummation of his marriage, and that this was something the
French never saw fit to record. The Spanish report cannot have been
based entirely on someone's conjecture because at least one item in it
was demonstrably true: judging by Héroard's notations, Louis did
sleep less frequently with Anne in 1620 and the earlier part of 1621.[19]
Whatever the reasons for that may have been, the couple's relations
seemed cordial enough, however, during the summer and fall.

In the late spring, Louis had set out on campaign to subdue a rebellion of Huguenot nobles and towns in southern France, and he asked
Anne to accompany him.[20] Marie de Medici went along too, since
Louis preferred to have her near him rather than conspiring against
him out of his sight. That did not make things as difficult for Anne as
one might expect. The three parties traveled and often lodged separately, as was customary on extended royal journeys because small
towns and villages or private castles and noble country manors could
not usually be expected to house and feed more than one royal suite
at a time. There was a good deal of visiting back and forth though. It
became a routine, while the army was besieging Montauban, for Louis
to ride over to the queen's lodgings to spend every other night, and for
her to visit him at his headquarters on the alternate days. It was a
pleasant interlude, especially since she had the company of her entertaining friend the duchess of Luynes. Anne was in excellent spirits
when at the beginning of November she wrote a lighthearted little
note to her sister-in-law's governess, Madame de Montglat, announc-
ing her return to Paris within a month.[21]

Rumor had it that twice in 1621 she suffered disappointment in her
hopes for pregnancy.[22] Héroard, however, did not record any such
occurrences in his usual detailed journal of the king's health. It would
have been strange if he had failed to mention an actual abortion or
miscarriage, since he meticulously reported everything that went into,
and came out of, the king, including issue borne by the queen. Perhaps the rumors were occasioned by delayed menstruation. Anne may

genuinely have believed herself pregnant for some days or even weeks, and may have been disappointed accordingly. And a great many people, herself included, no doubt also indulged in wishful thinking.

If 1621 had brought her a mixture of pleasure and unhappiness, the following year was no improvement. The constellation of Louis's loyalties shifted, and not in her favor. In December 1621 Luynes died of scarlet fever he had contracted during the siege of Montauban. Now that he was removed as an obstacle between Louis and his mother, Marie de Medici once again took the emotional ascendant over her son. She too returned to Paris, though not to the Louvre. She refurbished the magnificent Luxembourg Palace for herself and commissioned Peter Paul Rubens to paint a series of vast pictures showing the high points of her life from her arrival in France to the recent conclusion of peace between her and her son. Rubens used classical allegory as much as historical fact. Henry IV appeared as Jupiter, Marie herself as Juno, and the message of the series was clear: Marie had given a crown prince to France after some fifty years of sterility in the royal family; Marie after the assassination of Henry IV had piloted France successfully through internal troubles, had secured external peace by the Spanish marriages, and had triumphed over the evil spirits of calumny and discord and achieved the harmony in the royal family and in the kingdom for which she had longed. At least, that was how she liked to see herself, and Rubens presumably followed instructions.

Now that she was settled in Paris again, Marie wished to dominate public affairs as completely as she had done before her departure in 1617. To this end she began to importune her son to call her most trusted adviser, Jean Armand Duplessis de Richelieu, into the royal council and, since he was a bishop, to obtain the dignity of cardinal for him from Rome. Anne played no part at all in these weighty matters. Her function was to bear a crown prince. In every other respect, her position was marginal. It is true Louis XIII tried to use whatever diplomatic credit she might have in Spain, notably when in 1621 he had her endorse Marshall Bassompierre's mission to Madrid to oppose Spanish control over the Valtelline passes from Switzerland into Italy.[23] Anne's intervention had no effect on the negotiations, however, and in fact fighting on this matter broke out between France and Spain the following year. The Spaniards for their part apparently had given up the hope that Anne might influence her husband in their favor; there is no evidence that they expected anything from her at this time. Gone were the days when the Spanish ambassador in Paris suggested lines for her to speak to Louis so that she might render Spain good offices without risk to herself, as her father had intended.[24]

How did Anne reconcile herself to relative insignificance? How did she spend her time? We may assume that she had the consolation of religious practice. Her habits of piety during this period of her life are not recorded in detail. Presumably she followed the practices she had learned as a child, and certainly she took part in the religious activities dictated by royal ceremonial. We do know, however, that she liked to visit convents, as she had done in Spain and as her father had advised her to continue doing.[25] On one such occasion, she had met, and been impressed by, Mother Marguerite de Sainte-Gertrude, the abbess of Valprofond, a convent outside Paris.[26] Mother Marguerite had been appointed to her post by Louis in 1618 in order to reform the convent, which belonged to the Benedictine order. Anne met her at the ceremony in which Mother Marguerite was blessed as abbess and took such a strong liking to her that it became the beginning of a lifelong bond. In time Anne wished the convent to be moved to Paris, where it would be more accessible for her. On 7 May 1621, she therefore bought land, the so-called fief of the Petit-Bourbon, and in September the nuns moved into their new home. The only thing Louis contributed to this purchase was the cession of the seignorial rights that belonged to the crown.

It is suggestive that Anne took this step in early May of that year, so short a time after the death of her father. There is unfortunately no evidence to prove that she made this foundation as an act of piety in her father's memory, but we may assume that the purchase of land for the convent, now called by its older name of Val-de-Grâce, was associated with her grief and may have helped alleviate a sense of desolation. And she continued to support the religious community, transferring her attachment to the new superior, Louise de Milly, Mother Saint-Étienne, after Mother Marguerite died. When it became apparent that the existing buildings were inadequate, she promised to pay one-half the cost of a new convent. Construction on that began in 1624 with Anne herself laying the cornerstone. An apartment was eventually included for her use as a retreat. Since she was a very frequent visitor to Val-de-Grâce in later years, we may assume that she formed the habit of spending time there from the start.

Val-de-Grâce was an enterprise of which Louis evidently approved, at least in these beginnings. Not only did he cede the seignorial rights over the building site but in 1622 he granted the convent the right to elect its abbess rather than as heretofore receiving her by royal appointment. He approved less of some of Anne's other activities. Since the winter of 1618–19, her circle of ladies had become very youthful and lighthearted. This was not her doing. As we have seen, she had no choice about the appointment of Marie de Rohan as superintendent of her household nor was she consulted when Luynes's sister, Mademoiselle de Vernet, replaced the Spanish lady-in-waiting who was sent home in 1618. But Anne came to enjoy and depend upon the pair's company, particularly on that of Marie de Rohan. Marie and her sister-in-law drew other ladies like themselves into their set: Louis's half-sister Mademoiselle de Verneuil, and the princess of Conti, a sister-in-law of the prince of Condé and therefore a royal cousin. The princess of Conti was the oldest of the group, a widow of forty-four, but nevertheless as lively as the younger women and with a somewhat doubtful reputation. All four ladies gave most of their attention to sentimental involvements, jokes, and what the staider members of the court considered general frivolity. Amid all this gaiety Anne blossomed. She enjoyed hearing tributes to her beauty; she acquired gallants, albeit respectful ones: the duke of Montmorency, the aging duke of Bellegarde.

Marie de Rohan later recalled that it had taken her no end of trouble to induce the queen to enjoy talk of love affairs and to think that she herself might inspire sentimental attachments.[27] That Marie succeeded at all is perhaps surprising considering Anne's piety, strict upbringing, and the fact that she had been known to be very hard on gallant ladies at court. Apparently Anne came to see such things in a different light. As she explained subsequently, it seemed to her that flirtation was not a danger to a virtuous woman because even the court ladies in Spain who lived in the palace as strictly guarded as nuns took pleasure in boasting of their romantic conquests at court and no one thought any evil of it.[28] Her new friends amused her, flattered her, pointed out this or that courtier who they said was certainly in love with her. They played schoolgirl pranks together. Marie's sister-in-law the princess of Guéménée was reputed to be one of the most beautiful women at court. Lest she outshine them at balls, Marie and Anne used to approach her solicitously and tell her she looked ill; since she was impressionable, this device never failed to put her to flight.

Other amusements were earthier. It became known at court that Marie was giving Anne licentious reading matter, namely, the *Cabinet satyrique*,[29] an anthology that appeared annually in those years and to which even good though libertine poets, such as Régnier and Maynard, contributed. Some of the poems were satires, literary exercises on the classical model; some carried moral messages on the evils of prostitution and fornication. Most of the poems, however, were ribald celebrations of the pleasures of carnal love. They were often jokes, sometimes puns, and always explicit. Thanks to the element of wit, they are not what we would nowadays classify as pornography; and compared with sixteenth-century reading matter, they were neither novel nor especially shocking. Cultivated taste, however, was beginning to change in favor of greater decorum, and the growing strength of religious sentiment produced by the Catholic Reformation also had its part in making ribaldry socially unacceptable. Above all, it was feared that such reading might corrupt the queen's morals. Members of the royal court asked the papal nuncio to talk to the queen's confessor so that he might persuade her to dismiss her friends. Marie de Rohan's own father warned Louis himself about the unsuitable reading matter that his daughter had given the queen.[30]

Louis always disliked jokes with a sexual connotation. The thought that his wife could laugh heartily at such pleasantries cannot have made him feel comfortable, nor would he have appreciated epigrams with advice such as this:

> Get married, it's an honorable thing to do,
> I shall never be sorry to see it:
> But don't ever be so foolish
> As to marry your husband.[31]

Even before Louis received Montbazon's warning, he had begun to turn against Marie de Rohan: perhaps because she got on so well with the queen that he was jealous; perhaps as a way of repressing his own earlier fascination with the lady. For that matter, he was beginning to turn against Marie's husband. He took great pleasure in telling Luynes that Marie was making him a cuckold with the duke of Chevreuse.[32] This was a fact, but it was not kind to say so. As soon as Luynes died, Louis's hostility to the widow became more open. He wanted her to leave the Louvre altogether, and only when he was reminded that she could not do so as long as she remained superintendent of the queen's household did he permit her to stay on, although in meaner apartments. Mademoiselle de Vernet was sent away outright.

For the time being, however precariously, Anne kept the company of her friend Marie de Rohan. As a crowning joy, by March 1622 she knew certainly that she was pregnant. At that point, if universal report is to be believed, her friend Marie unintentionally did her a very ill turn. The physician Héroard's journal for 14 March shows a cryptic note regarding the queen's health, and two days later he reported that at three in the afternoon she had delivered an embryo of forty to forty-two days.[33] Louis was about to set out on a fresh campaign against the Huguenots of southern France, but he visited Anne later that day with every evidence of concern and good will. Only after he left Paris did he find out the probable reason for the miscarriage.

On the evening of 14 March, the queen with Marie de Rohan and Mademoiselle de Verneuil, had attended a gala reception in the Louvre apartments of the princess of Condé. When the queen returned to her own apartments, Marie thought it would be fun if they ran through the great hall of the Louvre. Although Anne did not wish to run, Marie and Mademoiselle de Verneuil took her each by an arm and ran with her down the length of the hall. The great room was not lit, and Anne stumbled on the dais that surrounded the throne—stumbled and fell.[34]

Considering what it meant to Anne's position to bear an heir to the throne, it seems hard to believe she could have been so careless of her safety. Indeed, the story might be dismissed as a fabrication by persons eager to discredit Marie de Rohan in the king's eyes were it not for the note in the physician's journal and for the fact that even Anne's later confidante, Madame de Motteville, indicated that the queen suffered this misfortune by running too much with Marie.[35]

It is, of course, possible that Anne's accident and her miscarriage were related by no more than coincidence. There may have been medical reasons for spontaneous abortion. Besides, midwives at the time attributed involuntary interruptions of pregnancy to a wide variety of causes in addition to accidental injury from falls: vigorous dancing, riding in poorly sprung coaches or on horses with a high gait, too tightly laced corsets, harmful foods, and even excessive lifting of the arms. Great ladies who were unused to physical exertion were therefore advised not to strain themselves by trying to dress their own hair.[36] Any one of these things might have been held accountable for Anne's miscarriage. Coincidence or not, however, what mattered was that Louis believed the miscarriage to have been the result of her fall. He blamed her companions for having encouraged her in thoughtless behavior, and he blamed her for having lost his child. Worst of all, Héroard thought it would have been a boy.[37]

Chapter Five

Buckingham

ANNE'S MISCARRIAGE AND its aftermath pointed up a growing problem in the royal marriage. It was becoming clear that Anne allowed herself to be led by people she liked, and that Louis was not one of those people. As Madame de Motteville later tried to explain it, since the king seemed to have no use for the queen's heart, she gave her attachment to ladies who abused it: far from encouraging her to please her husband, they were setting her against him in order to control her more completely for their own benefit.[1] Anne did not see it that way. She was apparently too grateful for friendship to perceive any ulterior motives. When things went wrong, as they did in 1622, she paid the penalty for her friends' misdeeds. And she continued in her ways: where she placed her affection, there followed her will.

Louis evidently had not discovered this key to Anne's character, or was unable to use it. She for her part, feeling misunderstood and rejected, fortified herself behind her own defenses. The couple thus lived increasingly at cross-purposes. For a while after Anne's miscarriage, Louis retreated into cold and painful anger. He did not confront her directly; his punishment fell on her companions. Marie de Rohan must leave court, and Mademoiselle de Verneuil must be married off with all speed. On 25 March, nine days after Anne's miscarriage, Louis wrote her curtly from Orleans: "The care I am obliged to take for the good of your household has decided me to make changes in it that will only be for the better, as you will eventually come to see."[2] Anne felt herself abused. As she saw it, Louis was striking at her through her friends. She did not think she had done anything wrong; she wanted to know what Marie de Rohan's fault was supposed to be and protested that as long as Marie continued to hold the post of superintendent of her household, she was bound to be in attendance at the Louvre.[3] For weeks messengers went back and forth between husband and wife, but Louis refused to enter on any explanations and kept repeating that his orders were only being given for Anne's good: "As I love nothing as much as you, so I can have no stronger concern than your welfare, which you will have recognized in the good order I desire to put into your household."[4] In the end Anne agreed to let Marie leave court and to see her only on rare occasions. Louis wrote that he was glad to learn of her disposition to obey him, assured her that he had not expected any other outcome, and again asked her to believe that he had nothing more at heart than her well-being and that forthcoming signs of his good will would convince her of his affection.[5]

However hurt Anne might have felt in her pride, she tried to make amends. Before he left on campaign and before the trouble over Marie de Rohan, Louis had again placed Anne in charge of government in Paris. Evidently thinking to please him, she carried out her duties conscientiously. Toward the end of April, she believed she had discovered traces of a plot against the king. An agent of the rebellious Protestant nobles had been found in Paris; she ordered his arrest and sent the letters he was carrying to Louis posthaste. Louis had not taken her into his confidence, however: he thanked her, as he said, with all his heart for the diligence she was showing in his service, but he knew all about the letters. They were merely credentials for the bearer in a secret negotiation the royal officials were conducting with the rebels. The king added he would have sent her annotations on the letters for her information; but because time was pressing, he did not wish to put her to the trouble, and she had only to send the agent on his way.[6]

After this rebuff, Anne did not offer any further initiatives. She might have learned something about the conduct of state affairs had Louis wished to teach her. Evidently, though, he did not want a politically active wife; and after this year, he no longer even appointed her as caretaker when he was absent on military campaigns. On the other hand, he was beginning to miss her physical presence. He sent for her to join him and by May was asking her to hurry her travel preparations "so that I shall have the happiness of seeing you soon, as I wish with all my affection."[7] Anne, of course, agreed to come, but there were delays. In early July, Louis had softened to the extent of permitting Marie de Rohan to accompany his wife on the journey with other ladies of the court: "The desire I have to see you does not allow me to let you stay far away from me any longer."[8] Louis was not letting Marie de Rohan rejoin the court just to please his wife, however: he said he was doing it for the sake of the lady's new husband, the duke of Chevreuse.[9]

Marie de Rohan had taken her own measures to improve her position.[10] Her lover, the duke of Chevreuse, like his sister, the princess of Conti, belonged to the Guise family, whose members were princes of Lorraine as well as great noblemen in France. Lorraine was still imperial territory, and the Guises therefore always considered themselves of almost sovereign rank as the relatives of the duke of Lorraine, a ruling prince in the empire. The king acknowledged these claims by calling the Guises cousins. In the previous century, moreover, a girl of their family had married James V of Scotland and borne him a daughter, Mary Stuart. The Guises had succeeded in wedding their niece to King Francis II of France and as royal in-laws had thought to dominate the court. These hopes were disappointed with the early death of Francis II, but Mary Stuart had returned to Scotland as queen, remarried, and produced a son, James VI, who in 1603 had succeeded Elizabeth and become king of England. To the English royal family, therefore, the descendants of the Guises in France were cousins in fact and not just in courtesy.

By marrying into such a well-connected clan, Marie de Rohan secured for herself an unassailable position in society. The king would have to deal warily with her, whatever his resentments. In addition, Chevreuse stood very well with Louis thanks to his unswerving loyalty during the king's conflicts with Marie de Medici. Although Louis opposed the marriage, it took place in Paris on 20 April 1622 without his consent. Then Chevreuse proceeded to beseech the king to pardon his disrespect. Although it took him several months, he succeeded in his suit as we have seen.

Louis's reunion and reconciliation with Anne waited longer. Despite his growing impatience to see his wife, delays and postponements intervened. He had wanted his mother and Gaston to meet him as well. First Gaston fell ill; then the queen mother needed more time for preparations; finally military operations caused the rendezvous to be changed repeatedly. Meanwhile, in October the besieged city of Montpellier fell to the king, and the great Protestant nobles agreed to make peace. Louis announced the treaty of Montpellier to Anne, rejoicing that it would leave him freer to give her proof of his affection.[11] He had to make a detour through Provence and Dauphiné, however, for a meeting with the duke of Savoy on diplomatic business. Not until 6 December 1622 did Louis meet Anne in Lyon, where she had arrived with the queen mother. According to some accounts, the encounter between husband and wife was glacial, in no way enlivened by the play performed that evening for their pleasure.[12] Perhaps after long separation they were unable to show their feelings; perhaps now that they were face to face, their feelings were mixed. Nevertheless, that night Louis slept with Anne as he did at four-day intervals during the next several weeks. A reconciliation of some kind had evidently been achieved.

Louis and his mother were apparently on good terms also. She had obtained her wish: the king had nominated her chief adviser and protégé Richelieu for the cardinalate. Confirmation arrived from Rome together with the cardinal's hat, which Louis presented to Richelieu during this stay in Lyon. We do not know whether Anne had any feelings about Richelieu's elevation or whether she had any awareness of him at all beyond the fact that he belonged to her mother-in-law, whose influence was growing stronger and stronger.

In other respects Anne's trip to Lyon must have been gratifying, for her presence next to Louis on public occasions underlined her importance as the king's wife. Envoys from Geneva who had come to greet the king of France celebrated Anne in their address as the goddess of peace at Louis's side.[13] The city of Lyon itself gave Anne and Louis a magnificent reception upon their formal entry, with triumphal arches, processions of all the local dignitaries, the most flattering speeches, and, in conclusion, elaborate fireworks set off from barges on the Rhône in which, according to the program, a crowned sun signified the virtues of the king and the dawn and stars represented the beauty of the queen. As a more tangible evidence of their devotion, the city fathers presented Louis and Anne each with a solid gold lion. Anne's gift carried with it a not altogether delicate hint at the kingdom's hopes for a dauphin, for her lion held a shield on which the queen could be seen sleeping while a hand emerging from a crowned cloud placed a medal on her arm showing a dolphin.[14] For the time being, however, no dauphin announced himself.

On 10 January 1623, the royal family was back in Paris, and the ensuing carnival season turned out to be more brilliant than usual.[15] The king presented his ballet with the theme that year of the Bacchanals, and on 5 March the queen appeared in her own ballet: the three festivals of Juno as a bride. Among the spectators were two gentlemen traveling incognito through France who had stopped in Paris to see the sights. Since they were incognito, the court did not take the notice of their presence that it would normally have done, for one of them was Charles, the prince of Wales, and the other was James I's favorite, the earl of Buckingham. The two did not stay long. They were on their way from London to Madrid in order to ask for the hand of Anne's younger sister, the infanta Maria, in marriage for the prince of Wales. Anne may not have been aware of the pair's visit; certainly they were not presented to her. She made an impression on them, however, for they reported home to James that they had watched "the queen and

Madame [Henrietta Maria] with as many as made up nineteen fair dancing ladies, amongst which the queen is handsomest."[16]

Anne was preoccupied with other concerns at this time. The duchess of Chevreuse was about to lose her post as superintendent of the queen's household. Anne's lady of honor, the dowager duchess of Montmorency, had brought suit at law to have the superintendency abolished on the grounds that it was incompatible with her own charge. She might better have left matters alone, for arbitrators decided that both ladies should resign their offices. Louis took the opportunity to assign the superintendency to a venerable gentleman, Chancellor d'Aligre, and at the end of November named a worthy and respectable matron, Madame de Lannoy, as the queen's new lady of honor.[17] It was a defeat for Anne. Although she still had the frequent company of the duchess of Chevreuse, her friend was no longer a member of her household, and much court routine thereby became less entertaining. The legal conflict itself must have placed Anne under considerable strain. In July 1623 the Venetian ambassador, who always heard the latest gossip, reported to his government that the queen had fallen unconscious in her apartments and injured her head. When she came to, nothing could be found wrong with her except for the bruises that resulted from the fall itself. There was speculation among the doctors that she might have suffered an attack of epilepsy, but it seems that no one ventured a definite diagnosis.[18] She never gave any other sign of such a malady either before or later. Most probably she had an attack of nerves brought about by the emotional pressures under which she lived.

While Anne was learning to put up with Madame de Lannoy and Chancellor d'Aligre, other changes were taking place at court. At the end of April 1624, Louis, yielding to his mother's long urging and to his own need for competent political advice, called Cardinal Richelieu to the royal council.[19] Anne had known Richelieu as her original grand almoner. He had been obliged to resign that post and to leave his place on the royal council in 1617 following Marie de Medici's disgrace. During the intervening years, he had spent much time in his diocese of Luçon reforming the clergy and writing works of religious controversy. He had also gradually displaced Marie de Medici's less capable advisers and had eventually succeeded in making himself as necessary to the son as to the mother. He had remarkable gifts of intellect and judgment and now at last had the opportunity to show himself as easily the most distinguished statesman of his age. Within months he rose to first place in Louis's council and dominated policy decisions.

Almost immediately Richelieu pressed his immediate predecessor La Vieuville's resumption of an old scheme of Henry IV for a marriage alliance between France and England. Such an alliance would strengthen France's diplomatic position in Europe in general and her hand in dealing with Spain in particular. Since the prince of Wales's wooing of the infanta had come to nothing, Richelieu advised a cordial reception to initiatives Louis now received from England for the hand of his younger sister Henrietta Maria.[20] Marie de Medici always had liked the idea of this match and had been sorry when it was dropped; the French Protestant nobles liked it as well and so, for that matter, did devout Catholics though for different reasons. Catholics hoped that through marriage with Henrietta Maria the future king of England at the very least would allow more toleration to Catholics in his own kingdoms. Against this favorable background, ambassadors spent the rest of the year and part of the next working out the provisions for a marriage treaty, settling questions regarding the dowry, the bridegroom's settlement on the bride, the extent of the privilege she should have to practice her own religion, and the benefits Louis requested should be extended to Catholics in England.

While the diplomatic work was progressing, Anne's friend the duchess of Chevreuse took as her latest lover Lord Holland, the English ambassador to Paris. Holland was close to Buckingham, a fact that gave Madame de Chevreuse what seemed to her a brilliant inspiration. Since Henrietta Maria would have to be married to the prince of Wales by proxy before she could leave France and since it was most probable that the proxy would be given to James's favorite and the prince of Wales's good friend the duke of Buckingham, what would be more suitable than that Anne herself should be introduced to the delight of a romantic love affair by being thrown together with Buckingham?[21] The scheme worked, although the factual evidence about what ensued is considerably less colorful than the imagination of later ages has suggested.

George Villiers, recently created duke of Buckingham, had a notorious reputation.[22] He had risen in the service of James I from small beginnings, and there could be no doubt that his most valued actions had been performed in the king's bedchamber. James doted on him and showered honors and gifts over his whole family. Charles, the prince of Wales, at first disliked Buckingham heartily; but Buckingham had great charm, and when he exerted himself to win the prince over, Charles came to look upon him as his best friend. No one ever suggested seriously that the relationship between Charles and Buckingham was overtly homosexual. It seems rather to have been a case of emotional dependence by the younger man on the older one. Besides, Buckingham was bisexual, to say the least. His seductions and love affairs were legendary, and it was his good fortune to have a loving and tolerant wife who turned a blind eye to all of them. He enjoyed daring and grandiose gestures such as his incognito trip with Charles to Spain, and could be relied upon to appreciate the gallant scheme the duchess of Chevreuse was proposing.

She and Lord Holland set to work in tandem. While Holland filled Buckingham's ears with reports of Anne's charms and supposed interest in his person, Madame de Chevreuse importuned the queen to receive Buckingham cordially when he should come. She sang his praises to Anne as the handsomest, most gallant man in Christendom; assured her that he was already in love with her even though he had glimpsed her only briefly two years earlier; and made light of Anne's scruples, maintaining no harm could be done to anyone by a bit of light flirtation. Neither Louis nor his advisers wanted to see Buckingham in France, not because they necessarily knew anything about the sentimental intrigue that was being spun, but because they had heard he was a hot-headed man, unreliable in negotiations, and feared he would upset the delicate last-minute bargaining concerning the marriage contract.[23] They could not refuse to receive him as the bearer of Charles's proxy, however, and Buckingham ordered a vast and magnificent trousseau for his entry into Paris and the subsequent festivities. He meant to take a suite of more than four hundred persons including gentlemen, servants, and musicians. For his personal adornment, he had twenty-seven outfits among which the most dazzling, meant for the wedding itself, was a suit of white satin velvet studded with a fortune in diamonds.[24] Strings of pearls were attached so lightly at the shoulders that they would be sure to break when the duke found himself in a crush of courtiers: scattering pearls was an impressively lavish form of tipping.

James I died in the spring of 1625, shortly before his son's wedding. Although Charles, now King Charles I, adhered to the arrangements that had been made, Buckingham himself was prevented from leaving for France in time by the rush of business connected with James's funeral and the establishment of the new reign. The bridegroom's proxy fell to the duke of Chevreuse, whom Charles was delighted to recognize in this way as his cousin. Henrietta Maria's betrothal ceremony took place in the Louvre on 8 May. From the descriptions we catch a rare glimpse of the French royal family: the bride in cloth of silver with gold embroideries, Louis in cloth of gold trimmed with silver, Marie de Medici in her usual black, Anne wearing silver-embroidered scarlet satin and a gold-striped black veil that must have set off her fair skin and dark blond hair.[25] On the following Sunday, 11 May, Henrietta Maria married Charles I of England by proxy in front of the doors of Notre-Dame cathedral with a papal dispensation for the fact that Charles was Protestant.

Buckingham missed all this. He arrived in Paris two weeks later on 24 May in time to escort the bride to London. At Louis's request, Chevreuse lodged the duke in his mansion near the Louvre; and for seven days, the king, Marie de Medici, Richelieu, and Chevreuse outdid one another in entertaining the English guest. Buckingham was then in his thirties, a handsome blond stud of a man whose animal magnetism was unmistakable. Anne's cloak-bearer, La Porte, recorded his impressions of the duke, whom he called "the best built and the best looking man in the world." According to La Porte, Buckingham appeared at court with so much charm and splendor that he inspired "admiration in the people, pleasure and something more in the ladies, jealousy in lovers and even more so in husbands."[26]

As far as anyone ever knew, Anne and Buckingham met only in public at the entertainments that were being given in his honor. Observers remarked, however, that, from the time Buckingham was first presented to the queen, the two seemed to get along as comfortably as though they had known one another a long while.[27] That was small wonder, since their mutual friends had been paving the way for the acquaintance. The same observers also noted the queen's obvious attraction to Buckingham, who, for his part, was paying her elaborate court. Although the most jaundiced onlookers had to admit that nothing actually improper was said or done, so much familiarity seemed shocking, and Anne was criticized for not paying enough attention to appearances.[28]

Louis's health was poor during the latter part of May, and he may not have been present at all the entertainments. But even if he did not see with his own eyes what was happening, he soon heard all about it. He could hurry Henrietta Maria's departure, and did so. He could not, however, break with the ancient custom that daughters of the royal house who married abroad be accompanied by their female kin to the border of the kingdom. On 2 June, therefore, Henrietta Maria, escorted by her mother and Anne, departed on her way to take ship at

Boulogne. Her suite included not only Buckingham but also the duke and duchess of Chevreuse, who were to stay with her in England until she was settled. As a precaution, especially necessary in that company, Louis had given strict orders that on no account was Buckingham ever to see Anne alone during the journey.[29]

For the most part, Louis's instructions were easy enough to follow, since the three royal parties traveled by separate routes as usual. But they met in Amiens, where they spent some days resting and enjoying the elaborate reception the city had prepared. Anne and Marie stayed in a house that possessed a large riverside garden, and the court enjoyed walking there in the evenings. On one particularly mild and pleasant night, Anne, who liked to walk late, was in the garden with her ladies. Buckingham led her; Madame de Chevreuse followed on the arm of Lord Holland. When Anne and Buckingham turned a corner from one walk to another, the others did not immediately follow. Suddenly Anne cried out; everyone rushed up to ask her what was wrong and Buckingham silently faded into the darkness.[30]

Scandal circulated about that incident for years, particularly because no one seemed to know exactly what had happened. Some conjectured that Buckingham had actually tried to rape the queen, though that does not seem likely considering the number of people who were within call and the danger of immediate discovery. Anne herself recalled the episode for Madame de Motteville much later. Her account agreed with La Porte's memoirs to the effect that Buckingham, using what seemed a favorable opportunity, had taken a liberty—that is, presumably had tried to embrace or kiss Anne, who became frightened and called her people.[31] Very likely it came as a shock to her to realize that this was not a safely romantic flirtation but that Buckingham's physical passion was in earnest. Though she reacted as a virtuous married woman should, she may well have felt pleased and excited to have been found desirable. She was at the height of her beauty then, an opulent beauty, judging by the portrait Rubens painted of her about this time. And her husband did not appreciate her.

From Amiens, Henrietta Maria proceeded to Boulogne alone with her suite. When it came to the leave-taking, Buckingham tried to declare his feelings to Anne at the door of her coach. Though she did not encourage him, she showed enough emotion so that her companion, the princess of Conti, declared she could vouch to the king for the queen's virtue from the waist down but would not be answerable for the part from the waist up.[32]

Nor was this the end of the matter. Contrary winds delayed Henrietta Maria's departure from Boulogne, and Buckingham made an opportunity to return to Amiens uninvited as the bearer of dispatches. He arrived late one evening, requesting an interview with Marie de Medici to present greetings from her daughter. Marie de Medici received him, although she was indisposed and had retired to her bed. From Marie's apartments Buckingham went on to Anne's. Anne had also retired early and instructed her ladies to refuse him admittance. He became so insistent, however, that Anne sent to her mother-in-law to ask her advice. Marie replied that Anne might as well receive Buckingham even though she was in bed since she herself, Marie de Medici, had just done the same thing. It was not a prudent piece of advice for anyone to give who had Anne's welfare at heart. Buckingham was admitted, threw himself on his knees in front of the bed, and declared his undying love for the queen, who, according to him, was the ideal woman for whom he had been looking all his life. The lady-of-honor, Madame de Lannoy, tried to get him off the floor, reminding him that it was not the custom in France for gentlemen to kneel to the queen. He retorted that he was not a Frenchman and was not bound to obey all the laws of France. In the end Anne grew angry, or pretended to, and sent him away.[33]

Of course, Buckingham's behavior could not be concealed from Louis. He heard about it in detail even before Anne and the queen mother came to join him at Fontainebleau. Understandably he was jealous. His mother assured him that nothing had happened to injure his honor, that Anne had been so well guarded that she could not have done wrong even if she had wished to. And, Marie added, she herself when young had been importuned by admirers: obviously women could not be held accountable for the feelings they might inspire in men.[34] Louis did not find that reflection comforting, however. He did not confront Anne directly with his anger. Instead he sent his confessor to her with orders to dismiss those members of her household who, in his view, should have guarded her better. Three of her ladies had to go as did her cloak-bearer, one of her equerries, and a servant.[35] Once again she felt that her husband was striking at her through people she liked.

In England, meanwhile, Buckingham nursed resentment at the treatment he had received in France. He vowed to return and advertised his love for the French queen. According to French sources, everything he did for the next three years was designed to force the French government to let him come back for negotiations of one kind or another. They accused him of fomenting misunderstandings between Charles I and Henrietta Maria, of obstructing the execution of treaty provisions in favor of English Catholics, and finally of instigating war against France on the pretext of aiding the Huguenots—and all for the sake of romance.[36] That was too simple an explanation; Buckingham may not have been the most astute stateman of his age, but he was not a complete fool. Although the marriage between Charles and Henrietta Maria did indeed have an unhappy start, the English, and Charles himself, blamed the new queen's French household for that.[37] Nor did Buckingham necessarily do anything deliberately to prevent good understanding between the couple. Charles was so dependent on Buckingham as his friend that any wife would have found it difficult to establish herself within that relationship. There is some evidence, moreover, that Buckingham tried to act as mediator, though not with great success.[38] As for his policies regarding English Catholics and French Huguenots, they were determined by the pressure of opinion in Parliament and in the country at large, not by personal pique.

As it happened, these political imperatives were compatible with Buckingham's romantic ambitions. He exchanged messages with Anne and showed himself very eager to be invited back to Paris, where he hoped to discuss the outstanding problems between France and England and to persuade Louis to a military alliance against the Habsburgs. In January 1626 he charged his friend Lord Holland to prepare the way for him, and to assure the French queen of his continuing devotion. Holland sent bad news however:

> I have been a careful spy to observe intentions and affections towards you. . . . I find many things to be feared, and none to be assured of a safe and real welcome. For the [king] continues in his suspects, making, (as they say) very often discourses of it, and is willing to hear villains say that [the queen] hath infinite affections, you imagine which way.[39]

Concerning Anne's feelings, Holland reported,

> You are the most happy unhappy man alive, for [the queen] is beyond imagination right and would do things to destroy her fortune rather than want satisfaction in her mind.[40]

However promising that might have sounded, the general auspices for a visit from Buckingham were so doubtful that Holland concluded, "Do what you will, I dare not advise you. To come is dangerous. Not to come is unfortunate."[41] Buckingham chose not to come.

The French government did not wish to welcome him for a variety of reasons. Not only was Louis jealous, but Richelieu gave it as his considered opinion that Buckingham was a madman.[42] On more objective grounds, neither Richelieu nor Louis judged the time ripe for a military alliance with England, nor did they appreciate English offers to mediate between the French crown and its rebellious Protestant subjects. After such rebuffs England and Buckingham had ample reason to adopt an increasingly hostile attitude toward France. Buckingham in fact began to contribute to plots that were hatching in France against the authority of Richelieu and of the king himself, plots to which he was introduced by Madame de Chevreuse.

Buckingham had gotten on very well with Madame de Chevreuse during her stay in England, so well that, according to rumor, he was sharing her as a mistress with Lord Holland. Both Madame de Chevreuse and her husband were altogether much cherished at the court of Charles I. Charles may not have appreciated Henrietta Maria's French household, but he expressed the highest regard for his cousin Chevreuse and was charmed by the wit and gaiety of Chevreuse's wife. Reports of Madame de Chevreuse's manner of living reached Paris, where Richelieu exclaimed that she was discrediting the French court by acting like a whore. She would have liked to stay longer in England, but Louis recalled her husband and her in the summer of 1625. She kept up her English contacts, however, and put them to use as opportunity offered. Probably she also maintained communication of a sort between Buckingham and Anne, though there is no evidence of it.[43]

What Anne herself felt, or how deeply she had been touched, we have no means of knowing. Her only remark on the subject was a guarded one: if a virtuous woman could love a man other than her husband, she confided to a friend, then for her Buckingham would have been that man.[44]

Many years later, the duke of La Rochefoucauld wrote in his memoirs that the French queen had given Buckingham as a farewell present a set of diamond points for laces that had been a gift to her from Louis. One of Richelieu's informants, a mistress whom Buckingham had discarded, saw him wearing the points in London and managed to cut off two, which she sent to the cardinal. According to La Rochefoucauld, Richelieu, seeing an opportunity to ruin the queen whom he distrusted, suggested that Louis ask her to wear the diamonds he had recently presented to her. Buckingham, meanwhile, having noticed the loss of two of the jewels, had the ports of England closed while a jeweler made exact copies. Then Buckingham reopened the ports and sent the jewelry back to Anne, who promptly showed it to Louis and thereby checkmated the cardinal.[45] La Rochefoucauld was twelve years old and not at court when all this supposedly happened. It was a dramatic story and inspired Alexander Dumas to write *The Three Musketeers*. There is no evidence to support it, however, and no other writer of the time ever mentioned it. La Rochefoucauld moreover seems to have assumed that as early as 1625 Richelieu felt a settled hostility toward Anne. This was not the case. On the other hand, thanks in large part to her friend Madame de Chevreuse, Anne was becoming involved in much more serious matters than purloined jewelry or romantic dreams.

In 1625 Louis was beginning arrangements for the marriage of his brother Gaston.[46] The bride had been chosen by Marie de Medici long ago: it was Mademoiselle de Montpensier, sole survivor of a junior branch of the Bourbon house and the richest heiress in the kingdom. Not everyone approved of the idea. Gaston was heir apparent in the absence of a dauphin. To marry him off at seventeen and risk his having children while the king himself remained childless seemed to some advisers an imprudent enhancement of Gaston's position. Anne had always gotten along well with her young brother-in-law, who was more fun-loving and lighthearted than Louis, but she too feared that Gaston's early marriage and the likelihood of his having children would put her even farther into the shade. By her own admission, she did what she could to prevent the Montpensier match, trying to work on Gaston through his governor, Marshall Ornano.[47]

In this effort she was more than seconded by Madame de Chevreuse. Since her return to France, Madame de Chevreuse had been feeding Anne's sense of grievance and giving it a focus. She never saw herself at fault in having led the queen to indulge in the Buckingham romance. Instead she blamed all the humiliation Anne had suffered in consequence on Cardinal Richelieu. She and Anne began to cultivate their dislike of the cardinal and to indulge in hopes and sometimes plans for his fall. Since Marie de Medici was pushing the marriage project, it was assumed that Richelieu as her protégé would not survive in the royal council if the match failed. Besides, Madame de Chevreuse herself had a candidate for the hand of the rich Mademoiselle de Montpensier. Her solution was to find friends in Gaston's entourage who would persuade him to refuse the marriage, or at least to ask for impossible benefits if he should consent. The plan worked. Gaston's people had their own reasons for opposing this particular marriage, and Gaston himself had been lukewarm about it from the beginning.

Now he came to feel that his dynastic importance was not being suffi-ciently recognized. He asked for a great appanage and also wished to be admitted to the royal council. His friends meanwhile were making efforts to enlist the support of Louis's half-brothers, the duke and the grand prior of Vendôme, as well as the Bourbon count of Soissons and the duke of Longueville. And through Madame de Chevreuse, they were sending out feelers to Spain and England. They talked of depos-ing Louis and at the same time getting rid of Richelieu.[48]

No one has ever been certain that Gaston's friends truly meant to depose the king, let alone kill him. Louis and Richelieu believed this, however, when they received information about the plotting in Gas-ton's circle. In the spring of 1626, they began to close in on the sus-pected conspirators. First, Gaston's governor, Marshall Ornano, was arrested, then the Vendôme brothers, and finally in July the count of Chalais, who was the king's master of the wardrobe. Chalais confessed everything, and more than could be proved. He testified that the queen had known and approved of the plot to depose Louis and put Gaston on the throne instead, and he alleged that the plan had called for marriage between Anne and Gaston once the deed was done. Be-fore his execution, he retracted his testimony, saying he had given it falsely in the hope of pardon. Nevertheless, Anne was summoned to appear before the royal council in the presence of the king himself, his mother, and Richelieu. To induce a properly pliant frame of mind in her, she was not given the armchair to which she would normally have been entitled, but had to sit on a small folding stool like an accused prisoner at the bar. The interrogation did not, however, break her spirit. She denied any knowledge of the alleged conspiracy, and as for wishing to marry Gaston, she exclaimed scornfully that she would have gained too little by the change.[49] She may have told the truth; there is no evidence to the contrary. But although it seems unlikely that she could have been a party to schemes for her husband's deposi-tion, she might well have been aware what role the Spanish govern-ment hoped she would play if Gaston ascended the throne. In the following year, 1627, the Spanish ambassador Mirabel explained to Anne the instructions Prime Minister Olivares had sent him: in case Louis XIII died without male issue, Spain would recognize Gaston as his successor, and Anne was to remain in France and marry the new king if possible.[50] It would have been strange if Mirabel had not at least mentioned such an eventuality earlier.

For the time being, Gaston surrendered and married the Montpens-ier heiress. He received the rich duchy of Orléans as well as Blois and

Chartres for his compliance. Madame de Chevreuse for her meddling was ordered to live in Poitou at one of her brother's castles. Instead she fled dramatically over the frontier to Lorraine and claimed shelter from her husband's cousin, the reigning duke. Louis again made changes in Anne's household, and the rift between husband and wife deepened. He did not believe Anne's protestations and to his dying day could not be convinced of her innocence.

Chapter Six

Crises and Conspiracies

THE YEARS 1626 TO 1637 WERE a bleak decade for Anne. She lived in an atmosphere of suspicion and constraint created by conflicts of personalities and politics. She herself blamed Richelieu for her difficulties. That explanation was too simple, although it may have been convenient insofar as it enabled her to avoid facing more painful realities. It was Louis who had placed Richelieu in the center of the political stage; it was Louis who kept him there and showed time and again that he valued his minister above his wife.

As Richelieu consolidated his position in the government, opposition to him grew correspondingly stronger: from great nobles who felt their influence slighted or whom he had offended, from disappointed office-seekers, and from men who disapproved of his policies.[1] These opponents gathered naturally around members of the royal family who were known to share their sentiments and whose prestige could be useful in maintaining a faction: Marie de Medici, first of all; Louis's brother, Gaston of Orléans; and Anne. Anne, for her part, played a background role. Unlike her mother-in-law or her brother-in-law, she did not claim a place on the royal council, nor did she instigate rebellion. However, she listened approvingly to criticism of Richelieu and obstinately kept up relationships with people who were his enemies—not just because they were his enemies but because she felt they were her friends. This was unfortunate for her because Louis regarded opposition to Richelieu as opposition to his own will.

Richelieu's situation was a difficult one. Above all he had to earn and keep the king's trust, in itself not an easy matter. But because Louis still seemed to depend heavily on his mother, Richelieu also had to endeavor to stay in the good graces of his former patroness, even though in the long run her jealousy made this impossible. With the king's brother, Richelieu tried admonitions, negotiations, rewards, eventually also to no avail. As for the king's wife, if he could not win her support, he had at least to prevent her from doing him harm.

Richelieu's notes and memoirs shed no light on his decisions in this matter. Perhaps he tried the path of conciliation first. People whispered at the time that he was in love with the queen, that he had been jealous of Buckingham and could not forgive Anne for having scorned his own feelings.[2] Gossip, of course, merely may have attributed such a motive to Richelieu because gallantry was in fashion and therefore readily understandable. Madame de Motteville later reported she had heard the queen recollect that Richelieu had once come to her with the air of a suitor and had made her a very passionate speech to which she was about to reply in anger and disdain when the king entered the room, and later she never had dared to resume her inter- rupted reply lest she give Richelieu the satisfaction of knowing that she remembered the incident at all.[3] Possibly the scene took place as Anne recalled it; possibly she misunderstood or read more into Riche- lieu's words than he intended. Richelieu would have taken a terrible risk in becoming her lover: the mere attempt would have given her the power to compromise him beyond redemption with the king. We do know he feared such a trap on at least one occasion. In April 1631 Richelieu received reports that the queen was taking it amiss that he did not visit her, and the Spanish ambassador advised him to cultivate the queen's acquaintance more, to go to see her whether or not the king was present. The ambassador assured Richelieu that she would welcome suggestions about what the king and the minister expected of her—in fact, would gratefully receive directions for her conduct. In his notes Richelieu remarked that he thanked the ambassador without showing that he saw the purpose behind these words.[4] Whether justly or unjustly, he was evidently afraid of a plot to lure him into a compromising position.

In her own household, Anne made no secret of her aversion to Richelieu. Perhaps she remembered her mother's at least partially successful struggle against the duke of Lerma and thought to emulate her. At any rate, she never believed Richelieu's assurances that he was always ready to employ his good offices with the king on her behalf; and he, on his side, never trusted her protestations of obedience to the king's wishes and esteem for himself. None of this appeared in the letters they exchanged as form required when Anne addressed him according to his rank as cousin, inquired after his health, and ex- pressed concern for his well-being.[5] But Richelieu had spies among her servants and knew perfectly well that she resented him and lis- tened to anyone who spoke against him, and moreover that she was maintaining against the king's wishes a correspondence with Madame de Chevreuse and that lady's friends. Richelieu accordingly took steps to supervise the queen more closely.

When, in September 1626, Anne's lady of honor Madame de Lannoy died, the lady-in-waiting, Madame de Sénécey, was promoted to her place and Madame de Sénécey's post went to a newcomer, Madame du Fargis.[6] From Richelieu's point of view, Madame du Fargis should have been an excellent watchdog and thoroughly reliable: she was not of the highest nobility and therefore should have been grateful for favors; she was pious, or seemed so, having spent three years in a Carmelite convent before her marriage. She came well recommended by Cardinal Berulle, Richelieu's old colleague, and above all she was a great friend of Richelieu's favorite niece, Madame de Combalet. Nor was the choice of Madame du Fargis an unfeeling one as far as the queen was concerned. Madame du Fargis's husband was French ambassador at the court of Spain, and she had spent time with him in Madrid; through her husband she was related to the marquise de Rambouillet, whose salon had already become the center of fashionable literary life. Besides, Madame du Fargis's sister-in-law was the wife of Philip Emmanuel de Gondi, general of the galleys, and the Gondis were a notably pious couple, the first patrons of Vincent de Paul in his charitable enterprises. The queen herself, of course, was pious; she had acquaintances among the literary set; and she liked to be reminded of Spain. Madame du Fargis, therefore, presumably had enough resources to make herself agreeable to Anne and was expected to report and to keep Richelieu posted on Anne's activities.

It would seem, however, that Richelieu was not a good judge of women: Madame du Fargis went over to the queen's camp. She ingratiated herself with Anne, and Anne discovered that she liked her. Madeleine du Fargis did not displace Madame de Chevreuse in the queen's affection. Being pockmarked, she did not have Madame de Chevreuse's beauty, nor did she have her gift of infectious gaiety; but she did possess a forthright, even earthy, sense of humor that Anne, who was no prude, evidently found appealing. And so Madame du Fargis became a secondary friend. She did nothing to stop Anne's secret correspondence while Madame de Chevreuse, for her part, was spinning the most ambitious international intrigues.

In 1627 Madame de Chevreuse was using her network of friends in high places to facilitate an alliance between Lorraine, England, and the French Huguenot nobles.[7] The purpose of this alliance was to be simultaneous military action against Louis in order to discredit Richelieu, who presumably would be unable to meet the three-front onslaught. Louis would thus be forced to dismiss the minister.

The project was by no means implausible. The duke of Lorraine was chafing under French demands for the cession of fortresses and passage rights for French troops. On the opposite side of France, on the southwestern coast, the Huguenot city of La Rochelle was already in revolt against the king's authority, although Huguenots in general had not yet taken to arms. As for England, Charles I and Buckingham were committed to the relief of their coreligionists in La Rochelle who were under siege by Louis's army. Open hostilities between England and France existed from the time in 1627 when Buckingham tried to break the siege of the city by bringing an English fleet into the harbor and landing an expeditionary force. It only remained to coordinate these strands into a concerted effort.

There was much coming and going of couriers between the parties interested in the alliance, and Richelieu believed that Anne was serving as a link between Madame de Chevreuse and the great noble Huguenot family of Rohan. He came close to proving it too. In the spring of 1628, in an effort to break the hostile intelligence network, a small detachment of royal troops crossed the border of Lorraine and abducted an English courier, Henrietta Maria's equerry Lord Montague, and brought him back to a French prison. Anne was devastated when she heard of his arrest. She sent her cloak-bearer, La Porte, to Montague secretly to find out whether the papers he was carryng implicated her, and to adjure him not to mention her name during any interrogations. La Porte found old friends among Montague's guards and thus was able to gain access to the Englishman. Montague was reassuring: to Anne's great relief, as La Porte later recalled, for she had feared that she would be sent back to Spain if her name was discovered.[8]

Contrary to the hopes of the conspirators, the affairs of the allies did not prosper. The year 1628 ended in triumph for Louis and for Richelieu. Buckingham was assassinated in August and his successor in the English admiralty was no more able than he had been to break the siege of La Rochelle. The starving city capitulated, and Louis entered it on 2 November 1628. The following April he made peace with England. Because he did not wish Madame de Chevreuse to owe her return from exile to the intercession of Charles I, Louis forestalled the English and allowed the lady to reenter France at the end of 1628. She was to keep away from court, however, and to reside on her estate at Dampierre.

The secret correspondence between her and Anne nevertheless continued. In 1629 it apparently concerned the affairs of the king's brother, Gaston of Orléans. His wife's death in childbed in 1627 had left Gaston a widower with a daughter. Now he declared he had fallen in love and wished to marry the princess Marie Gonzaga, daughter of the duke of Nevers, who had a claim to the succession of the duchy of Mantua in Italy. Louis, Richelieu, and Marie de Medici opposed this project because it seemed a needless complication in the already complicated French politics in northern Italy. That did not deter Gaston.

Louis and Richelieu spent much of that year in campaign against rebellious Huguenot cities and nobles in southern France and had left Marie de Medici in charge of the administration in Paris. When a crisis developed, the queen mother therefore dealt with it. She informed Richelieu that it had come to her knowledge that Anne, at the instigation of Madame de Chevreuse, had arranged with the Spanish ambassador Mirabel for Gaston to elope to Flanders for his marriage with Marie Gonzaga.[9] On her own initiative, the queen mother placed Princess Marie and the duchess of Nevers under honorable confinement in the fortress castle of Vincennes outside Paris. Unfortunately this action had the undesirable effect of leading Gaston to leave France in anger and seeking refuge with that ready friend of French malcontents the duke of Lorraine. It took lengthy negotiations to induce Gaston to come back in 1630.

Madame de Chevreuse, claiming to be the faithful champion of Anne, was involved in this as in every conspiracy that troubled the authority of Louis XIII and Richelieu. Her ostensible motive was always the same: to injure Richelieu, although in practice tangible benefits were usually at stake for her particular friends, whether in the shape of a rich marriage, high office, or the gratification of animosities. From a distance of three and half centuries, her conduct seems frivolous and irresponsible; but since Louis and Richelieu always had to take into account private interests of great families, they were forced to take her activities very seriously indeed. Nevertheless, her sort of personal antagonism to Richelieu, however spectacular, was a surface phenomenon as compared with the growing opposition Richelieu encountered from the devout party.

The devout did not form a party in the modern sense.[10] They certainly did not have a political organization. As the term *parti devot* was used in Richelieu's time, it referred to a loose configuration of Catholic lay people and clergy who worked in the forefront of religious reform and who by the nature of their religious commitment also harbored certain political goals: abroad, peace and cooperation with the Catholic powers of Europe, notably the Spanish and Austrian

Habsburgs; at home, good government, that is to say, honest officials, a reduction of the tax burden, efficient justice, and the elimination, or at least curtailment, of toleration for Protestants. Not all the devout expressed such ideas so explicitly. Those who did, such as Louis's keeper of the seals Michel de Marillac, may be said to have had a vision of Christian politics, of government policies oriented to religious values.

After the death of Henry IV in 1610, the devout had gravitated to Marie de Medici as the natural center of power, and she had found their support congenial: she did not have to buy their loyalty as she did that of the great princes or the Huguenots. As we have seen, it was the zealous Catholics, the devout, who applauded the Spanish marriages most unreservedly. When Richelieu began his career in Marie de Medici's service, he traveled in devout circles and was glad to use their influence to further his advancement. Even after he rose to power in the king's council, one of his closest collaborators was the notably devout Michel de Marillac. To all appearances he trusted Marillac completely. When Chancellor d'Aligre was believed to be implicated in the Chalais conspiracy, Richelieu had the seals of state taken away from d'Aligre and confided to Marillac, who also replaced d'Aligre as head of Anne's council and superintendent of her household.

Nevertheless, the devout began to suspect that Richelieu did not adhere to their party as fully as they had supposed. They did not think he followed a sufficiently restrictive policy against the French Huguenots and blamed him for the lenient Peace of Montpellier that Louis had signed after the latest round of Protestant rebellion in 1626. Their disappointment grew with the "Peace of Grace" in 1629 whereby Louis, who had subdued not only La Rochelle but also the heavily Protestant cities of southern France, deprived Huguenots of the military and political privileges they had enjoyed since the days of his father but left them in possession of religious toleration and civil liberties. Instead of urging the king to extirpate heresy, Richelieu moreover was negotiating alliances with such Protestant states as Sweden and the Netherlands, and was leading the king to defend French interests in northern Italy at the risk of war with Spain. It seemed that Richelieu was willing to sacrifice peace, and with it the chance for domestic reforms and tax relief, to the ambitious goal of challenging Habsburg predominance in international affairs. The devout found this policy orientation unpalatable, as in fact did most taxpayers, whether devout or not. Michel de Marillac therefore spoke for a large sector of public opinion when in the royal council he opposed every step Richelieu proposed to take in foreign policy. And for a while, it looked as though Marillac would win, for he had the queen mother on his side.

Marie de Medici supported Marillac not because she favored peace or domestic reform or religion but because she feared she was losing her influence over her son to Richelieu. She regarded Richelieu as her creature, and what she had made, she could break. The struggle between them came to a head in 1630.[11] For once Marie and Anne were on the best of terms and in complete agreement. They had accompanied Louis to Lyon, from where he and Richelieu were conducting a campaign in Savoy and Piedmont. In September the king fell dangerously ill with a high fever against which all remedies were unavailing. His mother and his wife nursed him and loudly accused Richelieu of having caused this illness by leading Louis into the war and tiring him out with military operations. On 30 September, Louis seemed to be at the point of death. Illness had drawn him closer to his mother and his wife; he asked Anne's pardon for not having lived with her as affectionately as he ought to have done. She replied she had been at fault but above all she blamed the cardinal for having sown misunderstandings between them. Marie's friends meanwhile looked forward to seeing Richelieu arrested as soon as Louis breathed his last, and it was understood among them that Anne would marry the new king, her brother-in-law Gaston of Orléans.

Instead of dying, however, Louis got better. It turned out his fever had been caused by an intestinal abscess; when the abscess burst, he began to recover. His mother and his wife continued to nurse him, and while he was in the emotionally vulnerable condition of convalescence, they continually implored him to dismiss Richelieu, the author, according to them, of all the troubles in the kingdom and in the royal family. Louis temporized. He said he needed Richelieu for the time being, at least until the present campaign was concluded.

After the royal family returned to Paris in November, Marie pressed for a conclusion. On 11 November she gave Louis a choice, either Richelieu left the council or she herself would leave Louis. When Richelieu entered the room and tried to justify himself, she made a scene of such venomous rage that Louis asked the cardinal to withdraw while he tried to calm his mother. Marie believed she had triumphed, and that evening she celebrated with her friends in the Luxembourg palace.[12] What Anne did or thought we do not know, nor is there any evidence that her mother-in-law took her into her confidence during these days.

On leaving his mother, however, Louis had sent a message to Richelieu ordering him to meet him at Versailles. When Richelieu appeared, Louis assured him of his confidence and support: the king had made his choice between his mother and his minister.[13] While Marie celebrated her supposed victory, Louis convened the royal council, deprived Marillac of the seals of state, and had him taken to prison. On hearing how the tables had been turned on the queen mother, one of her supporters exclaimed, "This has been Fool's Day." Some of the fools paid grim penalties. Marshall Bassompierre followed Marillac to prison, and Marillac's brother, Marshall Louis de Marillac, suffering chiefly from guilt by association, was tried on trumped-up charges and executed. The king took the initiative himself in these matters, whether out of vengeful anger or from a desire to ensure the future safety of his minister.

Next Louis turned his attention to the queen's household. At the end of December 1630, he decided to remove Madame du Fargis, who, it was well known, had helped feed Anne's hostility toward the cardinal. Anne felt deeply offended. She took counsel with her mother-in-law and then sent a message to Richelieu saying she had heard someone had been spreading slander about Madame du Fargis and that she was to be sent away. She, the queen, wished Richelieu to know that the greatest pleasure he could give her would be to prevent this dismissal and that she begged him to do so. She added that up to now people had treated her as they liked, but she wished Richelieu to know that she had resolved no longer to tolerate this and that she was not in such poor case that she might not one day have the means of showing her resentment.[14] Richelieu received the message and duly recorded it in his notes. Louis's decision stood, however, and Madame du Fargis received her orders to leave court. Anne exploded in anger to all who came near her. She would never forgive Richelieu, she said, never; and she repeated loudly on every possible occasion that now she had nothing left to fear, that she would know how to revenge herself when the time came.[15] It all got back to Richelieu, of course, who kept a careful list headed "grievances of the reigning queen against the cardinal."[16]

The purge in Anne's household extended even to a child, Françoise Bertaut, the future Madame de Motteville, Anne's later friend and biographer.[17] Françoise was then about nine years of age. Her father, Pierre Bertaut, was a gentleman-in-ordinary of the king's bedchamber, and Anne early in her life in France had come to know and value Bertaut's wife, Louise, because Louise could speak and write Spanish. When

Louise Bertaut presented her little daughter Francoise to the queen, Anne had an income assigned to the girl and in 1627 had her appointed as one of the women of her bedchamber. Anne enjoyed the company of children, but this particular child had an especially endearing attribute: Françoise knew Spanish, thanks to her mother's instruction. No doubt the king and the cardinal feared the girl might be used as a messenger between the queen and the Spanish ambassador or other suspect persons. At the beginning of 1631, therefore, Françoise Bertaut lost her place in the queen's service and was sent to stay with relatives in Normandy.

Dismissal was also pending against one of Anne's apothecaries, apparently because he was suspected of carrying messages as well as medicines. Rumors of his dismissal sent Anne into transports of fear. She told her servants and all her visitors that it was clear the cardinal was taking away her apothecary because he wanted to have her murdered. Presumably she meant that any new apothecary who might be appointed would have orders to feed her poison. And why should Richelieu wish to see her dead? Because he wanted to marry his niece Madame de Combalet to the king.[18] That was a wild accusation without a shred of evidence to support it. It sounded of a piece with the vituperations Marie de Medici had screamed at Richelieu on Fool's Day. Anne made so much noise about the matter, however, that Louis permitted the apothecary to keep his post, at least for several months longer, provided he entered the Louvre only when delivering medicine in the company of the queen's physician. He was not permitted contact with the queen, for he had to hand over the medicine to Madame de Sénécey, the lady-in-waiting, nor was he to meet the queen at any place outside the Louvre. If the apothecary obeyed these orders faithfully for two months, the king added, he might prolong the man's tenure.[19]

During these months Anne spent a good deal of time closeted with Marie de Medici. The two women fed each other's anger, fear, and thirst for revenge, and they waged feminine war against the king. When Louis asked Anne to join him at a play, she declined, saying she did not feel like it. For someone who loved the theater as much as she did, this was a strong measure, and Louis was visibly annoyed. Next day he invited her again with the same result, and the two queens were heard to agree they had better things to do than to give the king pleasure while he was giving them trouble.[20]

Marie for her part still hoped to wear down her son's resistance and induce him to dismiss Richelieu. Louis found the situation intolerable and resolved to isolate his mother. The royal family and court had gone to Compiègne. There on 23 February 1631 against all rules of etiquette, Anne was awakened at dawn by a loud knocking on her door. According to her own later recollection, she felt sure this meant bad news—at the least an order to return to Spain.[21] It was bad news, but not for herself. The king requested her to lose no time in dressing, to leave the castle without seeing her mother-in-law, and to meet him at a neighboring monastery where he was waiting for her to join him in order to return to Paris: reasons of state obliged him to leave Marie de Medici behind. Anne obeyed except in one particular—she took leave of her mother-in-law. To cover herself, she sent to Marie to ask that her mother-in-law request her to come. Marie did so. She crouched terrified in her bed and greeted Anne with "Is the king leaving me here and what does he want to do with me?"[22] Anne confirmed that the king was indeed leaving his mother at Compiègne, and so they parted.

Nothing worse was in store for Marie than an order to leave for Moulins in central France, where she could live quietly and enjoy her wealth provided she kept out of politics. Marie, however, refused to go. Gaston of Orléans took up her cause and proclaimed his outrage at the treatment his mother was receiving. Once again he fled abroad, this time to the Spanish Netherlands, from whence he launched protests and appeals against Richelieu. Marie meanwhile tried to bargain with Louis; getting nowhere, in July she decided to follow her son's example. She too fled to Brussels.

Contrary to her expectations, Louis never allowed her to reenter France. In subsequent years he repeatedly offered to have all her revenues paid to her in Florence if she would settle in her native city, but she found this recourse unacceptable. Without regular means of support and surrounded by intriguers and adventurers, first in Brussels, then in England, she lived as a wanderer for over a decade and eventually died in Cologne in relatively poor circumstances.[23]

How much Anne, upon reflection, regretted Marie's departure from France is impossible to say. Marie de Medici had not been a good mother-in-law to her—in fact, for years had kept her in the shade as though she were a negligible quantity. Although enmity against Richelieu had brought them more closely together of late years, if Richelieu had disappeared from the scene, their friendship would probably not have survived him for long. As matters now stood, however, Marie's flight did nothing to increase the reigning queen's influence at court but merely left her exposed and alone between the king and Richelieu. Louis may have hoped that Anne would become more docile. Instead she retreated within herself and remained obstinately defiant.

Richelieu was astute enough to see that she might be guided through affection. He prevailed upon the king to permit Madame de Chevreuse to return to court to console Anne for the loss of Madame du Fargis. Madame de Chevreuse could be counted on to keep Anne amused, and she gave Richelieu the most solemn promises that she would answer for the queen's good conduct. For a time, as far as Richelieu could tell from informants' reports, the lady seemed to be keeping her side of the bargain and was persuading the queen to please the king by staying on better terms with his minister. Certainly the queen's humor improved. As for her conduct, after some months Madame de Chevreuse felt able to assure the king and Richelieu that, from her personal knowledge and observation, she could vouch for it that Anne maintained no intelligence with Spain, or Gaston, or the queen mother, or anyone whomsoever.[24]

As it happened, that was not true. With or without the knowledge of Madame de Chevreuse, Anne was in communication with Madame du Fargis. That lady had taken herself to Lorraine and with the help of the Spanish ambassador in Paris had gone on to Brussels while her husband engaged himself in the service of Gaston of Orléans. Those circumstances alone would have made any correspondence between her and the queen suspect, for in 1631 and 1632 Gaston and his friends were deep in plans to invade France and raise a rebellion with the purpose of forcing Louis to abandon Richelieu and come to terms with Marie de Medici. The invasion took place in June of 1632, but the rebellion misfired and the enterprise ended as Gaston's ventures usually did with his going unscathed and his associates abandoned to the king's justice.

In the midst of these events, Madame du Fargis's correspondence with friends in Paris came to light.[25] No letters from her to the queen or from the queen to her were actually found, but Richelieu knew that Anne had both received and sent some. Moreover, in the captured letters there were ample references to Madame du Fargis's efforts to keep the queen's resentment against Richelieu alive. She had sent memorandums for the queen detailing the queen's grievances against Richelieu; worst of all, she mentioned the old plans for a marriage between Anne and Gaston should anything happen to Louis.

The king sent a formal delegation of inquiry to Anne: Richelieu, the new keeper of the seals Châteauneuf as the chief judicial officer of the kingdom, and two marshalls of France.[26] They showed her Madame du

Fargis's letters and questioned her about them. Anne was very helpful. She verified the handwriting, identified some of the pseudonyms that had puzzled the investigators, and professed horrified and suprised shock at Madame du Fargis's irresponsible talk regarding herself, Anne, and Gaston. As to the memorandums of the queen's grievances against Richelieu that Madame du Fargis had sent, the queen disclaimed them all. When Richelieu begged her most humbly to speak freely right then and there if she had any complaints to make of him, Anne replied she would be very wicked to say anything against him since he had given her no cause.[27]

Seeing there was no direct evidence to prove her actual collaboration with Madame du Fargis or Gaston, Anne was not molested further in the matter. She professed to be very grateful to Richelieu for the consideration he was showing her. She realized, as she confided to Madame de Chevreuse, that there had been sufficient grounds to treat her otherwise.[28]

Anne's show of humility did not mean she was giving up her secret correspondence; indeed, she soon had occasion to expand it. Madame de Chevreuse, ignoring her promises to Richelieu, had ensnared the new keeper of the seals Châteauneuf and was playing on his ambition to the point where he conspired to take Richelieu's place.[29] This plot too was discovered. In February 1633 Châteauneuf found himself under arrest, and he spent the next decade in confinement. To Madame de Chevreuse nothing worse happened than orders to leave court and retire to one of her husband's estates near Tours. Louis had come to detest her and only grudgingly permitted Anne to see her for a farewell. Against his wishes, as might have been expected, Anne stayed in touch with Madame de Chevreuse as she did with Madame du Fargis.

Every loss Anne suffered only made her cling more tightly to secret weapons of resistance. Perhaps what she much later told Madame de Motteville was true: that she lived in constant fear of being repudiated and sent back to Spain and that she took comfort only from the hope that her brother Philip would let her govern the Spanish Netherlands when her aunt, the regent in Brussels, came to die.[30] But she cannot have believed altogether in such a prospect, for at the same time she seems to have convinced herself that her family connections would keep her safe. When she had complained of ill treatment in 1631 and people advised her to bear her lot more patiently, to remember that her mother-in-law was not being treated any better, she had dismissed the advice out of hand: there could be no comparison between her and her mother-in-law, she said, because Marie had never had the kind of backing she herself possessed.[31] Apparently she expected her brother Philip IV to intervene forcefully on her behalf if the need should arise.

Affection as well as pride kept her attached to her family: she had no strong emotional ties in France, since the king apparently disdained her and her friends had been taken away from her one by one. From the letters she wrote her brother Ferdinand, the cardinal infante, between 1634 and 1637, we can see how much she relied on the family bond.[32] Her Aunt Clara Isabella Eugenia had died in 1633, and the cardinal infante replaced her as Philip's regent in Brussels. Thanks to Madame de Chevreuse's and Madame du Fargis's widespread connections, Anne wrote him regularly. She continued to do so even after Louis formally declared war on Spain in 1635, when communication with Brussels became more difficult because there was no longer a Spanish ambassador in Paris. With the knowledge of Charles I and Henrietta Maria, a good many letters went by diplomatic pouch from Brussels to London and thence to the English embassy at Louis's court and back again. This was not the only courier route used, though apparently it was the most reliable one.

To Ferdinand, Anne poured out her heart. She apologized for writing so often and implored him every time to send her news of his health and well-being. Surely he would do her that favor if he knew the happiness it gave her to hear from him. Thus, for example, in January 1635 she wrote that she waited for news from him every day because the consolation of hearing from him meant so much to her that having it, she could bear anything: "This wish fills me as much as the hope of salvation, the greatest I have in this life."[33] Later in the same month, she tried again. She could not keep herself from sending letters so often she explained, because, during the little bit of time she spent writing to him, it seemed to her that she was actually speaking with him; she had no better or greater comfort, since she was so much out of favor that she could not well be more so. And she added, "God knows the affliction it is to me to know you are coming to the frontier and that I cannot go to meet you."[34] She ended with the hope that some day it would be in her power to see him and to tell him what she was for the time being forced to conceal.[35]

Despite her pitiful pleas over the years, she had on the average only one letter from Ferdinand to every three or more of hers. Even then, they were apt to be short notes that in no way matched her own intensity of feeling. Nevertheless she persisted in her obsession, and every letter she sent to him involved her in even more voluminous correspondence with Madame de Chevreuse in Tours and Madame du Fargis and the former ambassador Mirabel in Brussels. There were constant questions as to why the cardinal infante had not written, pleas to persuade him to write, and endless discussions about couriers and safe routes. In addition, Anne had to respond to a constant stream of requests for favors, especially from Madame du Fargis.

Anne's friends made the most of her great emotional need. Madame de Chevreuse and Madame du Fargis wrote her the most extravagant protestations of the degree to which they missed her and constantly reminded her that they had been and were still enduring the hardships of persecution and exile for her sake. They may have been fond of her in their way, but they used her for their own interests: Madame de Chevreuse in order to add substance to her incessant intrigues, and Madame du Fargis to give herself a position and means of support in Brussels. Time after time the latter importuned the queen to recommend her to the cardinal infante; she even dictated what the queen should write and reminded her of her impoverished condition—she had, she said, no servant, no coach, no suite, not even the price of a dress.[36] Anne obliged as often as possible. How could she help it when Madame du Fargis was sending her bits of gossip about the cardinal infante's court, offering to send her his portrait, and urging him to write to his sister?

It should have occurred to Anne that, despite all precautions, so much coming and going of letters was sure to be noticed. Apparently she was willing to risk discovery, so strong was her feeling that she was an outcast, living a life of exile. No doubt it would have been different had she had children, more particularly, a son. Madame du Fargis herself said as much in the one disinterested piece of advice she gave the queen in their whole correspondence. Writing in December 1636 about the latest intrigue around Gaston of Orléans, who had meanwhile returned to France, Madame du Fargis added in her usual forthright language: "But for God's sake, to put an end to the disputes, make a son. You will be the star of your parish and all the rest is not worth a straw."[37]

Chapter Seven

Barren Years

TO MAKE A SON: FOR ANNE and Louis that seemed to be more easily said than done. Hopeful rumors had spread at court in 1626, in 1628, and again in 1630, all to no result. In the spring of 1631, Anne once more believed herself pregnant; her women and the king's physician, Bouvard, Héroard's successor, believed so too.[1] But once again she resumed menstruation.

The number of such "accidents" reported since 1619 might suggest a history of spontaneous abortions, though we have no means of knowing whether Anne actually suffered from an inability to carry a child. Midwives believed that if a woman had miscarried once her organs were likely to get into bad habits so that she would miscarry in subsequent pregnancies as well.[2] That may or may not have applied to Anne's case after her miscarriage of 1623; no diagnosis to that effect by either a midwife or a physician is on record.

It was, of course, recognized that physical illness could also terminate pregnancy; but Anne, in contrast to the king, enjoyed robust good health. Perhaps her so-called accidents were merely symptoms of an irregular menstrual cycle. Considering the conditions under which she and Louis lived, it is less surprising that she did not bear a child than that she had reason to believe herself pregnant at all.

The royal couple's intimate life was frequently interrupted by Louis's illnesses and military campaigns.[3] Not to mention the intestinal abscess that nearly caused his death in 1630, he suffered from fevers, troubles of digestion, nervous oppression, and, as the years went by, from gout. According to Héroard's journal for 1627, the king slept with the queen twice a month from January through May and then not at all for the rest of the year.[4] Similarly detailed records no longer exist after Héroard's death early in 1628. His successor, Bouvard, presumably kept working notes in order to document eventual pregnancy, but they are not extant. We know, however, that the king and queen continued to be often apart, although in 1630 and the following years Anne usually accompanied Louis on his longer campaign trips. That did not necessarily mean they shared quarters; the queen and court ladies had to stay in a safe spot to the rear whenever Louis went close to the scene of actual military operations. Besides, the custom of having royal personages and their suites travel by separate routes prevented companionship except during stays in larger towns. In addition to such external obstacles, the tensions between Anne and Louis made their marriage seem more and more like a battleground, and no less so because the battles were indirect.

The Lyon reconciliation of September 1630 turned out to be short-lived. Louis's decision in favor of Richelieu and against Marie de Medici caused him great anguish. For weeks after Fool's Day, he rehearsed the events of that crisis in season and out of season to anyone who came near him. But apparently he neither sought nor received solace or understanding from his wife: Anne had sided with Marie in Lyon and continued to make common cause with her in Paris. Even after Marie left France, Anne, as we have seen, continued in covert resistance to the cardinal, and it so happened that all her friends were his enemies.

Then as in later times, Anne's conduct was judged diversely according to the allegiances or prejudices of the observer. Her partisans, such as Madame de Chevreuse, portrayed her as a martyr to Richelieu's coldly calculated persecution, a view that became the basis for nineteenth-century romantic legend.[5] French historians on the other hand, eager to celebrate Richelieu as the founder of French national greatness, on the whole have blamed Anne for trying to undermine the cardinal and thus obstructing the true destiny of her husband's kingdom.[6] And there is a third point of view, based on pious regard for what Christian marriage required of women. Writing in this vein, Anne's friend and first biographer Madame de Motteville deplored Anne's pride and youthful rashness. Although Madame de Motteville in general treated Anne's marital troubles sympathetically, she believed that the queen contributed to her own unhappiness: by defying Louis's will and persisting in her opposition to Richelieu, "she showed she did not understand sufficiently that for a good wife the wishes of a husband when supported by reason must be a law to receive and follow with submission."[7]

Louis would have agreed with that statement. He was forever sending Anne unpalatable instructions with the notation that they were for the good of his service and her own benefit. All the moral teaching in the seventeenth century held obedience to be a wifely virtue, second in importance only to fidelity, and a woman as pious as Anne might have been expected to know it. Her disobedience, however, did not proceed simply from pride and disregard of duty; contrary to what Madame de Motteville thought, Louis's will was not always reason-

able, and the kind of obedience he required from his wife often surpassed normal human capacity.

Most of Louis's personal relationships were double-faced, combining passionate attachment or even dependence with distrust and hostility. In almost every case, ultimately the distrust and hostility became
predominant. This happened with his mother; with his first great favorite Luynes and Luynes's widow, Madame de Chevreuse; with all his
later favorites; and at times it seemed to be happening with Richelieu.[8]
Whenever Louis's affections changed, he expected his wife to follow
suit. Thus Anne for years had to defer to Marie de Medici beyond
reason and against her own inclination, and when she had finally
found common ground with her mother-in-law, was forced to let her
go. It had been the same with Madame de Chevreuse and the friends
Madame de Chevreuse had brought into Anne's circle, and the pattern
was to repeat itself subsequently. To submit to Louis wholeheartedly
in such continual reversals of feeling would have meant abdicating
any integrity of personality or acquiring the detachment and charitable comprehension of a saint.

Obedience, of course, need not be wholehearted: it could be
guarded, deployed as a matter of deliberate policy. Richelieu used this
method in picking his way among the objects of Louis's passions and
aversions. Richelieu, however, had an ambitious sense of mission to
sustain him and disposed of an extensive network of informants and
clients to help keep him abreast of Louis's moods. Above all he understood the king sufficiently to be able to manipulate him, at least to
some extent. Even with all these advantages, the nervous strain on the
cardinal was enormous; and when he himself met Louis's hostility, he
came close more than once to losing his hold.

Anne, on the other hand, lived by her heart more than her head: she
tended to follow impulse rather than rational reflection. She could
dissemble, but it never came naturally to her to proceed along a rational calculated course of conduct. Where Louis was concerned,
therefore, she had no access to an impersonal perspective: she was
not detached; she was involved. She had expected his affection and
trust and resented not receiving either; she wanted stability in her
relationships and resisted arbitrary changes. Apparently she never
realized that she was asking more than Louis was able to give. In fact,
so little did she understand the complexity of his emotional life that
she came to believe he had never loved her at all.[9] Anne evidently
found it easier to think of the few years of happiness in her marriage as
an illusion than to grasp that Louis could combine love with distrust

and coldness. Louis meanwhile confided to personal servants that he found the queen attractive but had not dared to show it for fear of offending first his mother and then Cardinal Richelieu.[10] That sounds like a convenient excuse, but most likely Louis himself could not have explained the full range of his feelings. He never gave up the hope of siring an heir, however, and therefore continued to visit his wife.

Whether or to what extent Anne and Louis carried their mutual disappointments and hostilities into their intimate relations is not known. Unless they were able to declare a truce, their encounters could hardly have been joyful occasions. Love, of course, need not necessarily accompany sex. In recent years, moreover, numerous studies have been written to show that companionate marriage is a relatively modern invention and that the concept of it scarcely existed before 1700.[11] In pre-modern times, medical, moral, and religious authorities indeed saw marriage in a generally utilitarian light. Everyone agreed the chief purpose of marriage was the procreation of children, and doctors pointed out the hygienic advantages of marriage for affording sexual relief to men without the danger of excesses in debauchery. That did not mean they regarded women as purely passive objects. On the contrary, it was widely believed that for the best chances of conception women had to be passionately aroused to a climax because, according to the prevailing understanding of the reproductive process, both male and female seminal fluids were needed for generation to take place. At least some Catholic theologians went so far as to hold it lawful for a wife to manipulate herself if her husband had not satisfied her. For these authors emotional fulfillment or the use of sex to bring husband and wife closer together was not at issue, and even physical harmony between husband and wife could be minimal. Social customs moreover tended to promote emotional distance in marriage, particularly among the well-born, where husbands and wives followed separate routines, had separate quarters and separate staffs of servants, and, in the case of royalty, lived in separate households.

Nevertheless, however much seventeenth-century theories of marriage may have differed from ours, the practice was not necessarily as cold-blooded as might be assumed. People seem to have expected a certain amount of good will between husbands and wives, even if only as a promise for the birth of children. Thus with respect to Louis and Anne, whose lack of children had serious political significance, public opinion apparently became a matter of concern. The king's subjects evidently had some notion that all was not right with the royal domestic life: only that can explain the repeated assertions to the contrary published in the *Gazette de France* during 1631 and 1632.

The *Gazette* was a weekly newsletter created in July 1631 with the blessing of Louis and Richelieu as a means of shaping public opinion. Both men contributed to it on occasion without bylines, and Richelieu himself edited the information and comments presented. One of the earliest issues of the *Gazette* offered its readers a brief sketch of the royal couple, who were spending the summer in the country at the castle of Monceaux: the king was in excellent health, went hunting almost every day, and generally gave evidence of being in first-rate mental as well as physical condition. Above all, his piety was earning him the reputation of being the best man in his kingdom, and "since the queen shares this quality, it is not to be wondered that not a single subject lives on better terms with his wife than their majesties do with each other."[12] In the following year, the *Gazette* went into greater detail. When Anne accompanied Louis on his campaign against the duchy of Lorraine, the *Gazette* reported, "The affection their majesties have for one another is such that they can bear to be separated only when the king goes to make foreign conquests, and even then the queen wants to see them from the frontiers."[13] And when they rejoined company after having traveled by separate routes, "they greeted one another as though they had not seen each other for a long time."[14] Later in the same year, while Louis and Anne were on progress through southern France and spent some time in Montpellier, the *Gazette* noted:

> They bear such affection to one another that they would not put up with being housed apart, and since Montpellier has no Louvre, several houses have had to be joined and the separating walls knocked down to provide sufficiently large quarters for them.[15]

Having traveled separately on the return trip, they met at Versailles in mid-December, and their joy was inexpressible.[16] It made a reassuring picture for the literate public in the provinces, although it is doubtful whether subscribers in Paris, having readier access to gossip, believed what they were reading.

This much at least was true in the *Gazette*'s presentation: Anne indeed was anxious to accompany Louis on his trips, and thereby showed that she clung to a wife's privilege.[17] In order to make life pleasanter and perhaps also to stimulate her husband, Anne was even willing to encourage Louis's friendship with another woman provided it did not go too far.

In 1630 while the royal family was in Lyon, Louis had noticed a newcomer at court, a granddaughter of Madame de la Flotte, one of Marie de Medici's ladies. The girl was Marie de Hautefort, about fourteen years old at the time, already beautiful, with ash blond hair, vivid blue eyes, and a pink-and-white complexion, and apparently precociously prudent as well as virtuous.[18] Louis liked to see her when he attended the queen's circle, a conversational gathering that customarily assembled in the queen's salon during the late afternoons. After Marie de Medici left France, Louis presented the girl to Anne with the request that she love her for his sake,[19] and he appointed her grandmother Madame de la Flotte to the post of lady-in-waiting vacated by the dismissal of Madame du Fargis.

At first Anne was not pleased, though as usual she had no choice in the matter. Before her own departure, however, Madame du Fargis had already advised Anne to make the best of the king's infatuation, reminding her that "with whomever he might fall in love, he can make love only to you."[20] Given Louis's religious scruples and other inhibitions, this was true. Besides, Marie de Hautefort herself was a model of chastity and, far from encouraging dalliance, seemed to take pride in rejecting even serious suitors. Louis would seek her out when he visited the queen's apartments and talk to her about his dogs, his birds, and the hunt—but from a distance, for he did not dare approach her too closely.[21] Marie de Hautefort did not find the king's shyness touching. Although she liked the prominence royal favor gave her, she felt no tenderness for Louis. Instead she attached herself to the queen, much to Louis's chagrin. Louis held it against Marie that she sided with Anne, and was sensitive to reports that she carried to Anne all that he said and laughed with Anne at his weaknesses. But when he reproached the girl with such behavior, she would retaliate with coldness and disdain, nor did she hesitate to tell him to his face when she thought he was wrong.

Anne, who was in too dependent a position to use such tactics, may well have found Marie's conduct as vicariously satisfying as Louis found it galling. In any event, Anne showed herself complaisant. A friend of Marie de Hautefort, her anonymous seventeenth-century biographer, recorded an incident that used to be thought charming: the king entering the queen's rooms one day, saw Marie de Hautefort showing her a letter. He asked to read it, but since it contained joking congratulations on her rise to favor, Marie was embarrassed to let the king see it. She folded the note and hid it in her bodice. Anne thereupon pinioned Marie's hands and invited Louis to help himself to the letter. He tried, not with his hands, to be sure, but with the silver fireplace tongs, the queen holding the girl all the while. The letter had slipped too far down however so that the king gave up and Anne let the girl go, laughing at the discomfiture of the pair.[22]

The story may not be accurate in fact. Another contemporary of Marie de Hautefort reported the same incident as having taken place at a later time in different circumstances and without participation of the queen.[23] The first version, however, has the ring of psychological truth as far as the relationship between Louis and the two women was concerned. Certainly Anne benefited when Louis was on good terms with Marie, for then he made every effort to be gallant, and in the entertainments he arranged, the queen with all her ladies necessarily had to be included. There were hunting parties, picnics, and concerts that featured songs composed by the king set to poems he had written in honor of Marie de Hautefort. On the other hand, such pastimes ceased whenever Louis was displeased with Marie. Then gloom descended on the court while he brooded alone and wrote out lists of his grievances.[24] As the years went by, their quarrels became more frequent, usually conducted through messengers, with formal reconciliations arranged through the mediation of Richelieu. Marie made no effort to enlist the support of Richelieu; moreover she refused to report the king's doings and sayings to the cardinal. Eventually, therefore, Richelieu thought it best to promote a favorite who would be less troublesome to the king and more docile toward himself. In 1635 he backed persons who were pushing forward a new candidate for the king's affections, Louise Angélique de La Fayette, a niece of Madame de Sénécey, Anne's lady of honor.

Louise, a pretty brunette, had been one of Anne's maids of honor since 1629.[25] Now, hearing her praised as it seemed from all sides, Louis began to pay attention to her. This time it looked as though he had found the perfect friend. Louise de La Fayette was young, impressionable, very pious, and, unlike Marie de Hautefort, tenderhearted. When the king told her about his anxieties and burdens, she pitied him. Moreover, she respected his confidence and kept her distance from Anne. In this case it was Anne who retaliated, not in Louis's fashion but in her own, with a teasing that in at least one instance verged on cruelty.[26] Mademoiselle de La Fayette had one defect: she suffered from a weak bladder that betrayed her whenever she laughed. An accident of this kind happened to her one evening when the king and a large company were assembled for the circle in the queen's apartments. As soon as Louise de La Fayette moved from her place, the queen noticed a wetness on the floor and called attention to it. One of Louise's friends quickly offered the explanation that it was lemon juice—Louise carried a lemon in her pocket and it had somehow been crushed. Anne sent her cloak-bearer, La Porte, to investigate; and he, truthful man, reported it was not lemon juice. Louise de La Fayette was mortified and Louis offended. He was all the angrier because he could not quarrel openly with the queen on such a subject. And so the hidden war between the king and queen continued.

The court spent more and more of its time in the country at Saint-Germain, sometimes in the summer at Fontainebleau. Louis liked Saint-Germain, where he and the queen usually stayed in the new residence built by his father rather than in the forbidding ancient castle in which he and his brothers and sisters had been brought up as children. From Saint-Germain he would ride to visit Richelieu at the cardinal's estate of Rueil for conferences, or go off on hunting trips to Versailles or other game parks or to the estates of friends. He came to Paris only rarely and did not stay long when he did come.

The air at Saint-Germain was thought to be particularly healthy, and the gardens and park were beautiful, as was the view of the Seine winding its way toward Paris. Except during the carnival season, however, when the king and court put on the customary ballets, life at Saint-Germain was apt to be fairly dull for anyone who did not go hunting regularly with the king or share the king's hobbies such as making artillery models and composing prayers based on Bible texts. Anne certainly found it dull, the more so because since 1631 her household had been reduced as an economy measure.[27] The fact that she no longer had counselors or masters of requests may not have affected her daily routine very much, but the loss of six out of twelve maids of honor and all twenty-four attending ladies, six of whom would have been on duty at any given time, reduced the possibilities for diversion in her own apartments.

Anne came to Paris as often as she could, that is, whenever Louis went hunting for several days. She had his permission, of course, but he was well aware how eager she was to get away and resented it. For example, Louis wrote to Richelieu in January 1635 when carnival preparations were under way:

> The queen is not leaving until Monday, and myself Tuesday. She expects to amuse herself in Paris in my absence; she will be well caught when she sees me coming. Someone told me last night that she was planning to rehearse the ballet every day at this one's and that one's house, followed by a good collation and the theater afterward.[28]

Then he added, "I beg you not to mention this to anyone for it would come out who told me."[29]

Paris was important to Anne for more than entertainment. The city provided better facilities than Saint-Germain for her secret correspondence. She could send and receive messages with less risk of being observed, and moreover she could write letters and see visitors almost in privacy at her favorite convent, the Val-de-Grâce. Although in May 1635 Louis sent a herald to Brussels with a formal declaration of war against the king of Spain, the outbreak of open war did not deter her from communicating with her brother. It only made her life more painful, for she could not help showing sadness whenever news came of Spanish defeats, and Louis naturally took her reaction amiss.[30] The war in fact accentuated a problem that had been developing for years. Her statement to her brother the cardinal infante in January, 1635 that she was in as much disgrace as it was possible to be reflected not only her personal relationship with Louis but political realities as well.

The basis for Anne's marriage had been the French-Spanish alliance. Granted, the government of Philip III and later of Philip IV had not always behaved toward France in the spirit of the instructions Anne had received when she left Spain. More than once, and as lately as 1627–28, Spain had encouraged and treated with Protestant rebels against Louis's authority. There had also been fighting between France and Spain over their respective interests in Switzerland, Savoy, and northern Italy, although, contrary to the fears of Richelieu's opponents, general war between France and Spain had not resulted from French military intervention in Mantua and Montferrat. It was also true that Brussels, the capital of the Spanish Netherlands, had become a haven for French malcontents and intriguers—Marie de Medici the first among them. None of these difficulties in themselves necessarily called for a reversal of the fundamental relationship between France and Spain. That only developed when Richelieu began to define French international interests in a new light. New, that is, as compared with the recent past, for he had ample precedents from the reigns of Francis I and Henry IV.

According to Richelieu's view, which Louis found convincing, religious affinity and dynastic connections were less important than France's place in Europe.[31] If the Spanish and Austrian Habsburgs were allowed to win the war they were currently waging against most of the Protestant princes of Germany, France would be faced with overwhelming Habsburg power. In that case, Louis would find himself trailing in the wake of the Habsburgs as a second-rate king, and would forfeit all the claims to influence in the empire and in Italy that his predecessors had established. If Louis wished to be respected in Europe, therefore, he would have to support the antagonists of the Habsburgs in the great war and if necessary join in the war himself. Louis did so although at the time it was a matter of hot dispute whether the choices Richelieu urged on him would harm the kingdom more than benefit it. French historians ever since have accorded Richelieu the highest praise for having guided, or rather returned, France into the path to her true destiny, so that at last "the error of the Spanish marriages was retrieved."[32]

Richelieu never said that Louis's marriage had been an error, but certainly the diplomatic assumptions on which the marriage had been based did erode with the new orientation of French policy. Anne felt it. It seems she relied a good deal on the dynastic treaty aspect of her marriage. Not unlike an ambassador on foreign soil under a diplomatic convention, whenever she thought she was being ill used, she called attention to her powerful relatives who would surely not leave any injuries to her unavenged. She had not been able to supplement the formal dynastic framework of her marriage by developing any personal position of strength, childless and apparently unloved by her husband as she was. It is not surprising, therefore, that she felt herself in an increasingly precarious situation after 1630, and feared Louis might repudiate her.

There is no evidence that either Louis or Richelieu ever considered such a thing. However, a curious rumor reached the royal council in Madrid in May 1633. The Spanish ambassador at the Vatican reported having heard from a monk that the French king had instructed his envoy in Rome to negotiate for a divorce from the queen. The Spanish ambassador added that he did not believe this report well founded but noted the same rumor was running in Venice.[33] The government in Madrid decided to wait for more information and must have been satisfied that there was no cause for alarm for the matter did not come before the royal council again.[34] Rome and Venice, of course, were famous and often unreliable gossip factories, but the story had also surfaced in France, and in more tangible form.

According to the *Gazette* of 4 June 1633, a state prisoner, one Don Juan de Medici, had been brought to the king at Fontainebleau on 31 May. Don Juan had been arrested at Troyes while traveling under an assumed name and was found to be carrying plans of French cities and fortifications as well as letters defaming the king and the government. The contents of the letters were not yet available for publication, with one exception:

> In one of the letters it is supposed the king has sent to Rome for three things, as malicious as they are improbable: to wit, to repudiate the queen, to declare the duke of Orléans unfit and incapable of succeeding to the crown, and to have permission to protect the Lutherans.[35]

Other papers in Don Juan's possession indicated he had come from Brussels. That circumstance, together with the nature of the items cited in the letter, suggests an attempted propaganda campaign by partisans of Marie de Medici and Gaston of Orléans in order to rouse feeling against Richelieu. In any event, Richelieu considered it so important to give this story the lie by publishing it that the *Gazette* of 4 June had to be reissued to include what was in effect a late bulletin.[36] How Anne took the incident is not recorded. Four years later, however, she had genuine cause for fear: her secret correspondence was discovered. Considering that both Louis and Richelieu at different times and without each other's knowledge extended covert peace feelers to Spain,[37] Anne's own efforts to maintain communication with her family hardly seem treasonable. But she was not supposed to engage in independent action, and moreover was disobeying specific orders when she wrote to her friends—and she knew it.

Tradition has it that Richelieu's agents in the early summer of 1637 intercepted one letter—according to one source, from her to Mirabel; according to others, from her to Madame de Chevreuse.[38] The agents also found out the identity of the first link in Anne's chain of couriers: it was her cloak-bearer, La Porte. Tradition is wrong, however, in one important respect: Richelieu already had a lengthy file, dating from 1634, of intercepted correspondence between the queen, the cardinal infante, Mirabel, Madame du Fargis, and Madame de Chevreuse.[39] The question is why he had not announced his discovery to Louis at once.

In keeping Anne's secret for more than three years, Richelieu was either waiting to gather the maximum ammunition against her with a view to controlling her or he was more benevolent toward her than she ever supposed, seeking only to keep himself informed. In any case, it is not clear what finally precipitated action. Perhaps the identity of Anne's messenger really had been unknown earlier, so that the authenticity of her letters could not be proved absolutely. If Richelieu's later remarks to the Venetian ambassador are to be believed, however, it was the king himself who began to suspect La Porte and the queen and thus launched the inquiry.[40] Of course, Louis's suspicions may have been fed by someone. Possibly Richelieu's knowledge made the cardinal increasingly nervous, especially since in 1637 he had to contend with serious threats to his place in Louis's confidence.

The danger came from two persons close to the king: Louise de La Fayette and the king's new confessor, the Jesuit Father Caussin. They had taken it upon themselves to reconcile Louis with his mother, and they held before his eyes the unchristian nature of the policies in which he was supporting Richelieu: the war against Catholic kingdoms, the alliances with Protestants, the excessive demands on his subjects' resources to pay for the war, and his steady refusal to allow Marie de Medici to return to France.[41] Those were vulnerable points. Louis himself felt inner doubts at times, particularly about the problem of his mother. It was not only that he remained tied to her by a peculiar bond of love, hate, and guilt; he shared the belief held by all pious people at the time that filial duty was an obligation in conscience. Whatever he might have suffered at Marie's hands and however certain he might be that she would never live quietly in France and give up her hunger for power, as a dutiful son he should have welcomed her back.

Of course, Louis was more than a son; he was a king, and could justify his conduct quite truthfully by reason of state. But a doubt remained, and along with it resentment against Richelieu, who had been the immediate cause of his break with his mother. To Louise de La Fayette and Father Caussin, Louis indeed confided a long list of grievances against Richelieu, whom he represented as a ruthless taskmaster who respected neither his king's feelings nor dignity. He, Louis, was a martyr to the cardinal's ambitious tyranny—at least so he said, and he appears to have enjoyed Mademoiselle de La Fayette's expressions of compassion and Father Caussin's sympathy. But they did not find it easy to get him to proceed to the logical question: Why suffer such tyranny? He would not admit that he identified with Richelieu and approved of his courses, nor yet would he abandon them.

Richelieu meanwhile kept himself well informed, and, lest Louise succeed where Marie de Medici had failed, he decided to encourage her sometime desire to enter the religious life. A curious duel of clergymen ensued. Her own confessor and Richelieu's client, the Dominican Father Carrier, pushed her on while Father Caussin tried to hold her back, advising her to test her vocation a while longer. In the end Louise's own relatives, intimidated by Richelieu, joined in urging a speedy decision. On 19 May 1637, therefore, the *Gazette* carried a brief notice: "Damoiselle de La Fayette, one of the queen's maids of honor, has become a nun in the convent of the Visitation, and is greatly missed by the king, the queen, and the whole court."[42] It took longer to remove Father Caussin, but his superiors eventually sent him into exile in Brittany; and by the end of December, Louis had a new confessor.[43]

Anne had not been involved with Louise de La Fayette and Father Caussin; there was no love lost between her and Louise. As for the question of Marie de Medici, Richelieu had two intercepted letters from Anne to Madame du Fargis in which Anne declined an invitation to help negotiate Marie's return to France, alleging her own lack of credit with the cardinal.[44] That should have satisfied Richelieu. Nor did her correspondence constitute any real danger to diplomatic or military security. Although occasionally she heard from Madame du Fargis or from the cardinal infante about Spanish campaign plans, it could only have pleased Richelieu to read, for example, that as late as the end of May 1637 the cardinal infante still had not got his troops ready to move for that year's operations.[45]

When Anne herself showed interest in diplomatic affairs, it was clearly for personal reasons. In July of the same year, she wrote Madame du Fargis that she had heard rumors of a closer understanding between England and France. She begged Madame du Fargis to let her know whether this was true and if in such case England seemed likely to break off relations with Spain, for she feared such an event would interrupt the chain of secret couriers that was passing through the English embassies in Paris and Brussels.[46] Several months earlier, the queen had expressed a similar fear to the cardinal infante concerning the French occupation of Lorraine. It was important for the king of Spain, she wrote, to help the duke of Lorraine because his duchy was a way-station in her correspondence with Flanders through Madame de Chevreuse.[47] As it happened, Mirabel forwarded a copy of this letter to Philip IV's minister Olivares in Madrid, although carefully without the signature, and with the veiled reference that Olivares would know from whose hand it came.[48]

Richelieu had a transcript of Anne's original letter, and by the end of June or the beginning of July, he also had a transcript of Mirabel's communication. In view of it, Richelieu perhaps believed Anne's correspondence was assuming an importance he could no longer conceal. On the other hand, considering his difficulties with Louise de La Fayette and Father Caussin, he may have thought the occasion opportune for deflecting the king's resentments from himself to the queen. In his memoirs Richelieu did not mention any motives, or even his role; he noted only that the king, acting on information from various sources, had the queen's cloak-bearer, La Porte, placed under surveillance.[49]

Anne must have suspected something for, near the end of July, she exhorted Madame du Fargis to warn Mirabel "for God's sake, not to speak of me in any connection whatsoever and for good reason. I shall say no more."[50] Her caution came too late, however; she was already trapped.

On 11 August, Anne left Paris to join Louis at Chantilly, and before leaving she entrusted La Porte with a letter to Madame de Chevreuse. That had been anticipated. Before La Porte had a chance to pass on the letter, he was arrested by order of the king and taken to the Bastille for interrogation.[51] On the same day, the archbishop of Paris and the chancellor of France, Pierre Séguier, entered the convent of Val-de-Grâce, ordered a search of the queen's private apartment there, and proceeded to question the mother superior and the nuns. The officials were looking for incriminating papers and codes of cipher, but none were found at either Val-de Grâce or in La Porte's lodging. They also wanted full confessions from La Porte and the mother superior, not just to confirm what was already known, but in the hope of obtaining additional information such as names and addresses of intermediary agents, confirmation of suspected places where the queen might have been writing letters, and the identity of anyone who might be linked closely enough to the queen to cover for her. In short, Séguier was conducting a fishing expedition as much as an inquisition.

At first both the mother superior and La Porte denied any guilty knowledge at all. Under solemn threat of excommunication and by all that was holy, the mother superior swore that to her knowledge the queen had never written letters in the convent; indeed, she passionately defended the queen as a woman of great virtue who was being falsely accused. She was more forthcoming after she had been deposed and sent for detention to a castle outside Paris. Even then she conceded only that the queen had in fact written letters on occasion though she did not know to whom or about what, and that she had transmitted letters to and from the queen but did not know the names of the bearers.

La Porte meanwhile continued to hold out despite threats of torture and repeated interrogations in the Bastille and in Richelieu's palace. He maintained that he had only run errands for the queen as was his duty as a servant, and that he knew nothing beyond that. Only after he was allowed to receive trustworthy assurances from Anne that he was free to speak because she herself had confessed did he finally talk. His testimony proved disappointing, however; it provided no fresh information but merely corroborated what was already known. To make sure of that, Marie de Hautefort had crept out of the Louvre at dawn one morning, disguised as a servant girl, and had succeeded in smuggling him a letter by which Anne let him know the extent of her own admissions—for she was indeed making admissions.[52]

A story later became current that Anne had been present when Val-de-Grâce was searched, and had been subjected to the indignity of turning out her pockets and removing the fichu from her bodice to prove she was not concealing any papers.[53] That was not true. She was out of the way in Chantilly in a state of growing alarm. When she found out about La Porte's arrest, she sent to Richelieu for an explanation, assuring the cardinal that she had used La Porte only to keep in touch with Madame de Chevreuse and had not written to Flanders or Spain through him or any other person.[54] There was no answer.

The king did not come near Anne, and courtiers avoided her apartments. For days she remained alone with the women of her household and cried. On the Feast of the Assumption, 15 August, Anne took communion and then, having summoned her secretary, swore by the sacrament she had just received that she had not written secretly abroad. She instructed the secretary to repeat her words to Richelieu. She also called in Louis's confessor Father Caussin and made the same statement to him under the same oath.[55] Caussin was convinced, though Richelieu was not.

Two days later Richelieu gave Anne to understand through her secretary that he already knew more than she was telling. At this point Anne gave in: she asked Richelieu to come to her and promised to admit what she had done. He appeared the next day, accompanied by secretaries of state Chavigny and Sublet de Noyers as witnesses.[56] The cardinal later recalled that she received him with a great show of good will and assured him that although she had indeed written to her brother the cardinal infante, it had been about things of no consequence, such as requests for news of his health. Richelieu told her he knew better; he offered her his mediation with the king and promised the king would forget all that had happened, provided she told the whole truth. Step by step he led her to confirm the contents of her intercepted letters: yes, she had written to the cardinal infante and to Mirabel; yes, she had complained about her situation; yes, she had expressed herself in terms that must displease the king; yes, she had referred to the question of Lorraine; and yes, she had expressed distress at the prospect of an Anglo-French alliance. Richelieu wanted to make sure she could not claim the letters were forgeries fabricated by himself in order to discredit her, as she had tried to do with Madame du Fargis's letters of 1631 and 1632. In fact, he referred to that old episode and got the queen to acknowledge that those letters too had been genuine.

Anne was in a rare state of confusion, torn between anger, embarrassment, and her need for the cardinal's good offices. Several times she exclaimed, "How good you are, cardinal," and offered him her hand in token of her sincerity.[57] Out of respect, so he said, he did not take it. There she stood, shamed and humbled before the man she considered her worst enemy, and she still had to face Louis.

Chapter Eight

The Child of Miracle

LOUIS'S ANGER TOOK A VERY humiliating form. He spared Anne nothing: spoken admissions were insufficient for him, and he kept her waiting while he had everything put into writing.

On 17 August, Anne was obliged to sign a full confession, first in draft and then in the form of letters patent:

> On the assurance which our very dear and beloved cousin, the cardinal duke of Richelieu, who came to us at our request, had given us that the king, our very honored lord and husband, had commanded him to say to us that just as he [Louis] has already forgotten several times some of our actions which he found displeasing, and notably what happened concerning Madame du Fargis in the years 1631 and 1632, he is still disposed to do the same provided we declare frankly what intelligence we may have had since without the knowledge and against the will of his majesty whether inside or outside the kingdom, the persons whom we have employed therein and the chief things we have known or that were reported to us:
>
> We, Anne, by the grace of God queen of France and Navarre, confess freely without being constrained in any way to having written a number of times to Monsieur the cardinal *infante*, our brother; to the marquis de Mirabel, to Gerbier, English resident in Flanders; and to have received frequent letters from them. . . .

The details followed, and at the end Anne added in her own hand:

> We admit without reservation all of the above, as things we acknowledge frankly and voluntarily to be true. We promise never to repeat such faults and to live with the king, our very honored lord and husband, like a person who wishes to have no other interests than those of his person and his state. . . .[1]

Below her signature, witnessed by her secretary, Louis wrote his endorsement:

> Having seen the frank confession that the queen, our very dear wife, has made of what has displeased us in her conduct for some time, and

the assurance she has given us that she will be guided in the future by her duty toward us and our state, we declare to her that we are forgetting entirely everything that has happened, not wishing to remember it, but to live with her as a good king and good husband should do with his wife. . . .[2]

His signature was also witnessed, so that the whole document had the appearance of a formal treaty.

Now at last Louis went to see Anne, taking Richelieu along. It was a strained interview. Anne begged Louis's pardon, and he said he forgave her; but Richelieu, acting as peacemaker, had to insist before Louis would kiss his wife in token of their reconciliation. What the two had to say to each other may be inferred from the memorandum Louis sent Anne later on the same day. He spelled out precisely what he meant by dutiful conduct:

> I do not wish the queen to write any more to Madame de Chevreuse, chiefly because this pretext has served to cover all the letters she has sent elsewhere.
> I wish Madame de Sénécey [Anne's lady of honor] to account to me for all the letters the queen writes, and that they be closed in her presence.
> I also wish Fillandre, first chamber woman, to report to me every time the queen writes, seeing it is impossible for her not to know it since she keeps her writing desk.
> I forbid the queen to enter any convents until such time as I may permit it again, and when I give her permission, I wish her to be always accompanied by her lady of honor and her lady in waiting in the rooms she may enter. I beg the queen to remember well, when she writes or has others write for her to foreign countries, or sends her views by any means whatsoever, direct or indirect; that she herself has told me that she will hold herself as having forfeited with her own consent the oblivion of her bad conduct that I have accorded her today.
> The queen will know also that I do not wish her to see Crofts and other agents of Madame de Chevreuse in any way whatever.[3]

Anne had to endorse these instructions: "I promise the king to observe religiously the above contained."[4] Even for an age when women were required to show great respect for their husbands, and allowing for the special courtesy and reverence due a king, Louis's insistence on such elaborate protocols was unusual. He evidently craved the assurance of formal contracts, for he used them also in his quarrels with Madame de Hautefort and other favorites.[5] They never worked for long, and particularly this contract with the queen did not seem to be producing a genuine renewal of trust and liking. Despite the kiss of reconciliation, it was noticed that Louis visited his wife only in company, and even then he did not speak to her.[6] It seemed she was more in disgrace than ever, and she had no defenses left.

In the aftermath of what one of Anne's former correspondents called "the *can-can* at Val de Grâce,"[7] the number of people on whom she could depend had shrunk. Access to the nuns of Val-de-Grâce was forbidden to her.[8] La Porte had a lengthy stay in the Bastille, and eventually was sent off to the country in retirement.[9] Madame de Chevreuse had taken alarm and fled to Spain, and spent the following six years in traveling abroad. Worst of all, the Spanish relatives on whose backing Anne had prided herself seemed unable to do anything for her. The Spanish government in fact denied the existence of any secret correspondence whatever with her.

Richelieu had been negotiating possibilities of a truce with Olivares, and the French agent in Madrid lodged a complaint concerning unauthorized Spanish intelligence with the queen. Olivares replied with a mixture of irony and outraged virtue. If Richelieu was alleging that Spain had used the queen of France to gather intelligence, he was either not showing his usual great astuteness, or he must be joking. It was clear, Olivares said, that the Spanish government would have derived short-lived and doubtful results by using such a means where the risks were known to be certain and great. "And," Olivares added, "Spain had no lack at any court of other channels, better informed and more involved in actual business, which do not run immediately between the king of France and the cardinal." He, Olivares, therefore felt confident in assuring Richelieu on oath that no one in Spain had procured or maintained any intelligence with the queen of France, "nor can it seem good to his Catholic Majesty that any of his ministers or vassals should risk causing trouble for the queen, his sister, even if much were to be expected from such a risk."[10] Under the circumstances, Olivares could hardly have said anything else, but neither did he make representations to Richelieu's agents concerning any ill treatment the queen might be suffering as a result of what he called unjust suspicion.

It must have been clear to Anne, perhaps for the first time since she entered France, that her welfare in this world depended entirely on her husband. She cried a great deal, and Secretary of State Brienne later remembered having tried to console her with the reflection that surely heaven would not let so many tears go unrewarded.[11] Either hindsight colored his recollection or he had spoken with great faith, for no human agency could have predicted what actually happened. Some time in the late fall of 1637, Louis and Anne resumed marital relations; and by the end of January, there could be no doubt that she was pregnant.

People who knew Louis and the circumstances of the royal marriage were amazed; one incredulous wit punningly referred to Louis's accomplishment as a remarkable piece of "sleight-of-bed."[12] Decades later certain pamphleteers alleged that the real father of this child was Richelieu, or even Richelieu's successor Mazarin, and not Louis.[13] These were politically inspired slanders, however: Anne loathed Richelieu; in 1637 Mazarin was in Rome, not Paris;[14] and Anne herself lived under much too close surveillance for irregularities of any kind to pass unnoticed. At the immediate time, no one seriously questioned the paternity of the child to come, although people were naturally curious to find explanations for an event most of them had ceased to expect. The *Gazette* gave considerable credit to the royal physicians for having brought the health of the king and queen to such a point that the couple could produce a child.[15] But even the physicians had only been instruments of God, who had rewarded the piety of Their Majesties and answered the prayers of all good people with this "marvel, when it was least expected."[16]

Posterity has preferred more circumstantial explanations, and the one that has enjoyed the greatest currency attributes a major role to the good offices of Louise Angélique de La Fayette, the Visitandine nun who had been Louis's favorite. Louis missed her presence so greatly that as soon as the first period of her novitiate had passed, he called on her regularly in the Convent of the Visitation in Paris.[17] They would talk for hours in the convent parlor, the king on one side of the grille that separated the public part of the room from the convent enclosure, and she on the other. No one knew the subject of their conversations since Louis's attendants withdrew to the farthest corner in order to give the king some privacy, although Richelieu for one believed Louise was continuing to exhort the king to follow Christian policies. In the light of subsequent events, it was also assumed that she urged him to a true reconciliation with his wife.

According to one contemporary, Louis paid one of his usual visits to the convent early in December 1637 on his way from Versailles to Saint-Maur. As it happened, the weather turned stormy, and the longer Louis stayed, the worse the storm became. Louis had to concede that it was out of the question for him to continue his trip, but where was he to stay the night? His apartment in the Louvre had long since been dismantled; beds and other furnishings were not kept in place permanently, but were put in storage or sent to whatever palace was being used—and Louis had not been expected to stay in the Louvre. As Louis's captain of guards Guitaut repeatedly reminded him, however, the queen was in residence and would be glad to offer her husband hospitality. In the end Louis let himself be persuaded. He sent word to Anne at the Louvre, she welcomed him, and that night they shared the same bed.[18] Nine months later, so the story goes, the future Louis XIV was born.

The incident may actually have occurred though with some slight variation. The *Gazette*, whatever its character as a propaganda instrument, usually furnished accurate information concerning the king's itinerary. According to the *Gazette*'s report, the king and queen were at Saint-Germain from 9 November until 1 December, when both went to Paris. On 2 December, Louis left Paris for Crône, not Saint-Maur, and from Crône went on to Versailles on 5 December while the queen still remained in Paris.[19] Louis may well have stopped in Paris on his way from Crône to Versailles, and his rooms at the Louvre may have been cleared of furniture since his departure three days earlier. Even if Louis did spend the night of 5 December with Anne, however, it does not necessarily follow that it was the first time since the crisis of Chantilly in August. His physician, Bouvard, calculated the approximate term of Anne's pregnancy from a possible beginning in late November, and he must have had grounds for doing so.[20]

There is also another account, less dramatic and therefore less popular than the first, of the effective reconciliation between Louis and Anne. According to Marie de Hautefort's anonymous seventeenth-century biographer, Marie took it upon herself to ask Father Caussin to remind the king how dangerous his coldness to the queen was for the welfare of the kingdom and the salvation of his own soul. She had picked the eve of a major church holiday for her request, judging that the king would take the occasion to confess himself and thereby give Father Caussin an opportunity to speak. All went as planned, and as a result the king spent the night with the queen. The following day a monk sent an urgent message to the queen, warning her that he had had a revelation that she was pregnant and that she should be careful about going out. She therefore excused herself from accompanying Louis on an outing to Versailles, and the sequel proved the monk had been right.[21]

There is an important church holiday in December, the Feast of the Conception of the Virgin on 8 December, which Louis may well have honored with particular devotion that year because on 10 February he had signed a solemn vow placing France under the protection of the

Virgin in the hope of her intercession for peace. Marie de Hautefort, however, was not a likely person to have discussed the king's marital problems since she was so ostentatiously modest that she refused to write even the most innocent letters to men, and would leave the room when anything was mentioned of which an unmarried woman should have no knowledge.[22] In any event, we may draw two possible conclusions: Louis had no lack of pious friends to prompt his conscience, and besides, considering that he was not only visiting Louise de La Fayette but also beginning to notice Marie de Hautefort once more,[23] simple physical need may have led him back to his wife.

The question remains why the couple should have proved fertile at this time, after fourteen years had passed since Anne's last undoubted pregnancy and miscarriage. In contrast to seventeenth-century opinion, modern curiosity is not content to refer such matters to divine Providence. Drawing on Freudian theory, one recent historian has suggested that Louis's achievement of paternity was perhaps his most difficult political triumph because the personality problems he had developed in childhood troubled his relationship with his wife as well as other people.[24] That does not explain, however, why 1637 should have been the fruitful year, especially since Louis had already been on the way to becoming a father in 1623: he had not been responsible for Anne's miscarriage. But it may have been Anne who, for psychological reasons of her own, had not been ready to become a parent. On the other hand, one can speculate along less theoretical lines whether the physical relationship between Anne and Louis assumed a new intensity at this time. Anne, who had no worldly recourse except her husband, may have given herself more completely than she had in years; and Louis, who liked to train birds of prey and surrounded himself with dogs, may have found it especially stimulating to feel her so much in his power.

Judging by her later acts of thanksgiving, Anne for her part was convinced that she owed her pregnancy to divine mercy. On the whole, the king's subjects shared her sentiments. After the king publicly announced the queen's pregnancy, at the end of April when the child quickened, prayers rose on all sides in thanksgiving and to ask for a safe delivery.[25] Even earlier a flood of relics had started to pour into Saint-Germain, starting in early February with the belt of the Virgin from LePuy, customarily lent to all French queens when they were with child.[26] Evidently for safety's sake, the queen did not set foot outside Saint-Germain for the entire time. That was less dull than it might have been, thanks to the round of congratulatory visits from all the great nobility that began at the end of January. And Louis was in such good spirits that he put on two ballets for the carnival season instead of the usual one.

In his first joy, it seems he showed Anne some tenderness, but his attention was soon preoccupied with the revival of his former feelings for Marie de Hautefort. She stood so high in his good graces that in March, without being solicited, he granted her the reversion of her grandmother's post as lady-in-waiting to the queen. While Madame de la Flotte lived, Marie would share in the exercise of her office, which entitled her from then on to be called Madame.[27] For once Anne had reason to be pleased with one of the king's appointments in her household. That was not to be the case in a far more important matter—the establishment of a household for the child to come.

Madame de la Flotte, who was ambitious, used her granddaughter Marie to ask for the post of governess, which entailed control over the rest of the staff as well as over the whole household expenditure. Marie's influence did not extend that far, however. Richelieu trusted neither her nor her grandmother and prevailed on the king to choose a candidate whose loyalty was more certain: the dowager Marquise de Lansac, daughter of the late Marshall de Souvré, who had been governor to Louis in the king's own youth. For the sake of form, Anne had to summon Madame de Lansac herself and present the letter of appointment. In mid-July, therefore, the lady waited on the queen, equipped with a detailed memorandum, annotated by Richelieu, instructing her what to say and do in order to win the queen's confidence.[28] Similar care was taken over the choice of the assistant governess, Damoiselle de la Chesnaye, widow of the first valet of the king's chamber.[29] Meanwhile a panel of eminent physicians met to select the royal wet-nurse. They picked a well-born matron, Damoiselle de la Giraudière, the wife of a royal treasury official in Orléans and daughter of a former royal steward and ambassador.[30] By that time it was the latter part of August, the earliest point at which, according to the doctors, Anne's confinement could be expected.

Next to the queen herself, the most important person at this stage was the midwife. Yet we know nothing about Anne's midwife save her name: Dame Peronne, who, if her name is an indication, probably belonged to a dynasty of midwives long established in Paris.[31] Anne's physicians played a secondary role, not being required for the delivery itself but only for prescribing medication or other supportive treatment if needed. Indeed, Anne's first physician, Pierre Séguin, was dangerously ill at this time, and she was petitioning Louis to give

Séguin's nephew the right of succession to the post. As he did with everything, Louis referred this matter to Richelieu, who was with the troops on campaign. Richelieu obligingly advised Louis to consent, "because she wishes it, and it regards the conservation of her person which concerns her more than anyone else. It will be an effect of your majesty's goodness, and has no bearing on affairs of state."[32] That was on 2 September so that the letter hardly had time to reach Saint-Germain before Anne's child was actually born, presumably without attendance of either Séguin uncle or Séguin nephew.

Anne's surgeon may have stood by in case she required bloodletting but midwives ordinarily did not ask surgeons to assist in the delivery itself unless there was a very difficult problem. There is no evidence that Dame Peronne found that indicated. Presumably she supervised the preparations that, although not mentioned specifically on this occasion, were standard procedure for confinements.[33] Since the normal vast, canopied, and curtained four-poster bed was unsuited for the midwife's work, a special cot had to be set up: wider at the head, narrowing from the middle to the foot, with the bottom end so arranged that the mother could brace her feet while keeping her knees flexed. In addition a delivery chair might be kept ready for use if, for example, labor was prolonged and the mother tired. Last but not least, the royal nursery had to be fitted out in white damask, with upholstery on all surfaces lest the child hurt itself when it came of age to walk.[34]

The great ladies of France, princesses and duchesses, began to gather at Saint-Germain for the queen's confinement. Gaston of Orléans arrived on 22 August. His friends had been trying to console him with the unkind thought that even if Anne was delivered successfully, it would probably only be a girl.[35] Such an event, of course, would leave Gaston as heir presumptive, since royal daughters could not inherit the crown. Louis himself had spent part of the summer with the army near the Flanders frontier, and Anne had worried lest her time came before he returned.[36] He came back to Saint-Germain on 18 August, however, and then proceeded to fret because the queen was not as near delivery as he had been led to believe. He would have liked to leave again, he wrote Richelieu, just to get away from all those women.[37]

What chiefly put Louis out of humor was his latest disagreement with Marie de Hautefort. Marie's behavior had not changed since 1635; she still did not mind provoking him with a cold manner and critical remarks and had done so on the day of his arrival. Consequently, while every one else was concerned about the queen, Louis spent a week nursing his grievances against Marie de Hautefort.[38] After he made peace with her, his spirits improved dramatically, but then he went hunting and came down with a fever. And the waiting went on. Anne had grown very large and was feeling uncomfortable; she was also becoming depressed because, so she said, she feared that she would die in childbirth.[39]

During the last week of August, the sacrament was exposed in all the churches of Paris, and continuous public prayers were begun for her speedy and safe delivery. At last, late on the evening of Saturday 4 September, Anne felt the first pains, and shortly after eleven the next morning, she gave birth to a son.

Louis had stayed with Anne since dawn and had just gone to his dinner when he was called back by a message that the birth was about to take place. At the entrance to the queen's room, Madame de Séné-cey greeted him with the news that he had a son, and Dame Peronne showed him the baby, whose beauty and size, she said, were remark-able.[40] Gaston, who had been obliged to witness the actual birth, con-gratulated his brother with apparent sincerity, although malicious spirits noted that he seemed to be a bit melancholy.[41] Then the dauphin was baptized, fed by his wet-nurse, placed on a silver charger, and carried to his apartments, where Madame de Lansac was waiting to receive him. Louis visited him there four or five times that day, so delighted was he to be a father.[42] But Louis had to be reminded to kiss his wife.[43]

Announcements went out to all the dignitaries of the kingdom and the great officials of the crown, as well as to the courts of Europe. Meanwhile the happy news spread from Saint-Germain to Paris and to all of France with almost literally the speed of sound, carried as it was by the peals of every church bell in the kingdom. In the town square in front of the old castle of Saint-Germain, a fountain decorated with silver dolphins spouted wine at the king's expense, an act of generos-ity that was imitated by private citizens in Paris and elswhere. In Paris one man even had wine running from his roof. There seemed to be no end to thanksgiving services, rejoicings, illuminations, fireworks; and emblems of dolphins reigned supreme.[44] For months congratulations poured in, brought by delegations from within the kingdom and by extraordinary ambassadors from abroad, culminating in the presenta-tion in July 1639 of the pope's traditional gift to the firstborn sons of French kings: baby clothes and furnishings of silk, cloth of gold and silver, and crimson velvet. Only the child's grandmother remained silent. Louis had asked Richelieu what he should do if an envoy came from his mother;[45] but he need not have troubled himself, for she sent no one.

In all the celebrations, religious feeling provided the keynote. The *Gazette* reflected this strong sentiment in its announcement: "What we no longer dared to ask except as a grace of which we considered ourselves unworthy, has been given to us as a sure token of heaven's special protection over this crown."[46] The editor compared the birth of the crown prince to that of Moses, Samuel, and John the Baptist in its miraculous aspect. For the public the dauphin represented an assured royal succession and the hope of future tranquillity within the kingdom. For Anne however, the child meant much more: he was her vindication and her salvation—in this world, if not in the next. Although she never put that into so many words, her actions spoke for themselves, and we may measure the intensity of her feeling by the religious observances with which she tried then and later to show her passionate gratitude for prayers answered.

Her first opportunity came when she celebrated her *relevailles*, the ceremony in which a woman was blessed after childbirth, and which marked the end of her period of lying-in. On Sunday 26 September, her household and a number of prelates gathered in her apartments, where an altar had been set up. She received the bishops on her knees and then carried her son to the altar, where she offered him to the service of God. Having heard mass and received Communion, she again took up the child for the rest of the ceremony, and she did it with such touching caresses while tears stood in her eyes that her whole court broke into sympathetic weeping at the sight. Then the gospels were read over the dauphin, and observers noted that the queen held him without assistance the entire time—three-quarters of an hour.[47]

Anne did not display maternal tenderness merely for show. The dauphin was the center of her life, and, as far as she could, she gave him a very different childhood than his father had experienced.

Outwardly the two were raised under similar conditions in infancy. Like his father before him, the dauphin lived in a separate nursery establishment. Aside from his governess, the assistant governess, the wet-nurse and her substitute, he was also served by a nursery maid, eight chambermaids, a physician, and a steward for his silver.[48] Such an elaborate household was reserved for princes, though wet-nurses were used also in noble or well-to-do families. Some few critics of this custom pointed to the dangers that might arise from ignorance or poor health on the part of the nurses; nevertheless, it was practically unthinkable for a woman of quality to nurse her children herself—whether it seemed degrading to subordinate her daily routine to such a demanding, animal function or whether out of the belief that a nursing mother could not conceive another child.[49]

According to modern opinion, placing babies in the hands of a wet-nurse tended to prevent the formation of strong emotional bonds between children and their parents, particularly with their mothers, because the nurses effectively became substitute mothers to the babies.[50] That may have been true in general, and it certainly seems to have been true of Louis XIII; but it did not happen with his son.

Lastly, the dauphin like all children whatsoever was wrapped in swaddling bands for the first months of his life so that his movements were restricted. Swaddling bands were long bandages, and a child wrapped in them looked like a small mummy, especially since at least some of the time its arms were enclosed as well. The main purpose of swaddling was to make sure that the child's limbs would grow straight; no one believed that an infant would grow up with straight legs, or to walk on two feet instead of four, without such early constraint.[51]

Nowadays the use of swaddling bands is held to have aggravated the harm done by wet-nurses because a child so constricted was deprived of mobility as well as sensory stimulation from the world around it, a deprivation that, according to modern ideas, must have outweighed any possible psychological benefits derived from the security of the wrapping. The suggestion has even been made that the use of wet-nurses together with the practice of swaddling may help to account for the proneness of seventeenth-century people to distrust one another and flare easily into rage or violence.[52] If Louis XIII grew up distrustful, however, that was probably not an effect of swaddling. Infants were not immobilized all the time in any case; they had to be unwrapped when they needed changing. Moreover since the swaddling bands were not intended to impede circulation, they were wrapped loosely enough so that an active baby could kick them apart, as Louis XIV did by the time he was seven months old.[53]

Above all, neither separate establishments, wet-nurses, nor swaddling precluded a close relationship between mother and child, provided the mother was loving. That was the difference between the infancy of Louis XIII and his son—his son had a loving mother.

Unlike Marie de Medici, Anne was often in her son's nursery. One of her attendants wrote at the beginning of April 1639: "The queen hardly leaves him. She takes great pleasure in playing with him and taking him out in her carriage whenever the weather is fine; it is the whole of her amusement."[54]

In other respects the circumstances of her life had not improved. In November 1638, as soon as decently possible after her recovery from childbirth, Louis had dismissed her lady of honor, Madame de Sénécey. The king had held a grudge against Madame de Sénécey since 1637, when she had helped urge Louise de La Fayette into the convent; moreover he suspected her of encouraging the queen in her apparently insurmountable dislike for Richelieu. While Anne was pregnant, Madame de Sénécey had been left in place, lest her dismissal upset the mother-to-be. In November that was no longer a consideration, and so she went. In her stead Anne had to accept a dependent of Richelieu, Madame de Brassac, and madame's husband, the count of Brassac, was installed as superintendent of Anne's household.[55] At last Richelieu had what he felt was reliable surveillance of Anne's movements, actions, and thoughts. More than that, the Brassacs could try to influence her in the cardinal's favor as much as possible since by virtue of their posts they had a great deal of access to the queen. Brassac reported to Richelieu almost daily and eventually felt able to assure him that Anne truly meant to live on good terms with the cardinal and be guided by him in all things.[56] Brassac was mistaken, but Anne did begin to find him and his wife useful as channels to the cardinal in case of need.

The next blow fell in November 1639, when Anne lost her friend Marie de Hautefort. Louis had grown tired of the eternal round of quarrels and reconciliations with Marie, and besides she belonged too much to the queen. He had opened his heart to a new friend: Henri d'Effiat, marquis de Cinq-Mars, and had sworn to him that he would not give his confidence to any other person.

Cinq-Mars owed his rise to Richelieu.[57] The cardinal had supervised his education after the death of the boy's father, Marshall d'Effiat, whom the cardinal had considered his good friend. The boy grew into a very handsome and lively young man. Richelieu thought he knew him well enough to trust him and began to put him in the king's way, starting with his appointment as master of the king's wardrobe in March 1638. It took some time, but gradually Louis found Cinq-Mars's company more appealing than Marie de Hautefort's and ordered the lady to leave court.

This new friendship did not mean that the king was neglecting his own family. From the end of May to the beginning of November that year, he was away on campaign; but whenever he stayed at Saint-

Germain, he visited the dauphin's nursery. He seemed to be pleased with his son, who, at seventeen months, managed to hand him the napkin at table.[58] And at the end of January 1640, the court rejoiced at the news that the queen was showing signs of being pregnant once more.

This time there was less anxiety on everyone's part. Anne remained quietly at Saint-Germain while Louis, Cinq-Mars, and Richelieu left for the annual campaign at the beginning of May. The pilgrimage church of LePuy did not send the Virgin's belt until September, and Anne did not receive the money to pay for her childbed until almost the end of August, and then only after repeated appeals to Richelieu through the Brassacs and in half the amount she had requested.[59] This time, moreover, the king did not fear to upset her. He returned to Saint-Germain on 7 September and two days later took along his friend Cinq-Mars to visit the dauphin. The child had just been weaned the day before and may have been fretful for that reason; or perhaps he did not recognize Cinq-Mars: at any rate, when Cinq-Mars tried to caress him, he cried. Louis took this as an affront to himself. When the governess, seeing his wrath, attempted an apology, he merely answered "I'm not blaming you"; but on the way out, he met the queen, stopped short in front of her, and with a face contorted by passion told her, "The dauphin can't stand the sight of me. He is getting a very peculiar upbringing but I shall see to it."[60]

Anne was thunderstruck; she retreated in tears to her apartment, saying to Madame de Brassac that she well knew what that meant; they wanted to take the dauphin away from her.[61] She was right: that was precisely what Louis had in mind, as he wrote Richelieu.[62] She herself begged Richelieu to intercede for her, and the threat blew over—particularly since the next time Louis visited his son the child was all smiles.[63]

Shortly thereafter, on 21 September, Anne gave birth to a second son. In the face of universal rejoicing, she may have reflected that now she had presented her husband with yet another hostage for extorting from her what he considered good behavior.

Chapter Nine
Motherhood

PUBLIC REJOICING WAS ALMOST as great for the birth of the second prince, Philippe of Anjou, as it had been for the first. Now the royal succession seemed doubly secure, a manifest sign of divine blessing on the monarchy, "for three years ago it would have been difficult to persuade their majesties of what we see today: namely, that they would give us two princes like so many columns to assure our conquests. . . . "[1] As the queen herself later recalled, the king showed greater happiness at the coming of his second son than at the birth of the dauphin, so pleased was he at finding himself the father of two children when he had used to fear he would die the father of none.[2] His pleasure in fatherhood, however, did not lead to increased cordiality toward his wife—far from it. Louis distrusted Anne as much as ever, and when in November 1641 the cardinal infante Ferdinand died of a fever in Brussels, Louis broke the news with brutal directness: "Your brother is dead."[3]

Louis's affections were preoccupied with the marquis de Cinq-Mars.[4] The king had not gained by the exchange of Marie de Hautefort for Cinq-Mars. Louis was passionately attached to the young man, wanted to confide all his thoughts to him, and to share his company at court, at the hunt, and on campaign. Malicious tongues added that the friendship went beyond that; but there was never any reliable evidence to support such an assertion, and Louis's very real piety made an overt homosexual relationship extremely improbable. Short of that, however, he loved Cinq-Mars and was as jealous and as demanding of him as he had been of Marie de Hautefort.

Cinq-Mars on his side proved an ungrateful subject. He was a lively young man who liked magnificent clothes, drinking parties, and late nights in Paris with his mistress. He found the king's devotion and frugal habits inexpressibly boring. As soon as Cinq-Mars felt sure of Louis's favor and had secured the prestigious office of grand equerry, or master of the royal stables, he became more and more petulant and ill-tempered. Once again there were long interludes at Saint-Germain when quarrels between king and favorite cast a pall of gloom over the court, with the full panoply of protocols, of grievances, mediation by Richelieu, and formal treaties of reconciliation. At least Louis could not blame Anne for any shortcomings in his friend's behavior. She never showed any resentment of the favorite, but neither did she cultivate him. Cinq-Mars was Louis's problem, and Richelieu's.

When Louis was away on hunting trips, which happened frequently, or on campaign, as he was from May to November in 1641 and from early February in 1642, the queen followed a peaceful routine at Saint-Germain. Her life centered on the royal nursery, established in the old castle. She went to Paris for only the most compelling reasons and under unimpeachable auspices. Thus it was an exceptional treat when in January 1641 Anne spent a week in Paris to attend a thanksgiving service at Notre-Dame for the birth of the duke of Anjou, and to enjoy a grand entertainment Richelieu gave in her honor.[5] The festivities took place in Richelieu's new theater, recently completed with the latest devices for scenery and stage illusions. There the queen, escorted by her brother-in-law Gaston and surrounded by a large company of noble ladies and gentlemen, saw a performance of *Mirame*, by Desmarets de Saint-Sorlin.[6]

Desmarets was one of Richelieu's literary protégés, even in some sense his collaborator, for Desmarets's plays were generally believed to have been inspired by the cardinal himself. No expense was spared in the production of *Mirame*, with a stage setting of formal gardens, complete with grottos, statues, fountains, and a long perspective to the sea in the distance where at the appropriate time two fleets could be seen in motion, while dusk gave way to night, moonlight, and dawn.

For any one who loved attending theatrical performances as much as Anne did, the spectacle should have been a great pleasure. The subject of the play, however, made court gossips wonder whether Richelieu had intended to insult the queen rather than compliment her. Mirame was a princess of Bithynia loved by two heroes: one hero was besieging her father's city while the other was its defender. She herself loved the besieger and spurned the defender, though apparently in vain, for her preferred lover suffered defeat at the hands of his unsuccessful rival. Scandalmongers at the time took the play as a *roman à clef*, reading the list of characters as Anne of Austria, the duke of Buckingham, and Richelieu himself, and they saw the allusion as a public mockery of the queen.

In his prefatory dedication to Louis, the author asserted firmly that the plot of the play was an invention. It is true the roles did not exactly parallel real life. Mirame was the daughter of the king of Bithynia, not his wife; and her rejected suitor Azamor, king of Phrygia, had no counterpart at the French court. On the other hand, it was suggestive that the hero, Arimant, was, like Buckingham, a royal favorite, and had originally come to Bithynia for a wedding. And the actual heart of the drama was even more suggestive: Mirame's loyalties divided between love and the safety of her father's state, or as her father saw it, loyalties insufficiently divided. He complained to his constable, Acaste:

> She who seems to you like a heavenly flame,
> Is a fire fateful for all my family
> And perhaps for the state; in a word it is my
>   daughter.
> Her heart that gives itself up to the love of a
>   stranger,
> Drawing him here, puts me in danger.
> While everywhere I show myself invincible,
> She lets herself be conquered.[7]

That speech was bound to put the audience in mind of Buckingham's attempts to relieve La Rochelle. Indeed, listeners were free to recall more sinister intrigues as the king continued:

> Acaste, it is too true; by various means
> People are attacking my state both within
>   and without;
> They suborn my subjects; they plot my ruin,
> Now covertly, now by open force.[8]

Clearly the Buckingham story had served as at least partial inspiration for *Mirame*. The only question is whether Richelieu meant the play as an insulting reminder to Anne of past mistakes, or as a gallant vindication of her honor. Mirame after all was portrayed in a most flattering manner: her only crime was love; otherwise she was entirely virtuous. Her love, moreover, had a happy ending, with peace and marriage, for Arimant turned out to be the long-lost brother of Azamor.

The rest of the evening's entertainments would also seem to belie any malicious intent on Richelieu's part. After the play and refreshments, Anne opened a ball with the first dance and then presided over the rest of the evening from a throne on the stage. It is difficult to imagine that Richelieu could have meant to humiliate the queen in such a setting, not only before the court but also in the presence of distinguished foreigners, prisoners of war who had been brought expressly from Vincennes to be impressed: the imperial generals Werth and Enkenfort, and the Spaniard Don Pedro de Leon.[9]

Besides Anne was now the worthy mother of two princes, and took care to be on good terms with the cardinal ever since she had thrown herself on his mercy to help her keep the dauphin. The count and countess of Brassac, her secretary Le Gras, and secretary of state Chavigny continued to keep her under surveillance and reported to Richelieu, but she gave them no apparent reason to doubt her protestations of heartfelt gratitude and her assurances that she would henceforth put herself in the cardinal's confidence and let herself be guided entirely by his advice.[10] She even came to like Madame de Brassac, so that life in her circle at Saint-Germain was by no means unpleasant.

There were also new faces in the queen's apartment. The cuts made in the queen's household in 1631 had been restored in 1640.[11] This meant, among other things, that Anne once again had a bevy of attending ladies, although only a few of the original incumbents were reappointed. Altogether Anne's household had increased vastly since her first establishment as a young bride, not so much in the number of women as in the size of the legal and clerical departments and the purveyors of goods and services. The latter were kept on retainer; detailed records dating from 1642 give us some idea of what the queen required.[12] For herself and her maids of honor, she employed: one goldsmith, two jewelers, two dealers in silk fabrics, four mercers, one dealer in braid trimmings and one in jeweled trimmings, one ribbon and fringe weaver, three makers of lingerie and other linens, five embroiderers and one embroideress, one specialist in cutwork and pleating, six tailors, one tailor-seamstress, one seamster, four painters, one mason-painter, one gilder and mirror-maker, one hoopskirt-maker for the queen and two for the maids of honor, one mask-maker, two needle-makers, one trunk- and box-maker, one perfumer, one pastry cook, two confectioners for preserved fruit, one confectioner for candies, and a dancing master for the maids of honor. Since the queen's shoemaker was also especially paid to make shoes for the dwarfs, we know that Anne still had dwarfs in her household, presumably female ones, according to royal Spanish custom.

These same records also reveal something of the domestic routine at Saint-Germain, including the spring cleaning when the upholsterers came to make running repairs on the furniture and wash the queen's bedspread, bedcurtains, and the bouquets of plumes that ornamented the bed's tester. When the queen wanted a change, she had a new bedspread made. It seems she did not use a magnificent present from France's new ally, Portugal—a large ebony bed covered with sheet silver and furnished with gold taffeta from China—for she had the bed wrapped up and evidently sent it into storage. She kept her children in mind too. She had the dauphin's little chair upholstered in green velvet, trimmed with fringe and gilded nails, and the only new piece of furniture she ordered during the year was a walker upholstered in crimson velvet, presumably for Philippe.

The dauphin was by now three years old, going on four. When he reached his seventh year, he would be entrusted to a governor and begin formal education in the charge of tutors. Louis was already considering possible governors, although as yet he had made no definitive appointments. Apparently he did not consult the queen, who had her own ideas on the subject. She spoke about it to a number of persons, among them the Jansenist Arnauld d'Andilly.[13]

One of the men Anne consulted, and it was not Arnauld, wrote a short treatise for her entitled "Maxims of Childhood Education and Direction."[14] The identity of the author is not known; whoever he may have been, however, he was not negligible. Judging by his essay, he had knowledge of theology, medicine, and ancient philosophy and literature; he also seems to have had some practical experience with small children. In addition, he was acquainted with the court and the habits of the king and queen, which he did not hestitate to criticize in one or two respects. Last but not least, his educational advice reflected the new religious emphasis on moral development, and thus was well ahead of much contemporary pedagogy. We do not know to what extent his maxims were actually followed in the dauphin's nursery. We can be certain, however, that they matched Anne's own views of what was important in the upbringing of her eldest son, for, as the author explained in his dedicatory preface, he had composed the little book specifically at the queen's request as a sequel to an earlier, more theoretical work.[15] He described this sequel as an unadorned, modest effort meant for her eyes alone, and indeed the manuscript was never published, but was bound in red leather, tooled in gold with the queen's arms, and preserved in her library. None of the many other treatises written then or later concerning the future Louis XIV's education was commissioned or treated in this way, so that the "Maxims" may be said to have a special importance and deserves some attention.

The treatise dealt with

the devotions, morals, actions and small studies of Monseigneur, the dauphin, until the age of seven years with a summary of the principal and general terms of the theological and cardinal virtues which those who will have the honor of being near his royal highness will begin to teach him and make him practice at this young age by their care and skill.

Although the title did not say so, the treatise included advice on the dauphin's physical care, daily routine, and general activities. Those were not the most important subjects, however. About a fourth of the manuscript dealt directly with the task of grounding the dauphin in religion and morality—a concern evidently prominent in the queen's mind when she requested the work. Although the author gave learned explications for the virtues of faith, hope, charity, prudence, temperance, justice and so on, at the end of each section he suggested ways in which such abstract notions might be made clear to a small child. In every instance the method was to make abstractions concrete by enlisting the child's senses, affections, and experience. His relationship to his parents, for example, was used to illustrate hope: he owes his life to them, and they care for him lovingly; but he can never be absolutely certain of completely possessing their good graces, for majesty is jealous of its dignity and prerogatives and is easily offended. With his parents, therefore, he lives in hope.[16] Any jealousy the dauphin might feel toward his younger brother should also be turned to account in order to teach him the danger of overconfidence and the meaning of hope.[17]

Understanding of charity was to start with the observation that he loves God and his father and mother because they love him;[18] temperance involved not eating or drinking too much, covering oneself modestly, and being courteous to others;[19] and prudence required the beginnings of introspection: learning to distinguish good from bad actions in others and in himself.[20] The dauphin was to learn in similar fashion the negative counterparts of the virtues: sin was what displeases God and his parents, and he could visualize evil as a dark stain on a beautiful cloth.[21] As for his devotions, he was to be taught simple prayers and a simple catechism, but would learn reverence most of all from observing the behavior of his household during mass and at prayer—for which reason it was important to choose and train his attendants carefully and also to let him have his own mass because at the court's mass in the royal chapel too many people behaved irreverently despite the good example set by Their Majesties.[22] In connection with the dauphin's catechism, his governess might also show him holy pictures and let him kiss them and encourage him to feel tenderness and affection for their subjects.[23]

The author of the "Maxims" thought the dauphin could begin reading lessons by the age of five at the latest, and once he had mastered reading, he could start to learn writing and a little Latin. The author emphasized, however, that these studies should at this early stage be treated more like a game than a systematic effort, for the object was to accustom him gradually to attention and self-discipline while avoiding any kind of coercion. Children who were frightened or bored in their early lessons often lost any taste for study, and work thereafter profited them little: "We see enough examples of this without looking further afield than the royal house of Bourbon."[24] The dauphin should not be exposed to such a risk, and Their Majesties' praise should be his main incentive, with a show of authority left only as the last resort.

On the subject of authority and correction, the author of the "Maxims" advised their majesties to try every kind of persuasion and admonition before ordering a beating for disobedience or mischief. He did not believe that corporal punishment had as powerful or salutary an effect on the behavior of the young as their fear of displeasing the people whom they loved.[25] Furthermore, if correction did become necessary, the dauphin's governess should administer it only in private, not before other people, because "children's sense of shame is their strongest spur to the good and it must be preserved because once they lose it, all is lost."[26]

Such precepts were very different from the principles that had governed the upbringing of Louis XIII. "Spare the rod and spoil the child" had been the motto of Henri IV, and the king did not worry lest the boy lose his sense of shame. From her approval of the "Maxims," we may infer that Anne did not wish to see this motto applied to her son, and for once Louis may have agreed with her. No one has ever reported that Louis ordered his son to be beaten as he himself had been. In other respects too, the "Maxims" implied that mistakes had been made in Louis XIII's rearing that ought not to be repeated. Thus, for example, the author allowed that the dauphin might learn music and could do no better than to imitate his father, who was a master of the art, but only up to a point: he should not be encouraged to acquire more facility than needed to judge performances by professionals, for "a prince of his quality has more important things to learn."[27] In other words, it would be well if the dauphin did not learn to busy himself with composing songs and hymns, as his father liked to do. It had also been noted that the dauphin's constitution, to use the medical terminology of the day, tended to be dominated by the melancholic humor, and that he seemed inclined to become sad, pensive, and solitary. Every effort should be made to counteract these tendencies by companionship and activity, and on no account should the dauphin be left to walk or sit alone and daydream idly.[28] Clearly the intention was to make the dauphin more sociable than his father.

The "Maxims" also suggested specific ways in which the dauphin, although as yet in the nursery, might be prepared for his future role as king. He should be taught that he must always keep his promises because "the good faith of the prince is the foundation of his monarchy";[29] he should hear about his father's and grandfather's battles and victories; and it would be well if geographies of France, Spain, Europe, and all parts of the world, as well as short histories of the kings of France and of neighboring states, were composed for him.[30] Nor should exercise for the development of his body be neglected, for "if we consider what is brewing in our day, what is preparing for his reign, we could wish that he had the body of Hercules."[31] Accordingly he was to be encouraged in horsemanship and in other activities such as dancing and hunting—only those kinds of hunting, however, that did not involve trickery or deception of the prey, since such practices were ungenerous and brought a prince no glory.[32] He should also be introduced to weapons, particularly if the king set up demonstrations and undertook the explanations himself.[33] In short, the training for kingship envisaged in the "Maxims" was quite conventional; there was no question of producing an infant prodigy or a future philosopher-king, but rather a prince who would be pious, reasonably informed about his kingdom and the world, acquainted with sociable pastimes, a good horseman, and familiar with the art of war. It was a practical view of royal upbringing, and the queen evidently found it satisfactory since she followed that orientation when the death of Louis XIII left her free to order her son's education.

For the time being, to be sure, she had no such power. It was not even certain that she would be allowed to keep her children near her. During the first half of 1642, her worst fears in this respect threatened to become fact, as a by-product of the latest round of conspiracies.

The years 1641 and 1642 were as fertile in noble plots as in uprisings among the people.[34] The strain of financing the continuing war was making itself cruelly felt. Not to mention lesser incidents in other places, the province of Normandy had rebelled against new taxes in 1639; men of all classes had resisted royal officials, the populace had massacred tax-gatherers, and not even the stern measures of legal retribution supervised by Chancellor Séguier in person could guarantee against similar outbreaks in the future. Since 1636 the king had been protesting that he was waging war only to get a good peace, but as yet peace was nowhere in sight. Although possible arrangements for a peace conference had been discussed secretly for some time among the belligerents, no such conference had met thus far; each side hoped to win some decisive victory before sitting down at a peace table. In addition to resenting the economic burdens this imposed, many Frenchmen were still persuaded that France should not be fighting Catholic powers: a war against the emperor and the king of Spain was to them the wrong war.

In time-honored tradition, the king stood above blame; opponents of the war heaped all their anger and hatred on Richelieu. Conspiracies by great nobles against the minister, therefore, particularly if led by princes of the royal family, were especially dangerous at this point because they could count on wide levels of support if they showed the least prospect of succeeding. When the count of Soissons, the king's cousin and namesake, joined forces with the duke of Guise and the duke of Bouillon, sovereign prince of Sedan, and with Spanish subsidies brought an army into France to force the dismissal of Richelieu, the conspirators called themselves princes of peace. Only Soisson's death in battle in July 1641 prevented widespread rallying to his support. The queen and the king's brother, Gaston of Orléans, seem to have kept aloof from Soissons's efforts; at least no evidence has ever linked them to it. But it was otherwise with the sequel in which Gaston played the titular lead while the king's favorite, Cinq-Mars, worked out the details.

Cinq-Mars had become increasingly ambitious. He had persuaded the king to allow him to enter the royal council, and he wanted to become a duke and peer, even constable of France, in order to be worthy of the woman he wished to marry—princess Marie Gonzaga, sovereign duchess of Nevers, former object of Gaston's matrimonial plans, and a great friend of the queen. Richelieu considered Cinq-Mars's pretensions outrageous, especially since the young man had refused to act as his confidential informant concerning the king's doing's and sayings. Moreover, Richelieu did not hesitate to lecture Cinq-Mars on how to behave toward the king. Cinq-Mars therefore came to detest the cardinal; he would have liked to see him eliminated and may even have dreamed of taking his place as first minister.[35]

Cinq-Mars was overreaching himself, overestimating his own capacity as well as the strength of the king's attachment to him. He seemed, however, to be receiving encouragement from the king himself. As he had done four years earlier with Louise de Lafayette, Louis had taken to complaining to Cinq-Mars about Richelieu's tyranny. Nor did the king dismiss suggestions that Richelieu might be prolonging the war out of self-interest, to keep himself indispensable. Finally Cinq-Mars even tricked the king into making remarks that could be construed by Cinq-

Mars and his friends as guarded approval for the cardinal's eventual assassination.[36]

By this time Cinq-Mars had secured the support of Gaston of Orléans, the duke of Bouillon, and numerous other enemies of Richelieu. Both Gaston and Marie Gonzaga kept the queen informed, and Anne gave more than tacit approval to the plot. She recruited one of her most trusted friends, the future duke of La Rochefoucauld, who had already compromised himself as the confidant of Madame de Chevreuse.[37] Only the intervention of another trusted friend, Secretary of State Brienne, prevented her from signing a sheaf of blank papers to be used by Cinq-Mars's agents for letters to army officers when opportunity should arise.[38] The years had not taught her prudence when people came to her protesting their devotion. She merely took the precaution of asking Gaston and Cinq-Mars not to reveal her complicity whatever happened. Gaston trusted her enough to send her a copy of the conspirators' draft treaty with Spain, and that was a dangerous piece of knowledge indeed.[39]

The duke of Bouillon had agreed to provide a retreat in his fortress of Sedan for Cinq-Mars and the others if things went wrong, but since Sedan could not hold out forever in case of a siege, it seemed desirable to secure a proper army. And so Gaston and Cinq-Mars had addressed themselves to Spain. Just as Louis and Richelieu were encouraging rebellion in Catalonia and Portugal, so now were Philip IV and his minister Olivares prepared to deal with the French conspirators. The result was an agreement by which Philip IV promised his brother-in-law Gaston of Orléans both cavalry and infantry, money for the upkeep of these as well as other troops, and large bonuses for Gaston, Bouillon, and Cinq-Mars.[40] Gaston was to command this army and might keep in his personal possession whatever lands it won, thus dismembering the kingdom that his father Henry IV had laboriously put back together after the wars of religion. On their side the French conspirators undertook, if successful, to conclude a peace with Spain in which both sides would return conquests made during the past years, whereby Spain would be the gainer because she had lately been losing ground. The French intervention in the empire would also be affected, since France was to abandon her Protestant allies. In subscribing to all this, the conspirators affirmed that they intended no prejudice to the king and kingdom of France or to the interests of the queen:[41] rebellion against the king would not have been respectable, but war to liberate the king from evil advisers was another matter. How Spain, whose resources were even more exhausted than those of

France, would have found the men and money stipulated is a question that never came to the test.

Early in June 1642, while Louis, Cinq-Mars, and Richelieu were in southern France conducting the siege of Perpignan in Spanish-held Roussillon, a mysterious messenger reached Richelieu and brought him an equally mysterious document. On 12 June, Louis XIII received the information it contained, and that evening ordered the arrest of Cinq-Mars and the lesser conspirators. Cinq-Mars went into hiding but was taken the next day; meanwhile special messengers went out to arrest the duke of Bouillon in Italy, where he was commanding the French army. Bouillon extricated himself by ceding Sedan to the king of France, and Gaston, when confronted by all the evidence of the conspiracy, made a full confession throwing all the blame on Cinq-Mars. That young man, together with his adviser de Thou, went on trial for high treason, was found guilty, and was executed on 12 September.

What everyone was curious to know and no one outside Richelieu's immediate circle found out, was how the cardinal had discovered the existence of the Spanish treaty and the list of chief conspirators. Various leaks were suspected, though the officially encouraged inference seems to have been that a Spanish courier had been intercepted somewhere, and that his diplomatic pouch had been searched.[42] One or two people guardedly hinted that a more highly placed personage had been involved. For once this does not seem to have been Gaston of Orléans; the rumors pointed to the queen.[43]

When Louis left for the Roussillon campaign in February 1642, he had shown no suspicion of Anne; all his distrust was apparently directed against his brother Gaston. The king evidently feared that should anything happen to himself, Gaston might attempt to seize the dauphin and the duke of Anjou. Consequently Louis instructed the royal governess, Madame de Lansac, that if Gaston came to visit the queen at Saint-Germain and wished to pay his respects to the dauphin, she was to call in the guards to stay with the child and must be sure not to let Gaston enter the nursery attended by more than three persons.[44] The captain of the guards, for his part, received strict commands not to leave the princes and to disregard any order for their possible transfer to another residence or to the care of other persons. Even if such an order arrived written in the king's hand, the captain was to ignore it unless it came together with a private token—half of a coin of which the captain had the matching portion.[45]

In the course of the spring, however, Louis turned against Anne also. He sent her word that he wished her to leave the children and join him in Provence.[46] The king's order came as a terrible blow to her, "one of the sharpest and most painful she has ever received."[47] Fearing that her journey would be the beginning of a permanent separation from the boys, she excused herself from traveling for the time being because her distress had made her ill. For more permanent relief, she tried the same means that had workd so satisfactorily in 1640: through intermediaries she addressed herself to Richelieu, pleading for his intercession with the king so that she might be allowed to stay with her sons.[48] She also sent a gentleman to the cardinal directly with a similar message.[49] This time, however, she received no reply from Richelieu beyond advice to do as the king wished, and her fears increased. Anne continued to put off the journey, all the while protesting that she had every desire to obey the king, if only she were in better health.[50] In vain did the Brassacs try to console her; in vain did they as well as Richelieu's niece Madame d'Aiguillon and the prince of Condé urge her to yield. Anne still pinned her faith on Richelieu's intervention and meantime could not be persuaded to stir.[51]

Anne professed to believe that Louis himself had made the decision to separate her from her sons, though he was perhaps encouraged by Cinq-Mars.[52] It is, of course, possible that the inspiration came from Richelieu. Although the cardinal did not know the precise nature of the plot against him, he was aware of growing coldness on the part of Louis, and of a faction building around Cinq-Mars. It may be that he assumed the queen must be involved, and thought she might be the most accessible link to be put under pressure. Anne vehemently denied any such involvement when gossip connecting her with Cinq-Mars was brought to her attention on 7 June. She immediately ordered Brassac to inform Richelieu that she did not believe Cinq-Mars had enough influence over the king to harm the cardinal, and that even if Cinq-Mars, out of ill will and ingratitude, should be plotting against the cardinal, the king could be relied on to judge better according to his true advantage and needs. For her part, Anne declared,

> she protests by her faith and conscience that even if [Cinq-Mars] were as powerful as could be imagined, . . . she would never dissociate herself from [Richelieu] and would remain staunch and attached to his interests, without ever changing her feelings, well knowing that [Richelieu] will do the same for her and will never abandon her.[53]

She had her secretary, Le Gras, write also, and on 9 June she herself sent a letter to Richelieu.[54] Four days later a messenger arrived at Saint-Germain with Louis's permission for her to stay there with the dauphin and his brother.[55] Anne's lingering indisposition was cured instantly, and she poured out declarations of undying gratitude to Richelieu. She attributed her happiness entirely to his efforts on her behalf, an assumption the Brassacs shared.[56]

It may have been coincidence that by 11 June, Richelieu had in his hands a draft copy of the Spanish treaty. Louis did not learn of it until the following day,[57] at which time his messenger to Saint-Germain already must have been well on his way, to be able to arrive on 13 June. What prompted Louis to relent toward the queen is therefore as mysterious as what had caused his decision to separate her from her children in the first place. Nothing proves that the draft copy of the treaty came from Anne, though the possibility cannot be excluded, considering the comings and goings of couriers between Saint-Germain and Provence. Not all the couriers were official, if the report is to be believed that Richelieu's protégé Cardinal Mazarin was helpful to Anne at this time, and that Mazarin's friend Walter Montague carried messages between him and the queen.[58] It may or may not have been a special service on her part to which Le Gras referred when he wrote to Richelieu in July: "As you know better than anyone else the singular esteem in which she holds you, I shall say only that it could not be desired greater. . . ."[59] And Brassac's remarks of the same date were similarly ambiguous: "there is reason to thank God, to see her so absolutely confirmed in the resolution which we have always wished to implant in her, which is the only one she ought to have taken, and which she has declared very opportunely to His Eminence."[60]

A case has been made either way concerning Anne's role. To some authors it seems plausible that Anne took such desperate means because she believed Richelieu knew more than he did, and also because she might not have been sorry to see Gaston compromised at this juncture: the king's health had been precarious all year, and in a prospective regency, Gaston would be a rival for her authority.[61] On the other hand, it has been pointed out that Louis would have been unlikely to do his wife any kindness, such as permitting her to keep her children, had he known her to be associated once again with secrets involving Spain.[62] But he may not have known. Richelieu went to a good deal of trouble to protect the identity of his informant, even though revelation would have made the interrogations of Cinq-Mars and de Thou easier.[63] If Anne was indeed the source of the cardinal's information, it would not have been the first time that he kept her secrets, at least for a while.

Apparently neither Gaston nor Cinq-Mars ever suspected Anne of betraying the plot, and rumor may have done her an injustice. But a doubt remains. According to a contemporary anecdote, Richelieu himself acted as though he knew something to the queen's discredit. After his return from southern France, when she visited him in his country house at Rueil, he received her without rising from his arm-chair. Instead of excusing this departure from etiquette with a reference to his poor health, which would have been true, he reminded her that in Spain cardinals enjoyed the privilege of being seated in the presence of queens. Allusions to her Spanish affiliations, however, no longer frightened Anne. She replied with dignity that she had completely forgotten Spanish customs and become entirely French.[64] But the reporter was not an eyewitness. Richelieu may not have intended any disrespect, and there is no way of knowing what he and the queen really communicated to each other.

Chapter Ten

The Changing of the Guard

LOUIS'S HEALTH WAS NOT IM-
proved by the affair of Cinq-Mars and its aftermath. The decision to
prosecute his friend caused him great anguish, perhaps all the more
because, as Richelieu insinuated, he, Louis, had contributed to the
young man's scheme. Richelieu insisted he no longer felt safe; he
threatened to resign unless the king promised never to have another
favorite, always to protect his ministers' confidentiality, and to keep
them informed of anything he heard said to their detriment. Louis
resisted for weeks before he gave in to the humiliating demands, and
the strain on both men was such that everyone wondered which
would die first, the king or the cardinal.[1]

Louis had suffered another loss that summer: Marie de Medici had
died in Cologne on 3 July. The court went into mourning while arrangements were made to have the remnant of the queen mother's
household accompany her body back to France.[2] Marie's death simpli-
fied the political situation. In exile she had been a constant source of
embarrassment to Louis and a reproach to his conscience, as well as a
rallying point for malcontents. Besides, if she had outlived him, as had
not seemed impossible, she would certainly have claimed a share of, if
not the supreme, authority in the regency for her young grandson.
Nevertheless, Louis did not show relief at her departure from the
scene; the news of her death increased the melancholy he already felt
over the fate of Cinq-Mars and aggravated his ailments. Perhaps it also
increased his bitterness toward Richelieu, who had imposed so many
hard choices on him for the sake of policy. His eventual reconciliation
with the cardinal was more outward than inward, and when it became
apparent that the cardinal was indeed mortally ill, the king's visit to his
old servant's deathbed lacked cordiality.[3]

Richelieu died on 4 December 1642. Anne felt no regret at his passing, although apparently she did not indulge in open rejoicing.[4] That
would have been a mistake because, contrary to the hopes of all Richelieu's enemies, Louis changed neither his policies nor his personnel.
Anne had no greater share in the king's confidence after Richelieu's
death than before. It was not even safe for her partisans to show their

sympathies too openly. She did have partisans, in fact an increasing number of them since the deteriorating health of Louis and of Richelieu had made it virtually certain that sooner or later she could expect to become regent. Some of her friends were still in exile or barred from court in disgrace—most notably the king's illegitimate half-brother, the duke of Vendôme and Vendôme's sons, the duke of Mercoeur, and the duke of Beaufort, not to mention Madame de Chevreuse with various of her close associates, Madame de Hautefort, and Anne's faithful cloak-bearer La Porte. Others, however, remained available; and whatever sentimental attachment they professed for her service, rational calculations tended to play a large part in determining their allegiance.

The count of La Châtre typified their situation, although he was blunter than most in explaining his motives.[5] He was Louis's master of the wardrobe during the 1630s, but in looking about for further lucrative opportunities, he concluded that he had too many connections among Richelieu's enemies to hope for any favors from the cardinal. After the birth of the dauphin, however, La Châtre reviewed his own prospects and decided that his best chance of future fortune lay in attaching himself to the queen's interests since the king did not seem likely to live long and she would most probably be regent for her minor son. Moreover it would be an advantage to join her party early, for La Châtre believed the queen to be, as he said, the best and gentlest person on earth and the most incapable of forgetting those who had attached themselves to her in the days of her eclipse. Through discreet intermediaries, therefore, he offered her his good offices if and when required. The queen accepted gratefully. She was even more pleased when, after the death of Richelieu, La Châtre proposed to use his interest with Louis to buy the colonelcy of the Swiss guards. One of the captains of the king's French guards, Guitaut, was already a secret friend to her cause, and the loyalty of the guards' commanders was very useful to have if time should bring trouble.

Others followed the same course La Châtre had chosen, even men belonging to the royal council. Two of the four secretaries of state, Loménie de Brienne and Sublet des Noyers, were well disposed toward the queen's interests. The Brienne family were not strangers to Anne: Madame de Brienne, noted for her piety, stood high in her regard; a Brienne daughter served her as maid of honor for a time; and Brienne himself had offered her consolation at the low point in her fortunes, in 1637. Brienne had never been one of Richelieu's creatures; he had kept his post, which his father had held before him, by attending strictly to his work and keeping himself clear of conspiracies. Unfortunately Brienne lost some of his caution at the wrong time. He put himself forward too much in an effort to reconcile the king with the duke of Vendôme—or so, at any rate, the king believed—and consequently in February 1643 had to sell his office of secretary of state and retire.[6] It was not a total loss for Anne; Brienne stayed in the offing, ready with expert advice should it be needed, and he could have done no more for her at that juncture even if he had remained on the council. His colleague Sublet des Noyers found out just how slippery the ground in the council was where Anne's interests were concerned. Hoping to safeguard his own position, des Noyers informed the queen of plans under discussion for limiting her power in the eventual regency. Louis took this interference very ill. Although des Noyers had been a friend and companion in his devotions, he accepted the secretary's resignation.[7] It was April 1643 by then, and the question of the regency had become a pressing issue.

The king had not been well that winter, and the holidays at Saint-Germain had passed very quietly. The carnival season did not bring the usual ballets and entertainments to lighten the gloom, for the court was still in mourning for the Queen Mother. Until the middle of February, the king managed occasional hunting trips to Versailles, but thereafter he took to his bed with what was announced as a slight indisposition. It was actually far more serious. On the basis of descriptions of the king's symptoms, modern historians estimate that he was in the last stages of intestinal tuberculosis.[8] His own doctors did not despair of him as yet, and in fact after a month he was sufficiently improved to dine in public and give a number of audiences. He was too weak, however, to perform the customary Holy Week ceremonies, and it was the dauphin, not he, who washed the feet of thirteen men on Maundy Thursday, 2 April.[9]

All during this time, the king had not ceased to transact state business or to meet with his council, and the prime item on the agenda was how to settle the regency. Louis trusted neither his wife nor his brother to keep the kingdom as a good steward for his young son.[10] Gaston had conspired against the crown so often and had so lately been treating with the Spanish enemy; and Anne was as bad or worse—her husband was sure she was still a Spaniard at heart. On the other hand, to exclude Anne and Gaston would invite trouble also: it would violate precedent for a widowed French queen not to act as regent for her young son; and if Gaston was left out, he might head a rebellious faction as the new king's aggrieved uncle. Louis's dilemma seemed insoluble until two of his advisers offered a compromise: why not create a regency council that would include the queen and Gaston but restrict their freedom of action?

The pair who suggested this expedient were men whom Louis had inherited from Richelieu: Secretary of State Chavigny and Cardinal Mazarin.[11] François Le Bouthillier, count of Chavigny, belonged to a clan that had served Richelieu's family for generations. His father, Claude Le Bouthillier, was superintendent of finances, roughly the equivalent of a modern secretary of the treasury, and Chavigny himself had entered the royal council as a secretary of state in 1632 at the remarkably youthful age of twenty-four.[12] Richelieu entrusted him with the most confidential work, including the management of Gaston of Orléans, for which purpose he made the young man Gaston's chancellor. After Richelieu's death, Louis XIII continued to rely on Chavigny, particularly in foreign affairs. Although he apparently did not like Chavigny very much personally, the secretary was undoubtedly an extremely able man.

Not unnaturally Chavigny's ambition matched his ability. He considered himself the man best fitted to step into Richelieu's shoes as first minister. There seemed little chance of that while Louis lived, since the king now preferred to be his own first minister, but things would be different under a regency: neither of the interested parties, Anne or Gaston, would be able to direct government personally, for lack of experience if for no other reason. Between the two Chavigny felt more confident of being able to control Gaston, entrenched as he was in Gaston's official household and fortified by long habit of browbeating the prince. Chavigny therefore set out to arrange the kind of regency that would give him the best chance though it catered to the prejudices of the king. It is not clear whether Chavigny simply discounted the queen, or whether he relied on his friend and colleague Cardinal Mazarin to enlist her cooperation. In either case Chavigny made a serious mistake.

Mazarin had been a newcomer to Richelieu's team.[13] Born Giulio Mazarini of a poor but respectable family on his father's side and noble lineage on his mother's, he had been raised and educated in Rome with his younger brother and four sisters. Early on he showed himself so gifted, both in intellect and in the capacity to attract good will and friendship, that his family looked to him to improve their fortunes, and he did not disappoint them. After a brief false start as an officer in the papal army, he found his true vocation in diplomatic service under the patronage of the Colonna, the Sacchetti, and the Barberini—all powerful names in the church, but particularly so the Barberini, who were the nephews of Urban VIII. Mazarin never took priestly orders higher than the simple tonsure that enabled him to hold benefices and domestic office in the Vatican, although he was obliged to wear clerical dress after he received the title of monsignor in 1633. Urban VIII, after all, had any number of priests at his disposal; he wanted Mazarin not for religious duties but for his extraordinary skill in negotiation and his evident personal commitment to the cause of peace in Italy and in Europe.

It was in the interest of peace that Mazarin had first come to France, accompanying Cardinal Antonio Barberini to interviews with Louis XIII and Richelieu in Lyon in January 1630, with the mission to propose a truce in the conflict between France and Spain over the succession of Mantua. Mazarin's efforts did not bear fruit at this time, but he came away from the encounter deeply impressed by Richelieu's personality and political sense. During the following months, Richelieu in his turn was impressed when the young man persevered in his mission, nothing discouraged either by obstacles or by the cardinal's outbursts of ill-temper, and returning patiently each time to the negotiation at hand. Mazarin's personal bravery in riding between French and Spanish forces about to join battle at Casal finally brought about the desired truce and confirmed Richelieu's respect.[14] From then on Mazarin was welcome in France even when the Vatican sent him on errands of peace that Richelieu did not wish to entertain.

Louis had taken to Mazarin from the start, and for once the queen shared his sentiments. The story ran that Richelieu introduced Mazarin to her with the comment, "You will like him, Madame; he looks like Buckingham."[15] The words were remarkably insolent, and it is not certain they were really spoken. Anne may not have met Mazarin until Louis presented him to her in 1632. As for Mazarin's resemblance to Buckingham, judging by portraits, what the two men had in common was the style of their hair, moustache, and goatee; their features and shape of face were as different as their characters. Mazarin was hardworking, even-tempered, and as affable to his enemies as his friends—none of which could ever be said of Buckingham. Moreover, although Mazarin had winning ways, they were a form of social charm and nothing like the sheer animal virility that had made Buckingham so famous. But even if the resemblance to Buckingham was doubtful, Mazarin had his own advantages in the queen's eyes: he had finished off his studies with two years in Spain as companion to one of the young Colonnas at the University of Alcalá, had happy memories of his stay, and could speak Spanish. Above all, whenever he appeared in France in the early 1630s, he came as the pope's emissary to preserve peace between France and Spain, and this was a matter close to the queen's heart. She obviously trusted him, for she confided to him her anguish at seeing the two kingdoms headed for major conflict. In his report to Rome, Mazarin noted how struck he had been by the gravity, moderation, and good sense with which she discussed the matter.[16] Up to now no person of importance at the French court had troubled to remark whether Anne had good sense or not. It would seem that Mazarin was the first to take her seriously—reason enough for her to regard him kindly.

Between missions Mazarin kept himself in the queen's remembrance by sending elegant trifles from Rome, perfumes and jasmine-scented gloves. There was nothing extraordinary in that, however; he did the same for court ladies of his acquaintance and for the wives of friends such as Chavigny; and to Richelieu and other men, he presented paintings and statuary, both on his own behalf as well as that of the Barberini.[17] He needed his contacts, and they repaid his care and cultivation.

Without abandoning his convictions about the desirability of peace, Mazarin decided to cast his lot with the French monarchy: he liked the French, their customs, and their manner of living. Above all, he almost worshiped Richelieu as the ablest, most resolute statesman of the day and the most apt to give full scope and recognition to his, Mazarin's, talents should he employ him. And Richelieu reciprocated. After war did break out in 1635 and while Mazarin was still in papal service, Richelieu found him very useful in looking after French interests in Rome and elsewhere, and also in the secret negotiations for an eventual peace that Richelieu liked to keep going with Spain and the empire. These good offices earned Mazarin the enmity of the Spanish faction at the Vatican, which made his life miserable until Louis XIII nominated him for a cardinal's hat in 1639 and invited him to come to France.[18] More than that, the king issued him letters of naturalization, thereby enabling him to hold benefices in France and dispose of property free from the legal restrictions imposed on foreigners.[19] Urban VIII was slow to grant Louis's request; when he appointed the king's nominee to the college of cardinals in December 1641, the candidate had already been in France for two years and Giulio Mazarini had become Jules Mazarin.

Richelieu put Mazarin to work on the most delicate matters. It was Mazarin who arranged the preliminaries for the peace congress that was to open at Münster in Westphalia, and he was on the point of leading the French delegation there when other problems and duties intervened.[20] He accompanied the king and Richelieu to Roussillon and made himself useful there. According to one of Gaston of Orléans's servants, Mazarin helped the queen with Richelieu when she was fighting to keep her children in the spring of 1642.[21] In the wake of the Cinq-Mars crisis, Mazarin conducted the negotiations with the duke of Bouillon and Gaston of Orléans that led to their reconciliation with Louis with the minimum of scandal. It was he whose visits lightened Louis's melancholy during that unhappy summer, and it was also he who attended Richelieu most faithfully on his deathbed, although the king's coldness toward his old minister might have made that seem an impolitic thing to do.

Richelieu considered Mazarin invaluable and, finding himself on the point of death, apparently urged the king to keep the younger man in France by giving him formal employment.[22] Whether on Richelieu's advice or on his own initiative, upon Richelieu's death Louis called Mazarin to the royal council and thereby made him a minister of state. Since Louis had always had a guilty conscience about the war against the Catholic Habsburgs, Mazarin's orientation toward peace pleased him, all the more so because Mazarin shared Richelieu's and Louis's notion of the place France ought to occupy in European affairs and the advantages the kingdom should derive from a peace settlement.

Richelieu's enemies, of course, felt nothing but chagrin at seeing the king's council firmly in the grip of Richelieu's creatures: Le Bouthillier, Chavigny, Mazarin, Chancellor Séguier, and, for a while at least, des Noyers. These men together with the remaining council members, Secretary of State La Vrillière and Brienne's replacement, Secretary of State Duplessis de Guénégaud, had charge of the kingdom's business when Louis's health failed in the late winter and early spring of 1643. They did not all enjoy the king's confidence to an equal degree: his inner circle of advisers consisted of Chavigny, Mazarin, and des Noyers until des Noyers dropped out, and with this group Louis most often discussed the problem of the regency.[23]

At first Louis did not like the suggestion of a regency council put forward by Chavigny and Mazarin any better than the other alternatives before him.[24] A council would in effect put the regency into commission and limit the queen's authority and freedom of action, but on the other hand, custom and general expectation were undeniably on her side. Louis's own mother had been an unrestricted regent, and symbolic imagery at her court had underlined her natural right to the position. Thus, for example, the fireworks celebrating the engagement of Louis and the infanta Anne in 1612 had included allegorical figures of the sun and the moon, which pamphlets helpfully explained as representing respectively the king and the queen, with the further note that the moon was the most fitting symbol for queens of France

> because just as the moon borrows its light from the sun when it falls into conjunction with it, the queens of France derive whatever authority they have from the kings their husbands as soon as they are married. The setting sun gives way to the moon and confers on it the power of shedding light in its absence. The queens of France often succeed to the authority of their husbands after their death if the heirs to the crown are still young and are by a special prerogative declared regents of the kingdom and of the person of the kings, their children.[25]

But the king's memories of Marie's regency were not happy ones, and in the present case he could not bring himself to lend any light to his queen. And so the argument continued to go round and round until, after the middle of April, Louis had grown so weak that he had to recognize it would be unwise if he waited much longer to make up his mind. He decided in favor of the regency council.

When Anne had found out about the proposal for a regency council, she had been deeply offended by the implied insult to herself and had asked her friends to cease paying the customary courtesy visits to its authors, Chavigny and Mazarin.[26] Whether she protested directly to Louis himself we do not know; it is improbable, considering that she had never stood up to him before in a face-to-face encounter.

At some point during this period—the exact timing is unclear— Mazarin entered into communication with Anne. He made his approach through the papal nuncio and her own grand almoner, Auguste Potier, bishop of Beauvais, who both undertook to assure her of Mazarin's good will.[27] On their recommendation she resolved to trust Mazarin. Talking the matter over with Brienne, she explained her reasons: she needed someone close to the king who could keep her informed of the king's last intentions, and who was not tied to Gaston of Orléans or that other possible rival for power, the prince of Condé.[28] Having gained that much, Mazarin somehow managed to convince Anne that the most important thing was to have the king name her regent, regardless of the conditions attached: after the king's death, nothing would prevent her from establishing her complete power by one means or another.[29] There was a good deal of truth in this. Louis

XIII could not actually forbid Louis XIV, however young, to issue what orders he pleased about his mother. According to French constitutional law, no king could bind his successor, since each king was held to possess the authority of the crown full and entire. Louis must have known this, but perhaps he did not believe that Anne would have the wit, or the energy, or the cooperation of enough people, to overturn his arrangements.

Meanwhile Anne visited the king every day, going from the old palace of Saint-Germain, where she was staying with her sons, to the new palace, where Louis had taken her apartments as his sickrooms.[30] He enjoyed the view from there when he sat up on his chaise-longue, for the windows of her cabinet looked across the Seine to wooded countryside and in the distance to the towers of Saint-Denis, the last resting place of his predecessors, which he was soon pointing out to his servants as his next home. His niece, Mademoiselle, frequently drove out from Paris to see him also, a mutually enjoyable custom that her father's fall from grace had interrupted in recent years.[31] Gaston himself was allowed to reappear at court and so were the duke of Vendôme and his sons, while the great nobility began to gather in the anterooms waiting for the end.

On 19 April, Louis's physician-in-chief finally admitted to him that his illness was mortal, news that did not surprise the king, who ordered the queen, his brother Gaston, his cousin the prince of Condé, the ministers of state and a delegation from the Parlement of Paris to attend him the next day to hear his wishes concerning the regency. On 20 April, therefore, they all assembled, the queen seated in an armchair at the foot of the king's bed, while secretary of state La Vrillière read the king's declaration: for the duration of his son's minority, the king appointed the queen regent with Gaston of Orléans as lieutenant-general of the kingdom, but, although

we have every reason to expect from the virtue, the piety and the wise conduct of our very dear and well beloved spouse and companion, the queen mother of our children, that her administration will be fortunate and beneficial to the state; . . . because the charge of regent is so heavy, the well-being and the whole preservation of the kingdom depending on it, and because it is impossible that she should have the perfect knowledge so necessary for the handling of such great and difficult business, which is only acquired by long experience, we have judged it appropriate to set up a council at her side for the regency, by whose advice and under her authority the great and important affairs of state will be resolved according to majority vote.[32]

The members of the council were to be Condé, Cardinal Mazarin, Chancellor Séguier, Le Bouthillier, and Chavigny; with Gaston of Orléans presiding, or in his absence Condé, or in both their absences Mazarin. The council was to have universal competence: questions of war and peace, internal matters including taxation and budget, appointments to all major offices and to vacancies on the council itself. Ecclesiastical benefices were to be the particular province of Mazarin, whose advice the regent was to take when making church appointments. Lastly, for the sake of tranquillity within the kingdom, the duchess of Chevreuse was to be kept out of it until peace was concluded; and if the regent and council permitted her to return after that, she must never be allowed to reside near the court. Similar precautions were prescribed for Madame de Chevreuse's friend the former keeper of the seals Châteauneuf.[33]

The reading of the document, with its implication of the king's impending death, drew tears from some of the assembly. The queen cried too, although perhaps as much from vexation as grief. She and Gaston took the oath to observe the declaration, however, and signed the document after Louis, whereupon it was witnessed and sent off to the Parlement to be registered as law. Whatever anyone else felt, Louis seemed pleased with himself, as after a job well done.[34]

The next thing was to get the dauphin baptized. He had, of course, been sprinkled at birth; but in accordance with the custom of the time, he had not yet received his name. Now, therefore, the king ordered that his son be called Louis Dieudonné, that is, "Louis Gift-of-God," and chose the godparents: the princess of Condé as godmother and Cardinal Mazarin as godfather. On the following day, 21 April, the queen, the godparents, and the court accompanied the dauphin to the Gothic chapel of the old palace. In consideration of the king's illness, it was a simple ceremony, the only concession to splendor being the silver gauze robe the dauphin wore over his usual clothes.[35] Before the first almoner of France, the bishop of Meaux, and an array of other prelates, the boy affirmed that he renounced the devil and all his works and believed in the Apostles' Creed, whereupon the bishop of Meaux placed salt on his tongue, anointed his head, chest, and shoulders with holy oil, and named him. Afterward the queen and Mazarin with some of the other participants went to see the king and reported to him how everything had gone and how well behaved his son had been. An anecdote circulated later that the dauphin had also come, that his father had him seated on the bed and asked him "What is your name? to which the child supposedly replied "Louis XIV." And the king retorted "No, my son, not yet."[36] It never happened. The detailed eyewitness account of events in the king's sickroom makes no mention of the dauphin's presence after his baptism, and it would seem the boy was sent back to the nursery.

Although the anecdote was pure fiction with regard to the relationship between Louis and his son, it did reflect accurately enough the state of mind of the courtiers, who simply attributed to the four-and-a-half-year old child their own impatience to see his father die. They were growing very impatient indeed, for the king was taking his time. The day after the baptism he was sinking, and he gave his blessing to his wife and children. He received the last rites on 23 April. On 24 April, however, his strength returned somewhat, and he lingered for almost three weeks longer, his repeated ups and downs keeping people in an agony of suspense. All those persons who were still in exile from the court waited with bated breath for the turn in their fortunes, although the most pathetic cases were Madame de Hautefort and the queen's cloak-bearer La Porte. Hearing rumors that the king had died, they set off posthaste from Normandy for Paris, only to find upon arrival that the king was still living. And so they sadly returned to their province.[37]

As for the queen, on whom all their hopes rested, she seemed sincerely stricken with grief. On 7 May, Anne moved to the new palace, into a room near the king's so that she could look in on him more frequently and spend more time with him. She kept part of the night watch too, and when she was not there, was constantly sending her servants for reports of Louis's condition. Toward the end she did not leave at all but sat at the head of his bed while his clergy took turns praying with him and supporting his spirit with pious discourse. What astonished everyone was that she did not mind the sickening stench from the king's bed, although she was famous for her love of cleanliness and her passion for perfumes. Louis by now suffered from constant diarrhea and, because he was as cleanly as she, felt embarrassed and asked her repeatedly not to come too close to his bed because, he said, it smelled too bad. She gave no sign of noticing anything amiss, however, and stayed.[38]

On his last day, 14 May, Louis took leave of Anne in front of all the notables of the court who had crowded into his room. She kissed him and spoke to him at length, although no one could hear what she said since her face was so close to his on the pillow that their tears ran together. Then he said goodbye to his sons, his brother, and the others, and devoted himself to the prayers for the dying. Anne remained until Louis lost speech and hearing, when Gaston of Orléans and Condé led her, shaking with sobs, to her own room.

Later Anne often recalled that when she saw Louis dying, she felt as though her heart were being torn from her body.[39] Perhaps the intensity of her grief surprised her. One way or another, she and Louis had caused each other a good deal of pain; but at the end, with their struggle done and with the priests' message of penitence and forgiveness in their ears, they may have won their way back to some of the tenderness of their youth when Anne was the Amaryllis for whom Louis wrote songs of love.

Nevertheless Anne had not been preoccupied exclusively with emotion during the last weeks of Louis's life. She had managed to improve her position with respect to the impending regency. She gave no sign of such activity, however, evidently drawing on her long experience in keeping vital matters to herself. Even Gaston's people noted that

> the queen behaved marvellously well at this time and did everything a good woman should. She listened to everyone [who spoke to her of political affairs] and replied only rarely, showing little interest in the things of this world while her husband found himself in the state in which he was.[40]

Appearances to the contrary, she was preparing for the future. Now that the Vendôme clan was back at court, she had suitably lofty leaders for her party. They might be relatives on the wrong side of the blanket, but they were of royal blood just the same and could be considered in some measure a counterweight to her brother-in-law Gaston. One of the Vendômes, the young duke of Beaufort, particularly offered himself as her champion.[41] He, if anyone, resembled Buckingham, if not in face at least in character: he was well built, athletic, bold, and dashing, and he flattered himself that the queen looked on him with more than kindly interest.

As it happened Beaufort was neither intelligent nor honorable, but the queen had not yet had occasion to notice that. She needed someone with an armed following, for she was coming to distrust Gaston's intentions. More gentlemen than usual were accompanying Gaston, and they seemed to be quarrelsome. Might he be preparing to use force to get control of her children and contest the regency? Fearing for their safety, she commended her sons to the care of Beaufort and his friends when she moved from the old to the new palace to be near the king. She also wanted La Châtre to put the Swiss guards on alert.[42]

She may have been doing Gaston an injustice: nothing was ever proved against him in this matter, although his record of loyalty was certainly far from reassuring. From then on, however, Beaufort considered himself especially privileged with the queen and acted as though he were confident of directing her future government.

Whether Anne herself saw Beaufort in this capacity is doubtful. During these weeks she had taken to referring all place-seekers and petitioners to her first almoner, Potier, bishop of Beauvais.[43] In her service since 1624, Potier had consoled her in all her tribulations and impressed her with his piety. Richelieu had never disturbed him because, as unkind tongues put it, Potier was too much of a mediocrity to be worth the cardinal's attention. Presumably, however, Potier on his side refrained from meddling in business of state. Through long association, therefore, Anne trusted Potier; and since she was now giving him patronage work to do, most people, including Potier himself, believed that she meant to make him her first minister. It remained to be seen whether or how Potier and Beaufort would accommodate each other.

Potier and Beaufort were assuming, of course, that Anne would be free to dispose of government ministries, that the regency council would go; but they may not have known all the means by which she was trying to ensure that result. Without consulting them, she enlisted the support of the Condé family. Although she did not approach the old prince directly, she could count on the princess, who, like Madame de Vendôme, had become a friend over the years. It was the heir of the house who had to be won over, the duke of Enghien, to whom Louis XIII had recently given command of the French army on the Flemish frontier. Anne worked on Enghien through intermediaries who had to proceed very cautiously: the king would have suspected treason if he had found out that his general was negotiating with the queen before leaving to fight the Spaniards. It proved fairly easy to persuade Enghien that the good of the state and the good of the house of Condé obliged his family to oppose Gaston of Orléans. Enghien agreed to the bargain Anne proposed: she undertook to prefer him to Gaston in marks of confidence and esteem and to give him those employments from which she could exclude Gaston without an open break, and Enghien for his part promised to attach himself inseparably to her interests and to look to her and no one else for advancement at court.[44] Although oral and not in writing, it was a formal contract between patron and client, made at Gaston's expense, with Beaufort nowhere—or so Enghien believed.

Having secured the son, Anne had Potier arrange a conference for her with the prince of Condé and got him to agree to the dissolution of the regency council after the king's death.[45] Gaston too agreed, on the assurance that he would keep his appointment as lieutenant-general of the kingdom and would be made head of the council of war.[46]

The next step was to make sure of the cooperation of the Parlement of Paris. Anne could count on the sympathy of many of its members, whose hatred of Richelieu's memory made them look kindly on anyone who had suffered at the cardinal's hand, and she also benefited from the influence of those judges who were in any way connected with her service, such as her household chancellor Bailleul, or Potier's brother Novion. The ground was well prepared when on 9 May, she sent one of her almoners to the royal advocate-general Omar Talon, with an explanation of what would be wanted as soon as the king died.[47]

For a woman with a reputation for indolence, Anne was being remarkably active. Was it her own idea to divide and conquer, or did she have advice? As their memoirs show, she took neither her old friends nor her new ones completely into her confidence. That left Cardinal Mazarin, who had pointed out to her in the first place the possibility of annulling the king's will. Apparently he kept in touch with her although there is no record of any meetings.[48] Whether it was Mazarin who was steering Anne's course of action is therefore impossible to tell.

What is more certain is that Anne was beginning to trust Mazarin despite his connection with the late Cardinal Richelieu: at least she was considering him as one of her ministers, even if not as first minister. It would seem she was moved in this by the persuasions of Mazarin's friends, people whom she had known for a long time and whose opinion she valued: Beringhen, the king's first valet and man of confidence, argued that Mazarin's competence in affairs of state was too valuable to waste;[49] Father Vincent de Paul urged her not to seek indiscriminate vengeance against Richelieu's former dependents and exhorted her to Christian forgiveness;[50] and Walter Montague, an English expatriate who had been associated with Buckingham and Madame de Chevreuse, pointed out that Mazarin was the minister most likely to work seriously for peace. Upon inquiry, furthermore, Montague assured the queen that in character and disposition Mazarin was quite different from Richelieu.[51]

Anne therefore decided to keep Mazarin on her council, but she acted so circumspectly that among her partisans only the former secretary of state Brienne guessed her intention. The others either discounted such a possibility or believed her when she explained that she meant to use Mazarin only for a while, for the transition from the old government to the new. Besides, she added, Mazarin was talking about returning to Rome and serving French interests at the Vatican.[52] But Brienne read the queen's mind more astutely. While he himself did not like Mazarin, as a good courtier he helped the queen get what she wanted. On his advice Anne sent Beringhen to Mazarin secretly and obtained a written promise: Mazarin engaged himself to serve her when she called, and meanwhile agreed to the apparent loss of his position when the regency council was dissolved.[53]

Anne's preparations against the moment of the king's death were now complete. When she took her tearful farewell of her husband, she already knew that she would be able to disregard his last wishes. We have no reason to assume that she was a hypocrite in her display of grief; realism is not necessarily incompatible with feeling. In many respects her marriage had been a long war, but she was the survivor: she had won, and victors can afford to be generous.

Anne stayed in the new palace of Saint-Germain until word came that Louis XIII had expired. Then she returned across the gardens to the old castle and to her children, stopping for prayers in the chapel. She had paid the dead man his due; it was now the turn of the living. In her apartment, surrounded by all the dignitaries of the court, Anne was the first to kneel in homage to her son Louis XIV.[54]

Chapter Eleven

The Queen Regent

ANNE DID NOT LINGER IN Saint-Germain longer than necessary. On 15 May she brought Louis XIV to Paris in the company of his brother, his uncle Gaston of Orléans, the prince of Condé, and all the available dukes, peers, and marshalls of France.[1]

For months death had seemed to hover over the capital as Parisians saw repeated signs of mortality in high places: Richelieu's funeral in December, the convoy bearing the body of the queen mother Marie de Medici from Cologne to the royal mausoleum in Saint-Denis in March, the cortege of Anne's late brother the cardinal infante Ferdinand, transporting his coffin from Brussels through Paris to Spain early in May—and now Louis XIII was following his mother to the crypt in Saint-Denis.

On 20 May the monks of Saint-Denis held Louis's funeral service, attended by all the officers of his household and a great gathering of archbishops and bishops, after which alms were distributed in the late king's name to more than a thousand poor folk.[2] Following custom, the immediate members of the family did not attend. Royalty never went to funerals, even of their closest kin: kingship was incompatible with death. To be sure, the great dignitaries of the royal household each deposited his insignia of office on the king's bier to cries of "the king is dead," but then they took them up again when the herald proclaimed "the king lives." By the time this ritual had been completed over the body of Louis XIII, his successor had already performed his first judicial act of majesty by setting the procedure in motion for overturning his father's will. The time of sickness and death was over: new life had begun.

No one greeted the advent of the regency with more joy than the group that wits were already beginning to call *Les Importants* because of the airs they were giving themselves.[3] The *Importants*, the duke of Beaufort at their head, included practically everybody who had felt himself injured or slighted under Louis XIII and Richelieu, and did not belong to the following of either Gaston of Orléans or the prince of Condé. For Beaufort and his friends, the moment of vengeance seemed at hand, and they were convinced that Anne felt the same way. Since Beaufort seemed to stand so well with the queen, the *Importants* confidently expected her to despoil Richelieu's relatives and former dependents in their favor, beginning with the places on the royal council. Orléans and Condé meanwhile cherished their own hopes of aggrandizement, each at the other's expense, nourished by the queen's confidential if contradictory promises.

During the week of her return to the Louvre, Anne said and did nothing that could disturb anyone. All options were apparently still open when on Monday 18 May she led the king to a formal session with the Parlement of Paris for removal of the restrictions placed on her authority by the late king's declaration concerning the regency.[4]

In ages past, widowed queens had spent the first forty days of mourning dressed in white, lying on their beds, and had kept secluded in their black-draped apartments for a year. But custom and fashion had changed, and seclusion was impossible for a regent in any case. Anne therefore brought her sons to the Parlement, first stopping at Saint Louis's Sainte-Chapelle, where the bishop of Beauvais celebrated mass for the royal procession. Arrived in the hall of justice, she placed the king on the throne of state and took a seat to his right, surrounded by Orléans, Condé, the duke of Vendôme, and the other peers and dukes. Potier, the bishop of Beauvais, stood to the king's left; it looked as though he was being destined for important duties. Young Louis had been taught what to say: "Gentlemen, I am come to show you my affection; my chancellor will tell you the rest." Thereupon Chancellor Séguier presented the king's request that the council of regency established under his father's will be dissolved so that, in accordance with precedent, his mother would be left in free and entire charge of himself and the business of state. The judges and the peers voiced their approval, as had been expected.

Now it remained to be seen how the queen would reconstitute her council. Orléans was sure to remain on it as lieutenant general of the kingdom, and Condé as first prince of the blood; but the *Importants* were convinced they would be able to replace Richelieu's creatures— Séguier, Mazarin, Chavigny and his father Le Bouthillier—with their own men. Later that same day, the queen indeed made an announcement: she, in the king's name, wished Cardinal Mazarin to remain as minister, and to act as head of the royal council in the absence of either ranking member, Orléans or Condé.[5]

Everyone was stunned. Even in Anne's inner circle, only Brienne and Beringhen, who had helped prepare the way for it, suspected that she was going to make this appointment. Beaufort and his associates deluged her with complaints and countersuggestions: she did not refuse any of them outright but excused herself by explaining that she needed Mazarin at least for a while because of his experience, particularly in foreign affairs.[6] This seemed plausible, especially since she added the bishop of Beauvais to the council, as though to groom him for stepping into Mazarin's shoes when he had learned enough about statecraft. The queen even let it be understood in Rome that Beauvais would be the French crown's next nominee for a cardinal's hat.[7] Moreover, from the point of view of the *Importants*, Anne seemed to be making a good beginning when, during the ensuing weeks, she replaced the old superintendent of finances Le Bouthillier with the chancellor of her own household, Bailleul, and required Le Bouthillier's son Chavigny to sell his post as secretary of state to her loyal supporter Brienne.[8]

Although Chavigny for years had been showing increasing signs of jealousy at the rise of his and Richelieu's protégé Mazarin, Mazarin tried to save Chavigny from disgrace. He reminded the queen that Chavigny was not only able and experienced but intimately acquainted with all the secrets of state, so that it would be safer not to alienate him completely.[9] That was precisely the trouble, however: Chavigny knew things that Anne wished to forget. Some memories must have rankled especially, for she took the trouble at about this time to go through Louis XIII's papers and destroyed the originals of the humiliating confessions and agreements she had been forced to sign in 1637.[10] What few people had known, and probably fewer remembered, Chavigny had witnessed and countersigned those documents. Nor could it have counted as a recommendation with her that he had been privy to her anguish at the time of the Cinq-Mars plot in 1642. There was no help for it; Chavigny had to give up his office. Only his importance in Orléans's household and the intercession of Mazarin induced the queen to leave Chavigny on the royal council as a minister without portfolio, an equivocal position that he kept until he was arrested for conspiracy five years later.

There were other significant changes too. Madame de Lansac, the governess whom Richelieu had designated for the royal children, had never taken pains to please the queen; Anne now replaced her promptly with an old friend, Madame de Sénécey, the lady of honor whom Louis XIII had exiled in 1639. Since Madame de Sénécey insisted on recovering her former post as well, another Richelieu appointee had to go: Madame de Brassac. The Brassac case was special however, and showed that Anne was not animated by blind animosity against everyone who had ever served Richelieu. She liked Madame de Brassac and would have preferred to keep her, had not Madame de Sénécey forced her hand. Although Madame de Brassac left, however, Monsieur de Brassac stayed on as superintendent of the queen's household.[11] That evidence of discriminating judgment on her part went largely unnoticed, as Anne recalled to court victims of Richelieu's severity: in addition to Madame de Sénécey were Madame de Hautefort, Madame de Motteville, and La Porte.

After weeks of hesitation and contrary to the instructions left by Louis XIII, Anne also sent to Brussels for Madame de Chevreuse. She took the precaution of warning her friend indirectly not to expect to find the queen as she had left her: new responsibilities had brought changes.[12] Madame de Chevreuse did not really believe that, nor did the other returned exiles. When they eventually had to recognize that Anne no longer shared their opinions and interests, and was generally less docile and avid for friendship than they remembered, they did not look for the explanation in any development of her character but fastened on an external cause: the rival influence of Cardinal Mazarin.

Mazarin's progress could be measured by his public appearances in the queen's company. He had not been present during the session with the Parlement on 18 May when his political future had still been officially obscure. By 27 June when the memorial service was held in Notre-Dame concluding the first forty days of mourning for Louis XIII, Mazarin was one of the two masters of ceremonies who offered the queen holy water at the entrance to the cathedral and escorted her to and from her place.[13] On 18 August he was prominently present when the queen attended the thanksgiving service in Notre-Dame in honor of the latest French victory, the capture of Thionville.[14] And a week later, on 25 August, the feast day of Saint-Louis, Mazarin took part in a traditional observance that had special significance for the royal family: he accompanied the queen and the court to vespers in the Jesuit church of Saint-Louis that Louis XIII had founded.[15] One did not have to be a courtier to read the signs of Mazarin's favor.

The *Importants* and Anne's other old friends could not understand how she could support a man who stood for the continuation of Richelieu's policies at home and abroad—policies under which she had suffered and which she had opposed for the past twenty years. She was herself perhaps surprised at her own gradual reorientation. At any rate, she felt timid about it, for she continued to placate her friends with vague promises and intimations that her mind might not yet be fully made up concerning the first ministership. Moreover she seemed to have genuinely believed that people who professed to be devoted to her service should and would follow her lead: she asked them to visit Mazarin, to be cordial to him, in short to accept him as one of their own.[16]

Mazarin did not share Anne's illusions. Despite his naturalization, he was a foreigner in the kingdom, an intruder. He knew that his only source of power lay in the queen's confidence, and he set out to win her trust so completely that she would do nothing without him. We can follow his strategy from the little memorandum books he kept to jot down notes for talks with the queen, reports on what important people were saying and doing, reflections on events, and plans for actions to be taken in military campaigns and other business.[17]

On the evidence, Mazarin was an extraordinarily hardworking man, probably a great deal more so than his would-be competitors. He had taken over the direction of war and diplomacy, even of internal affairs, and from the first his correspondence was voluminous. His private memorandum books show that politics and related problems were never far from his mind: page after page covered with tiny script, in Italian, sometimes Spanish, later on French; written mostly in ink but occasionally in pencil, which would indicate that he made entries while traveling in his coach. When he presented himself to the queen in the light of a probationer, therefore, assuring her that he would withdraw to Rome if after three months she did not find his services satisfactory,[18] he could feel certain that if work alone counted, she would not easily find his equal.

But, of course, work did not count alone: an emotional bond was necessary. Mazarin therefore asked the queen to treat him as a friend, not simply a minister—to share with him all her thoughts. He was constantly placing himself at her feet, figuratively speaking, and reminding her that, since he had left home and family, he had no other attachment except to her service, in which it was his fervent wish to spend his life.[19]

No doubt Anne found his professions of devotion extremely flattering. There was no question that she liked him; everyone noticed it although no one could say how great or how lasting the liking might be. Moreover Mazarin had the advantage of her—she apparently never fully realized the extent of her power over him: only if she employed him could he use his talents as he wished. He needed her as much as she needed him, yet at the beginning of the regency she worried lest he really meant to return to Rome as he sometimes said.[20] Even years later, when he had to go into temporary exile during the civil wars, she still did not see, until he desperately reminded her, that without his first ministership he counted for nothing, especially in Rome.[21]

Perhaps Anne did not understand Mazarin's situation because she felt overwhelmed by her new responsibilities. She did not have much confidence in her own judgment or abilities. More than one observer praised her natural good sense and regretted that she did not value it sufficiently.[22] If she was not diffident by upbringing, her experiences in twenty-eight years of marriage to Louis XIII would surely have made her so. Undeniably also she lacked training and experience in government, and it was Mazarin who helped her out of that predicament by becoming her teacher as much as her servant.

Every evening Mazarin met with the queen for what was called the small council. It was very small indeed, just the two of them in the queen's private cabinet, with the doors left open for the sake of decency, and her women within call.[23] These meetings were a sign of Mazarin's growing influence, and people did not fail to note that they preempted time the queen had used to give to the bishop of Beauvais.[24] Ostensibly Mazarin was there to brief Anne on foreign affairs, his acknowledged field of specialization, but, as his notebooks show, he actually advised her on everything.

Anne was not totally ignorant of the workings of government.[25] She was familiar with the personnel of the royal council, and knew not only Brienne but also the other three secretaries of state who conducted all routine business. She knew the greater nobility too, all those who had household posts at court or held provincial governorships and commands in the army. She had acquaintances among the judges and other officers of the Paris Parlement as well as some of the other royal courts, and her travels in the provinces of eastern, western, and southern France had brought her into contact with local dignitaries. No doubt she would have been unable to draw up a table of organization reflecting the administration of the realm, nor would she have been able to trace the path of a royal edict from the council to the localities, or of an appeal from the localities to the council. But nobody expected her to know such things, or to bury herself in paperwork as her grandfather Philip II had done. What people did expect from her were decisions on general policy and on the distribution of patronage. Such matters, however, required judgment: even to entrust them to a minister involved at least some conception of political conduct. But Anne had no informed opinions, only prejudices; she had never had the opportunity to learn to see the political world in other than personal terms or to judge decisions by their consequences and ramifications in a larger frame of reference. If Mazarin wanted her to delegate power to him, he first had to make her understand what power really meant; and so he undertook to give her a political education.

During the first weeks of the regency, Anne, out of gratitude, was disposed to grant all requests from her friends or anyone who professed to have served her in the past—offices, pensions, it seemed they had only to ask in order to receive. They remembered that time as a glorious spring, and one man who later turned against Anne recalled that then only one comment was heard on every side: "The queen is so kind."[26] Criticisms were also heard, however, and not merely from people who wished her ill. Observers with nothing to gain or lose noted that the queen was giving away millions that the state could not afford, and feared that if she kept this up, she would find herself in the position of her late mother-in-law, who spent all the reserves accumulated by Henry IV and was left without resources or credit.[27]

Mazarin put a stop to this largesse. He represented to Anne that if she insisted on pleasing everyone she would be bound to fail and would spend a most unhappy life. Furthermore she would lose the respect of the very persons she gratified if they found her so easy: she must know how to refuse as well as to give. He urged her not to grant requests without taking time to consider them, or better yet, to let it be known she was deferring expensive gifts until France was at peace and the treasury in better shape.[28] In short, he wished the queen to calculate the effect of her bounty and to bestow it where and when it would bring the best political advantage.

Mazarin thought also that the queen should make herself less easily accessible: too many persons had the right of entry to her inner apartments, and she allowed her ladies too much familiarity. Now that she was regent and subject to solicitations from every side, she owed it to herself, he suggested, to hold herself a bit more aloof than in the days when she had no power.[29] He found that not even all members of the royal council treated her with sufficient respect; some spoke too arrogantly for his taste during sessions at which she was present. In his opinion this would be remedied if she showed her firm support for him by appointing more people to the council whom he could control,[30] and meanwhile he cautioned her against speaking of military and diplomatic matters too freely. She should discuss such questions only at the highest level, with Gaston of Orléans, the prince of Condé, and Mazarin himself.[31]

All this was good advice, even if self-serving. Anyone who would be minister-favorite—or prime minister, as we should call it—needed to monopolize as much as possible all patronage, appointments, information, and decisions: if he was not the main channel for the monarch's grace and will, he was nothing. Mazarin was following Richelieu's example, although unlike Richelieu, who had sometimes bullied Louis XIII, he never used such tactics with Anne—it was not his style. He tried to persuade, he implored, and above all he explained.

Richelieu too had given lessons to Louis XIII, including lengthy memorandums setting forth the options when difficult problems had to be decided. Anne's lessons from Mazarin in the summer of 1643 were more elementary and often more pragmatic. He showed her the complexities of maneuvering among the interests of the great families to prevent their aggrandizement at the expense of the crown. The duke of Bouillon, for example, was asking for the restoration of his autonomous principality of Sedan, which he had ceded to the French crown in 1642 as the penalty for his involvement in the Cinq-Mars conspiracy. Mazarin, it will be remembered, had conducted that negotiation, and at the time the duke had been glad to get off with his life and liberty. Now, however, the duke claimed to have been a victim of Richelieu's injustice, and expected the queen, who after all had sympathized with the conspirators, to right the wrong. The duchess of Bouillon came to court to plead for her husband, and Anne was inclined to give in until Mazarin pointed out to her what a dangerous example such leniency would set for the other great nobles. The princes, such as Condé and Vendôme, and even Gaston of Orléans, would take it as license to conspire against the royal authority with impunity; and if the queen committed such an error, it would surely cost her all reputation.[32]

Anne saw the point of this and did not give back Sedan, but meanwhile she came under similar pressure from the duke of Lorraine, who wanted to be reinstated as sovereign prince in Lorraine, now under royal administration after numerous negotiations, cessions, and military campaigns. The duke of Lorraine had powerful allies close to the queen: his sister was Gaston of Orléans's second wife, newly received into the family with great ceremony; and above all, the duke's old friend Madame de Chevreuse was pleading his cause most ardently.

Mazarin had to repeat all the arguments he had used in the case of Sedan, and he noted that he would have to speak with vigor.[33] Anne saw reason here too; she was not going to dismember her son's kingdom to please her friends.

She found it more difficult to understand why she should not deprive Richelieu's relatives of important places in the state when such longstanding supporters as the Vendôme family seemed so much more deserving. What the Vendômes wanted were the offices held by Richelieu's cousin, Marshall de la Meilleraye: the governorship of Brittany and the grand mastership of the artillery, as well as those in the hands of Richelieu's nephew the duke de Brézé: the grand admiralty of France with the governorship of the fortified port of Le Havre, and the governorship of the three bishoprics of Metz, Toul, and Verdun, strategically located on the northeastern frontier.[34]

It was true that the duke of Vendôme had been governor of Brittany, and that Richelieu and Louis XIII had removed him for disloyalty; but if he now recovered that position while his sons Beaufort and Mercoeur divided up the other great dignities between themselves and their friends, the family would become as formidable as the Condés or Gaston of Orléans. They pursued the queen relentlessly with their demands, and they had powerful allies: the bishop of Beauvais, Madame de Chevreuse, the king's governess Madame de Sénécey, Madame de Hautefort—in fact, the whole cabal of the *Importants* and all its adjuncts.

Hatred of Richelieu was their constant theme. Beauvais said publicly that the memory of Richelieu and his works should be eradicated from the kingdom,[35] and the duke of Nemours, Vendôme's son-in-law, thought that the Richelieu castle should be razed and the houses of the late cardinal's relatives pulled down along with it.[36] Madame de Sénécey meanwhile undertook to nurture corresponding sentiments in the young king. She let him listen to satirical songs about Richelieu, and taught him to say that the minister had wanted to be king and pope. One day she pointed out to the child a portrait of Richelieu: "Look at the dog," to which the little king replied, "Give me my crossbow so I can shoot him."[37] The queen herself was not immune to feelings of this kind, and besides she was being reminded on every side of the gratitude she owed old friends. At least she did not commit herself outright; she hesitated and, when pressed, responded that she would think about it. As late as June 1643, Mazarin still could not get her to tell him her intentions; he thought she was wavering and did not fully trust him,[38] although perhaps she simply did not know her own mind. She found it easier to decide after he explained to her what was at stake.

Mazarin reminded Anne that Richelieu's relatives were people of importance in their own right: competent marshalls and admirals of France were not negligible, especially in wartime. The queen would do better, he advised, to win them over rather than to make enemies of them; and since they and their clan also had circles of clients and dependents, if she attached them to herself she would have a whole ready-made party of her own.[39]

The Vendôme family, by contrast, was unreliable. They had been involved in conspiracies before, and could not be trusted to respect the royal authority to any greater degree in future if it ran counter to their ambition, no matter what protestations of personal devotion Beaufort might make to the queen. Besides, whatever Gaston of Orléans might feel or do if the Vendômes got what they asked, the Condé family would be sure to take offense. Richelieu's nephew Brézé was Enghien's brother-in-law. What was even more important, Mazarin represented to the queen, was that if she allowed herself to be drawn into the partisan interests of the Vendômes and deprived La Meilleraye, Brézé, and the duke of Richelieu for no reason except their relationship to the late cardinal, she would be violating the crown's basic obligation to maintain justice. In the position Anne now occupied, she could no longer afford to let her feelings govern her actions; the crown should be impartial, and Mazarin implored her to speak against no one, to take no sides, to let it be known that she esteemed all her servants, and that considerations of friendship would not lead her to make any decisions contrary to justice and contrary to what she judged useful for the state and the welfare of her son.[40]

Anne evidently found Mazarin's arguments convincing. When Richelieu's niece Madame d'Aiguillon came to court to plead for the young duke of Richelieu in whose name she was holding Le Havre, Anne received the lady kindly, the more so since Madame d'Aiguillon assured her of her own as well as her nephew's unwavering devotion and loyalty.[41] In the end, the queen let the duke of Richelieu and his aunt keep Le Havre, although that meant disappointing the young La Rochefoucauld, her own friend as well as a relative of Madame de Sénécey and a cherished protégé of Madame de Chevreuse. Anne also continued Brézé as a grand admiral of France, and on Mazarin's advice adopted a solution for the governorship of Brittany that outmaneuvered the duke of Vendôme completely. As a result of delicate negotiations conducted by Mazarin, and in return for a ducal title, Marshall de la Meilleraye agreed to resign the government of Brittany to the queen. Instead of giving the office to Vendôme, the queen kept it herself and appointed La Meilleraye as her lieutenant-governor for the province.

Anne used the same tactic three years later in 1646, when the grand admiralty fell vacant after Brézé was killed in naval action. At that point the prince of Condé claimed the office of grand admiral for his son Enghien as a family inheritance on behalf of Enghien's wife, Brézé's sister. Rather than let such a dignity pass by inheritance, Anne kept it in her own hands and had herself named by the king's letters patent "Grand Master in Chief and General Superintendent of the Navigation and Commerce of France."[42]

Mazarin did not confine his political lessons to pragmatic advice suited for particular problems. His specific suggestions arose from his general conception of the royal authority and the nature of politics in France—a conception, not to say a theory, that he explained repeatedly to Anne in the first months of her regency. He took it as an axiom that the power of the crown should be absolute, that is to say, independent, not subject to encroachment or control by any institution, group, or person, whether parlements, noble factions, or great princes. He noted that all these persons and groups had interests running counter to the interests of the crown, for they always worked to increase their own importance at the expense of the king's authority and opposed his absolute power, except insofar as they could use it for their own purposes.[43] As Mazarin saw the situation and endeavored to make the queen see it, the parlements, the princes, the governors of provinces, and, for that matter, the noble leaders of the Huguenots, all were trying under various pretexts to undo her late husband's program and turn the clock back to the time when France "although in appearance governed by a king, was actually a republic"[44]—in other words, the time when Marie de Medici had been regent. Accordingly, Mazarin warned Anne not to yield too much, otherwise she would be unable to recover lost ground. And she had to consider her responsibility to her son. Nothing would hurt the young king more when he came of age, as the successor of a strong absolute monarch, than to find himself dependent on his own subjects because of her bad government.[45]

Historical judgment has been ambivalent about Mazarin's political lessons to the queen. Nineteenth-century French historians in particular, with a bias toward constitutional monarchy or republicanism, tended to read back the issues of 1789 into the 1640s and somewhat uneasily depicted the "ambitious Italian" arousing the "Spanish woman's" passion for absolute power as though the notion of absolute monarchy had been a foreign importation.[46] In fact Mazarin said the same things that native sons had said before him—notably Richelieu and even Richelieu's opponent Marillac—and at least the hope of setting the crown effectively above factions and magnates dated back beyond Louis XIII to Henry IV and the sixteenth-century monarchs. However ambivalent French historians felt about that heritage, they all took pride in the growing strength and the territorial expansion of the French state. On the whole, therefore, they approved Mazarin's position on royal authority at least as far as external affairs were concerned, though they would have done so more wholeheartedly had he not been a foreigner, and Italian at that.[47]

To do Mazarin justice, he was not speaking of destroying a viable tradition of representative or participatory government. There was no such thing in France. No matter what slogans the magnates published for the sake of general welfare, the experience of Marie de Medici's regency had shown that they lacked both the ability and the inclination to subordinate private interests to any truly common cause. Mazarin was quite correct in his analysis of their and the parlements' wishes in 1643: in the words of the disappointed La Rochefoucauld, they wanted a minister who would "re-establish the old form of government which Cardinal Richelieu had begun to destroy."[48]

Although Mazarin was indeed ambitious, he did not exaggerate when he represented himself to the queen as the man best suited to carry out the policies he was outlining to her. His most intelligent rivals, Châteauneuf, des Noyers, and Chavigny, were too deeply involved in partisan politics to see absolute monarchy as a positive unifying force for a whole people. He, Mazarin, did have this vision. To make the kingdom's fortunes prosper in the highest degree, he noted, "it is needful only that Frenchmen be for France.[49]

That Frenchmen be for France—it was a more modern expression than anything even Richelieu had used, conjuring up a sense of patriotism that went beyond the traditional category of kingship and obedience. Although few people at the time would have understood exactly what he meant, Mazarin evidently had a concept of the monarchy as the embodiment of something greater than itself, something that would later be called the nation. If Frenchmen were to be for France, the regent had to be for France too. Anne was already learning to subordinate her personal feelings to political needs in domestic matters, and Mazarin was teaching her to do the same in foreign affairs.

Louis XIII at his death had left French forces committed to varying degrees on four fronts: in southwestern Germany, on the Spanish Netherlands frontier, in Catalonia, and in northern Italy. Although the major warring powers and their allies had agreed on a general peace congress to be held in Westphalia, the delegates had not met as yet. To satisfy his conscience, Louis, while he lay dying, had sent to Brussels in a vain effort to hasten the peacemaking process. The military advantage seemed to lie with the Spaniards, who were preparing to lay siege to a gateway into northern France: the fortified town of Rocroi in Picardy. The young Enghien averted the danger of invasion by relieving Rocroi in a brilliantly executed battle five days after Louis died, a victory that was hailed as a magnificent omen for the new reign.[50] Nevertheless the question loomed, asked anxiously by France's allies and hopefully by the Spaniards, whether the regent would choose to continue the war.

Richelieu had never succeeded in reconciling all sectors of public opinion to the war's burdensome cost or its moral justification as a genuinely necessary enterprise. Many of the clergy still thought the war ungodly, and Louis XIII himself, as we have seen, shared their scruples to his dying day. The anti-Richelieu party among nobles and officials also opposed the war, condemning it as a device invented by Richelieu in order to make himself indispensable to the king. Now Mazarin was trying to do the same thing, they said; but in foreign policy as well as domestic government, they wished to return to the days before Richelieu came to power, and to liquidate the war, like the rest of Richelieu's heritage, as soon as possible.[51] At least some of them favored an immediate separate peace with Spain even at the price of losing whatever had been gained in eighteen years of fighting: Châteauneuf was of this opinion, for example, and count d'Avaux, one of the named delegates to the Westphalian congress, and of course Madame de Chevreuse.[52] They thought they could count on the queen, judging by her attitude in the past and her well-known attachment to her Spanish family. Anne did in fact, frequently and in public, express her great eagerness for peace—behavior about whose implications Mazarin, however, lost no time in enlightening her.

During the very first days of the regency, Mazarin made notes to tell the queen that she must think only of her title as the king's mother and make people forget that she was the sister of the king of Spain.[53] Mazarin himself was not enamored of war. He had founded his career in France on his proven skill as peacemaker and negotiator, and he remained alive to the ideal of peace as the most desirable condition for

Christendom. But as both his public and his private correspondence shows, he always believed that peace negotiations called for mutual give-and-take, not for the imposition of terms by one side and abject yielding by the other. In the present case, therefore, he begged the queen to speak openly of continuing the war against Spain, and to make it plain that in the interests of the king and of justice she would not consent to the restitution of French war gains.[54]

Nor would Mazarin hear of a separate peace, however advantageous to France, at the expense of Sweden, the Netherlands, and her other allies: on the contrary, the allies must be reassured. He reported to the queen that their ambassadors in Paris were already saying, "The queen will be for her son against Spain, but for her brother against all others,"[55] and suggested suitable replies she could give them when she received them in audience. Anne took these lessons to heart. By the time Madame de Chevreuse returned to court in mid-June 1643, Anne was on guard against diplomatic propositions coming from her old friend, much to the lady's unbelieving surprise.[56]

Madame de Chevreuse did not give up easily, either on a separate peace or on her hopes of recovering her influence over Anne. Allied ambassadors in Paris, Sweden's Hugo Grotius and Venice's Giustiniani, claimed in their dispatches that Madame de Chevreuse was acting in the service of Spain as well as in her own interests.[57] They were right, though they did not know all the details. The Spanish government was proposing to use Anne's regency to the advantage of Spain, and it remained to be seen whether Mazarin's lessons had fortified the queen enough to resist her brother's appeals to old loyalties and affections, not to mention her own piety.

Chapter Twelve

The Sister of the King of Spain

T HE SPANISH COUNCIL OF state had greeted the news of Louis XIII's death with joyful relief. As the members gave their opinions, one by one, the chorus rose: this death is a blessing of Divine Providence for Spain because it will bring peace.[1] At the very least, the regency government in France could be expected to be weak, troubled by rivalry between Gaston of Orléans and the prince of Condé as well as other factions, less able to prosecute the war and more willing to come to terms than Louis XIII had been. The likeliest advantage to Spain, however, would certainly come from the Most Christian Queen herself, Anne of Austria. The count of Chinchon summed it up: "Undoubtedly the lady queen of France still has the heart with which she was born."[2] All the councillors therefore advised Philip IV to choose some man of skill and discretion to carry a message of condolence to his sister; though the two kingdoms were at war, the ties of blood between Philip and Anne and their mutual affection would make such an action plausible, and Anne would surely be deeply touched by it.[3] With this opening the envoy then could proceed to bring up the matter of peace, and in a subsequent meeting the council elaborated on the instructions Philip should give him.

Philip soon decided on his messenger: Don Diego de Saavedra Fajardo, already a designated delegate to the peace congress in Westphalia, who had a safe-conduct to travel from Spain to Brussels via France and could make an unobtrusive detour to Paris. Don Diego was to deliver the king's condolences and assurances of brotherly love; then, when Anne gave him the expected encouragement, he was to point out all the trouble that internal factions could give her and suggest that her own interest as well as her love for the king of Spain should incline her to make peace. If she did so, she would always find Spain ready to serve her when she needed help.[4]

To the Spaniards Anne was an agent-in-place, a dynastic chess piece whose usefulness for the past twenty-eight years had been disappointing but which could now be deployed to good advantage. Only one of the councillors, the marquis de Castañada, was humane enough to consider the possible danger to Anne. He insisted that the mission be conducted in the utmost secrecy, "so that the queen would not lose the love and credit in which she is held in France."[5] Thus it was concluded to proceed, with the approval of Philip. Don Diego subsequently added a suggestion of his own: it would be useful for him to make an approach to Mazarin also, he thought, because Mazarin was believed to be ambitious; and since his future in France seemed insecure, he might welcome offers of Spanish backing for his career.[6] As it happened, Don Diego had known Mazarin in Rome. The council therefore advised Philip that it would be a good idea if he authorized Don Diego to visit Mazarin on the pretext of renewing old acquaintance.[7]

All these deliberations took time, and Don Diego did not actually reach France until July 1643. He came too late. Perhaps he would have been too late even in May, but by July the Most Christian Queen was definitely not susceptible to overtures from Spain.

Don Diego was foiled from the moment of his arrival in Bordeaux, where he was met by Monsieur Riqueti, an envoy from the French court.[8] Riqueti, who was an officer in the king's bodyguard, had accompanied the body of the cardinal infante Ferdinand on its journey through France, and now had orders from the queen to escort Saavedra from the Spanish to the Flemish border. Most likely Mazarin had briefed Riqueti on what to expect, for he inquired in the most persistent although friendliest manner whether Don Diego did not by chance have orders to proceed by way of Paris. No, indeed, Don Diego protested: he was minister of peace with a safe-conduct from the king of France and must follow the usual route posthaste to Brussels. Upon being pressed, however, he admitted that he did have a mandate from the Spanish king and queen to deliver their personal letters of condolence to Queen Anne and kiss her hand if he should happen to be passing through Paris, not with any purpose of initiating negotiations but purely as an expression of the Spanish court's affection and his own reverence for the queen. To Riqueti's objections that he was not traveling in sufficient state to receive or return official visits from the great dignitaries of the French court, Don Diego replied that he meant to spend less than a day in Paris without calling any attention to himself, simply to meet Mazarin, kiss the queen's hand, and continue on his way. In that case, said Riqueti, he had best send a summary of his orders and intentions to Mazarin, so that the minister could consult the allied ambassadors and take the opinion of the council of state.[9]

Don Diego complied, only to receive a disappointing answer. The Swedish ambassador had seen no harm in a condolence visit, but the Dutch ambassador had objected; and upon deliberation the council of state decided that in order to keep the confidence of France's allies, the queen should receive neither visits nor letters from Spain.[10]

By way of softening the blow, Anne sent one of her gentlemen to see Don Diego with assurances of her regrets. For her own part, she said, she would have been glad to welcome her brother's messenger. As matters stood, however, she had no choice but to follow the advice of her council. There could be no doubt that she as well as Mazarin had understood the ulterior motive of the proposed visit, for she added that having been kept away from state affairs for so long, she was only a poor, confused woman with no knowledge or any influence at all on diplomatic negotiations. Moreover, she could not countermand council resolutions by her own will, nor could she afford to give occasion for comment by appearing Spanish in her sympathies.[11]

Don Diego was not easily put off. As a last resort, he suggested that she might receive his messages through Mazarin: surely no one could think ill of a brother's concern for a dearly beloved sister, particularly since the brother had not started the war and was continuing it merely in natural defense of his territories and in order to recover what had been taken from him. Richelieu was to blame for the war, Richelieu and those ministers who followed his maxims and claimed that Spain did not really want peace. Now was the time, Don Diego implored the queen, to clear up this tragic misunderstanding.[12] His appeal had no success, and what he heard about the queen's actions while he was still waiting for her reply was not encouraging either.

As soon as Don Diego reached Cambrai in the Spanish Netherlands, he reported to Philip IV: Mazarin was clearly following in Richelieu's footsteps and had brought the queen to agree with him to such a point that she was actually protecting Richelieu's relatives and, Don Diego concluded bitterly, "is leaving all sign of devotion [for Spain], so that your Majesty would do better to consider her a stranger than his sister."[15]

Having failed to move Anne directly, the Spanish government was ready to resort to indirect means. The ministers apparently found it difficult to believe that Anne herself had changed. It must all be Mazarin's fault; if only his influence over her could be removed or at least counteracted! Madame de Chevreuse offered to do just that, for an unnamed price, and Philip IV's council advised him to accept.

The duchess made her approach through one Antonio Sarmiento, a

Spanish official who had become her friend, possibly her lover, during her late stay in Brussels. In mid-September 1643 Don Antonio journeyed to Saragossa, where the Spanish court was staying, and presented a memorandum to Philip IV, reminding the king that even before Louis XIII died, Spain had been gathering information concerning French subjects who were likely to stand high in Anne's favor and who could be subsidized by Spain. According to Don Antonio, there could not be a better prospect than Madame de Chevreuse: now that the queen had recalled her to court, the duchess would infallibly recover first place in the queen's favor and would thereby have more power than any of the ministers. Grateful as Madame de Chevreuse was to Spain for help in her previous troubles, she could be counted on to keep the Spanish court supplied with useful information and, above all, "to nourish in the queen the love and cordiality that used to be and still is between brother and sister."[14] That would be to the greatest advantage for Spain because Mazarin, the minister to whom the queen was confiding all diplomatic negotiations, was poisoning her mind against her homeland and family.

Here Don Antonio cited arguments allegedly used by Mazarin that have the tone of authenticity. There are echoes of them in Mazarin's notebooks; evidently Anne repeated to Madame de Chevreuse what the minister had told her, and Madame de Chevreuse passed it on to Sarmiento. According to the latter's report, Mazarin argued that the king of Spain had long ago forgotten Anne, and in war and diplomacy regarded her not as a sister but as queen of France, a kingdom with different views and interests than his own.[15] And even if Philip still did bear Anne the love of a brother, it did not shape his policy: Spanish policy was formulated by ministers who were more attentive to the welfare of their own kingdom than any other and would not mind deceiving Anne. Therefore she must put love for Spain behind her and remember that if she entered into any private secret dealings with the enemy, she was risking the perdition of her sons, to whom, after all, she owed more than to her Spanish relatives.[16]

Naturally enough, Don Antonio considered this to be pernicious advice. He could not bring himself to believe that she was fully reconciled to taking it; he thought he could detect signs of continuing good will for Spain. Thus, for example, the queen had shown kindly interest in his correspondence with Madame de Chevreuse, and she was quite openly preparing to send Philip a portrait of the young king, Louis XIV.[17] According to Don Antonio, Mazarin himself was not sure of the queen, for when he, Don Antonio, had recently passed through Paris, the minister had gone to great trouble to prevent the queen from giving him an audience.[18] If Mazarin was determined to keep all Spaniards away from the queen, she ought at least to have the opportunity to stay in touch with them through Madame de Chevreuse's correspondence. In short, Don Antonio represented Madame de Chevreuse's services as essential to Spain, and, he concluded, it would not be amiss to launch a propaganda campaign in France against Mazarin—something to the effect that the queen should use good Frenchmen, such as Châteauneuf, instead of this foreigner.[19] Châteauneuf, it will be remembered, was Madame de Chevreuse's candidate for first minister.

Without delay the Spanish council voted to thank Don Antonio and approve the use of his correspondence with Madame de Chevreuse for communication with the queen of France.[20] That was as far as the project got, however, for meanwhile events had been developing so rapidly in Paris that Don Antonio's information was out of date.

During the first week of September, Madame de Chevreuse's faction had been undone, its members either arrested, banned from court, or in hiding. The queen was only waiting a decent interval before ordering Madame de Chevreuse herself to retire into the provinces. Although this setback lessened the duchess's usefulness for Spain, it did not discourage her personally. She remained convinced for almost another decade that she could govern Anne if only Mazarin were removed from the scene. For a woman reputed to be intelligent and knowledgeable in the ways of the world, she was singularly obtuse where Anne was concerned. She learned nothing from her failures during the first summer of the regency, yet they were many, for she pulled every string that used to move Anne in the old days only to find that none of them worked any longer.

As we have seen, Madame de Chevreuse miscalculated when she counted on the queen's hatred for Richelieu and love for Spain. Even Anne's ladies noted that her affection for her brother no longer weighed as much with her as it once had done.[21] The duchess might have thought she had another asset: the queen used to depend on her for entertainment. But that did not seem to be the case any more either. Anne was not isolated and friendless. Not to mention the crowds of people clamoring to see her on business and the noblewomen such as the princess of Condé, whose company she enjoyed, she had her sons; and for interesting conversation every evening, she had Mazarin. Lighthearted amusements or festivities were out of the question, with the court still in deep mourning. Even when Madame de Chevreuse arranged a garden picnic for the queen, the party turned into a social disaster because Madame de Chevreuse's stepmother, the duchess of Montbazon, behaved badly to Anne's friend, the princess of Condé. Anne felt highly offended, sided with the princess, and left without tasting so much as a dish of preserves.[22] Formerly Anne had enjoyed Madame de Chevreuse's malicious wit, but now she appreciated it less as the lady took to ridiculing Mazarin.[23] In growing frustration, Madame de Chevreuse tried to exploit the queen's piety, using Beaufort's mother, the devout duchess of Vendôme, as a link to the "party of saints" that was already urging the queen to get rid of Mazarin and make peace with Spain.

Properly speaking, the devout were not a party at all, nor did they as a group have a formal political program such as the one that had been proposed years before by Marillac. Even that unofficial secret organization, the Company of the Holy Sacrament, if one can believe its surviving records, stayed clear of politics: it merely lobbied, through Anne's grand almoner, the bishop of Beauvais, for the continuation of Louis XIII's campaign against dueling as well as for other pious projects.[24] In general, the devout were men and women, laity or clergy, who actively supported spiritual revival in the French Catholic church: the application of high standards in the appointment of bishops and the training of priests, the reform of old monastic orders and the foundation of new ones, more regular and more fervent religious practice in all layers of society, and a public morality disciplined according to Christian principles.[25] By 1643, however, the devout had begun to be divided among themselves into ultramontanists and gallicans, pro-Jesuits and Jansenists, depending on whether they emphasized papal authority or royal authority in the French church, and whether they preferred a generous or an austere interpretation of divine grace.

Besides, the devout were not all equal in the depth of their commitment: some few, such as Philippe Cospéan, the bishop of Lisieux, or Vincent de Paul, were so saintly as to be unworldly; but for many others, devotion was no hindrance to ambition and factional alignment. Anne's grand almoner, the bishop of Beauvais, was an example of the latter group, casting his lot with the *Importants*, and he had numerous companions. The equally devout and ambitious chancellor, Pierre Séguier, on the other hand, supported Mazarin in order to keep custody of the state seals in the face of competition for Châteauneuf. On the whole, however, most of the devout who held positions of public importance tended to the opposition: they remembered Richelieu's treatment of Marie de Medici and the fate of the brothers Marillac; they still resented Richelieu's strong hand in church affairs, and abhorred the war against the Habsburgs as an ungodly enterprise. Sometimes passion quite blinded them. The bishop of Beauvais, for instance, maintained vehemently that all things must be restored to the way they had been before Richelieu came to power. He had no ready reply, however, when a court wit among his hearers remarked ingenuously that in that case La Rochelle and other fortified towns must be returned to the Huguenots.[26]

Mazarin knew that Beauvais and other bishops were meeting in Paris in the summer of 1643, and he also knew what they were saying against himself and the policies he advocated. His notebooks show how much he feared the influence of these people, particularly their possible influence on the queen.[27] It seemed all the more dangerous because it was being reinforced by the devout women who surrounded her: her lady of honor Madame de Sénécey, her associate lady-in-waiting Madame de Hautefort, her friends at court and in society such as Madame de Motteville and Madame de Brienne, and the mother superior and nuns of Val-de-Grâce and the other convents she loved to visit. They all, some unwittingly, others knowingly, made common cause with the faction of the Vendômes and Madame de Chevreuse in a grand effort to win the queen away from Mazarin, and they looked to the queen's own religious feeling as their best ally.

By any except the highest standard, Anne was a very pious woman. It is true that mysticism, the hallmark of many Catholic reformers of the time, never attracted her. Nor was she interested in theological questions; the bitter controversy between Jesuits and Jansenists over the nature of divine grace touched her only insofar as it called for the intervention of royal and papal authority, and she protected the noted Jansenist Arnauld d'Andilly for years simply because she liked and respected him.[28] Although she left theology to the experts, however, she fervently observed all the religious exercises enjoined or advised by the Council of Trent—in other words, the most orthodox and most modern orientation available.

Anne heard mass every day, sometimes more than once; attended services and sermons in the leading churches of Paris and in her favorite convents; and punctiliously observed all the required feasts of the ecclesiastical calendar as well as many of the optional ones.[29] Much of this was part of royal protocol, but it was not laid down by protocol that she should fast rigorously during Lent against the advice of her physicians, or that she should take Communion every Sunday as well as on the great holidays.[30] She communed weekly entirely by choice, following a practice warmly urged by many spiritual directors though far from being a widespread custom. She had a special devotion for the Virgin, and consequently, whenever she resided in Paris, she heard mass at Notre-Dame every Saturday without fail.[31] She also had a devotion for the Rosary as well as an extensive collection of relics ranging from fragments of the Cross to a finger of Saint Anne.[32]

As soon as she was widowed and free to do as she pleased, she enrolled herself in every confraternity of note, starting with the Confraternity of Notre-Dame and the Confraternity of Saint-Denis, in which latter she had the king inscribed also.[33] And she resumed her visits to convents, a pleasure she had not enjoyed since Louis XIII's prohibition of it in 1637. The prohibition had soon been modified to extend only to Val-de-Grâce, but Anne had decided that if she were not allowed to go to Val-de-Grâce, she would not go to any other convent either.[34] Now she made up for it with frequent visits to the Carmelites, the Visitation, and above all, Val-de-Grâce, where she sometimes also took along the young king.

The nuns had been her friends in adversity, as indeed had the bishops of Lisieux and Beauvais, as well as many other devout persons who opposed Richelieu. From Anne's present feelings as well as from her background, the devout, therefore, had every reason to expect that she would let herself be guided by them. Their confidence seemed all the more reasonable because, during the first month of the regency, it looked as though Anne, a widow with young children, was placing herself under the protection of the church, and the most regenerate part of the church at that. Aside from having made Beauvais a minister of state, she consulted with Lisieux and Paul de Gondi, the former general of the galleys and patron of Vincent de Paul, now turned into an austere Oratorian priest.[35] And she had asked Vincent de Paul to direct her conscience after having called on him to assist Louis XIII on his deathbed.[36] The only jarring note in all this for the devout was her support of Cardinal Mazarin.

Although personally Mazarin was a punctiliously observant Catholic, when it came to government he, like Richelieu before him, refused to let religion or religious pressure groups dictate policy. Direct appeals to the queen on matters of state, made in the name of religion, were therefore unavailing as long as Mazarin was at her side to head them off. The papal nuncio had found that out when he urged her to accept her brother's letter of condolence and, for the sake of Christendom, to consider a separate peace.[37] In consequence the devout concentrated on dislodging Mazarin, using as their instrument the queen's own conscience. The bishop of Lisieux headed the effort, all unaware that, according to Mazarin's information, Madame de Chevreuse was seconding him by coordinating convents and pious ladies through Madame de Vendôme and other Vendôme connections.[38] People such as the queen's lady of honor Madame de Sénécey came apparently spontaneously to him and to Vincent de Paul and beseeched them to warn the queen that her evening interviews with Mazarin were giving rise to public scandal, and to make her promise that she would no longer receive Mazarin in private audience. On the strength of his reputation as the "saint of the court," Lisieux did admonish the queen, whom he had always called his "dear daughter."[39] The queen's ladies kept Vincent de Paul similarly informed of the latest gossip in court and city, and Father Vincent too admonished Anne, armed with the moral authority of a spiritual director.[40] At the Carmelites the prioress, Mother Maria of the Passion lectured her on the same theme until the queen burst out weeping and declared that she would not return if she were addressed again like that.[41] But wherever she went, she could not escape the pious chorus of criticism and advice.

At home in the Louvre, Madame de Hautefort told Anne that Mazarin, at forty-one, was too young for his association with her not to provoke scandal. Anne tried to laugh that off by saying Mazarin did not love women since he came from a country where other inclinations were fashionable.[42] It was no laughing matter, however, when Anne found an anonymous letter in her bed, detailing the infamous gossip that was circulating about her and Mazarin, and begging her to send him away for the sake of her reputation, the salvation of her soul, and the good of the state. Smuggling in the letter had been the work of her faithful old servant La Porte, who was less blindly devoted to Anne than to Madame de Hautefort.[43]

Even in her little private chapel, the queen was not safe from pursuit. She found her friend Madame de Brienne there one day, asking leave to speak frankly. Leave being given, Madame de Brienne told Anne all the aspersions that were being cast on her virtue. By now such a recital could have been no novelty for Anne, but according to Madame de Brienne, the queen blushed right into the whites of her eyes. Anne protested in tears that there was nothing sinful in her feelings for Mazarin, and swore solemnly by the relics on her altar that she would never permit him to speak to her of anything except matters of state.[44]

It was Anne's unshakable defense against all attacks on her conscience and reputation: she was innocent, and therefore gossip could have no importance. She said it in so many words when she grew sufficiently angry, as she did with La Porte one day in reply to his reproaches that she was providing food for talk: people who do no evil have nothing to fear, she maintained. When he insisted that whatever the reality, the public judged by appearances, she became so irate that she drummed on the window with her fan instead of answering.[45] She was being quite true to herself, for she had had the same reaction almost twenty years earlier during the scandal over Buckingham's attentions. Time had done nothing to lessen her obstinate self-righteousness, and so her devout friends failed in their object: she did not send Mazarin away.

It was also characteristic, however, for Anne to be evasive under pressure. She seemed to yield to opposition, to agree with the last speaker when challenged. As Richelieu could have testified, that did not mean she changed her mind on the basic issues involved: she was merely avoiding unpleasant confrontation while protecting whatever lay closest to her heart, using the tactics of a small hunted animal without much confidence in its weapons. Consequently she had the reputation at one and the same time of being biddable and dissembling, an apparent contradiction that few people understood as well as her servant La Porte, who observed that "she stood firm only for things in which her affections were extraordinarily engaged."[46] In the present case, however, it was still far from clear on what object or which party Anne had settled her affections.

Mazarin was in an agony of suspense as he noted that the queen did not always tell him what her friends said to her or she to them, and that despite his entreaties that she look upon him as a true confidant, she seemed to be keeping him at arm's length and would not speak to him about anything other than affairs of state.[47] He counted the hours she spent at the Visitation, and especially at Val-de-Grâce in conference with the mother superior. When the queen returned from such visits, he thought she seemed less well-disposed to him, and it filled him with disquiet to hear from informants that she offered only feeble excuses when the nuns taxed her with continuing the policies of Richelieu and maintaining him, Mazarin, in office.[48] He begged the queen to make up her mind once for all because the prolonged uncertainty about her ultimate intentions was keeping the hopes of too many rivals alive and therefore undermining the authority of her ministers.[49] Perhaps she had made up her mind, but she either could not or would not declare it unequivocally. She found it very difficult to burn her bridges until circumstances forced her hand.

Whereas Mazarin was patient, Madame de Chevreuse and her ally the duke of Beaufort had become impatient for action: they organized a conspiracy to assassinate Mazarin. Most of the men whom they recruited for the purpose among their dependents and acquaintances were accustomed to such work, seasoned by participation in more than one abortive plot against the life of Richelieu. They expected the queen to be grateful to them once it was all over, for they were proposing to rid her of a dangerous encumbrance that threatened public tranquillity.

There was an established ethic of tyrannicide in France going back to the sixteenth century: if a minister could be branded as an unworthy royal favorite, a usurper and abuser of power, his assassination was not murder but righteous execution.[50] Conspirators against Richelieu had justified themselves with this argument. As it happened, however, he kept himself well guarded and died of natural causes. The last "tyrant" to have paid with his life had been Concini, Marie de Medici's favorite, and his assassination had been arranged, possibly with the connivance of Louis XIII, by Madame de Chevreuse's first husband, the duke of Luynes. Like Concini, Mazarin was Italian and served a regent. Anne's old friends pointed out to her this parallel between her own situation and Marie de Medici's. Marie would have had a peaceful, happy regency, they said with a fine disregard for facts, if she had not persisted in supporting the detestable foreign upstart.[51] It was a parallel that occurred to the most respectable people. In Paris a faction of the Parlement urged that the old law directed against Concini and barring foreigners from public office be reactivated, and a number of bishops meeting privately endorsed the proposal.[52]

The *Importants* thus had a favorable climate for their operation. In the event, they failed, partly because one of their agents had scruples and deliberately missed several opportunities, partly because of sloppy organization, and partly because Mazarin had warnings.[53] He took the problem to the queen. Within days, on 2 September 1643, Anne ordered Beaufort's arrest in her own salon in the Louvre, in the presence of Madame de Chevreuse, Madame de Hautefort, and others.[54]

Beaufort spent the next five years in the fortress of Vincennes, and his fellow conspirators either fled the country or went into hiding on the estate of his father, the duke of Vendôme. The Vendôme family in fact, as well as the rest of the *Importants*, were sent out of Paris to provincial exile. Madame de Chevreuse had to go also, along with her protégé Châteauneuf. She left the court unwillingly, unable to believe her misfortune and in no way blaming herself. From their surveillance of her, Mazarin and the queen knew that she was continuing her intrigues abroad as well as at home. After a year and a half, the queen therefore ordered her to remove to a royal castle, a threat of confinement that galvanized Madame de Chevreuse into fleeing the kingdom once more.[55] From her refuge in the Spanish Netherlands, she proposed the most daring schemes to Madrid for the defeat of France and the overthrow of Mazarin, until civil war in France brought her back in 1649 like a stormy petrel.

But that was far in the future. Meanwhile, within two weeks of Beaufort's arrest, the regent in the king's name ordered all bishops staying in Paris to take up their legitimate duties and return to their dioceses. The bishop of Beauvais had the distinction of receiving the first invitation to leave.[56] The "Cabal of the Important People" thus came to an end, to the apparent satisfaction of almost everyone except themselves and the devout. Mazarin had apparently been right in advising the queen that Frenchmen only respected boldness; now that he had escaped assassination and the queen had openly committed herself, even the Paris populace jeered at Beaufort on the way to Vincennes. Equally important, in the diplomatic corps the ambassadors of French allies gave a sigh of relief and waited upon Their Majesties with congratulations.

The second day of September 1643 has been noted as a major turning point in Mazarin's career.[57] To be sure, opposition to him did not disappear. The Vendôme family, the remnant of the recent cabal, his enemies in the Parlement and among the bishops, all simply stayed in the background and bided an opportunity. Anne's ladies and retainers went on nagging her, and so did the nuns. None of the deeper problems had been resolved: the rivalry between the house of Condé and Gaston of Orléans, the general tendency to insubordination among the greater nobility, or the chronic dearth and disorder of the public finances. Nevertheless, the queen's actions had given a direction and clarified the line of authority. Above all she and Mazarin had bought time—practically the most important thing for a regency government.

But the second of September also marked a turning point in Anne's own life. She had put behind her the orientation with which she had come to France twenty-eight years earlier, the orientation embodied in the instructions her father had given her upon her marriage. Gone were the assumptions that France was an adjunct of Spain, that whatever was good for Spain was right, and that she in her own person represented the interest of her Spanish family. Anne had emancipated herself from her youth, and there could be no doubt about it—the queen was for France.

She received much abuse for it in her day from adherents of the old ways, and only grudging credit from posterity. Even the most patriotic French historians, fully approving of the course on which Richelieu and Mazarin had set the kingdom, have deprecated Anne's conduct because they considered she acted blindly out of passion for Mazarin and not from rational conviction. Her most sympathetic defender, the nineteenth-century historian Victor Cousin, expressed this reservation very eloquently:

> . . . If Anne of Austria did not love Mazarin, if she had the wit to appreciate him in the sole light of reason, if she sacrificed all her friends to him without any compensating affection, if in 1643 she defended him against the *Importants* and in 1648 and 1649 against the *Fronde* because she had recognized in this foreigner a misunderstood man of genius, the only one able to save the monarchy and to keep France in the place that rightfully belonged to her in Europe: if this constancy, unshaken by the most terrible storms and maintained over a decade did not proceed in her from love, the great motive and the great explanation of female conduct, then we must consider Anne of Austria an extraordinary person, one of the greatest minds, one of the greatest souls ever to occupy a throne, a queen equal or superior to Elizabeth. For our part, after mature reflection, we do not dare to go so far. . . .[58]

If love was indeed the motive and explanation of Anne's conduct, at least she had chosen her object wisely. Without a reserve of prudence, acting merely as an irrational, susceptible female—a female, too, of a certain age—she might as well have fallen in love with Beaufort, who certainly gave himself all the airs of a romantic suitor. But the distinction between motives of heart and mind is apt to be an artificial one. Anne confessed that she loved Mazarin, although she swore to Madame de Brienne that it was a love of the spirit and not of the body.[59] Few contemporaries believed that. Mazarin's apparent hold over her was so much easier to understand if it was sexual. Mazarin was, after all, an attractive man, and she, despite her forty-two years, was still described as a fine figure of a woman: stoutish and with more than a double chin, but a fine figure nonetheless.[60] And there were precedents in the royal family. Louis XIII's sister Christine, the duchess of Savoy, was famous for her lovers, the first of whom in her husband's lifetime reputedly fathered all her children. Louis's other sister, Henrietta Maria of England, at the very least had gentlemen followers to whom she permitted fond if not ultimate liberties.[61] On the nature of

Anne's relationship with Mazarin, however, all must be conjecture because there is no conclusive evidence for or against, either direct or circumstantial.

Much has been inferred from secret correspondence between Anne and Mazarin, although with no really solid foundation. Those letters belong to a later period, however, and will be considered in their place. For the early stages of the relationship, there are no clues except gossip, a good deal if not all of it deliberately planted by the *Importants*, and appearances—and since Anne had a sovereign disregard for such things, appearances proved nothing.

In the latter part of September 1643, Anne fell ill: a slight indisposition caused by her "assiduity in devotions and affairs of state," announced the *Gazette*,[62] jaundice brought on by the vexations she had endured for the past several months, said the courtiers.[63] Rumor had it that it was nothing of the kind, however, and that the queen was pregnant by Mazarin.[64] It could hardly have been true jaundice, for she was recovered by the end of the month, but neither did she turn out to be pregnant. At the relevant time, Mazarin himself set down in his current notebook the cryptic phrase "jaundice from excess of love."[65] Whether he was summarizing the talk against himself, as he sometimes did, or whether he meant to turn a compliment for the queen by telling her that her care for his preservation had caused her illness, is not clear. What is least likely is that he meant the phrase literally, as some historians have taken it.[66]

It was true Mazarin had protested to Anne that he would not stay in France if he came to feel that she was using his services merely out of necessity without liking him personally,[67] but winning the queen did not need to be a matter of outright sexual seduction. There are more subtle ways of attaching a woman.

Nothing in Anne's life suggests that she resembled her sister-in-law Christine of Savoy in sexual appetite. On the other hand, all observers agreed that she liked to flirt and enjoyed receiving male attention. Mazarin certainly gave her that, along with his lessons in statecraft. But he also gave her something she had not experienced since she had taken leave of her father on the Spanish border: he entered into her feelings. The clue we have to this comes from Don Diego de Saavedra's report to Philip IV on the failure of his mission to Anne. In the message the queen had sent him explaining why she could not receive him, she had dwelled on her distress at thus refusing her brother, and added that Mazarin greatly pitied her.[68] At the time Mazarin was sparing no effort to convince her that she must change her loyalties. He listed all the cogent arguments in his notebooks, as we have seen, but the secret of his success evidently lay in his manner of presenting them. Judging by her remark, he neither lectured nor condemned her for loving her family; he gave her to understand that he knew how she felt in the present difficult circumstances. Sympathy of that kind was precisely what had endeared such friends as Madame de Chevreuse to her in the past. Finding it offered now, offered by Mazarin together with the promise of a glorious heritage for her son, it is small wonder that she consented to follow his lead and came to regard him as indispensable.

Their relationship lasted until Mazarin's death in 1661. In many ways its working side remains as enigmatic as its personal aspect—a fact we may regret, for it makes it difficult to estimate Anne's contribution to the task of governing. From passing references in Madame de Motteville's memoirs and in Mazarin's notebooks, we know Anne took part in meetings of the royal council, at least when it sat as a small policy-making group and not in its larger capacity as a clearinghouse for reports and orders.[69] There are no minutes, however, of these policy sessions. Consequently we have no evidence of the queen's voice on such occasions or any way of documenting on a regular basis how she collaborated with Mazarin. As for their daily conferences, from Mazarin's notebooks we can learn only what he planned to say to the queen, not what she replied. She herself did not keep notes. We may infer from the fact, for example, that the members of Richelieu's family kept their posts or from Anne's refusal to see her brother's envoy, that she was convinced by the persuasions Mazarin had outlined in his notebooks. Judging by six of her surviving twelve letters to the cardinal, all dating from a later period, this became the established pattern of their collaboration: he proposed and she followed. Thus when Mazarin was away on campaign alone or with young Louis XIV, she forwarded messages and political correspondence to her minister,[70] asked for instructions,[71] and sometimes gave her impressions or opinion of the matter in hand.[72] When it happened that in Mazarin's absence she had taken an action of which he disapproved, she humbly apologized;

> Your letter of the 24th which I have received has given me much pain, because 15 [the queen] did something you had not wished. But you may be assured that it was not done with any intention of displeasing you. . . . and 15 will have no rest until he knows that 16 [Mazarin] does not think badly of what he has done.[73]

In this instance the difference between Anne and Mazarin concerned mercy: Anne had pardoned four former rebels, and Mazarin thought they should have been left in exile a while longer.[74] From one case, however, we cannot deduce that the queen always took the more merciful part in political decisions. In short, we know too little about Anne's collaboration with her minister to make informed judgments concerning her role in detail.

In general, the way Mazarin worked with Anne may be characterized in the same terms that have been used to describe the methods of Richelieu with her late husband and of Olivares with her brother: "Both ministers developed . . . a tutorial relationship to royal masters who were also royal pupils."[75] Unlike Louis XIII and Philip IV, however, who on occasion made their will felt and gave their ministers difficulties, Anne seems to have been consistent in her deference to Mazarin's political acumen. As they had begun in the summer of 1643, so they continued—Mazarin supplying the expertise while Anne supported him with her authority.

Chapter Thirteen

Comforts and Cares of State

HAVING WEATHERED HER first crisis as regent and made plain her intention to uphold Mazarin and all that he represented, Anne settled in to enjoy her new life and make herself comfortable. She had the means to do so now that the opportunity had come to repair her finances. The annuity from her dowry and the revenues of her marriage settlement were converted into a widow's portion, and exchanges were made for income that had been mortgaged.

The income was sizable, concentrated mostly in central France and Brittany, including the duchy and domains of Bourbonnais, the counties of Forêt, Haute and Basse-Marche, the duchy and county of Auvergne, the barony of La Tour, the county of Dourdan, the domains of La Fère, the forest of Saint-Gobin; Marle, Han, and Calais; and the counties of Nantes and Rennes and the barony of Fougères—the latter three domains in Brittany that formerly had been assigned to Marie de Medici.[1] In principle, the income from the widow's portion equaled the previous revenues from Anne's dowry and marriage settlement: one hundred seventy-nine thousand three hundred seventy-five *livres tournois* per annum. In the absence of accounts, we do not know how much of those previous revenues actually reached the queen or had been mortgaged, so that the new settlement may have represented a gain. In 1646, however, Anne acquired an additional source of income when, on the advice of Mazarin, she kept the office of "Chief Grand-Master and General Superintendent of the Navigation and Commerce of France" instead of bestowing this great office on a member of Condé's family upon the death of the incumbent, the duke of Brézé.[2] The admiralty, as we may call it for short, was very lucrative indeed; for among other things, it gave her shares in all prize money obtained from the sale of ships and cargoes seized on the high seas.

Last but not least, Anne received compensation for the crown jewels that had been in her possession, which at the death of Louis XIII went to the new king.[3] The jewels in question were the diamonds set into the portrait bracelet that Louis XIII had sent to her in Madrid, and the precious stones in the pieces of jewelry Louis had given her under the provisions of their marriage contract. The young king verified the inventory in 1644 and ordered that this mother be paid the appraised value of the gems. All the jewelry that she had brought from Spain, however, including the great pieces that had been a formal part of her dowry, remained her exclusive property, like the jewelry she had bought herself or received from her husband during their marriage. In fact not much was left of the elaborate Spanish neck chains, girdle chains, and other ornaments; the rubies, diamonds, pearls had for the most part been taken out of their settings. Evidently Anne was not sentimental about old jewelry even though it had come from Spain, and did not mind having it reworked in accordance with more modern fashion. And now that she was free to please herself, she brought her living quarters up to date as well.

In October 1643 Anne moved herself and her children from the Louvre to Richelieu's palace, which had become crown property when Richelieu left it to Louis XIII.[4] At the time the Louvre was not a very comfortable habitation. Louis XIII had left construction on the northern and eastern wings uncompleted, so that the central court looked like a builder's yard.[5] The royal apartments themselves, in the southwest and south wings, had not been redecorated since Anne came to France and were sadly in need of renovation. By contrast, Richelieu's palace was modern, although that was probably not its only attraction for Anne. If she had left the Louvre merely because she disliked living on a construction site and wanted fresh, comfortable apartments, she would hardly have embarked on the course of remodeling and decoration that inconvenienced her life in Richelieu's palace for some years. But the Louvre can have held few pleasant memories for her, and it must have given her profound satisfaction to occupy the ground once held by her former enemy. Significantly, the palace changed names almost immediately. It had been known as the Palais-Cardinal, and the inscription over the entrance said as much. Now everyone called it the Palais-Royal, and the inscription disappeared. Richelieu's heirs brought suit, successfully, to have the inscription restored in accordance with the terms of his will, but in common usage the name "Palais-Royal" was there to stay.[6]

Anne installed the king in Richelieu's former quarters in the left wing of the palace and herself in a suite of rooms in the right wing, just behind Richelieu's theater—a very convenient location for someone who loved to attend plays as much as she did.[7] Her younger son, the little duke of Anjou, received rooms beyond hers on the righthand side; and Mazarin, after some months, was assigned quarters near the king. The latter decision raised many eyebrows, for the king's apartment and her own were linked by a long gallery to which Mazarin naturally had access. In her usual fashion, Anne ignored the gossip, resting her case on the explanation she gave the royal council: it was more convenient and, in view of recent attempts on Mazarin's life, safer to have him reside in the palace rather than walk the long way from his house beyond the palace gardens every time he had something to say to her.[8]

The gallery in any case was a public, not a private, space. Its windows faced the garden and gave onto a balcony protected by an arcade that Anne was having constructed so that she could walk in fresh air when the weather was bad. The gallery itself provoked much admiration once it was refurbished to the queen's taste. Its walls were paneled with wainscoting and hung with pictures; the ceiling was decorated by the court painter Simon Vouet and ornamented with crystal chandeliers, and underfoot the famous cabinetmaker Jean Macé created a floor inlaid with precious woods in a pattern of roses and fleurs-de-lys outlined with pewter threads.[9] Nothing of all this splendor has survived, nor have the queen's apartments. We do not know the exact number of rooms or their layout, although they included a smaller gallery, a great cabinet or drawing room, a bedchamber, a boudoir, an oratory, and a small cabinet hung in gray that she used as a mourning chamber to receive condolence calls from ambassadors and delegations.

According to contemporary descriptions, and several contracts for work to be done,[10] the rooms were paneled in the traditional way, with wainscoting about halfway up the walls, leaving the upper part of the wall free for tapestries or other hangings according to the season. All the other woodwork, including the window frames, was gilded, as were the stucco ornaments on the ceilings and cornices, the preferred shades being brown gold and matte gold, shades that remained fashionable for the rest of the century. At least some of the ceilings, as well as some wall panels, were painted. Although Simon Vouet did not do all the work, he got the major share of it. Thus for the queen's bedchamber, he painted Providence surrounded by numbers of children as the ceiling picture, and Prudence reducing the world to obedience for a panel above the mantelpiece. Elsewhere in the paneling, he painted small landscapes; and for the oval panels above the three doors, he was given a choice of subject: either the actions of illustrious women, or figures that would accord with the central theme of Prudence. Unfortunately we do not know which he chose. For the queen's small gallery, Vouet provided paintings depicting the three powers of the soul: Will, Intellect, and Memory, with smaller panels on related subjects. For the boudoir Vouet and others painted landscapes and children playing amid foliage, and for the oratory, their theme was the life and attributes of the Virgin.

Anne may have taken advice in choosing the subjects; Mazarin, for one, was a notable connoisseur and may well have contributed some ideas. Whoever their originator, themes such as Providence, Prudence, and the powers of the soul expressed the message that the queen-regent took her duties seriously and was equal to the tasks laid upon her. By 1646 most of the work on the queen's apartments had been completed, and they became famous for their elegance and beauty—a suitable frame for Anne in which to preside over her government and court and enjoy the company of relatives and friends.

It is true the royal family circle was rather limited. Gaston of Orléans came to the palace frequently for council meetings and conferences, but otherwise he had his own interests and his own set of intimates. Nor was Madame, his wife, an addition to the queen's circle. During one of his periods of self-imposed exile, Gaston had married a sister of the duke of Lorraine, against Louis XIII's wishes and without the king's permission. Although on his deathbed Louis XIII at last recognized the marriage, Madame was not permitted to enter France until after the king's death. She received a warm enough welcome, but no sooner had she settled into the Orléans residence in the Luxembourg palace than she developed what seems to have been agoraphobia.[11] She hardly ever left the palace and only very rarely managed to pay even a ceremonial visit to the queen. Instead the queen visited her when Madame was ailing or in childbed.

It was different with Gaston's daughter from his first marriage, Mademoiselle. Mademoiselle spent even more time with Anne than she had in the days of Saint-Germain when she was the king's and queen's little pet. She visited Anne daily, played with the young king and his brother, and took part in all the diversions that were organized.[12] Mademoiselle was not particularly close to her stepmother, and Madame for her part was preoccupied with an increasing brood of daughters of her own. It was Anne, as surrogate mother, who insisted on seeing Mademoiselle before she went off to balls, in order to inspect her dress and her hairdo, and make adjustments if necessary. On one especially glamorous occasion, she personally decked out the girl in all the diamonds belonging to the crown. For years too Mademoi-

selle accompanied the queen on her steady round of visits to churches
and convents until, in a brief access of enthusiasm, she announced a
desire to become a Carmelite nun—a notion that so outraged her
father that he told her he would ask the queen to stop taking her to
convents, where pious ladies were obviously turning her head.[13]

No doubt Mademoiselle clung to her aunt during the early years of
the regency, and Anne, for her part, reciprocated with an easy fondness. But it was a sweet-sour relationship at best and one that did not
improve over time. Mademoiselle never got over the shock of being
displaced in the queen's attention by the birth of young Louis. She
complained that the queen neither appreciated her attendance sufficiently nor took her into her confidence.[14] Recalling in her memoirs
the queen's kindness to her before the birth of Louis, Mademoiselle
accounted for it as a mere by-product of the queen's currently good
relations with Gaston.[15] Once she grew up, she added a fresh grievance: it seemed to her that the queen and Mazarin were not trying
sincerely to arrange an appropriate marriage for her.[16]

True, it was not easy to find suitable candidates for Mademoiselle's
hand. As the sole heiress of the ducal house of Montpensier, she was
the richest woman in France, not excepting even the queen. It was
unthinkable to let so much wealth and power fall into the hands of any
French noble family. Besides, since Mademoiselle was, if not a daughter of France, at least a niece of France, everyone agreed she had to
marry royally. Mademoiselle herself had secretly set her heart on marrying the young king. While the queen was pregnant with him, she
used to tell Mademoiselle, "You shall be my daughter-in-law"; and
when Mademoiselle visited the baby, she called him "my little husband," until Richelieu heard of it and took her to task severely for
loose talk unbecoming to a young lady of eleven.[17] But the idea had
taken root, and it chagrined Mademoiselle that in later years the queen
no longer seemed to favor it, that in fact the queen dreamed of marrying Louis to his cousin and her niece the Infanta Maria Teresa of Spain,
once peace should have been made between the kingdoms. Meanwhile, other marriage projects for Mademoiselle came to nothing—
with the widowed emperor, for instance, or the prince of Wales, soon
to be Charles II in exile.

Mademoiselle's tongue grew sharp with resentment. On one particularly dramatic occasion, the queen and Mazarin were interrogating
Mademoiselle concerning an alleged plot by one of her servants to
arrange a marriage between her and Archduke Leopold, the governor

of the Spanish Netherlands. This would have been a very serious matter if true, necessarily entailing secret understandings betwen Gaston of Orléans and the Spanish enemy. Mademoiselle denied any knowledge of such a plan, saying that her servant must be mad but that she herself was not. She may well have been telling the truth. To make certain of it, however, Anne tried to draw her out by appealing to her sense of loyalty to the servant: "What a pretty thing—here is a person who is attached to your service and by way of reward, you put his head on the scaffold!" Mademoiselle recalled all she had heard about the conspiracies in which Gaston and Anne had been involved in their time, and the executions that had resulted, and replied, "At least he will be the first."[18] Anne turned cool toward her niece after that.

Mademoiselle intermittently continued her verbal skirmishes until four years later, in 1652, she sided with her father against the king and queen in civil war. Meanwhile, however, she still appeared prominently at court events and fulfilled various representational duties because she was in effect the second-ranking woman in France since her stepmother, Madame, would not or could not appear in public.

The royal family circle enlarged somewhat with the arrival of Queen Henrietta Maria as a refugee from England in 1644.[19] Henrietta Maria brought her younger daughter, Henrietta, with her, and her sons Charles and James joined her at least periodically. That led to reciprocal rounds of ceremonial visits, not only in greeting, but subsequently on holidays, occasions when the king and queen departed or returned from a journey, or when anyone was ailing. For the rest of the time, however, Anne did not see much of Henrietta Maria. The little English court in exile was established at Saint-Germain, and therfore at some distance from Paris; and even Henrietta Maria's devotional visits to convents did not coincide with Anne's because the sisters-in-law patronized different religious orders. In short, the extended royal family provided occasional companions of suitable rank for the queen but not much intimacy or friendship.

Anne does not seem to have suffered under this lack, even though at the same time her ties to her Spanish family were growing more and more tenuous. Death made inroads there: in 1644 Anne's sister-in-law the queen of Spain died, to be followed by Anne's sole surviving sister, the empress, in 1646. Later that year the Spanish crown prince, Philip IV's only son, died as well. Anne showed a normal amount of distress, nothing out of the ordinary. Because France was at war with Spain and the empire, the court did not go into mourning on these occasions.

On the other hand, the queen of Spain had also been a daughter of France, so that for her memorial services were ordered at Notre-Dame cathedral with Mademoiselle delegated to attend as chief mourner. Whatever sentiment Anne still had for her brother Philip IV, and whatever hope she cherished of marrying Louis to her niece the Spanish infanta, her feelings apparently did not cause her the anguish they once had, and she certainly made no effort to communicate privately with Spain.[20] After all, the people who were really emotionally essential to her she had close at hand: Louis, Mazarin, and little Philippe of Anjou, in that order.

Nor did Anne lack congenial company for her daily activities[21]—the dowager princess of Condé was a frequent caller and accompanied the queen on many of her visits to churches and convents. Anne also enjoyed the society of the princess of Carignan-Savoy, wife of Prince Thomas of Carignan-Savoy, and of the princess Palatine, Anne of Gonzaga-Nevers, who had married the son of Frederick, the winter king of Bohemia. They were both lively and amusing ladies, even if not particularly devout. Mazarin's nieces were going to provide an addition to that circle; but the first of them did not land in France until 1647, and Mazarin did not produce them at court until they had been schooled for some years in French ways. Meanwhile the queen also kept her old set of friends and retainers, most notably the devout Madame de Brienne; Guitaut, captain of the queen's guard; La Porte, her former cloak-bearer who became the king's first valet as soon as Louis received his own household; Madame de Hautefort and Madame de Motteville, to mention only the most prominent. Whatever the degree of Anne's affection and loyalty, however, all these people occupied a very secondary place in her life—a fact to which a number of them found it difficult to resign themselves.

Madame de Chevreuse was not the only one to be jealous of Mazarin's influence with the queen. To be sure, Madame de Chevreuse had political power at stake more than personal feelings, whereas Anne's humbler friends were not that ambitious. They had their various reasons for disliking, or disapproving of, Mazarin; but one and all they resented it that she relied on Mazarin rather than on them for support and guidance. Material interest played a part too, for under Mazarin's tutelage the queen did not grant favors nearly as easily as some of them had hoped she would, and they resented it when she referred them to Mazarin for patronage.[22] Self-interest was not a problem for the most troublesome of Anne's friends, however: Marie de Hautefort quite simply disliked, and disapproved of, Mazarin and everything he represented. Mazarin's efforts to win her over met with no success. This would not have mattered had she been discreet, but she refused to compromise with what she regarded as evil and missed no opportunity to admonish the queen and make disobliging remarks about Mazarin.[23] Her nagging put the queen in a painful position. Anne was very fond of Marie de Hautefort, besides being grateful for her past loyalty. The young king and his brother for their part adored Marie, Louis going so far as to call her his mistress.[24] She was very good with children and exceedingly kind to persons in need or otherwise dependent on her, but with her equals and superiors, she felt free to speak her mind for their own good. Louis XIII had used to complain of her sarcastic tongue, and now Anne was finding out its inconveniences.

Anne went to the trouble of explaining at length to Marie her reasons for having chosen Mazarin: he was capable; because he was a foreigner, he had no factions in France and no interest except the interest of the crown; he could best support her against Gaston of Orléans on the one hand and the prince of Condé on the other because he was not tied to either man.[25] It was no use. Far from being convinced, Madame de Hautefort let herself be drafted as the spokeswoman for the clique of devout who were trying to bring Anne to dismiss Mazarin for the sake of her reputation and conscience.[26] For them it was matter of political alignment, notably, support for the "important people" and Châteauneuf. For Madame de Hautefort, it was simply a question of saving a friend, the queen, from moral ruin. Anne grew very tired of constant criticism from her lady-in-waiting. A first quarrel in August 1643 was patched up with tears and promises of amendment from Marie de Hautefort and forgiveness by the queen.[27] Marie found it impossible to curb her tongue, however, especially after the arrest of the duke of Beaufort and the other "important people," for she refused to believe that there was any truth in the charges that Beaufort and his friends had wanted to assassinate Mazarin. Mazarin was fearful in any case of the effect that pressure from the devout might have on the queen, and he thought it important to discredit Madame de Hautefort with Anne. From informants he had detailed reports on Madame de Hautefort's conversations in convents, and he made sure the queen came to hear whatever remarks were made about her.[28]

It was one thing to suffer criticism in private, but quite another for the queen to know that her friend was discussing her conduct in public. Marie herself made things worse when in the spring of 1644 she took advantage of a court outing to the park of Vincennes to remind the queen that Beaufort was imprisoned in that castle and to ask whether he could not hope for grace. Then she went on to spoil the picnic altogether by declaring that the thought of that "poor boy" languishing in his nearby cell had quite taken away her appetite and that if she ate, it would seem to her as though she were depriving him of his food.[29] For the time being, Anne held in her anger. Shortly thereafter, however, on an evening in mid-April, Marie de Hautefort begged a favor for an old manservant and, finding the queen unresponsive, told her with a disdainful smile that it was not good to forget old servants. The queen promptly replied that now she had had enough of her reprimands, and although Marie de Hautefort tearfully protested her good intentions, next day she received orders to leave the court.[30] She retired to a convent for a time to collect herself, then took up a private residence, and two years later married a distinguished general, Marshall Schomberg. As it happened, Schomberg was a trusted supporter of Mazarin, so that both the minister and the queen were pleased with Marie's choice. Anne graciously received her for a farewell visit on the eve of her marriage.[31]

Among Marie's friends, two or three remained irreconcilable and left court, but the others made their peace with Mazarin in one way or another and stayed. Even La Porte, who was so devoted to Marie de Hautefort that, in Mazarin's own words, "he would have cut his veins for her,"[32] stuck to his job for almost a decade until he went too far in his surreptitious attacks on Mazarin and was dismissed. As for Madame de Motteville, she decided that subjects must accept the will of their princes and temper criticism with discretion.[33] She adored the queen, and it has been convincingly suggested that her feelings of admiration for the queen's beautiful eyes and other attractions somewhat exceeded what was normal.[34] The queen did not reciprocate this infatuation; when Madame de Motteville told her she was keeping notes for an eventual biography of her, Anne replied that Madame de Motteville was very silly to want to waste her time that way, but if she insisted on doing it, she should at least not let friendship blind her to the queen's faults.[35] *The Memoirs for the History of Anne of Austria* indeed became Madame de Motteville's life work, and we owe to them many details about the queen that we would not otherwise know. But Madame de Motteville revenged herself on Mazarin for having preempted such a large share of her mistress's affections: she either damned him with faint praise or imputed base motives to him without reason, thus contributing not a little to the low character French historians gave him for a long time.

With the death of Count de Brassac in 1644, the way was clear for Mazarin to become superintendent of Anne's household and head of her household council. Now at last he had what he had asked for originally: a secure place in the queen's establishment from which he could counteract any effort by her daily associates to undermine his influence. The chief troublemakers were already gone or leaving shortly, although as household purges went, this one was mild compared with the inroads Louis XIII and Richelieu had used to make among Anne's attendants. Mazarin believed it was dangerous to drive people to despair and liked to build bridges of reconciliation whenever possible.[36] The queen for her part was long-suffering and also a bit disinclined to give herself trouble and unpleasantness. Above all, she was loyal to persons who had any share in her affections—a quality whose benefits Mazarin himself was to feel in time. Without strong provocation, therefore, no one stood in danger of losing his or her post. Anne settled down cheerfully with those who were left and proceeded to enjoy her widowhood.

As soon as the first year of deep mourning was over, she took the king on a holiday to Richelieu's country palace at Rueil on the invitation of Richelieu's niece. Mazarin accompanied them, and there was the usual gossip over the proximity of his quarters to hers.[37] Living space was indeed cramped for such a retinue of royalty and retainers; but although there was talk of removing to Saint-Germain, where they would all have been more comfortable, the queen preferred to remain at Rueil for several weeks. Except for an occasional brief visit to Henrietta Maria, Anne in fact did not set foot in Saint-Germain until civil disorders in Paris in the winter of 1648–49 made withdrawal to that castle strategically wise. Clearly Anne was not eager to relive her years of boredom there. No such prejudice attached to Fontainebleau, which from now on became the court's regular refuge from city heat in late summer and early fall. She loved the park and gardens there and eventually had her apartments fitted up as elegantly as those in the Palais-Royal. On hot days the court spent most of its time in the forest or bathing in the Seine, where modesty was preserved by the voluminous gray linen shirts everyone wore, from the queen and her ladies to the king's officers and attendants.[38] For the young people, there were tennis games and hunting parties and impromptu ballets, not to mention the more general pleasures of dinners, balls, concerts, and French and Italian plays. Visitors came too, Gaston of Orléans, for example, and the prince of Wales, as well as other foreign royalty and ambassadors.

Nor was life dull either when the court returned to Paris in the fall. Anne was passionately fond of the theater, and had performances put on as often as possible. She did not give up this pastime even during her year of mourning, although she would sit hidden behind her ladies for the sake of decency.[39] Conservative pious souls disapproved of such activities; the Louvre's parish priest, the curé of Saint-Germain de l'Auxerrois, went so far as to make an issue of it, protesting that the queen was setting a bad example by patronizing actors and acting within the very precincts of the royal palace. Far from giving in, Anne had the theological faculty of the Sorbonne canvassed, where a number of experts pronounced that there was no harm in watching decent plays.[40] Her spiritual adviser, Vincent de Paul, had no better luck when he tried to wean her away from her addiction to the theater.[41] There is no doubt that the plays she saw were indeed decent. Newspaper reports generally specified only that the queen and court had seen the French comedy or the Italian comedy. We know from the history of the French theater, however, what the repertory was likely to have been: pastoral romances and melodrama, aside from the new classical tragedies that Corneille was producing.[42]

Mazarin added to the queen's pleasure by recruiting Italian actors and singers for her and importing Italian productions, such as the pastoral play *Micandro and Fileno* and Julio Strozzi's *La Finta Pazza* in 1645.[43] Strozzi's piece, which combined spoken verse and music, had great success not only at court but with the public, less for the content than for the elaborate scenery and sophisticated stage machinery that surpassed anything that had previously been seen in France. Encouraged by this reception, Mazarin two years later imported the first real opera—a project he had cherished but dared not realize for years. It was Rossi's *Orpheus,* described as a tragicomedy in music in three acts.[44] It had been adapted for French production with the addition of a prologue showing a great battle won by the French, whereupon Victory descended from the skies and praised the king's arms and the queen's wise conduct of state affairs. Then followed the story of Orpheus and Eurydice, interspersed for the young king's especial delight with numerous comic interludes and ballets of animals.

This was all very well received, but what evoked the most admiration were the marvelous scene changes and stage machinery. The king and queen saw the opera a number of times in the spring of 1647, and thereafter the king had the stage machinery transported to Fontaine-bleau, where he had its operations demonstrated for the benefit of visiting dignitaries.[45]

Aside from these highlights, there were the amusements of the car-nival season, which was once again celebrated at court beginning in 1645 when the king gave a family dinner for the queen, his brother, his aunt Henrietta Maria, his uncle Gaston, and Mademoiselle, with an Italian play and a court ballet to follow. Also he gave a ball, at which he led out Mademoiselle.[46] The entertainments became more elaborate as the king grew older and himself took part in the court ballets; and they were not all confined to the carnival season, for visits from for-eign princes and ambassadors gave occasion to hold festivities de-signed for impressive display. The queen herself no longer danced, just as she no longer wore rouge, but she liked to see other people enjoying themselves.[47]

Plays and parties were only one side of Anne's life, however; she spent far more time on her devotions than on amusements. Aside from the daily mass she heard in her own oratory and the hours she spent in prayer there, her round of visits to churches grew more exten-sive as the years went by. There were holidays and saint's days when she attended as many as three churches, going to each for a different service.[48] Since the king's music was often sent to these churches to play or sing for her benefit, her churchgoing had its pleasurable as-pects. Her visits to convents continued also, most regularly and most often to Val-de-Grâce. Not to mention brief visits for services or ser-mons, she retreated to Val-de-Grâce on the vigil of major holidays such as Christmas, Easter, Pentecost, as well as for the anniversary day of the death of Louis XIII. Mazarin thought she was overdoing her devotions; in fact, he professed to believe that the devout were delib-erately keeping her occupied in that way so that she would have less time to work with him.[49] He did know for certain that the pressure on the queen's conscience to dismiss him was continuing, notably at Val-de-Grâce.[50] He therefore used every argument possible to detach her somewhat from her pious habits, pointing out to her, for instance, that France was not Spain, and that Frenchmen did not appreciate seeing their monarchs spending their time in churches and convents.[51] In fact, he added, people were beginning to make fun of her obsessive piety: "God is everywhere, and the queen can pray to Him in her own private oratory," he concluded.[52] He tried to appeal to her love for her son and her sense of duty:

> It is very important that the public be convinced that her principal aim is the welfare of the king and the state; and in that she will obey the will of God who has given her the government of this kingdom and of the king's education. That is the duty she must above all strive to fulfill, and she should persuade herself that every moment she gives to this supreme task is more pleasing to God than whole hours of prayers, visits to churches, sermons and vespers.[53]

Mazarin's concern about the impression her devotions were making on the public may have been genuine, although no contemporary criticism of her religious practices has come down to us. At any rate, the editor of the semiofficial *Gazette* was induced to reassure his readers that her religious observances did not prevent the queen from attending to the king's upbringing and caring for matters of state.[54] As far as the queen was concerned, it was all wasted breath. She may have accepted Mazarin's guidance in every other domain, but when it came to her religion, she went her own way with unshakable persistence. The *Gazette* finally made a virtue of necessity and credited her piety with securing the blessings of heaven for the kingdom.[55] Least of all did Anne curtail her visits to Val-de-Grâce. She felt herself cherished and protected there, away from the press of business, and she invested heavily to preserve and enlarge this part of her life.

Before Louis was born, Anne had vowed to build a church if she were given a son. Now she fulfilled that vow by building a new church and convent for Val-de-Grâce.[56] The church was dedicated to the Nativity, or literally "to Jesus being born to the Virgin Mother"; and when it was completed, it stood as the visual expression of Anne's passionate gratitude for desperate prayers answered. The chief architects were, in succession, Mansart and Le Mercier, who designed an elegant building in a somewhat restrained Roman baroque style. The dome was a smaller version of Saint Peter's, topping an edifice that was more square than rectangular because convent churches, not having large congregations, did not require a long nave. The interior decorations of the church celebrate the Nativity, from the bas-reliefs of Saints Anne and Joachim, Elizabeth and Zacharias, and Joseph and Mary in the vault of the short nave to the sculpture of the Holy Family with the Child in the manger over the altar. Cherubs range joyously over entablatures and cornices, and on the ceiling of the central dome, God the

Father sits enthroned and surrounded by the Son, the Holy Ghost, the Virgin, and the host of angels, and accepts the model of the church presented by Anne of Austria herself through the mediation of Saint Louis and with the support of Saint Anne. Over the whole structure, inside and outside, the initials "A and L" are intertwined, and there can be little doubt the "L" stood for Louis XIV and not Louis XIII.

It took two generations for all this work to be completed. On 1 April 1645 Louis XIV, then in his seventh year, laid the cornerstone; but the church as a whole was not consecrated until 1710—long after Anne's death. The first mass was said in 1665, however, in the chapel of Saint-Anne, with the queen mother present. There were lengthy interruptions in the building process as money ran out. We do not know the total cost of the church, but the accounts for the first four years of construction show that more than three-quarters of a million *livres tournois* were spent during that short time alone—enough to pay the ordinary salaries of the queen's household officers for six or seven years.[57] Most of it went into the foundations, which proved unexpectedly troublesome because, when digging began, three courses of ancient catacombs were discovered that had to be filled in. It was because of arguments about cost overruns and proposed economies that Mansart abandoned the work and was replaced by LeMercier.

The rebuilding of the convent itself, which Anne also undertook, went much faster. By 1647 her little apartment in the convent was so far advanced that the carpenters and cabinetmakers could go to work.[58] The suite was expansive, including a large cabinet, a smaller cabinet or dining room, a dressing room and a bedchamber. The only concession to monastic austerity was the absence of gilding on paneling and woodwork, although at least one ceiling, the one in the bedchamber, had pictures painted on it.[59] This was Anne's refuge from court life, where she could enjoy the company of a few chosen attendants and friends, converse with her favorite nuns, and also attend religious services. As a private retreat and a source of profound pleasure, Val-de-Grâce undoubtedly meant as much or more to Anne as the hunting lodge of Versailles had meant to Louis XIII. Perhaps it even reminded her of her grandfather Philip II's apartment in the Escorial, surrounded as that was by the great grid of the monastery of Saint Lawrence.

Anne's devotion had limits, however. Not even the nuns of Val-de-Grâce could induce her to abandon Mazarin, and in other ways too it became apparent that she was unwilling to subordinate politics to religion. Even Vincent de Paul found that out. Anne had contributed to

Father Vincent's charitable projects for years, and seeing her so well disposed, Father Vincent hoped to involve her more directly. In 1617 he had organized the first Company of Servants of the Poor, or Ladies of Charity. Since then such Charities, as they were called for short, had been formed in many provincial centers as well as in Paris. Father Vincent dreamed of establishing a Charity at court, as a directorate for the Ladies of Charity in Paris. He drafted statutes for it: Anne would preside, and the court ladies would be deputed in groups of three to superintend the various enterprises of the parish Charities.[60] Ladies of Charity devoted their own persons to their work. In Paris they provided the patients at the Hôtel-Dieu, the public hospital, with spiritual instruction and clean bed linen; they maintained a foundling home, operated soup kitchens, visited prisoners, and raised important sums for relief and rehabilitation in war-devastated border provinces. If a court Charity had come into being, Anne's ladies would have been kept very busy supervising and coordinating all these activities; and Anne herself would have had to contribute a good deal of personal exertion to administrative meetings as well as visits of inspection. Perhaps Mazarin had this project in mind when he claimed the devout were trying to preempt Anne's time. In the event, Father Vincent's dream of a godly and useful court came to nothing, whether because the queen pleaded Mazarin's admonitions to concentrate on her main duty, or whether she found it too distasteful to change her daily routine in order to accommodate Father Vincent's project.

In more serious matters, Anne stood out against Father Vincent also. When she had taken him as her spiritual director after she became regent, she had also named him to the council of conscience: a group of eminent clergy who met weekly or biweekly to advise the crown on the fitness of candidates for ecclesiastical posts that were subject to royal nomination. These benefices included the bishoprics and many of the abbeys in the kingdom, as well as numerous lesser dignities. The man immediately in charge of their distribution was Mazarin, whom Louis XIII had designated before his death as most suitable for the work. Mazarin kept that responsibility even though many of Louis's other arrangements were altered. He used his powers of patronage to consolidate his position, rewarding friends and keeping opponents hungry.[61] He did not necessarily do this in every case, but sufficiently often to distress the devout, who held that religious considerations should be his paramount guide. For Catholic reformers, of course, the nomination of spiritually committed candidates was a major goal, since on it depended the inner renewal of the church.

Judging by the surviving minutes, the council of conscience was not much of an obstacle to Mazarin since it ratified every nomination before it.[62] Appearances are misleading, however, for the minutes did not record preceding arguments. Vincent de Paul for his part refused to accommodate himself to political calculations. Time and again he protested one or another of Mazarin's nominations. On these occasions the queen backed Mazarin. At least once Father Vincent barely skirted disgrace when the queen heard that Mazarin was in very bad temper because Father Vincent's conscience did not agree with his own.[63] Anne took ecclesiastical patronage very seriously and made her own inquiries about candidates, notably candidates for a bishopric, whom Mazarin presented, but she upheld Mazarin's authority against all challengers.[64] His authority was, after all, the authority of the crown, her son's crown; and there is no question that in her heart, her son's interests came first.

It is significant that in Anne's new church at Val-de-Grâce the inscription facing the altar was to read: "He who created me has dwelled in my tabernacle." Those words were, of course, attributed to the Virgin, but their choice can be taken to mean that Anne felt the birth of her elder son had given her life.

Chapter Fourteen

The King Monsieur My Son

ANNE SPENT MUCH TIME WITH both her sons, and all observers agreed that they were more attached to her than princes usually were to their parents.[1] It was also noted that whereas she loved her younger son Philippe naturally as a mother does, she idolized Louis.[2] True, the distinction she made between her sons arose to some extent from the special dignities and ceremonials surrounding a reigning king. Even a king's mother was one of his subjects, although the first. She always rose when he entered her presence and in public never referred to him otherwise than as "the king, Monsieur my son." Such was the custom, but she gladly went beyond custom to underline Louis's miraculous birth and to emphasize his particular relationship to the Deity.

The most striking example of this occurred when Louis was confirmed and made his First Communion in 1649. Louis and his brother were confirmed together on 8 December in the chapel of the Palais Royal, Gaston of Orléans and Mademoiselle standing sponsor for the king, and the prince of Condé and his mother the dowager princess doing the same for Anjou.[3] The next step was First Communion, which newly confirmed children customarily received at Easter. For Louis, however, Anne made unique arrangements by special privilege. Louis received his First Communion on Christmas Day in his parish church of Saint-Eustache.[4] Since the full congregation was present, this was a public occasion, deliberately chosen for maximum edification at the sight of the young king taking the sacrament on the birthday of the Christ Child, who was the King of Heaven. Indeed, all of Paris had been associated with the event: in the days preceding, by order of the archbishop, every church in the city held a prayer vigil of forty hours, with the Sacrament exposed on the altar, in order to implore divine aid for the step the king was about to take. On the day itself, Louis stood alone without a rival; Anjou had to wait for his First Communion until Easter Sunday like other children. It was true that in 1649, in the midst of civil unrest, it was politically desirable to emphasize the monarchy's divine connection. Anne's chief concession to that consideration, however, seems to have been her decision to have Louis take his First Communion in Saint-Eustache rather than in the private chapel of the Palais-Royal.[5] The choice of Christmas for the ceremony on the other hand expressed her personal feelings about her son.

La Porte, Anne's former cloak-bearer, now the king's first valet, told her she was spoiling the boy. Louis liked to spend more time in the queen's apartment than in his own, so La Porte claimed, because his own people did not let him get away with any mischief whereas in his mother's rooms he met nothing but petting and praise.[6] Whether La Porte was right or wrong in his assessment, Louis certainly knew his mother well. If he wanted to cajole her into letting him have his way, he offered to contribute to her favorite charities when he should come into money.[7] That tactic did not always work, however, which leads us to conclude that the queen was not blindly indulgent. What she did do was to enter into his interests and amusements.

Although he was quiet and reserved in the company of people whom he did not know well, Louis could be very lively in his own familiar circle and much preferred physical exercise to sedentary activities. He became passionately fond of hunting as soon as he was introduced to it, but even earlier, and with his mother's encouragement, he had shown fascination for another kingly occupation—military exercises. He loved to beat on drums as soon as he was able to hold the drumsticks, and when he was five years old, he began to play "soldier" with a little troop of children of honor gathered around him, sons of good families somewhat older than himself.[8] The queen delegrated one of her chamberwomen, a Madame de Lasalle, to drill the company, which she did in exemplary fashion, a great ruff around her neck, a black plumed hat on her head, pike in hand and sword at her side. For safety's sake, Louis was not allowed to handle firearms until he was past the age of seven, but thereafter he enjoyed target practice with his companions in the gardens of the Palais-Royal. When he reached his teens, a miniature fort was constructed for him in those same gardens; and then Louis and his troop played defense and assault with real gunpowder, to the admiration of the court.[9] His favorite toys were military also. Pride of place went to a complete army—including infantry, cavalry, and artillery—created for him in silver by a goldsmith from Nancy.[10] That became an heirloom, passed on to his own son. For a sampling of Louis's less-exalted toys, we are indebted to the memoirs of one of his companions, son of Secretary of State Brienne, who recorded the little gifts he used to present to the king by way of paying court: some were educational, such as card games with pictures of geography, heraldry and history, but most were military—small swords, pistols, muskets, and miniature cannons, including a golden one drawn by a flea.[11]

Of course, all this military play had a serious purpose. A king was expected to be a commander-in-chief and could hardly win the respect of his noble generals, not to mention his soldiers, if he showed himself incompetent in that regard. It was as well for Louis that he enjoyed this aspect of his work. Before he was six years old, he was reviewing his guards regiments, escorted by his uncle Gaston, lord-lieutenant of the kingdom, the prince of Condé, Mazarin, and all the noblemen of the court.[12] Two years later, in 1646, Louis went on his first campaign, reportedly to encourage his troops.[13] The war front chosen was the closest to Paris, in Picardy, and Louis was kept safely in the rear and got no closer to the scene of military operations than Compiègne and Amiens. He was very eager to set out with his own convoy; the queen, Mademoiselle, and the court ladies traveled by another route, as did Mazarin, in order to make billeting easier on the way. They were all back in Paris in five weeks, to the great satisfaction of the *Gazette*, which rejoiced that the king's first journey had not impaired his health, and editorialized that, since kings must necessarily travel a good deal, it was reassuring that Louis showed stamina at so early an age.[14] The following year Louis returned to the same theater of operations, again accompanied by his mother, Mazarin, and Mademoiselle; but this time they stayed three months, and he got somewhat closer to the actual front, going beyond Amiens to Abbeville and Dieppe.[15] In 1648, with peace looked for at any moment, no campaign trip was scheduled. Louis made up for that, however, in subsequent years, both during and after the civil wars.

Until he was practically a grown man, his mother accompanied him. For more than a decade, with the exception of 1648, she spent a sizable portion of every year in travel—no mean feat for a woman of middle age and sedentary habits. Aside from the discomfort of lumbering coaches, the inconvenience of misplaced baggage, and the at least occasional inadequacies of lodging on the way, the royal parties often had to make do with makeshift quarters at their destination. Compiègne had a royal castle with which Anne was familiar, and in Amiens the archbishop's palace could be pressed into service; but smaller places such as Abbeville had no such spacious facilities. Nevertheless, Louis throve on these expeditions, and they apparently did no harm to the queen either.

Once arrived in any place where they planned to stay awhile, and the receptions, speeches, and compliments from local dignitaries over, Anne and Louis settled into a fairly comfortable routine.[16] He had military reviews to attend, which increased in number as he grew older. By the time he reached his teens, he was accompanying Mazarin on trips close to, or actually on, the fighting front. Anne meanwhile indulged her taste for visiting convents and developed favorites among them as she returned to the same cities year after year. In his first campaigns, Louis followed similar pursuits though not necessarily in the company of his mother. In fact, he and she often divided the field between them, taking it in turns to visit the local churches and monastic establishments. Such visits could be very enjoyable, since some of the monastries had beautiful gardens to show and offered refreshments to the royal guests. Anne had made such outings with her father before she left Spain, so that now she was letting her son discover pleasures dear and familiar to her.

Visiting monastic houses had not been a royal pastime in France for centuries. Mazarin, as we have seen, considered it a Spanish custom; and taking their cue from him, historians since have often deplored Anne's religious training of her son in what they have called Spanish-style religiosity.[17] By this they meant that Anne paid more attention to religious ceremonials and outward observances than to inner piety. As an accusation this is not altogether just, for it is impossible to assess the degree of Anne's inner piety or to know by whose standard it should be judged. Nor is the "Spanish" label attached to her practices particularly illuminating, since it mostly reflects the traditional desire of French scholars to differentiate their seventeenth-century Catholic reform from the similar movements in Italy, Spain, or Austria. Granted, the French reformers, such as Cardinal Berulle's Oratorians and their followers, tended to a somewhat austere and cerebral approach. Religious historians subsequently characterized them as the creators of a distinctively French school of spirituality, marked by disdain for "baroque" sensuousness and enthusiasm.[18] At the time, however, these particular reformers were in a minority; there were plenty of French people as attached to the saints, relics, processions, and other devotions as Anne herself was. It is true that her faith, whatever its other qualities, was of a simple kind. She had no interest in theology and privately deplored the current Jesuit-Jansenist controversies and the lack of charity displayed by some of their participants.[19]

Louis had a similarly practical outlook on religion when he was grown, but to what extent he learned it from his mother or to what extent it was a matter of his personality and temperament would be difficult to determine. Nor was there anything extraordinary in the religious exercises in which he took part as a child[20]—the daily mass he heard, the Advent and Lenten sermons in the palace chapel, belonged to standard royal protocol. Custom also in large part dictated the choice of churches he attended: the parish church on holy days such as Christmas, Easter, or Corpus Christi; the cathedral of Notre-Dame for occasional special services; the Jesuit church of Saint-Louis on the feast day of that patron of the royal house; and on numerous other occasions the church of the reformed Cistercians, or *Feuillants,* which French kings had frequented for generations. And some religious acts were expected from Louis as king, even at a young age. Thus on Good Friday 1644, for the first time as king he observed the traditional rite of royal penitence: washing the feet of thirteen poor boys, giving them alms, and serving them food, with the assistance of great officers of the crown.[21]

It was perhaps less usual that his mother enrolled him in pious confraternaties, such as the one dedicated to Saint Denis.[22] That did not, however, require continued personal exertion on his part. Meanwhile as the years went by, the *Gazette* noted approvingly, for the edification of the public, that Louis was showing the effects of his mother's lessons in piety and modesty by his behavior in holy places, and gave evidence of serious-mindedness because he liked to repeat things he had heard in sermons.[23] What he did not do, except on journeys, was to accompany his mother on her rounds of convents. He did not develop a permanent taste for visiting monasteries, and his mother's steadfast companion in that activity, as soon as he grew old enough, was Louis's brother Philippe.[24]

About Philippe's childhood even fewer details are known than about Louis's. The *Gazette* steadily publicized the brotherly affection between him and Louis, and it may well have existed along with the deference Philippe was expected to show for Louis as his elder and his king. Philippe had his moments of rebellion though, and on occasion the two brothers fought bitterly in the manner of boys, with pillows, fisticuffs, and even less polite exchanges.[25] Apparently Philippe never showed jealousy of his older brother's position and potential power; what he did resent was having to share their mother's company and attention not only with Louis but also with other people. In her memoirs Madame de Motteville noted a revealing incident when Philippe was still a small child: while he was recovering from an illness and the queen was visiting him, a number of noble ladies came to call and Philippe asked his mother to send the company away so that they could be alone by themselves. Anne explained that was impossible; the ladies had a right to be there, and she could not dismiss them. Philippe retorted that she sent him away on occasion, even though he was her son, so why could she not turn out these people? The solution Anne adopted was to leave herself, taking the company with her, explaining that it was the only way to cure Philippe of his little notions.[26]

Philippe's reflections as he stayed behind were not recorded, but it must have seemed to him as though his mother was always leaving him. For a number of years, he stayed in Paris while the court went on campaign, and he also remained there if he happened to be sick when the court was ready to remove to the country for a vacation. Anne was by no means unfeeling, and reportedly showed great distress at these separations. She visited him when he was sick, as in 1647 when she came from Fontainebleau to Paris for a few days because he was suffering from dysentery.[27] But when the king was ill, Anne nursed him herself, and there was no question of her leaving the king to nurse her second son. Her duties as regent may have been involved here as much as any personal inclination, though admittedly arguments of state could be small comfort to a child who wanted his mother.

In her memoirs Mademoiselle, wishing to explain Philippe's later homosexual proclivities, alleged that Anne and Mazarin deliberately encouraged effeminate tendencies in the boy so that he would not become politically ambitious and threaten Louis with any rivalry.[28] No one has produced evidence to substantiate this accusation. Moreover it is unlikely that the queen and her minister would have chosen deliberately to make Philippe effeminate; he was, after all, next in line to the throne, and it would have been very risky to do anything that might unfit him should the succession ever come his way. What actually happened was much less simple. According to the custom of the time, little boys were dressed in skirts until they were about five years old. Because Philippe happened to be a pretty child with long brown curls, it was natural for the queen's ladies, with whom he spent much of his time, to dress him up and treat him as a little pet. He enjoyed all this, especially since he was already giving evidence of what was to be a lifelong passion for jewels and finery.[29] Such tastes were not in themselves unusual for men, whose costume could be as elaborate as that of the ladies; most probably no one expected Philippe's character to suffer any serious damage thereby. Similarly the queen must have thought it harmless, if not downright praiseworthy, to make him her steady companion in her visits to churches and convents, where the sisters spoiled and petted him as much as did the ladies at court. When in his eighth year he was handed over to Louis's governor and the company of men, Philippe's habits and associations were already fixed, particularly since he remained his mother's escort on her religious rounds.

Formal education began after boys turned seven. In the case of royalty, this meant not only that princes were given into the care of a governor and provided with tutors, but also that a separate household establishment was appointed for them. Louis XIII had given thought to these matters, at least for his elder son; but his first choice as governor had fallen in battle, and nothing further had been decided by the time the king himself had died.[30] That made things easier for Anne and Mazarin, inasmuch as they found it unthinkable that an outsider control the young king's upbringing. Thus a new office was created: on 9 March 1646 Mazarin took oath from the queen as superintendent of Louis's and Philippe's education.[31] The queen announced her decision in the most glowing terms to the leading dignitaries of the state. As she wrote, for example, to the duke of Montbazon, governor of Paris and the Île de France, she had wished to confide the care of the king's education to someone who would strengthen Louis's good tendencies and inspire him by theory as well as example with the desire for glory and the art of ruling well. Therefore, with the approval of the duke of Orléans and the prince of Condé, she had chosen Cardinal Mazarin to superintend the education of the king and his brother, not only in view of his evident abilities but also because as the king's godfather he would have a special obligation to perform his duties well. She, the queen, felt all the more confident in entrusting him with such an important charge, since she had ample evidence of his zeal for the good of the kingdom. Because Mazarin had to devote the larger part of his time to affairs of state, however, she was appointing the marquis of Villeroi as the king's governor under the cardinal's authority.[32]

With the superintendency of the king's education, Mazarin's hold on power became complete; he was already superintendent of the queen's household, as well as first minister. He has been accused of neglecting his royal pupil's intellectual training, even his material welfare.[33] The main source for these accusations is suspect, however, because highly partisan: it was La Porte. La Porte never got over the high point in his life, the time in 1637 when by his silence, as he thought, he saved the queen and made possible her reconciliation with Louis XIII. He considered himself in a measure responsible for the birth of young Louis, took a proprietary interest in the boy, and felt himself entitled to proffer the frankest criticism and advice to his mother.[34] Mazarin had tried to make friends with La Porte, to no avail—La Porte persisted in regarding Mazarin as a foreign upstart and intruder, giving vent to the chagrined jealousy displayed by all Anne's old associates who had thought they owned her until Mazarin came along.

In La Porte's memoirs his animosity toward the cardinal is plain to see. He accused Mazarin of trying to make the king subservient, of surrounding him with spies and keeping anyone away from him who might teach the boy that he, not Mazarin, was the real master.[35] Furthermore, said La Porte, Mazarin was not at all interested in the king's progress at lessons, claiming that, since Louis was alert and asked many intelligent questions in council, he would learn what he needed to know from experience rather than from books.[36] Then too La Porte charged Mazarin with meanness in providing for the king's household necessities: the king's sheets were so worn that they tore; his dressing gown was mangy and outgrown before it was replaced; his carriages were allowed to fall into dilapidation.[37] Last but not least, La Porte covertly encouraged Louis to dislike Mazarin and could hardly contain his delight when the boy took to calling Mazarin "the Grand Turk."[38] Mazarin was well enough informed as to what was going on, but apparently did not attempt to discredit La Porte with the queen—probably because he realized how much she valued her old servant. Eventually, however, La Porte went too far. Without evidence he accused Mazarin of having seduced Louis sexually.[39] This time not even the queen could ignore La Porte's capacity for making mischief, and so in 1653 he had to give up his post and leave the court.

How much truth there had been in his other charges would be difficult to determine. He was not always reliable. For example, he maintained stoutly that Louis was kept in such isolation that, unlike his predecessors, he was not given children of honor for company, whereas from the memoirs of at least one of Louis's childhood companions, we know the contrary was true.[40] Perhaps the king's furnishings did get shabby; if so, it probably happened during the civil wars when the court was often on the move and money was hard to find. As for the king's education, it is true that Mazarin valued practical experience in government above theory, although that is not to say he expected Louis to grow up ignorant. Already before the king entered his teens, Mazarin was giving him an apprenticeship for his lifework. He had the king sit in council as soon as he was ten years old,[41] took him to the war fronts to let him see how military decisions were arrived at and how armies were organized and supplied, and later even taught him how to hunt in royal style by way of celebrating the feast of Saint Hubert, patron of huntsmen.[42] Book learning however, Mazarin was content to leave to Louis's preceptor, Hardouin de Péréfixe, abbé de Beaumont.

Péréfixe had been selected in 1644 from a large and varied field of candidates, many of them self-nominated.[43] To show their qualifications, most of them offered treatises on royal education, fairly conventional works on the whole, stressing the necessity of teaching the king to hate vice, love the traditional virtues, and care for his state like a good shepherd. Some were more pious than others; Arnauld d'Andilly, for instance, produced a program of political education that called on the king not only to look after his finances and his subjects' welfare in person but also to make God reign in the state.[44] In his memoirs Arnauld indeed claimed that the queen had once promised him the office of royal preceptor. Anne knew and respected him as a zealous lay partisan of religious reform, and one day while Louis XIII was still living, she remarked—so Arnauld said—that she knew no one to whom she would rather entrust the education of the dauphin than him.[45] Whether she had meant it as a promise or not, by 1644 Arnauld was too much a pillar of the Jansenist party and too much involved in religious controversy to be a viable candidate. She continued to like him, and even did him favors; but for her son's education, she had to look elsewhere.

Having eliminated the other candidates for political, religious, or personal reasons, Mazarin and the queen settled on Hardouin de Péréfixe, who had served in the late Cardinal Richelieu's household and was therefore a safe, dependable man. Admittedly he was not brilliant, although he was conscientious about fulfilling his duties.[46] The education he gave Louis has been condemned for being pedestrian and superficial, not designed to instill in the young king a love for the liberal arts and scholarship in general.[47] Although it is true that Louis was no great scholar, took no lasting pleasure in humanistic studies, and throughout his life was more open to practical than to abstract knowledge, these dispositions were in large part a matter of temperament and talent and hardly attributable entirely to failings of Péréfixe's part. Nor is it clear that anyone wishing to lead Louis into more bookish ways would have been doing him a favor. Scholarship was not likely to win him the respect of either the great nobles or officials of the crown. Apart from Mazarin's pragmatic lessons, what Louis needed was an education that would not separate him too much from most of the men whom he would have to lead, and that is exactly the education he got—a gentlemanly knowledge of Latin, history, literature, and mathematics, supplemented in due course by training in advanced horsemanship and military arts at the hands of the famous riding master Monsieur Arnolfini.[48]

There is no evidence that Anne interested herself in Louis's course of studies. Indeed, the particular contribution she made to her son's education lay not in the academic realm but rather in the psychological one. Whenever Louis XIII's shortcomings had used to annoy Anne, which happened frequently, she would promise herself that if God gave her children, she would be sure to raise them differently from the way Louis had been brought up.[49] It is La Porte who tells us so, and in this case his testimony is credible since it had no connection with his animosity against Mazarin. Besides, we know Anne sought advice on errors made in her husband's childhood and how to avoid repeating them. The author of the treatise on the dauphin's primary education that Anne commissioned had already pointed out several dangers to watch, as we have seen.[50] After Louis XIII's death, Anne sought out a man with expert knowledge on what had happened during the king's childhood: Nicolas Vauquelin des Yvetaux, a poet by then in his seventies.[51] Henry IV had tried out Vauquelin as tutor for his illegitimate son, the duke of Vendôme, and liked him so well that he had appointed him preceptor to the dauphin, the future Louis XIII. Vauquelin had not enjoyed his post for long; the devout wing of the clergy campaigned against him because he held freethinking views, and the boy's physician, Héroard, considered him a rival and an enemy. Shortly after Henry's assassination, therefore, Vauquelin lost his appointment. For his pupil, the duke of Vendôme, he had written a little essay in verse on princely education, whose main claim to originality lay in a hint of what might be called deism.[52] After his dismissal from court, he lived quietly in retirement, a poet no longer in fashion but still scandalizing the devout. Within a year or so of Louis XIII's death, however, Vauquelin, apparently upon request, produced a memorandum on the education of the prince that was in essence a critique of the education Louis XIII had received.[53]

According to Vauquelin, Louis XIII had had good potential that had been wasted because he never was taught the underlying causes of things.[54] For the new king, Louis XIV, he advised the choice of a preceptor clever enough to make the boy enjoy his studies.[55] At the same time, he warned that the preceptor as well as the governor must be in perfect harmony with the queen, to ensure the obedience of the young king and good understanding in the family. As a negative example, Vauquelin recalled that Héroard used to incite Louis XIII against Marie de Medici, warning the boy, for instance, not to eat any food that might be offered to him in her apartments. In Vauquelin's opinion, that was the beginning of the lifelong mutual suspicions and bad relations between mother and son—something that obviously should not be allowed to happen again.[56] Vauquelin also believed that Héroard had mismanaged Louis XIII's medical care. Louis had a deficiency in mucous secretions, so that Vauquelin thought he needed to be encouraged to clear his throat and blow his nose. Héroard, disagreeing, insisted that all impurities would be evacuated through the bowels, an insistence that Vauquelin held accountable for Louis's later chronic illnesses. Although it was clear that Louis XIV did not share his father's disabilities, had no stammer or other impediment to his speech, and altogether seemed to have a different temperament and a stronger constitution, Vauquelin nevertheless thought it important that the king's attendants made sure he blew his nose regularly.[57]

For recreation, bodily exercises that would build strength and grace such as dancing, horsemanship, and fencing would be excellent. Likewise play with toy soldiers, fortifications, and similar games was a good idea, although the king should be kept away from mechanical arts. In this Vauquelin agreed with the author of the "Maxims," for Louis XIII, in Vauquelin's opinion, had lowered himself by making such things as toy cannons with his own hand.[58] As for the king's studies, those studies that would prepare him to govern and do justice, Vauquelin stressed French over Latin. The king should have some Latin, as a necessary ornament, and also some knowledge of arithmetic and geometry; but mainly Vauquelin advised a course of reading in great authors, in French, ranging from Aristotle and Josephus to Montaigne, together with training in clear, unpretentious speech in accordance with current usage.[59] For competence in statecraft, however, Vauquelin urged the queen to let her son read current government dispatches.[60]

We do not know to what extent, if any, Vauquelin's advice was followed specifically in the program laid out for the young king. Although Louis did learn less Latin than French, he by no means followed the ambitious plan of reading Vauquelin had suggested. It is doubtful whether Péréfixe had the gift of making the king enjoy schoolwork, but, on the other hand, both he and Villeroi were hand-picked to make no trouble between their pupil and Anne or Mazarin. Probably Vauquelin's work told Anne nothing new and merely confirmed her in ideas she already held.

Whatever the merits of Vauquelin's diagnosis of Louis XIII's ailments, he was right in one observation: Louis XIV had a more robust
constitution than his father. He throve on exercise and was rarely ill; it
is true, of course, that he was not subjected to the regimen of enemas
and purges with which Héroard had dosed Louis XIII from infancy.
Louis XIV's only serious childhood illness was smallpox, the common
scourge of the times, though even in that he had what could be considered a mild siege.[61] On 11 November 1647 he complained of back-
ache, and though he insisted on watching a play that had been scheduled, he himself asked to leave before the performance was over. The
doctors took it for a slight indisposition, until rising fever and other
symptoms persuaded them that they were in fact dealing with smallpox. Louis was acutely sick for about two weeks, delirious part of the
time. His doctors deployed their best weapons to encourage the erup-
tion of the pox and break the fever. They bled the boy four times,
purged him with extracts of rhubarb and chicory, and prescribed
strengthening cordials with remarkable ingredients: solutions of
pearls and sugar, powdered bezoar, stagshorn and bitters of cedar.
The queen meanwhile requested that the sacrament be exposed in all
churches, which meant continuous prayers for the king's recovery,
and had the boy join her in vows to the Virgin. She spent practically her
entire time at his bedside and nursed him with her own hands, feeding him, giving him his medicines, and generally comforting him. She
charitably excused those of her ladies who feared contagion from attending her. Her son was not as generous—he kept track of the missing persons and later called them to account for their dereliction.[62]
Mazarin visited every day and, when the king was better, presented
him with an English horse that had to be led upstairs and into the
king's bedroom because he insisted on seeing it immediately.

By the first week in December, Louis's recovery was pronounced
assured, though weeks of convalescence would have to follow. His
brother had been removed from the Palais-Royal to the house of Monsieur de Mauroy, an intendant of finances, where he stayed for safety's
sake from the beginning of Louis's illness until February 1648. He
begged to see his mother, and Anne went to visit him every few weeks,
at first daring to speak to him only through a window.[63] She herself
suffered a fever as a result of fatigue, though that cleared up while
Louis was visibly recovering. The editor of the *Gazette*, recalling the
recent death of the Spanish crown prince, echoed the universal relief
in December when he wrote, ". . . Thus we see how well God loves
France, contenting Himself, as He does, with merely showing her the

rods of punishment with which He beats others."[64] It only remained to fulfill the vows that had been made, and thus on 12 January as his first outing Louis went to Notre-Dame with his mother for a thanksgiving service. Twelve days later it was the turn of Saint Genevieve, and in March, after Easter, they went accompanied by Philippe and Mademoiselle to give thanks at the shrine of the Virgin in Chartres.[65]

For Anne her son's sickness had been a fearful time. Looking back on it on New Year's Eve, as well as on other difficulties 1647 had brought, she told her ladies that she was glad to see the old year out and to enter the new. In the old year, she explained, she had had nothing but trouble: little success in the war and much worry over the illnesses of her children, whom she had feared to lose.[66] Perhaps Anne felt she had earned better things for 1648; but she need not have been so glad to enter this new year, for instead of good fortune it brought rebellion and ushered in a long civil war.

Chapter Fifteen

Disaffection and Rebellion

THE FRONDE WAS THE CULMI-
nation of all the forces of opposition that Mazarin and Anne had tried to quiet in 1643 but had not succeeded in eliminating. There were important issues at stake: peace, tax reform, resentment at administrative innovations, all sorts of grievances dating back to Richelieu. But to a remarkable extent, the issues presented themselves less in their own right than as adjuncts to the ambitions and desires of prominent persons: Gaston of Orléans, his daughter, Mademoiselle, the prince of Condé and his relatives, and Madame de Chevreuse, to mention only a few. Their Fronde was a veritable jungle of conspiracy, mutual bargaining and equally mutual betrayal, impossible to penetrate fully even with the guidance of the memoirs left by many of the chief actors. During the past quarter-century, historians have made efforts to bypass this jungle and get to apparently more objective fundamental causes—economic exploitation and class struggle; or conflicts between provincial and central administrations or within the administrative hierarchy itself.[1] That was not what contemporaries saw, however, especially not what Anne saw. She had to deal with a storm of hatred directed against Mazarin, and against herself for supporting him. Since these attacks compromised the royal authority, Anne viewed the Fronde very simply as disobedience to her son the king, and in her opinion the cure lay in a strong hand dispensing punishment. Circumstances forced her to conceal her wrath most of the time and to negotiate with the rebels, but she never really forgave any of them even when peace was restored and amnesty prevailed.

The first sign of more than ordinary trouble came in June 1648, when thirty-two delegates from the sovereign courts in Paris met in a self-constituted body, the so-called Chamber of Saint Louis, in order to work on the reform of the kingdom's administration and finances. With fourteen delegates the Parlement took the lead in what was essentially an illegal enterprise, for the law courts had no inherent legislative powers, no commission to take up the reform of the kingdom, not even the right to meet together for any concerted political action.

Although they claimed to be proceeding in the name of law against tyranny, their righteousness was far from pure: what had galvanized them into action was not some dramatic change in the state of the kingdom but a threat to their material interests. Earlier in the year, in a desperate need for revenue, the royal council had ordered the suppression of four years' salary for judicial officials of the major courts: Aids, Accounts, and Grand Council. The courts protested, and the Parlement, though its personnel was not affected in the same way, decided to make common cause with them. The regent vainly prohibited joint discussion; under the leadership of the Parlement, the courts moved from the immediate to more fundamental grievances, and the Chamber of Saint Louis was formed as a result.

It was natural for the Parlement to take charge of the protest movement. It was the senior court of law in the kingdom except for the royal council itself; it had the largest resort both for appeals and in first instance; and with the addition of the great nobles of France, it functioned as a court of peers when necessary. Although the Parlement had no legislative duties as such, it had the right to remonstrate before registering royal edicts. To be sure, the Parlement obeyed and registered whenever the king appeared in person and made his will known, but the Parlement nevertheless regarded itself as the guardian of established law.[2] That attitude had often led to conflicts with the crown in the past; the royal position was that the king had delegated some of his judicial powers to the Parlement and other courts, but had not thereby alienated these powers, for he continued to be the kingdom's highest judge. The Parlement could not deny that the king retained a residual power of justice, but sought to contain it within limits by protesting royal innovations such as the creation of extraordinary tribunals, the appointment of commissioners and intendants with judicial functions, and the evocation of cases from the courts to the royal council. Cardinal Richelieu had found such opposition particularly troublesome, and he and Louis XIII together had cowed the Parlement into quiescence. Under the regency, however, the Parlement was regaining its courage, asserting its privileges with vigor, and entertaining criticism, privately at first, of the regency government.

In 1643 Anne had had numerous partisans in the Parlement. Some were officials in her household or related to such, but for the most part, her sympathizers were former opponents of Richelieu, who, like so many of her old friends, assumed she would be only too glad to destroy all vestiges of Richelieu's work. The Parlement had been very cooperative in breaking Louis XIII's testament to free Anne from the regency council, although it would seem that even then Mazarin warned her against giving the court too much importance.[3]

Anne's choice of Mazarin as first minister and the continuation of Richelieu's policies—the prosecution of the war and the use of intendants for judicial and administrative purposes—speedily soured most of the judges and counselors. Mazarin knew that some of them, linked with the "Important People," spoke of reviving a decree issued in 1617 as a reaction to Marie de Medici's favorite Concini, to the effect that no foreigner could be minister of state.[4] Although Mazarin's foreign origin was the ostensible reason for the animosity against him, it merely covered the fact that the Parlement, taking his conciliatory manners for weakness, found him a convenient whipping boy for its old enemy Richelieu. Mazarin was able to establish a working relationship with the first president, Mathieu Molé, for whom he had the highest praise, saying, ". . . He loves the state. . . . "[5] But Mazarin could not win over any substantial number of Molé's colleagues, and by January 1648 the Parlement had grown so bold as to permit the advocate general, Omer Talon, to tell the queen regent in formal session that the monarchy must function within the limits of established law if it was not to become tyranny.[6]

Mazarin reportedly urged the queen not to defer too much to the Parlement lest she become unable to control it. He used the not quite parallel example of the English Parliament, which at the moment was successfully contesting royal authority.[7] Anne, however, seems not to have appreciated the Parlement's potential for obstruction. Perhaps she overestimated the strength of old loyalties among the judges, but in any case she had no patience with the ways of the legal profession. Her friend Madame de Motteville reported of the queen that

> in all her business with the Parlement, whose organization and petti-fogging spirit she never understood, she always wanted to ride rough-shod over the court, and expected that company to carry out everything ordered in her council.[8]
>
> She had great contempt for the judiciary, and could not conceive that this group of the king's subjects could inconvenience her or bring about any change in her affairs.[9]

With feelings like that, Anne found it hard to bear when in July the Chamber of Saint Louis made its report and the Parlement revealed major political ambitions.

Some of the propositions offered by the Chamber of Saint Louis dealt with finances: a call for the remission of one-quarter of the assessed *tailles,* the basic land taxes, as well as the annulment of the existing contract with the tax farmers. Furthermore, no taxes whatever were to be levied without having been verified by the sovereign courts, and a tribunal was to be set up to investigate and prosecute the malfeasances of financiers. The most important provisions, however, were those that touched the residual judicial powers of the monarch: demands for the abolition of intendants of justice and finance, and of all extraordinary commissions not verified by the courts; and guarantees that no person be kept in prison for more than twenty-four hours without being delivered to his natural judges. That meant the end of *lettres de cachet,* the royal warrants by which individuals could be arrested and detained indefinitely at the king's pleasure.[10]

Anne's first reaction was outrage. She wanted to strike against the Parlement immediately, but Mazarin pointed out that in this she did not have the unqualified support of Gaston of Orléans and persuaded her to await a more favorable opportunity. Meanwhile, Gaston was sent to the Parlement to ask for conferences. The outcome of these talks was the dismissal of Mazarin's friend Particelli d'Emery as superintendent of finances and his replacement by old Marshall de La Meilleraye, who was irreproachably honest but knew nothing about money. Since this sacrifice failed to pacify the Parlement, nothing remained but for the government to make further concessions. A royal declaration on 18 July accepted most of the Parlement's demands, though the crown insisted on retaining intendants of justice in six provinces and made no mention of the clause that would have ended *lettres de cachet.*[11] That did not satisfy the Parlement, and in view of its continued agitation, the queen regent brought the king into the court for a formal session on 31 July. What the crown presented was essentially a repetition of the earlier declaration with some additional sweeteners, such as financial benefits for the Parlement's personnel.[12]

Anne had announced widely beforehand that, as she put it, she was going to throw roses at the Parlement, but if it did not accept her kindness, she would know how to punish.[13] Neither Anne's threats, however, nor news of an imminent peace treaty with the empire that brought France substantial territorial gains, nor even a great victory won over the Spaniards at Lens by the prince of Condé on 20 August, at all disarmed the Parlement. That body insisted on gaining every one of its points, and in the meantime the government could get neither sufficient revenues nor credit from the financiers.

Anne was not altogether sorry that her "roses" were being rejected; by her own admission, she was looking forward to vengeance. She foresaw no serious problems of resistance, having as little respect for the Parlement's popularity as for the privileges that it claimed. She expressed the opinion that revolts were not easy to make in Paris: a guards regiment would suffice to restore order if necessary, and at worst, twenty to thirty pillaged houses would teach Parisians the cost of disobedience.[14] She was encouraged in her sentiments by Mazarin's former friend and her old adversary Chavigny, who recently had been readmitted to the royal council as a favor to his patron Gaston of Orléans.[15] Although Mazarin still preferred a waiting game, the council decided on the arrest of the three most vehement *parlementaires*: the judges Charton, Broussel, and Blancmesnil. The royal guards were to carry out the arrests on 26 August, immediately following the thanksgiving service in Notre-Dame for Condé's victory. It was hoped that no one would notice the deployment of the guards since they would be required to escort the royal party to and from the cathedral in any case.

The operation had unexpected consequences. Although Charton got away, Blancmesnil was taken and so was Broussel—but not before his housekeeper raised a hue and cry that alerted the neighborhood. Broussel was especially beloved among the populace for his opposition to taxes, financiers, and court luxuries; at the news of his arrest, therefore, people poured into the streets and set up barricades almost up to the gates of the Palais-Royal, effectively preventing the guards companies from dispersing the crowd. Although Anne herself took this news calmly and showed no sign of fear, courtiers began to feel alarm for the safety of the royal family.[16] At this point, when the government had clearly lost control of the situation, a self-appointed peacemaker appeared on the scene: the coadjutor of the archbishop of Paris, Jean-François Paul de Gondi, abbé de Retz.

Retz was the son of a very prominent and very devout family.[17] His parents had been Saint Vincent de Paul's first patrons in setting up works of charity, and his father, left a widower, gave up his position as general of the galleys to join the priests of the Oratory. Retz's aunt, Madame de Maignelais, also a disciple of Vincent de Paul, already was an almost legendary figure for her charities, and greatly loved by the poor. Retz himself felt no vocation for the religious life, but the family chose him to succeed his uncle the archbishop of Paris, and thus with the coadjutorship waiting, Retz duly pursued theological studies and was ordained. That did not prevent him from frequenting the ladies and enjoying numerous love affairs. He was discreet about his private life, however, and worked hard at enhancing his public reputation: he used to accompany his aunt Madame de Maignelais on her many errands of mercy, and by association acquired a good name among the people.[18]

Politics rather than religion interested Retz.[19] He felt himself called to do great things in the world, and the disorders of 26 August 1648 seemed to offer him a long-awaited opportunity. He presented himself at the Palais-Royal as a mediator, letting it be understood through friends that in reward he would like to be appointed governor of Paris.[20] Whether he thought already of replacing Mazarin as first minister is not clear, though the idea came to him soon enough.

Anne held Retz's father in high regard, but she detested Retz himself, a feeling he reciprocated. When he came before her, proposing to calm the populace if she would promise to release the prisoners, she lost her temper with him. As he described the scene, she screamed at him in a sharp falsetto that she "would rather strangle Broussel with her own hands, as well as all those who . . . ," and made as if to suit action to words.[21] Mazarin calmed her down, however, and they sent Retz off with an oral promise that the prisoners would be freed. Next day the Parlement in a body waited on the queen to plead for the prisoners, and she had to bow to the inevitable. Blancmesnil was released immediately, but it took longer for Broussel since he was on his way to the fortress of Sedan. On 28 August he too returned as a free man, and a hero, carried in triumph to Notre-Dame by the people. Then at last the Parlement ordered the barricades dismantled. Meanwhile a new expression had been added to the political vocabulary: Parisians called the resistance against the crown *Fronde*, a word normally meaning a slingshot used by boys, and having a connotation of irrepressible insubordination. It made its first appearance in its new sense in a street song:

A wind of *fronde*
Has come up this morning:
I think it blows
Against Mazarin.[22]

It blew against more than Mazarin. As he told the queen, the Parlement was assuming the functions of the sovereign, and he cited reports that some members spoke of transferring the regency to Gaston of Orléans.[23] Until steps could be taken to recover the royal authority, Mazarin advised Anne to take the king out of Paris. That could not be done immediately since Louis's brother had just come down with smallpox and Anne did not wish to leave him. Not until 13 September did she move the king, herself, and the royal council, first for a visit to the estate of Richelieu's niece at Rueil and than to Saint-Germain.[24] To the delegation from the Parlement that followed her with protests at this removal, Anne explained that it had been necessary to vacate the Palais-Royal for a thorough cleaning, and she asked the magistrates blandly why they should wish to deprive the king of a pleasure enjoyed by any private person, namely, to spend the rest of the fine season in the country?[25]

Gaston stayed in Paris to negotiate once again with the Parlement, a course on which he, Condé, and Retz had agreed in preference to confrontation. Far from recovering the royal authority, however, Gaston agreed to everything the Parlement wanted. The accord he and his colleagues brought to Anne for signature contained fifteen articles that met all the original demands of the Chamber of Saint Louis, including the abolition of all intendants of justice and finance, as well as the promise that no prisoner would be detained for more than twenty-four hours without being arraigned before his natural judges. In return the Parlement undertook to stop its political discussions. At first Anne flatly refused to sign a declaration so injurious to royal power. Never would she do that, she exclaimed, for it would make her son just a paper king.[26] Mazarin urged her to yield however, pointing out that she could tell Gaston and Condé she was signing under duress with mental reservations, in order to avoid internal troubles while the war against Spain continued.[27] On 22 October, therefore, she signed, and two days later the Parlement registered the declaration. After that it was an anticlimax when the royal family returned to Paris on 31 October.

During the following months, it became clear that nothing had really been resolved. The government was still short of revenues and found no financiers willing to do business with it. The Parlement was continuing its political discussions and complaining that what it considered the charter of liberty of 22 October was not being executed in good faith—which, as it happened, was true. Mazarin judged the time had come for strong measures. He had already suggested removing the Parlement from its base in Paris by ordering it to sit in a provincial city; as a more drastic alternative, the Parlement could be suppressed altogether and replaced with a new tribunal drawn from the personnel of the great council.[28] Because armed force would be necessary to crush a resistance the Parlement would no doubt organize, he urged the queen to enlist Condé's support so that she could use him as her general against the *frondeurs*. Mazarin even offered himself as a scapegoat if it would help persuade Condé: Anne was to complain to the prince that Mazarin was too lukewarm in his handling of the Parlement, and to plead that she needed a strong champion.[29] Presumably Anne followed instructions; she and the cardinal had concerted a similar scenario before she signed the October declaration, when she was heard to lament often that Mazarin was too kind and conciliatory.[30] Mazarin further hoped that the cooperation of Condé would spur Gaston to greater activity on behalf of the crown by way of emulation. To make sure of that, Gaston was being gratified by the admission of two of his friends to the royal council: his favorite, Abbé de la Rivière, and the king's governor, Villeroi.[31] Meanwhile Mazarin began to concentrate troops around Paris in preparation for the next step, which would be to take the king out of the city once more.

Mazarin's calculations paid off. Condé and Gaston agreed with Anne not only on the necessity for action but also on its nature. During the night from 5 to 6 January 1649, the queen and her sons left for Saint-Germain, where they were joined by Mazarin and Gaston of Orléans and his family, including Mademoiselle, who would have preferred to stay in Paris because she had *frondeur* sympathies.[32] The secret of the plan had been well kept. On the evening of 5 January, Anne had celebrated Twelfth Night with young Louis and her ladies in the customary fashion, dividing the traditional cake of the three kings and enjoying herself with great merriment when she was crowned queen of the bean.[33] She retired at her usual time, but when the doors of the Palais-Royal had been closed for the night and everyone could be assumed to be sleeping, she got herself ready, ordered Villeroi to waken the king and his brother, and left with them by the garden gate, where a closed coach was waiting. She was in great spirits, tasting the pleasures of revenge in anticipation. Mademoiselle, who traveled in the royal coach, reported sourly that she had never seen Anne so lighthearted; the queen "could not have been happier," Mademoiselle added, "if she had won a battle, taken Paris, and hanged everyone who had crossed her. . . ."[34]

Anne did not even mind the hardship of arriving in an unfurnished palace in the dead of winter. Because of the need for secrecy, it had not been possible to send ahead furnishings and hangings for herself and the others, nor was she able to take along any baggage. Mazarin had taken the precaution of providing camp beds for Anne, the king, the little duke of Anjou, and himself, but the rest of the party slept on straw—if they were lucky enough to find any. Food and fuel were scarce, for the town of Saint-Germain had not been prepared to supply the court. Moreover, no one had sufficient clothing or linens. It was not easy to repair these deficiencies either, since the Paris citizen militia was guarding the gates and preventing any belongings of the royal party from going out. They made an exception only for Mademoiselle, who prided herself that anything of hers was allowed to pass without question. To get a wagonload of her own clothes delivered, Anne had to ask Mademoiselle to declare the shipment under her name.[35] No amount of inconvenience, however, seemed able to disturb the queen's good humor.

In theory it was the Parisians who should have been suffering since royal troops were now blockading the shipment of food and other supplies into the city. But the Parlement had acquired noble partisans who did duty as blockade runners and with armed escorts got many a convoy through the royal lines. The Parlement's champions included the duke of Elboeuf, a member of the house of Lorraine, long at odds with the French crown; the duke of Beaufort, who had escaped from prison the previous spring; Condé's younger brother, the prince of Conti, and his brother-in-law, the duke of Longueville. The Parlement had been ordered to remove itself to the town of Montargis; only a handful of counselors obeyed, however, and the main body stayed where it was, condemned Mazarin as a disturber of the peace, authorized the formation of a small army, and sanctioned the takeover of the Arsenal and the Bastille. The one thing from which it shrank was the making of foreign policy.

The Spanish government was hoping to profit from France's internal divisions, and in February 1649 an agent arrived to sound out Mazarin about concessions he might be ready to make for peace. The overtures were not made in good faith, however, because at the same time Spain was treating with some of the noble *frondeurs*. Moreover Archduke Leopold, the governor of the Spanish Netherlands, sent an agent of his own to the Parlement, who addressed that body with the flattering message that the king of Spain believed its participation in peacemaking was necessary because it verified treaties.[36] The Parlement professed to be much gratified at being thus honored and sent the news to Saint-Germain, but there the matter ended. Leopold therefore prepared to cross the frontier and eventually opened his campaign for 1649 on French soil. The danger that represented, together with disturbances in provinces such as Normandy, Provence, Champagne, Poitou, and Guyenne, determined the government to open negotiations with the Parlement.

The Parlement was equally ready to negotiate. Its small army was no match for regular troops in skirmishes around Paris, and by the end of February, the royal blockade was making its effects felt. What the Parlement chiefly wanted was confirmation of the October charter, but its noble supporters added demands of their own: rewards for themselves and for their friends, including a pardon for Madame de Chevreuse, who once more had fled to the Spanish Netherlands in 1645 and now wished to return to Paris. The Parlement and the noble *frondeurs* were as one, however, in calling for the removal of Mazarin. In the treaty of Rueil, on 11 March, the government yielded on everything except the last point: Mazarin stayed.[37]

Then came the petitioners, from the sovereign courts, from the Paris city council, from the guild companies, asking for the return of the king. Since the royal court did not feel the capital was secure enough as yet, the king informed his good city of Paris that he would be pleased to return as soon as he had attended to military matters on the Flanders front.[38] Accordingly the whole royal party with Mazarin set out to follow the army. The campaign of that summer turned out to be inconclusive, but the royal family spent its time very agreeably in and around Compiègne, with the usual visits to convents and churches, as well as picnics and riding parties. Not until 18 August did Anne bring the king back to Paris, to a most enthusiastic welcome.[39] Two weeks later the municipality gave Louis a magnificent birthday party in the city hall, with a ball, a collation, and a program of fireworks in conclusion.[40] The celebrations did not mean that the Fronde was over, however; they merely signaled the end of the first act.

For the time being, the Parlement gave no trouble; it was the prince of Condé who caused problems. He felt the regent and Mazarin were not appreciating his services sufficiently, and he seemed to be insatiable in his demands.[41] The governorships held by him and his family already gave them potential control over a sizable portion of the kingdom. He was also to be grand master of the king's household when the king came of age and the full household was formed. The positions that would be under Condé's patronage in that post could be expected to bring him almost a million livres when they were sold. He wanted more, however: a strategic strong point in Normandy for his brother-in-law, Longueville, the admiralty for his family, and for himself the revival of the extinct dignity of constable of France, which would have given him power over the entire military establishment.

Condé did not get the admiralty or the constableship, but Mazarin, desperate to keep the prince's support, gave him something else: a written promise that he, Mazarin, would consult Condé on the naming of generals, ambassadors, governors, other officers of the crown and the royal household, even on ecclesiastical benefices, as well as on all other important matters.[42] With the queen's agreement,[43] Mazarin thus offered himself as a client to Condé; and if he had been serious and the promises had been kept, Condé would have held almost sovereign power. Gaston of Orléans, though nominally lieutenant general of the kingdom, would have been left on the sidelines. Mazarin circumvented the agreement, however. Secretly he advised Anne to assume the direction of business herself, at least in public, and coached her on how to deal with Condé in council meetings.[44] How far Condé was taken in is not clear. He displayed supreme confidence, however, and more than once treated the queen and the king himself with insolence.

At this point Madame de Chevreuse came to the rescue. For personal reasons she had long been on an unfriendly footing with the Condé family, and now saw a way to discomfort them while benefiting her friends. She offered Mazarin the loyal support of the late *frondeur* faction, including Beaufort and Retz, over whom she claimed to have control. Since the court thus would be relieved of the need for placating Condé, she urged the queen to arrest him. As the price for her good offices, Madame de Chevreuse asked for a place in the ministry for her old friend Châteauneuf and a cardinal's hat for Retz.[45] The queen and Mazarin found her proposition most attractive. There could be no question that Condé was a very dangerous, overmighty subject, and this fact outweighed the distrust they felt for Madame de Chevreuse. Anne undertook to win Gaston's support for the plan, which was not too difficult to do since he felt slighted by Condé's ascendancy. She even overcame her dislike for Retz sufficiently to grant him two secret interviews with every appearance of cordiality.[46] And so the bargain was struck.

The associates decided on the arrest not only of Condé but of his brother Conti and his brother-in-law Longueville as well. Given the importance of the intended victims, it was a daring enterprise. To protect himself if anything went wrong, Mazarin had the queen write him instructions that would appear to have forced his hand in breaking his promises to Condé. Just as though he had not been warning her against the prince for months, Anne therefore informed Mazarin

I am resolved at last not to follow your advice in this matter nor the advice of anyone else whomsoever, who would persuade me to gloss over any longer the inroads that the said princes are making into the authority of the king which is being entirely abased. I declare to you therefore that my last and absolute will is to assure myself of the persons of the said princes without further delay, believing there is no other way but this to save the crown for the king, Monsieur my son. . . .[47]

If Mazarin persisted in opposing her, she concluded, he would not only be displeasing her but would be giving her cause to suspect his loyalty.[48] The stage was thus set for the surprise arrest of the princes when they came to attend a meeting of the royal council on 18 January 1650.

Although Anne had been intrepid at the time of the barricades, on this occasion she felt so nervous that she took to her bed with a feigned sick headache, and had to suffer the embarrassment of having to entertain her old friend, the dowager princess of Condé, who had come to inquire after her health.[49] While the princes were actually being arrested, Anne withdrew with young Louis into her oratory, where mother and son prayed for the success of the action.[50] Condé offered no resistance, however; he said only, "So be it; just take me somewhere warm."[51]

Unfortunately, although Condé was thus immobilized, his friends and relations were not. His sister the duchess of Longueville hurried to raise revolt in Normandy while others encouraged troubles in Burgundy, Poitou, Guyenne—especially in its capital of Bordeaux. Local grievances and in some cases cooperation between the provincial parlements and the Parlement of Paris played into the hands of the noble *frondeurs*. Moreover, one of the kingdom's most distinguished generals, Turenne, defected; in April he and the duchess of Longueville signed a treaty with Spain by which they agreed to deliver whatever strong places they had in their control in return for Spanish troops and subsidies.[52] Anne, Louis, and Mazarin had to spend most of the year traveling from one end of France to the other in an effort to put down disorders and settle problems. In February they went to Normandy; March and April they spent in Burgundy; in June they traveled to Compiègne to be near the Picardy-Flanders frontier for the summer campaign; in July they left for Poitou and Guyenne, where they supervised the siege of the rebellious city of Bordeaux, which did not capitulate until 29 September. Gaston of Orléans stayed behind in Paris as caretaker and loyally did his best to raise extraordinary revenues.[53]

It was a grueling year. Louis suffered no ill effects from his itinerant life, but Anne fell ill on the way home in mid-October; and after her return to Paris, she was sick again most of December. Her own doctor having failed to find a cure, the king's physician was called in. He diagnosed an intestinal abscess, which he proceeded to treat with concoctions of rhubarb and a purgative, all the while making comparisons with the symptoms Louis XIII had suffered during his last illness.[54] Mazarin was deeply alarmed. He had gone on to Champagne to prepare the royal troops for a confrontation with Turenne, but he insisted on having daily medical bulletins with detailed reports of the queen's condition.[55] Fortunately Anne's constitution was strong. She survived both the treatment and the abscess—if it indeed was an abscess. By Christmas she was convalescent.

The news from Champagne was equally encouraging, for the royal army defeated Turenne and was retaking numerous places that had fallen into the hands of Condé's supporters. When Mazarin returned to Paris at the end of the year, therefore, he and the queen had reason to feel their exertions during the past eleven months were bearing good fruit. Mazarin in fact considered the outlook for the crown so promising that he thought the whole Fronde might be wound up in the near future.[56] It was not to be, however; for in the meantime, Madame de Chevreuse had changed her mind.

Chapter Sixteen

Mazarin in Exile

FAR FROM THE END OF THE Fronde being in sight, for Anne the hardest part was about to begin. On 30 January 1651, Madame de Chevreuse entered into an alliance with Gaston of Orléans and representatives of the prince of Condé. The parties agreed to work together for their common interests, set forth in the conditions they meant to put to the queen: Condé, his brother, and brother-in-law must be freed from prison; Mazarin must leave the ministry; Gaston of Orléans should have the preponderant voice in choosing members of the royal council; and Madame de Chevreuse's old friend, Châteauneuf, was to become first minister and her new friend Retz was to be made a cardinal.[1]

What had brought about this reversal of Madame de Chevreuse's long-standing hostility to Condé and his family was a project of marriage between her daughter and Condé's brother, the prince of Conti. As a further seal upon the alliance, Condé's son and heir was to marry one of Gaston's younger daughters. It had not been too difficult to secure Gaston's adherence to the coalition. He felt his services of the previous year were not sufficiently appreciated at court, and besides he had come to regret giving his consent to the arrest of the princes.[2] Now he took the lead in the campaign to force the queen's hand. On 1 February he informed her that he refused to participate in council meetings, and would not so much as set foot in the palace while Mazarin stayed in office.[3] Three days later the Parlement, with Gaston's endorsement transmitted by Retz, asked Anne for Mazarin's dismissal. In the meantime Gaston authorized the Paris citizen militia to put up barricades in the streets.

Anne was not inclined to yield. It was Mazarin who volunteered to leave, on the advice of Madame de Chevreuse, who urged him to leave court at least long enough to let the present storm blow over.[4] She evidently knew as little as ever about the character of her former friend the queen, for she assured Retz cynically that with Anne, out of sight was out of mind; that Mazarin once gone could be considered dislodged forever.[5] Mazarin apparently did not yet know of Madame de Chevreuse's recent alliance with Condé and Gaston, but this knowledge would have made little difference since it was manifestly difficult for the regent to continue conducting business without the cooperation of Gaston, who was lieutenant general of the kingdom. Mazarin and Anne therefore concerted a plan of action: he would withdraw from court to meet Gaston's demand, and if the queen found it necessary to free the imprisoned princes, she would have him transmit the order so that he would receive the credit for their liberation. If on the other hand his departure did not make Gaston more tractable, Gaston's further intentions would be suspect and the queen should prepare to take Louis and Philippe out of Paris secretly and seek refuge in Saint-Germain.[6] After an apparently innocuous conversation with Anne on 6 February, Mazarin himself left Paris quietly late in the evening.

Anne had shown no sign of emotion during their leave-taking.[7] She was, of course, expert in playing a part, and besides no doubt expected soon to see Mazarin again. Her plans for secret travel, however, did not work out as successfully as they had two years earlier. Gaston still being difficult, she was making preparations for departure when, on 9 February, the king's governor Villeroi intimated to Châteauneuf that something was afoot. Châteauneuf passed the word to Madame de Chevreuse, who notified Gaston, and the next step was to alert the citizen militia. Despite contrary orders from the queen, the militia turned out immediately to guard the city gates and cut off escape routes from the Palais-Royal. Anne ordered the royal guards doubled at the palace entrances but otherwise showed no alarm. Her ladies were less calm; to hearten them, she assured them nothing would come of the disturbances—the people's hysteria would die down because it had no foundation. She protested to everyone in sight that she had no idea of leaving Paris and would promise the people any guarantee that the king would remain in the city. Meanwhile, she added, the people could watch the gates all they liked.[8]

The unrest continued, however, and rumor had it that Gaston meant to seize the king. He was actually considering such a move but decided against it.[9] About midnight, though, he sent a rather ominous message to the queen, asking her to put an end to all these disturbances, which put him into despair. Anne replied that since it was Gaston who had armed the people, he should be the one to quiet them down. His fears of her leaving were quite unfounded, for the king and his brother were sound asleep and she herself was in her bed and in no state for travel. She invited Gaston's messenger to go to the king's room and see for himself. The messenger did so, and on his way back to Gaston's palace, tried to reassure the crowds in the streets. Some of the people however, preferring the evidence of their own eyes, entered the courtyard of the Palais-Royal and shouted they wanted to see the king. With great presence of mind, Anne commanded that all doors be opened to them and that they be taken to the king's room. There the men gathered around the bed whose curtains had been opened. As they watched the sleeping boy their truculence turned to tenderness and admiration, so that after a long interval they left, softly murmuring blessings.[10]

Finding her strategy so successful, Anne sent for two officers of the citizen militia who had taken up stations near the palace. She received them herself very amiably, assured them that she was more pleased to have them near her than if they had been the greatest princes in the world, and then had them shown in to see the king. After that, she sent them out twice to speak to the people still gathered in the courtyard and in the approaches to the palace. With that at last the crowds dispersed. By then it was after three in the morning.[11] It hardly seems credible that Louis should have slept through the comings and goings in his room. Perhaps he did not, but in any event he was already as self-possessed as his mother and also knew how to play a part when necessary.

Next day, in the face of Gaston's continuing threatening posture, Anne had no choice but to send Mazarin the order to release the princes who were being kept in the fortress of Le Havre. She also had no choice but to stay where she was. Indeed, for several nights she had to admit people who demanded to see the king asleep in his bed. Even after those visitations ceased, she and her sons remained virtual prisoners in the Palais-Royal for more than a month.[12] Not until late March did the citizen militia disband. By then Condé and his companions had returned triumphantly to Paris, and Mazarin had found refuge across the frontier.

Prospects for his return did not look good. On 11 March, with the endorsement and in the presence of Gaston and Condé, the Parlement had ordered Mazarin's arrest; if he could be captured, he was to be detained in the Conciergerie prison for judicial inquiry and eventual trial, and the same order applied to his servants, dependents, or anyone who continued to remain in contact with him.[13] Although he was not captured, the inquiry was instituted in his absence and continued the rest of the year. Already in 1649 the Parlement had branded Mazarin as a disturber of the realm, and now it amplified that indictment at leisure. The case it built up against Mazarin ranged from allegations that he had mismanaged the state's finances, dissipated revenues, exported money illegally from the kingdom, engaged in piracy, to the most serious charges: that he had misrepresented political and diplomatic conditions to the king and was preventing the conclusion of peace with Spain for his own personal aggrandizement.[14]

Unquestionably the finances were in disorder, with the government using the most dubious expedients to increase revenue while financiers and tax farmers profited hugely from interest on loans, discounts on monies advanced, not to mention graft. Mazarin did not create these problems; he inherited them. Even had he been gifted as a political economist, which he was not, he could not have cured these ills given the refractory nature of the tax system and the administrative structure, the weakness of a regency government, and military needs.[15] That, of course, was the point: if the war ceased, the government would not be so desperate for money. The choice Louis XIII and Richelieu had made almost twenty years earlier to put war ahead of internal reform, was as unpopular as ever. It is also true that Mazarin was accumulating a large private fortune and as the head of his house was doing his best to provide for his entire family. Altogether he brought to France his brother, one of his sisters with her husband, five nieces, and two nephews. The first of the nieces had arrived not long before the Fronde broke out and were still being schooled for a role at court when they were forced to join their uncle in his exile. According to the customs of the time, establishing one's relatives was a positive duty. Besides, insofar as such relatives were marriageable, they could be used to extend influence and cement alliances. It was therefore nothing extraordinary for Mazarin to take care of his family; on the contrary, it would have been extraordinary if he had not done so. They were foreigners, however, intruders as far as the French were concerned. As for Mazarin's personal wealth, the story of his finances remains to be written. He was not scrupulous in his money-making investments, though there is no evidence that he actually defrauded the government.[16] It was normal for first ministers and princes of the church to be rich; he himself would have said that he had earned his rewards by hard labor—a defensible point of view if only he had been native-born.

The other charges against Mazarin had little foundation, least of all the accusation that he was misleading the king and preventing the conclusion of peace. That allegation had in fact been the keynote of Spanish propaganda since 1643, echoed by the devout, and for different reasons by Madame de Chevreuse as well as every other dissident.

Notably Mazarin's former friend and colleague Chavigny had in 1649 produced a memorandum purporting to show Mazarin's incompetence in general and bad faith in the conduct of peace negotiations with Spain in particular.[17] Neither Chavigny nor Mazarin's other detractors troubled to mention the gains in territory and prestige Mazarin's policies had secured by the Peace of Westphalia, or that it was Spain that had withdrawn from the peace conference. Although Mazarin defended himself repeatedly and at length, in public as well as in private, against the charge that he was continuing the war with Spain solely for the purpose of keeping himself indispensable to the crown, the allegation persisted, not only during the Fronde but also in later historiography. The nineteenth-century historian Adolphe Chéruel tried to lay it to rest by examining the diplomatic documents. He pointed out that the secretary to the duke of Longueville, head of the French mission to Westphalia and no friend of Mazarin's, subsequently recalled that in the negotiations the Spanish aim had been to detach the French allies, not to conclude peace with France—an assessment echoed at the time in reports from Rome. Nor does any trace exist of secret instructions from Mazarin to the negotiators to undermine the peace talks with Spain; on the contrary, he sent them positive orders to persevere.[18] No doubt Mazarin was correct in judging that the Spaniards were insincere in their professed desire for peace with France; that rather than settle down to fruitful negotiations, they preferred to keep matters in suspense in the hope of profiting by France's internal troubles. Although Mazarin's arguments had convinced the queen, however,[19] they made no impression on his enemies.

While the Parlement was constructing its case, the public was being treated to a flood of pamphlets and other works that had begun several years earlier and showed no sign of abating. These pieces, collectively called *Mazarinades*, attacked Mazarin, the queen, and the entire direction of royal policy during the past twenty years. They were published anonymously, often with fictitious imprints or none at all, although in some cases the authors could be identified as known supporters of Gaston, Condé, or Retz. The repertory ranged from invective to satire. Nothing belonging to Mazarin escaped—his ancestry, family, habits, and motives were all decried. Perhaps the most harmless of the satires was the burlesque *Ballad of the Financiers:*

> Jules is leaving;
> Good-bye to the shop.[20]

Other satires were more vicious, such as the *Ballet Danced before the King and the Queen Regent, his Mother, by the Mazarinique Trio, Taking Leave of France, in Burlesque Verses.*[21] The leading characters had several entries with appropriate lines, Mazarin himself as a peddler of scents and waffles, his nieces as rope dancers and whores, and a chorus of financiers as charlatans and thieves.

Most of the *Mazarinades* had a political content, on the whole fairly unsophisticated and traditional in character. There were relatively few radical pronouncements, for the *frondeurs* in general were not republicans, nor in sympathy with the Puritan revolution going on across the English Channel.[22] The most ambitious work to come out of the Fronde was backward looking: Claude Joly's *Collection of True and Important Maxims for the Instruction of the King . . .*[23] Properly speaking it was not a *Mazarinade* but a full-fledged treatise of more than five hundred pages. Joly, a canon of Notre-Dame of Paris who sympathized with Retz, the princes, and the *Parlement*, went back almost a hundred and fifty years to the political theory of Erasmus and especially Claude de Seyssel. With the aid of frequent citations from these and other Renaissance authors, he maintained that it was the duty of God-fearing kings to make the cardinal virtues manifest in their rule, and to make their kingdom flourish, not to destroy it with taxes. They must take care not to support bad ministers who have only their self-interest at heart, for if the royal authority is used to perpetrate injustice, it becomes tyranny. What was amiss with the government now, according to Joly, was the prevalence of Italian or Machiavellian maxims dispensing kings from practicing virtue and keeping faith. Joly attributed this condition to the presence of Mazarin, who, he urged, should be removed permanently lest he corrupt the young king by training and example.

> If this infidel spirit no longer animated our court, whose former honesty has been completely perverted by the spread of his subtle poison, we could hope for some good reconciliation[24]

and an end to the Fronde. To avoid similar problems in the future, to prevent unsuitable persons from gaining access to the ministry, Joly recommended that the principle of election be used: for any given post, the sovereign courts (with the Parlement presumably taking the lead) would choose three candidates recognized as wise and honorable men, lawyers or officials experienced in public affairs, and the king would make his choice from this slate. In Joly's eyes the plan had particular merit because Charles VII had entertained it two hundred years earlier.[25] But however antique and respectable their origins, Joly's ideas, tending as they did toward limited monarchy, impressed the royal court most unfavorably. As soon as circumstances permitted, the work was banned and Joly himself was sent into exile in the provinces.

Aside from Joly, the authors of political *Mazarinades* generally avoided theory and concentrated on practical questions. The most striking example of the pragmatic approach, had been published anonymously in 1649 as an address to the Parlement: *Notice, Remonstrance and Request, by Eight Peasants from Eight Provinces, Delegated by the Others of the Kingdom, Concerning the Miseries and Problems of the Present Time. . . .*[26] The eight peasants, who were actually not peasants but spokesmen for the lesser nobility, prepared a long list of grievances and requests, high among which stood the demands that the Estates-General be called and that peace be concluded abroad. They credited the king and his mother with good intentions, however, and therefore went on to offer ideas for the internal reform of the kingdom: the nobility should be restored to its former importance in relation to the crown, that is to say, should have greater access to royal offices, and the numbers of lawyers and administrative officials should be reduced. On the other hand, the king should no longer grant pensions to princes and great nobles, since it was not right that he should have to pay them for obedience. Because the king, furthermore, ought to live in a palace that impressed foreign visitors, the financiers, churchmen, and lawyers should be made to pay contributions toward the completion of the Louvre's reconstruction. On the related subject of finances, the eight were willing to grant that commoners are the legs, feet, and liver of the body politic for its sustenance and support, but they thought this should not mean that as taxpayers they were altogether mutilated and bled white. The spokesmen had similarly firm ideas in matters of religion: they believed the king should maintain the Edict of Nantes and keep peace between Protestants and Catholics, but they recommended that the king banish Jews from the kingdom on the one hand and curb the activities of the Jesuits on the other. Foreign entanglements were not wanted either. The king should put an end to the exchange of resident ambassadors between France and other states. It was also wrong for him to employ foreign mercenary soldiers while France had a surplus of men, especially since, so the peasants argued, one Swiss soldier cost as much to keep as six Frenchmen. As for foreigners employed in his service in other ways, he should throw them out, for they only wanted to weaken France and let her fall prey to outsiders. That particular article of course was directed against Mazarin.

The more run-of-the-mill of the *Mazarinades* offered far fewer ideas than the discourse of the eight peasants. They shared two common themes: government by ministers was an evil innovation, and the sooner Mazarin left the kingdom, the better. To mention only a few, the titles speak for themselves: *The Christian Knight Speaking about the Miseries of the Times, to the Queen Regent;*[27] *Truth Speaking to the Queen,*[28] *The Laughter and Tears of France at the Conduct of the Queen and the Council of State, Revealing the Origin of our Miseries and of the Public Calamities;*[29] *The Queen's Mirror, Showing Her All the Disorders of her Regency and Giving Her Infallible Methods for Repairing them.*[30] Dire warnings were not lacking. Thus Marie de Medici was recalled from the dead to speak from her own unfortunate experience: *The Spirit of the Late Queen Mother, Speaking to the Queen, on the Condition of the Regency.*[31] Charles I of England, freshly executed, added his voice to show what could happen when monarchs disregarded the wishes of their subjects: *The Shade of the King of England as it Appeared to the Queen of France.*[32] And to point out alleged lessons of the more distant past, there was the *Chronology of Queens Brought to Misfortune by the Insolence of their Favorites, Dedicated to the Queen Regent to Serve Her as Example and Mirror.*[33] With a cavalier disregard for historical facts, the anonymous author cited a series of queens and princesses who had come to grief, so he maintained, because they insisted on following the bad advice of men whom they idolized: Hecuba, mother of Priam; Olympias, mother of Alexander; Agrippina, mother of Caligula; Joanna of Castile, mother of the Emperor Charles V; and Anne Boleyn, mother of Elizabeth. The author further urged the queen regent to consider that favorites were ungrateful creatures at best, interested in their own self-aggrandizement. She would lose nothing by banishing Mazarin from court and kingdom; on the contrary, all France would bless her.

There is no evidence that Anne read any of this literature. She did not need to do so in any case, since people about her were telling her substantially the same things. She had heard protests against Mazarin in the convents she liked to visit, and the devout even waylaid her on her travels. Mademoiselle reported one such incident, during the court's return journey from Bordeaux in 1650. A pious recluse, an invalid lady, insisted on seeing the queen in order to give her a solemn warning that she must send away Mazarin. Anne replied only,

"You do not know him; he has no other interest except that of the king."[34] She remarked later that the poor woman must have been instructed to speak as she had done.

Mademoiselle herself claimed to have talked to Anne frankly on that same journey. There was hardly anything left of the royal army, Mademoiselle pointed out, and the parlements in Paris and the provinces were not about to accept Mazarin's continuation in office. Indeed, the lesser courts would soon join the parlements, so that in the end Anne and the king would not be able to enter any place larger than a village: "For the sake of a difficulty that amounts to nothing, it is very strange to want to spend one's days traveling from village to village, thus exposing the authority of the king which is already so much in decline."[35]

The usually submissive and discreet Madame de Motteville also joined the chorus of reprobation. She ventured to suggest, after Mazarin's departure in February 1651, that Anne was well rid of him. The queen once again explained, as she had done in 1643, that it was very difficult to find a disinterested minister who did not belong to any faction. And, she added, "I believe I have an obligation to defend a minister who is being taken from me by force."[36] She was aware of his faults, she said, but knew him to be well-intentioned for the king's service as well as her own. Moreover, he had conducted the government very well as long as he had been left alone. He had been betrayed by the very people for whom he had done favors, and his misfortune obliged her to feel the more pity for him.

Anne's unshakable determination to stand by her minister puzzled her contemporaries, many of whom could explain it only by assuming that Mazarin had a sexual hold over her. The *frondeur* press made the most of such allegations and focused popular feeling against her even more than against Mazarin. A ditty composed by one of Gaston's men expressed that plainly:

> I don't blame the cardinal;
> He is a foreigner who wants revenge.
> I pardon his hatred;
> But I'd like to strangle
> Our whore of a queen
> Tra-la
> Our whore of a queen.[37]

Probably the most scabrous attack on Anne appeared in a pamphlet published in 1649: *The Queen's Keeper Tells All.*[38] The narrative, in verse, opened with the lines

> People, don't doubt it any longer,
> It's true that he's f.....d her
> And through this hole Jules s....s on us. . . .

From fornication the poem went on to sodomy, but its chief feature was a long monologue by the queen in which she confessed that she loved Mazarin more than her son or the state, and that for her minister's sake she was content to sacrifice every duty.

As it happened, the printer, Claude Morlot, was caught at work on the piece with his assistant. The two men were put on trial for *lèse majesté* and were sentenced to hang. On the way to their execution, however, they were rescued by a sympathetic mob. The Parlement of Paris, which had the jurisdiction, sent an apology to the queen for the mishap, but since it did not pursue Morlot further, the episode marked what could be called an open season on Anne's reputation.[39]

The attacks on her did not cease even after Mazarin went into exile. Scurrilous verses continued to circulate, such as these:

> But if he comes back, what shall we do?
> We will cut off his private parts.
> The king says: "Don't do that,
> Mama still has a use for them."[40]

The *frondeurs* wanted assurance that Mazarin's exile would be permanent, and their pamphleteers spared no arguments, as can be seen in *The Queen's Convulsions the Night Before Mazarin's Depature, with the Consolation She Received from the Appearance of a Good Saint, Which has Caused Her to Resolve not to Wish any Longer for Mazarin's Return, for Fear of Setting her Kingdom on Fire for a Third Time.*[41] In this pamphlet the queen awoke from a nightmare in which she had seen Paris become a desert and her subjects turned into wild beasts. Overcome with horror, she cried,

> "I am losing my son's state, my reputation, and my subjects' hearts, and all for the sake of a miserable foreigner. . . . Jesus, my Lord, who would have believed in the time of the late cardinal [Richelieu], seeing me all steeped in devotion, that I would thus take wing when I got my freedom, and that my widowhood would be so different from the time I spent married to the late king."[42]

There was a suggestion that one of the opera singers Mazarin had imported must have slipped her a love potion; there was also a hint that Mazarin only made show of reciprocating her feelings. In the midst of the queen's lamentations, Saint Genevieve, patroness of Paris, appeared with admonitions. The saint told the queen that she had usurped the regency against the wishes of Louis XIII and the Parlement (which was not true), and that, seeing she had done so badly with it, she should give it up if she wished to avoid the punishment of hellfire hereafter. The wrath of God would surely destroy her son's monarchy unless she let Mazarin go and devoted herself in future to satisfying her people's grievances. In the end the repentant queen resolved to change her manner of living. In the morning when Mazarin came to take leave of her, she told him that she was taking back her heart as voluntarily as she had given it.

Among all the obscenities spewed out in the *Mazarinades*, what was the truth? What was Anne to Mazarin, and what was he to her?

On the evidence of Anne's own letters to Mazarin, she loved him. Eleven of them have been preserved, each with its red seals and pink silk ties.[43] They were published in the mid-nineteenth century, with the addition of a twelfth letter that appears from its contents to be genuine but whose manuscript has never since been found[44]—a small remnant of what originally must have been a voluminous correspondence. Anne wrote the letters herself, in great secrecy while Mazarin was in exile, more openly after his definitive return whenever he was away from court with the army. French historians have uniformly deplored her unformed handwriting and erratic spelling, faults that they have taken as evidence of ignorance and a failure to assimilate French culture. In fact, however, Anne did not write much more badly than her late husband Louis XIII, and considerably better than some ladies of the high aristocracy who were French born and bred. If the letters are troublesome to read, it is because she and Mazarin used a private set of code phrases, words, and numbers to refer to themselves, their feelings, and other people. In her letters the numbers fifteen and twenty-two meant Anne herself; sixteen meant Mazarin; "the confidant" meant the young king. Mazarin used greater variety, calling himself Heaven, the Sea, or twenty-six; the queen, Serafin, Zabaot, as well as twenty-two; and the king, twenty-one, as well as "the confidant." Both Anne and Mazarin, however, used the same symbols to express devotion: for Anne a vertical line crossed by three short lines, for Mazarin four intersecting lines forming a star. They invariably ended their letters in that fashion, Mazarin with one or more stars and Anne with three crosshatched lines.

The first of Anne's surviving letters dates from January 1653.[45] Anne poured out her feelings when she wrote to Mazarin:

. . . I no longer know when to expect your return, since every day brings obstacles to prevent it. All I can say is that I am very upset about it and bear this delay with great impatience; and if sixteen knew all that fiteen suffers on that account, I feel sure he would be touched. I am so moved at this moment that I do not have strength to write for long nor much idea of what I am saying. I have received your letters almost every day, and without that I do not know what would happen. Continue to write to me as often since you console me in the state in which I am . . . [crosshatched vertical line and star] to the last breath . . . Adieu, I cannot go on. [star] well knows why.[46]

On another occasion, after she had asked for instructions concerning a decision that had to be made, she added:

. . . I confess to you that I should very much like to see the business succeed, more for the sake of sixteen than of fifteen, because every-thing he will ever have or possess belongs more to sixteen than him-self. I have no doubt you believe me, because you know to what extent [crosshatched vertical line] is. I would say more if I did not fear to worry you with such a long letter; and although I am very happy to be writing to you, it upsets me so much that the necessity for it goes on, that I should very much like to talk to you in a different fashion. I say nothing about that; for I fear I should not speak too rationally on that subject.[47]

And as Mazarin's arrival continued to be put off, Anne wrote:

. . . I have just received one of your letters of the twenty-first, in which you give me hope of seeing you; but until I positively know the day, I will not believe a word of it because I have been deceived so often. I wish it very much, and assure you that you never will be deceived by [crosshatched vertical line] since it is the same thing as [star].[48]

Mazarin's half of the correspondence is not extant for this period; on the other hand, a goodly number of his letters from his first exile have survived, permitting us to compare his and Anne's expressed sentiments. His description of his feelings was as fervent, though more fluent and eloquent than hers, as befitted a man who lived pen in hand. He had better command of himself, however, for he alter-nated his compliments with appeals and political advice in a fashion calculated to move the queen to action on his behalf. In May 1651, for example, he wrote:

. . . How happy I should be, and you how satisfied, if you could see my heart, for if I could write you about its condition, and say only half the things I have in mind, you would easily agree there never has been a friendship that comes close to mine with you. I confess that I should never have imagined it could go so far as to deprive me of all pleasure when I spend time doing anything other than thinking of you; but it is true, and to such a degree that it would be impossible for me to do anything whatever, if I did not believe it is for your service.[49]

Two pages of admonition and advice followed, urging her to exert herself more to hasten his return. Then came another passage of compliments, in which he claimed that it sometimes seemed to him it would be better for his peace of mind if Anne did not write to him at all, or wrote coldly—though he begged her to do no such thing. But for the next several pages he reverted to the practical problems of bringing his exile to an end. After that he concluded with an effusion that mingled passionate feeling and political purpose:

> . . . I would give my life to see you again, and before I die, to tell you things that assuredly no one has ever so much as imagined.
> Let me know, I beg of you for pity's sake, if that will be and at whatever price, and have the Confidant write it to me: for in the end, without this assurance and if I do not see you entirely resolved [to act] whatever happens, all that you may tell me about Spain [Anne's feelings] counts for nothing. Ah! If I could tell you all my thoughts on that subject, what relief that would be. The greatest consolation I have here is to read regularly every day the letters of the Spaniard [the queen] whom you know. They are, in my opinion, more beautiful than the letters of Balzac and Voiture; at least they sustain and touch me more. . . .[50]

Although alternation of emotional with practical passages was the method Mazarin generally followed in his letters to Anne, he showed especial skill in using even his protestations of devotion to envelop a political message. In July 1651, for example, he wrote:

> Ah! How I pity the condition of twenty-two! It gives me a thousand times more pain than my own state, and I tremble when I think it could get even worse through the bad advice of those people who flatter her in order to ruin everything.[51]

And in another letter shortly thereafter, he slipped in a reminder to Anne that she had obligations to him:

> Forty-six [Mazarin] tells me that he has suffered greatly from his misfortunes, but much more for those of twenty-two, and that the condition of twenty-six was strange indeed, finding himself persecuted without cease because he was so happy as to possess the friendship of Serafin.[52]

Of the two correspondents, therefore, Anne was the more spontaneous and Mazarin the more manipulative partner. For him it would
seem that her confidence and affection were means to an end: access
to the work that was his greatest passion.

The nineteenth-century historians who discovered the correspondence between Anne and Mazarin found it shocking that a minister
should be on such terms with a sovereign as to write her that he was
dying for her, or that he wished he could send her his heart, and that
the queen reciprocated in similar language. Even making allowance
for the florid epistolatory style of the mid-seventeenth century, they
concluded that the pair were either lovers or married. On the whole,
they leaned toward an assumption of marriage because they felt it less
distasteful to think of Anne's protestations of affection as coming from
the pen of a wife rather than a mistress.[53] The correspondence itself
does not offer any evidence of marriage between Anne and Mazarin. It
is true that in one of his letters, Mazarin wrote;

> He [Mazarin] is to be pitied, for it is a strange thing for this child to hide
> himself, married and separated at the same time, and constantly beset
> with obstacles to his marriage. It is to be hoped that now nothing will
> be able to prevent his seeing again what he wishes for more than life
> itself. . . .[54]

In the context, however, it would seem he was speaking metaphori-
cally, to express unswerving attachment. Indeed, the entire tenor of
his letters from exile speaks against the existence of a marriage.
Seventeenth-century husbands, whether espoused secretly or not, had
sacred claims and rights over their wives. If Mazarin had enjoyed the
status of a husband, with all of the attendant moral and religious authority, he would hardly have adopted the posture of a supplicant and
wooer as consistently as he did, nor is it likely that he would have
appealed so desperately to the queen's feelings. Nevertheless, the
theory that he was married to Anne has persisted, despite a lack of
solid evidence.

Anne's and Mazarin's contemporaries themselves speculated about
it. Someone indeed asked her director of conscience, Vincent de Paul,
whether it was true that he had married them, to which he replied that
is was as false as the devil.[55] Unfortunately he did not make clear
whether it was false that he had married them, or false that they were
married at all. More than a half-century later, however, Elizabeth Charlotte, the second wife of Philippe of Anjou, retailed it as fact that Anne
had married Mazarin.[56] Elizabeth Charlotte was a very witty and pro-

lific correspondent, attributes which have endeared her to historians as a source, but she was an unreliable reporter of historical fact. Most probably what she did in this particular case was to repeat ancient court gossip. Numerous scholars have taken her word at face value, however, and by way of confirmation have pointed out that since Mazarin, although a cardinal, was neither bishop, nor ordained priest, nor even a deacon, it seemed entirely possible for him to marry.[57] A further argument has been added by Louis XIV's most recent biographer, who noted that Anne and Mazarin brought Louis into their correspondence and that the three lived on such terms of mutual respect as to preclude any clandestine relationship. In short, they acted like a family because they were a family.[58]

At first glance, this is a very persuasive observation. Anne, Mazarin, and Louis did indeed live on close terms. Mazarin never forgot that his career depended as much on the good will of the young king as on the support of his mother. In his secret letters, he asked for news of Louis; worried if he did not hear from him; sent regards; and begged Anne to keep his memory alive in the boy's mind: "It will be very useful for you and for me if the Confidant esteems and trusts him [Mazarin]."[59] And several months later, ". . . I beg you to embrace the Confidant from me and to tell him a thousand things about the passion I have for him."[60] After eventually receiving his recall from exile, Mazarin ended his letter of thanks:

> . . . I beg you to tell your Confidant that the Sea will not see him without his relative [Mazarin] and that both will die a thousand times for him and for the person whom he loves the most. [crosshatched vertical line and star].[61]

Anne, on her side, when she wrote to Mazarin while he and the king were with the army, never failed to ask Mazarin to embrace the king for her. When Mazarin was at the front alone while the king remained at court, she transmitted messages:

> . . . The Confidant does not write to you because you cannot perceive any difference in our handwriting, any more than in our feelings, since they are the same for you and though only one hand writes, the hearts are united in friendship.[62]

Clearly the Confidant was in his mother's confidence.

The marriage theory, however, has been disproved quite conclusively. A modern Mazarin scholar has reviewed his status in the church and recalled the unquestionable fact that, although cardinals who were not priests sometimes married, they thereby ceased to be cardinals. Moreover, thorough examination of the relevant registers in the Vatican archives reveals that Mazarin took great pains to comply with the regulations pertaining to his office; and he was so unpopular at the Vatican during the late 1640s and early 1650s that there could be no question of his having received extraordinary favors or exemptions. Indeed, had he been guilty of any major irregularity, it would have come to light, especially since Gaston of Orléans and others were urging Innocent X to put him on trial in Rome. Lastly, some months before his death, Mazarin began to think seriously of becoming ordained, a step impossible to contemplate while Anne was still alive had they in fact been married.[63]

But if Anne and Mazarin were not married, were they lovers? A few ambiguous passages in their letters might be taken to point that way. First of all, there was Anne's exclamation, which so shocked the nineteenth century: "Adieu, I cannot go on. [star] well knows why."[64] And in Mazarin's letters, there are several suggestive passages:

. . . You never explain yourself and say more obliging things than when you hold back your pen and refrain from declaring certain sentiments.[65]

I shall see you in a fortnight no matter what happens. In saying that, I am beside myself. Think, I ask you, what will happen when twenty-six sees twenty-two. I shall say no more about it since you know the rest because of [crosshatched vertical lines] and [star], who are in perfect friendship despite everything that has been done to separate them.[66]

I am waiting with very great impatience to know what will happen at the meeting between the Sea and twenty-two; but I believe I can tell you ahead of time that twenty-two will be pleased with the Sea, because twenty-six, his good friend, has assured me of it. I have heard that the Sky [Mazarin] would very much have liked to see Zabaot in private; but that is believed to be very difficult.[67]

Such words and phrases, however, did not necessarily carry a specific sexual meaning. Psychological considerations also speak against an outright love affair. It was by no means unknown for royal ladies to have lovers. As we noted earlier, Anne's sister-in-law Christine of Savoy indulged herself in that way even during her husband's lifetime; and Anne's other sister-in-law Henrietta Marie of England at the least carried on a very cordial relationship with Mazarin's good friend Lord

Montague. But unlike Louis XIII's sisters, Anne was extremely devout. It is inconceivable that she could have lived for decades in mortal sin while at the same time taking communion every Sunday and holiday. Nor was hers the kind of tortured personality that alternates between sin and expiation. Her temperament was on the placid side, and by all accounts she liked a comfortable routine in her spiritual as well as her material life. Most likely she believed that, short of intercourse, loving Mazarin was not a sin. She had told Madame de Motteville once that in her youth she had never believed there could be any harm in gallantry; that people who had done nothing wrong had nothing of which to be ashamed and need not worry over the opinion of others.[68]

It would have been in character for Anne to have loved Mazarin without engaging in physical relations and without regard for appearances. Her old friend Madame de Chevreuse, an expert in such matters, was never sure that there was anything sexual between Anne and Mazarin.[69] Louis XIV's boyhood companion, the son of Secretary of State Brienne, later recalled that there had been much talk at court about the queen and her minister; that Louis himself was aware of it and occasionally referred to it; but that the whole affair was quite obscure and ambiguous. There is one revealing fact, however. At one point in his exile, Mazarin feared seriously that the queen had abandoned him. He was so upset that he put aside gallant phrases and wrote spontaneously, and what he appealed to was not her love but her kindness, her sense of justice, and the purity of her conscience.[71] And in a letter to a go-between, Mazarin added what he evidently considered the most telling argument of all for his reinstatement: Louis XIII had made him head of his council and chosen him to be godfather to his son in return for Mazarin's promise that he would serve the boy all his life. Surely the queen must remember that on his deathbed Louis XIII twice explained all this to her and exacted from her the promise that in her turn she would stand by Mazarin.[72]

Mazarin was indeed the godfather of Louis XIV. As a modern scholar has pointed out, that status put Mazarin and Anne in the forbidden degrees of kinship in the eyes of the church: marriage or fornication would have been incest. On the other hand, the relationship created a strong sprititual bond, the equivalent of a family bond, between Mazarin, Anne, and her son.[73] On this fabric Mazarin and Anne built their idyll of mutual affection: godparent and parent were united in a common obligation to protect the interests of the young king.

Chapter Seventeen

Coronation of Louis

EVEN IN EXILE, MAZARIN CONtinued to serve the young king and his mother. The Spaniards paid him the sincere compliment of offering him employment, an offer that he declined.[1] He spent his time keeping abreast of events in France and sent suggestions, not to say instructions, to Secretary of State Le Tellier, the minister Abel Servien and his nephew Lionne, as well as to Anne herself. He could not rely on the rest of the royal council. Secretary of State Brienne had always been Anne's man rather than Mazarin's, and the two other secretaries of state, Guénégaud and Phélypeaux, were bureaucrats who kept themselves to themselves. Chancellor Séguier had never been a particular friend of Mazarin, and besides he had his own troubles threading his way between the rival factions of the Fronde. As for the ministers who had been named to placate this or that camp, Villeroy and the abbé de La Rivière were Gaston's men; and Mazarin's enemy Chavigny was more or less representing the interests of Condé. In Mazarin's absence, however, Anne did not choose another first minister. Chavigny, who had hoped to step into Mazarin's shoes, felt so chagrined in his disappointment that he resigned from the council during the summer. Clearly Anne considered Mazarin her first minister whether he was present or not.

It was no easy matter for Mazarin to direct business from across the frontier. He complained that Lionne was not reporting everything he should, nor sending dispatches as diligently as could be wished:

> . . . As for your parading the various dates of your letters, you ought to add that you sent them all by the same courier; and I shall not tell you that if you wrote to me every day and kept the dispatches, I should not be very well informed.[2]

In his frustration Mazarin came to suspect Lionne as well as Servien of being lukewarm in his service; he believed they were speaking to Anne more of their own interests than of his, though he admitted that they were probably not actually betraying him. He continued to need them and Le Tellier, however, not only for information but also to back up the advice he was giving the queen. She was not used to methodical work and had to be encouraged by persons close to her.

In May, when it began to look as though Mazarin's exile would be protracted, he sent Anne a lengthy memorandum for her guidance.[3] In it he outlined the alignment of the *frondeurs*, analyzed the position of all the leading members of the government, and indicated how far, in his opinion, each one could be trusted. Clearly it was a novelty for her to read and digest so much material; she had become accustomed over the years to leaving all tedious business to Mazarin and relying on his oral reports. In his covering letter, therefore, Mazarin apologized for the trouble the length of the memorandum would give her.[4] He had had it copied by a secretary, he said, in order to make it easier for her to read. He implored her to reflect on it thoroughly, and to read the whole at least three times, even if that took her three days. He suggested that she take the time for this study during her religious retreats, since she could be assured "that it was important for the service of God, of the king" and of herself.[5] Above all, she was to keep the document hidden, so that she could use its contents as a secret touchstone to test the veracity and loyalty of her entourage. Apparently she followed instructions, for outsiders never knew of the memorandum nor indeed of the entire correspondence between Anne and Mazarin. Even Madame de Chevreuse still went about saying confidently that the queen would have forgotten Mazarin entirely within eighteen months—a remark that provided Anne and Mazarin with much amusement in their letters.[6]

Mazarin continually supplemented his general summary with specific advice and requests. He bade Anne to let him know, however, if she found the length of his letters troublesome and commiserated with her over having to exert herself so much. In fact, he would have liked her to exert herself more; " . . . You know what I have always told you without flattery about the intelligence of Zabaot, and my opinion of it: the only thing I could wish for is a little application."[7] But her capacity for application had limits. She did not become her own prime minister, work her way through dispatches, or even read official proclamations issued in the king's name. And although she was able to operate on the level of personalities, it seems she found it difficult to analyze political situations and deduce their implications and consequences. Those were weaknesses of which the *frondeurs* tried to take advantage, and for which Mazarin made every effort to compensate by his copious instructions.

Mazarin and Anne were agreed on a strategy for dealing with the

Fronde. It was simple and had been tried before: namely, to exploit differences between the *frondeurs* and to separate them from one another. This time Mazarin and the queen had help from an insider in the enemy camp, Anne of Gonzaga, princess Palatine. Her branch of the Gonzaga family had affiliations in France; she herself had married the prince Palatine, son of the unfortunate elector Palatine whose Bohemian adventures had precipitated the Thirty Years' War and who had lost most of his ancestral lands as a result. Anne of Gonzaga and her husband were clients of the king of France, which meant that she spent much time at court and had indeed been a very good friend of the queen during the past years. More recently, she had joined forces with Madame de Chevreuse and her friends, principally because she saw an opportunity to make herself sufficiently important to oblige the court to buy her off. This calculation bore fruit when Mazarin was exiled. The princess Palatine offered her services to him and the queen as confidential agent and negotiator in return for the promise that she would be named superintendent of the household of the young queen when Louis XIV came to marry. Mazarin trusted her with the code he and the queen used, and wrote to her, as well as to her man of business, almost as often as he wrote to Anne.[8]

What disrupted the coalition of the *frondeurs*, however, was less the princess's intervention than Conti's refusal to honor his agreement to marry Madame de Chevreuse's daughter Charlotte. Conti's and Condé's sister, the duchess de Longueville, was adamant in her opposition to the match and made sure to let her brothers know on just what friendly terms the intended bride had lived for years with the coadjutor Retz. The queen furnished Condé with a polite pretext for breaking off the engagement: the king, she assured Condé, would not permit this marriage.[9] Madame de Chevreuse was so enraged at the insult of having her daughter jilted that she led her friends in a campaign of vituperation against Condé, clamored for his arrest, and declared herself ready to back Mazarin. She and Retz had several interviews with Anne and struck a bargain: their section of the Fronde would agree to Mazarin's return on condition that Retz be named a cardinal and that Mademoiselle de Chevreuse marry Mazarin's nephew Mancini. In contrast to her performance in the past, Madame de Chevreuse kept her word until the death of her daughter in November of the following year, 1652, led her to retire into the country and abandon politics altogether. Her defection from the Fronde, however, still left the queen faced with the problem of dealing with Gaston and Condé and the dangerous political issues they were raising.

The year 1651 was especially critical for the monarchy because after the king's thirteenth birthday on 5 September he would enter his majority according to established custom. That meant the regency would come to an end, together with Gaston's commission as lieutenant general of the kingdom. From then on the king would, at least in principle, be head of his own government, with all the advantages of respect this would give him in the popular mind. The king's majority, however, had to be declared formally in the Parlement of Paris. It was the queen's object to ensure that the ceremonies would take place without friction or opposition, but Gaston, Condé, and their allies tried to use these last months of the regency to alter the constitution in a last bid for power.

Early in 1651, assemblies of the nobility had met in Paris and in the provinces with the encouragement of Gaston of Orléans. They had demanded first the release of the princes, and, once that was accomplished, they went on to ask for a meeting of the Estates General. The Assembly of the Clergy joined in this request, as did Condé, his brother, and brother-in-law. There had been talk two years earlier about a meeting of the estates, but this time it was more serious. All factions combined to put pressure on the queen, though they were somewhat at cross-purposes. Mazarin feared the *frondeurs* would use the estates to force the king to confirm all the declarations issued by the Parlement in recent times, declarations not only directed against Mazarin himself but also tending to limit the king's authority, " . . . so that the [king's] majority will begin with the destruction of the monarchy."[10] The clergy, however, vehemently opposed one of those declarations, namely, the one prohibiting cardinals from sitting on the king's council. Nor were all the judges in the Parlement enthusiastic about the prospect of having the Estates General meet. The Parlement had long ago come to see itself as the supreme guardian and arbiter of law, including constitutional law; and one distinguished judge, Nicolas de Mesmes, declared roundly that the voice of the Parlement was superior to that of the Estates General.[11]

Considering these corporate jealousies, the Estates General might not have been any more effective than they had been in 1614 in presenting a united front against the crown. Mazarin thought otherwise, however. In his opinion it would be far safer if the estates were not allowed to meet at all because Condé and his relatives, through the governorships of provinces that they held and their network of clients and dependents in subsidiary posts, could easily control a working majority of the deputies from the nobility and the third estate. If the queen could not avoid bowing to pressure, Mazarin advised her, she should consent to call a meeting of the Estates General but at least make sure that the date of its convocation was set after the king's thirteenth birthday, when he would be in a stronger constitutional position.[12]

Although at the time neither Mazarin nor the queen had specific inside information concerning the program of the princes for the Estates General, Mazarin's fears were in fact justified. Madame de Chevreuse's old friend Châteauneuf later revealed the princes' scheme to one of Mazarin's clients: first of all, the fundamental law was to be changed and the king's majority set at eighteen years instead of the customary thirteen. The king thus still being a minor for the next five years, he was to get a regency council of twenty-one members consisting of the queen, Gaston, Condé, and eighteen representatives of the estates, with the deputies of the clergy, the nobility, and the third estate each choosing six respectively. Within the council the eighteen men from the estates were to function as a standing committee to watch over the execution of the estates' decisions.[13]

Here indeed was a project capable of leading to the "destruction of the monarchy" or, at any rate, of the monarchy as Louis XIII and Richelieu had understood it. It did not come to the test, however, for the Estates General never met. The queen consented to their meeting and set the date for 8 September, several days after the king's birthday—a delay to which the Parlement did not object and which Gaston persuaded the nobility to accept. During the summer, therefore, election meetings took place all over France, even where unauthorized, as in the city of Paris.[14] If the electors compiled the usual *cahiers*, or books of grievances, little of their work has survived. A few noble *cahiers* exist, and the members of the French Reformed church as well as the estates of Languedoc apparently took this opportunity to present such books, for there are references to them in subsequent decisions of the royal council. It is not likely, however, that these were the only groups to draft a collection of grievances.[15] Certainly everyone concerned seemed to take the impending meeting of the estates quite seriously. The royal council solemnly ruled on procedure and adjudicated election disputes from August through September, with no hint even toward the end of this period that these activities might be exercises in futility.[16] In fact, 8 September passed without the king's showing any sign of departing for Tours to open the meeting of his estates. Although hope remained for a time that he was merely postponing the convocation, events soon made it impracticable for the estates to meet at all.

Throughout the spring and summer, Anne had given every appearance of good faith not only about the estates but also in meeting other demands of the *frondeurs* while following Mazarin's advice to play off the factions within the Fronde as much as possible. It seemed she was prepared to do anything to ensure the king's safe passage into his majority, especially since the ceremony required the cooperation of the Parlement. Thus in July, Anne yielded to often-repeated importunities and dismissed Mazarin's creatures from the royal council: Abel Servien, Secretary of State Le Tellier, and his nephew Lionne. At the same time, however, she managed to get rid of the troublemaker Chavigny. Chavigny had thought his opportunity had come; he seized upon the occasion of the apparent purge to put an ultimatum to the queen: either she name him first minister or he would retire to his country house. "The country house," Anne replied laconically, and so Chavigny departed.[17] She still had unofficial advisers who could be trusted to represent the interest and reinforce the advice of Mazarin: military men such as the marquis de Senneterre, marshall d'Estrées, marshall du Plessis Praslin; and the princess Palatine and her agent Bartet, as well as Mazarin's agents, Ondedei and Mileti. But even some of these people were coming under fire, and for the moment there could be no question of her creating her own party within the royal council itself as Mazarin was hoping she would do.[18]

Meanwhile, as we have seen, Anne was negotiating with Madame de Chevreuse and overcame her distaste for Retz sufficiently to grant him several secret interviews. She professed to believe in his and Madame de Chevreuse's good faith, and agreed to the bargain they offered: they would secretly help her work toward Mazarin's return, in exchange for which Retz would be made a cardinal, Châteauneuf would become first minister, the first president of the Parlement would be keeper of the seals, and a friend of the princess Palatine, la Vieuville, superintendent of finances.[19] Their common enemy was Condé, so that Anne felt strong enough to accuse Condé formally of treasonable commerce with Spain—an accusation that was true enough though unsupported as yet by more than shrewd suspicion. Condé asked for a trial to clear himself, but his behavior toward the king and queen became so discourteous as to approach lèse-majesté—a display that should have given Gaston of Orléans and the Parlement food for sobering thought.

Anne's secret alliances notwithstanding, the outlook for Mazarin did not seem to improve. Having secured the dismissal of Mazarin's creatures, the *frondeurs* continued to pursue Mazarin himself. Notably the Parlement wanted to commit the crown irrevocably against Mazarin's possible future return and petitioned the queen to confirm in the king's name all the sentences it had rendered against the cardinal. At first Anne temporized with an oral reply, promising a delegation from the Parlement on 17 August that she would soon publish the requisite decrees.[20] She had to keep the promise eventually. On 5 September, the king's birthday and two days before the ceremony of his majority, the Parlement registered with great satisfaction a royal letter confirming that Mazarin was excluded forever from the kingdom and forbidding anyone whomsoever from communicating with him.[21] On the same date, Anne sent the Parlement a letter discharging Condé from the accusation of treason. No one was to have an excuse for troubling the king's assumption of power.

Mazarin's anxiety over his prospects had been growing throughout the summer. He could not understand why the queen failed to impose her will to bring about his return. He warned her against the dangers of weakness, appealed to her affection, tried to arouse her fears that their separation might prove to be permanent if she did not show more resolution.

He had a first shock early in September when Secretary of State Brienne informed him that the queen wished him to go to Rome for what was assumed to be an impending papal election. Mazarine was horrified. What influence could he hope to exert in Rome, where Innocent X had so lately been advised to put him on trial? Where he would not have the backing of an assured position in France, and thus no power base in negotiations? He hastened to protest to Anne that he had lost his normal income and could not possibly appear in Rome, close to beggary, and expose himself to contempt. He begged her in the name of God not to urge him to go to Rome, "into the hands of my enemies, and to ask for alms in my birthplace, banished from France with ignominy."[22] He thought the plan was an artful device of his enemies for removing him even farther from France, a device whose implications Anne had evidently not penetrated. Perhaps she had not; it is possible that she had seen in the journey to Rome only an employment more honorable for Mazarin than exile in Brühl.[23] If so, his protest enlightened her, and she did not press the matter.

But his alarm on that occasion was as nothing compared with his feelings a few weeks later when news finally reached him of the royal declaration concerning him that the Parlement had registerd on 5 September. He was beside himself at this mortal blow, and he wrote Anne:

> The king and the queen, by an authentic act, have declared me a traitor, a public thief, incompetent, and an enemy to the peace of Christendom, after having served them with so much loyalty, with no self-interest, with so many great successes, and having taken so many pains and given so many signs of my passion for the progress of peace![24]

Moreover, the declaration was bound to reflect on the queen's judgment, "for everyone will accuse her of having honored with her affection, and protected the interests of a man whom in the end she was obliged to declare a miscreant."[25] He felt so ashamed that he wanted to die. He demanded a trial so that his innocence could be vindicated and his honor restored; he even offered to go to Rome if only he were rehabilitated. Above all he could not believe that Anne had read the actual text of the declaration; if she had, she would surely not have signed it contrary to all justice. If she had kept herself better informed, he wrote her, this disaster would not have happened.

Mazarin wrote to the king also, combining his congratulations on Louis's majority with a petition for redress.[26] Weeks passed, however, with no sign of action in his favor. Anne sent him private letters, assuring him that neither her affection nor her intentions regarding his recall had changed. She let him know too, through his agent Mileti, that she had had no choice in consenting to the declaration, but that she would never permit it to be confirmed by the king after the majority.[27] Although Mazarin thanked her profusely for her letters and professed to feel much relieved, his agitation scarcely abated until the middle of November when he actually received the king's command to rejoin the court.

Had Anne known all along what she was doing, or was Mazarin right in believing that she had let herself be surprised by his opponents? Unfortunately we have no information whatever about the way in which she made political decisions during this time, nor even about council discussions. In the absence of Le Tellier, Servien, and Lionne, Mazarin kept Anne advised through his agent Ondedei,[28] but it is impossible to tell how she used the instructions that came to her through this channel. In the case of the declaration against the cardinal, as Mazarin imagined the circumstances, his enemies on the council had given her only a bare outline of the document and had minimized its importance as much as possible. Since Mazarin knew Anne's habits, his conviction that she had not read the declaration but had trusted to reports on it[29] ought to carry due weight. On the other hand, it may be that she attached less importance to words, however injurious to his honor, than he did. It would not have been the first time that she used a lie when driven to extremity. If so, she gained her purpose, for it must be admitted that the king's majority passed very smoothly.

At the queen's request, from the feast of Saint Louis on 25 August to the ceremony on 7 September the monks of Saint-Denis kept the relics of Saint Louis exposed in order to obtain extraordinary graces for the king by the saint's intercession.[30] No special festivities marked the king's birthday this year; celebrations were reserved for 7 September. On that day Louis rode in cavalcade from the Palais-Royal to the Palais de Justice on the Île de la Cité.[31] He made a splendid figure, dressed in a coat so covered with gold embroidery that neither the cloth nor its color could be seen, and he was in such high spirits that he made his Arab horse prance and rear several times on the way for the sheer pleasure of it. Arrived at the Palais de Justice, he opened the full royal session of the court with the fateful words:

> Gentlemen, I am come into my Parlement to tell you, that according to the law of my state, I wish to undertake the government myself, and I hope from God's goodness that it will be with piety and justice. Monsieur the Chancellor will tell you my intentions in more detail.[32]

Séguier, the chancellor, did so. Then the queen, leaning forward a little in her seat, addressed her son:

> Monsieur, this is the ninth year that according to the last will of the late king, my very honored lord, I have taken care of your education and the government of your state; God in his goodness having blessed my work, and preserved your person which is so dear and so precious to me and to all your subjects, now that the law of the kingdom calls you to the government of this monarchy, I surrender to you with great satisfaction the power which had been given to me for governing it: and I hope that God will give you the grace of assisting you with his spirit in strength and wisdom, to make your reign a happy one.[33]

The king replied:

> Madam, I thank you for the care it has pleased you to take of my education and of the administration of my kingdom. I pray you to continue to give me your good advice; and it is my wish that after me you be the head of my council.[34]

The queen got up intending to cross over to the king and salute him as the first of his subjects, but he came to her instead and embraced and kissed her. Next his brother Philippe came to bend a knee and kiss his hand, and he was followed by Gaston of Orléans, the prince of Conti, and all the other peers and officers of the crown who were present. The first president of the Parlement, Molé, spoke eloquently of the great virtues the queen had shown during her regency. The chancellor ordered the doors opened to the public while the 5 September declaration of Condé's innocence was read and thus confirmed by the king. In a notable omission, there was no reading of any declaration against Mazarin.

That night the royal family enjoyed a theatrical performance followed by fireworks and a bedtime serenade for the king while Parisians illuminated their windows and lit joyful bonfires in the streets. Next day, a Friday, the king, his mother, and the court, escorted by the city councillors, went to the cathedral of Notre-Dame, where Retz as coadjutor to the archbishop of Paris received them at the door. Anne spent the rest of the day at Val-de-Grâce, presumably with a full heart. Thereafter it was time to honor the bargains that had been struck during the summer.

On 21 September the king announced that he was nominating Retz for a cardinal's hat.[35] Meanwhile the royal council was reorganized to accommodate the friends of Madame de Chevreuse and the princess Palatine, particularly Châteauneuf. Châteauneuf, however, found that he had to make do with the position of chief of the council of dispatches—as the royal council was called when it met to consider routine business and to render decisions on appeals, petitions, and reports. He had of course hoped to become first minister, and he continued to cherish that hope in the face of every discouragement. Neither he nor Retz in fact abided by their agreement to work among the *frondeurs* for the return of Mazarin, since neither could give up the dream of displacing Mazarin permanently.

As for the prince of Condé, he had not attended the king's coming of age, making transparent excuses for his absence. Within several weeks and after a family council, he decided that his best interests lay in active rebellion. In mid-September he left the vicinity of Paris for his government in Guyenne, where he would raise his supporters and negotiate with the Spaniards; he had been in touch with Spain since the spring. Under these circumstances the royal court did not need to waste any further attention on the Estates General. Instead the king and queen with their entourage left on 27 September for the southwestern provinces in order to support the royal troops there and to counteract Condé's influence as much as possible.[36] On the way the king sent Mazarin the long-awaited letter inviting him to return to court, explaining that Condé's rebellion had made it clear the princes' demand for Mazarin's removal had merely served them as a pretext for perpetuating disorder.

Mazarin joyfully accepted the invitation. His relief after the months of strain and uncertainty was immense; all his subsequent letters breathed a new spirit of ease and calm. However, he asked for permission to delay his return while he recruited troops in Germany so that he could come back with at least a small army for the king's service and also for his own protection. He certainly needed protection, for the Parlement of Paris was growing ever more virulent in its hatred for him. The judges sent a deputation to the king asking him not to receive Mazarin and got a noncommittal reply: the king thanked them and said he would make his intentions known more fully at a later time.[37] The Parlement immediately sent further petitions, but meanwhile it had already forbidden officials in towns and strong places on Mazarin's route either to admit him or let him pass, put a price on his head, and ordered his library and other possessions in Paris seized and sold so that the proceeds could be applied to the reward for his head.[38] The Parlement's influence was not as great as it thought, however. Mazarin journeyed across France in January with relatively little trouble, barring an abortive ambush or two,[39] and on 30 January 1652 arrived in Poitiers, where the royal family was staying.

Louis XIV came out to meet him at two leagues' distance—a mark of respect usually reserved for fellow royalty—brought him into the city in his own carriage, and kept him company at supper.[40] Whoever may have witnessed the reunion between Mazarin and Anne, no one recorded it. What mattered, however, was that the family triumvirate was once again complete, with the godfather, mother, and son reunited.

Three days after Mazarin's arrival, Châteauneuf departed, unreconciled and unresigned. Both he and Retz from then on concentrated on Gaston of Orléans as their remaining possible avenue to power. Gaston for his part had professed himself outraged at Mazarin's reentry into the kingdom. In January he had made a treaty with Condé and joined the prince in revolt.

The predicament from which Mazarin now had to extricate the crown was a difficult one. Aside from the internal rebellion instigated by Condé in Guyenne and attempted by his supporters in other provinces, 1651 had brought nothing but military disasters. To the north, on the Flanders front, the Spaniards were retaking the strong places that France had laboriously acquired over the past decade; and to the south, in Catalonia, what remained of the French occupying force found itself being betrayed by the governor, a friend of Condé's. In southwestern France itself, Condé permitted Spanish naval vessels to enter the Gironde River and establish bases at Talmont and Bourg in the province of Saintonge. At the same time, he, as well as the municipal rebels who now controlled the city of Bordeaux, sent envoys to England with the mission of persuading Oliver Cromwell and the Commonwealth government to invade Guyenne and Saintonge. They held out hopes of territorial gain—these provinces had once been English possessions. Furthermore, Condé's emissaries in particular stressed how desirable it would be for the French Protestants of the region to find a champion in Cromwell, and asserted that these Huguenots only awaited an English landing in order to rise up in arms and shake off royal and Catholic oppression.[41]

At this juncture Mazarin's longstanding policy of minimizing religious conflict proved its worth. Since 1643 Mazarin had been urging Anne to treat the Huguenots with consideration, and indeed the royal council had repeatedly confirmed the Edict of Nantes by way of reassurance. Mazarin's own relations with leading Protestant nobles were excellent; he did not, for example, lack confidential go-betweens in negotiating with the Calvinist Turenne to abandon the *frondeurs* and rejoin the king's side. Since the loss of their military autonomy in 1629, the Huguenots had gotten out of the habit of following their nobles in armed adventures, though to be sure there were always pockets of dissatisfaction, particularly in the south and southwest of France. On the whole, however, the king's Protestant subjects had stayed remarkably loyal and peaceful during the disorders of the Fronde, nor were they showing any signs of following the prince of Condé's lures by the spring of 1652. To keep them thus well disposed, Mazarin persuaded the king, queen, and council in May to issue the Declaration of Saint-Germain wherein the king expressed thanks to his Protestant subjects for their good behavior, once again confirmed the Edict of Nantes, and through very careful wording allowed the Huguenots to hope for greater favors to come—possibly even a restoration of their past privileges. The royal council meanwhile accorded their petitions and appeals a benevolent hearing, as indeed it had been doing since the year before.[42]

The French Catholic clergy protested vehemently against this development, but the agents whom Cromwell sent into France to check out Condé's allegations that the Huguenots were oppressed had nothing alarming to report. That was an important advantage, for Mazarin was trying to enter into relations with the government of the Commonwealth not only to prevent Condé from getting English help but also if possible to secure an English alliance as well as naval aid in the hopes of saving Dunkirk from falling into Spanish hands. As it happened, Mazarin found it very difficult to persuade the royal family to enter into relations with Cromwell, the murderer, as they saw it, of their relative by marriage Charles I. Charles's widow, Henrietta Maria, was after all living on the king's bounty in the king's palaces and seemed to expect her French nephew to restore her son to the English throne. Reason of state eventually prevailed, so that in December 1652 France recognized Cromwell's government and sent an ambassador to London. That was too late to save Dunkirk, which had fallen to the Spaniards in September. The treaty of friendship with England for which Mazarin hoped did not come about for another three years, and the military alliance not until 1657. In the spring and summer of 1652, all this still lay far in the future; Mazarin had to deal with the immediate situation by sending what reinforcements he could to the war fronts and simultaneously trying to reduce Condé's bases within France.

The latter effort led to more success than the former; Turenne, reconciled with the court and in command of operations in the north, managed to pin down Condé and his auxiliaries around Paris. On 2 July it looked as though a decisive battle was going to be fought. The king, queen, and court had established themselves at Saint-Denis, on the outskirts of Paris. The queen spent the day in front of the high altar of the local Carmelite convent church while the king and Mazarin went to the heights of Charonne to watch the fighting that was taking place in the suburb in front of the gate of Saint-Antoine.[43] Eventually Condé's people found themselves so hard pressed by Turenne that their only salvation lay in a retreat into Paris, but the city council had steadfastly refused for months to admit the princes' army. Gaston of Orléans, safely ensconced in his quarters in the Luxembourg Palace, hesitated what to do. It was his daughter, Mademoiselle, who saved the day for Condé.

Mademoiselle was her father's most passionate partisan; it pained her when he did not live up to the heroic role that she thought proper for persons of their high rank. At twenty-five she was still unmarried, even though—or perhaps because—she was the richest heiress in France, if not in all Europe. Her vast fortune continued to make any marriage plans the highest matter of state; indeed, it put most possible candidates for her hand out of the running. One match, however, had been proposed to her that she herself found most attractive: the princess Palatine, in her efforts to divide the *frondeurs* and bring about Mazarin's return, had suggested in 1651 that Mademoiselle might marry the king. In her memoirs Mademoiselle claimed not to have taken this proposition seriously.[44] Other persons, however, took it very seriously indeed; Gaston thought it would be a good basis for bargaining with the court, whereas Mazarin expressed strong reservations.[45] Mademoiselle herself objected only to the manner of arranging the marriage, not to the intended bridegroom. She had after all called Louis "her little husband" until Richelieu took her to task for such immodest behavior. And between royalty an age difference of some eleven years was no great matter. During the summer of 1651, she noted with satisfaction how much pleasure Louis seemed to be taking in riding out with her and her friends. She thought he might be on the way to falling in love with her and, had his mother not put a stop to these excursions, might have come to realize that she was the best possible match anyone could propose for him save only for the infanta of Spain.[46] Having the king in love with her—that way of becoming queen, she wrote later, was more to her taste than the other, meaning the princess Palatine's matchmaking.[47]

Mademoiselle's own wishes are clear; whether she read the thirteen-year old Louis's feelings correctly is doubtful. Moreover, it apparently did not occur to her that under any circumstances rebellion might not be the best way to his heart. On 2 July 1652, therefore, no caution held her back, and she resolutely browbeat her father into sending her to the city council with the demand that they open the gates to Condé. She herself rushed to the Saint-Antoine gate to make sure that the guard obeyed these orders, and seeing that the royal troops were coming uncomfortably close, she went on to the Bastille, where she allegedly prevailed upon the commander to turn the guns of the fortress on the king's men. Whoever ordered it, the fire from the Bastille had the desired effect; all of Condé's men entered the city safely.[48] There was also an undesired effect: it had killed any possibiity of Mademoiselle's marrying the king.

Once in the city, Condé and his companions took over the government, partly by instigated violence, partly by intimidation. The Parlement cooperated by naming the duke of Beaufort governor of Paris, Gaston of Orléans lieutenant general of the kingdom, and Condé commander-in-chief of the armed forces. They set up a government council, proceeded to levy taxes, and permitted their army to loot the countryside around Paris, actions that did a great deal to erode what popular support for the Fronde still existed.

To put an end to an intolerable situation and isolate the most rabid *frondeurs* in the Parlement, the king ordered the Parlement to leave Paris and settle in Pontoise. During August an increasing number of judges and councillors obeyed, leaving a dissident rump Parlement in Paris. The loyalists at Pontoise were not, however, completely subdued; they asked the king to send Mazarin away once more, to remove any pretext from Condé and the other princes who were proclaiming that they were making war solely on the cardinal, not on the king. Mazarin agreed to go, though his second exile was very different from the first one. This time he did not travel as far; he went to Sedan and Bouillon, and some of the time the court stayed nearby at Compiègne. He continued to direct the royal council, which he left in the charge of Secretary of State Le Tellier and the unexceptionable Prince Thomas of Savoy-Carignan. It was understood that Mazarin's absence would be a temporary one, and above all he went without stigma: at Anne's insistence, Louis issued a declaration exculpating Mazarin from all charges the Parlement had preferred against him, and explaining that the king was acceding with the greatest reluctance to Mazarin's own request for permission to withdraw.[49]

Mazarin left the court on 19 August. Three days later Condé and the other princes declared themselves ready to put down their arms although at the price of such exorbitant concessions that they left the king no choice but to refuse. For all except the most fanatical *frondeurs*, their enterprise began to take on the appearance of a sinking ship. Retz, Châteauneuf, even Chavigny, approached the court with offers of accommodation: the court was not interested. Retz went to Compiègne to collect his cardinal's hat from the king and proposed to rouse royalist sentiment among the Paris populace, a proposition the king saw no need to accept. Royalist sentiment was already growing in Paris, partly owing to the depredations of Condé's troops, partly through weariness with disorder and fear of mob violence, partly thanks to the efforts of publicists who were being paid by Mazarin to present the case for the king's authority. On 24 September some four thousand citizens took matters into their own hands. Despite prohibitions from the Parlement and the city council, they met in the Palais-Royal, where they resolved to keep on meeting and to take up arms if necessary until legitimate city government was restored. In the face of such determination, the city council gave in. Condé's appointees resigned, and the remainder sent a delegation to the king to plead for his return. Louis agreed provided the city restored his governor as well as the councillors Condé had ousted, and also provided they induced Condé and his allies to remove themselves and their troops from the vicinity of Paris. By the middle of October, the city had fulfilled these conditions. On 21 October, therefore, Louis, the queen, and the court entered Paris, entered the capital by treaty for the third time since the beginning of the Fronde. That it was to be the last time was made plain to all by the sight of the king's military household: the royal guards lodged in the suburbs near the gates of entry; the gendarmes and the light horse set to guard the palaces in which the members of the royal family would reside—the Louvre for Louis and Anne, the Tuileries for Louis's brother Philippe, the Palais-Royal for Henrietta Maria.[50]

Great crowds lined the route from Chaillot to the Louvre. The royal procession took five hours, moving slowly so that everyone could see the king riding a grey horse and looking impressively serious. Even the fishwives had changed their allegiance. Whereas the duke of Beaufort had been their darling not long ago, they now idolized the king: one of their number broke through the line of guards to kiss his boot. From monasteries along the way, the monks came out bearing candles; the parish churches rang carillons; there were artillery salutes, illuminations, and bonfires.[51]

The next day the king offered amnesty to all former *frondeurs* who made submission within three days. Gaston of Orléans was one of those who accepted. To the last moment, Retz and Châteauneuf had tried to incite him to resist, but the game was so clearly lost that Gaston submitted and retired to one of his country estates. He left his daughter to shift for herself; she too went into exile in the country. Normal life could begin again, as the official *Gazette* rejoiced:

> . . . The king is in his Louvre, the soldier is at the gates, and the beating of drums and the fanfares of trumpets, which only recently gave sad warnings to citizens to be ready to watch and defend their property or their welfare, now only serve to excite transports of joy.[52]

And all this good outcome was owing to the prayers and exertions of the queen, that most virtuous of princesses: "It is she who has happily procured this amnesty, which sheltered you from prosecution for your past misdeeds. . . ."[53]

The Parlement of Paris found itself enjoined to obedience. The king by formal declaration forbade the court to interfere henceforth in political, financial, or administrative affairs, and its decisions and decrees in these areas since February 1651 were annulled. Nothing now stood in the way of Mazarin's return, and on 26 October the king invited him to come back. Mazarin chose to wait for a while however, first until his great enemies Châteauneuf and Retz had been arrested, and then because he was busy gathering men and supplies for Turenne, who was reducing numerous Condé strongholds in Champagne. Anne was growing very impatient at the delay; as she wrote in January of 1653, " . . . When one feels friendship, the sight of the people one loves is not disagreeable, even were it only for a few hours."[54] By the end of the month, she complained of having been disappointed so often that, despite his promise to come soon, she would believe him only when he set a definite date.[55] At last he arrived in Paris, on 3 February, met by the king two leagues outside the city. He rode the rest of the way in the king's own carriage, and was housed in the Louvre, where Louis gave a supper for him followed by fireworks. Mazarin's nieces arrived on the same day; they were lodged in the Louvre also, and the queen herself took them to their apartments.[56] Honor could not be carried to greater heights, and in the following days and weeks, Mazarin was inundated by visits from courtiers and private persons anxious to pay him their humble respects. The triumph was underlined by the gaiety of the carnival season. Not for years had the royal family enjoyed such a satisfying round of dinners, comedies, and ballets.

After the celebrations the task of pacifying the kingdom remained. The chief part of that was accomplished when the city of Bordeaux surrendered to royal siege on 31 July 1653. From then on it was largely a matter of negotiating with former *frondeurs* to give up whatever strong places they held by virtue of a royal commission. The war effort against Spain did not fare as well. The most humiliating reverse came in September when Condé, now openly fighting for Spain, took that same town of Rocroi where his great victory ten years earlier had seemed to open the reign of Louis XIV in a burst of glory. The court of peers was charged with Condé's case. In March 1654 it reached its verdict: it declared the prince of Condé guilty of lèse-majesté, deprived him of the Bourbon name and of the title "prince of the blood," and sentenced him to death in absentia.

As far as domestic tranquillity was concerned, there was now no reason to wait longer for the last ceremony that would confirm the king in the plenitude of his power: his coronation. It took place on 7 June 1654 in the traditional church, the great cathedral at Reims, in the presence of the queen, Philippe of Anjou, Mazarin, and all the dignitaries of the realm except Gaston and the other exiles and Condé.[57] The coronation regalia had been brought from the abbey of Saint-Denis outside Paris earlier: the crown of Charlemagne, the sword of state, the scepter and hand of justice, a brooch for the king's mantle, his spurs, and the book containing the order of ceremony. The other essential ingredient, the vial of holy oil for his anointing, came under solemn escort from the abbey of Saint-Rémy near Reims. Every detail of the ceremony was published in lengthy reports, to let all of France share in the great event: the order of procession, the clothes worn by the king, the anointing with the holy oil, the administration of the oaths by which the king swore to protect and defend the church and the kingdom, the coronation itself, the rendering of homage by the peers, starting with the king's brother, and the dozens of birds released as the people acclaimed the newly crowned and anointed king.

Except for mentioning, however, that a tribune had been set up near the altar from which the queen and special guests watched the proceedings, the reporters did not spare her any further attention. It was, of course, proper to focus the public's eyes on Louis, who was not only the chief actor but also the reason for being of the whole ceremony. What Anne felt as she watched her son being crowned, with Mazarin on the cardinals' bench nearby, we can only conjecture. But it may be indicative of her feelings that she had the coronation week celebrated as an octave, with religious observances for eight days.[58] During that time Louis performed the act that more than any other convinced the faithful that France once more had an anointed king: he went to the abbey of Saint-Rémy, where, it was said, almost three thousand scrofula patients awaited him. He touched all of them, to each one reciting the ancient formula: "May God cure you, the king touches you."[59]

Chapter Eighteen

A
Safe
Haven

AFTER MANY TRIBULATIONS, A safe haven: from 1653 Anne's life was a relatively peaceful one as she reaped the harvest of her efforts. Not that tranquillity could be taken for granted. In retrospect it is clear that the Fronde had been thoroughly defeated, but this was not evident at the time.

Reconciliation was the policy Anne and Mazarin followed. They took no vengeance on repentant *frondeurs*; even the most prominent, such as Gaston and his daughter Mademoiselle, merely had to stay away from court and reside in the provinces, and some of the humbler sort actually received charitable alms from the queen.[1] More particularly Mazarin set himself to win over the city of Paris. The city fathers had given him a great welcoming banquet in March 1653,[2] and he built on that foundation of good will by making sure that the interest on the widely held city bonds was paid more punctually. He also gave attention to public relations, encouraging the publication of pamphlets favorable to royal authority by allocating pensions to appropriate writers and scholars. But some old habits died hard. The Parlement, though subdued most of the time, was not entirely quiescent. At the other end of the social scale, rootless elements of the population, loosely termed "vagabonds," remained a reservoir for potential trouble if they found a leader to manipulate them. An armed riot on the Pont Neuf in September 1653 pointed up this fact. To create a more orderly city, therefore, police measures were instituted, such as prohibiting lackeys from carrying swords or firearms, and shutting up beggars in the new general hospital.[3] As for those men who should have been the first bulwark of public tranquillity, namely the parish clergy, enough of the curés engaged themselves in a protest movement at this time that there was question of an ecclesiastical Fronde.[4]

The movement centered around Cardinal de Retz, who was not a repentant *frondeur*. He had been arrested and sequestered in the fortress of Vincennes in December 1652, even before Mazarin's return to the capital, giving rise to great outcries from the Vatican against such an indignity perpetrated on a prince of the church. During his imprisonment his uncle, the archbishop of Paris, died in March 1654. As his coadjutor, Retz would normally have succeeded his uncle without difficulty; but as matters stood now, what ensued was a bitter contest between the archdiocese and the government. The cathedral chapter accepted Retz as rightful archbishop, but the crown persisted in declaring the seat vacant. A sizable portion of the chapter and the diocesan clergy went on supporting Retz, made petitions in his behalf, protested to Rome, and preached disloyal sermons. Retz himself escaped from prison and fled to Rome, where at the end of 1655 he was induced to choose a vicar for the archdiocese from a list of royal nominees. Although that improved the religious climate in Paris, some contention remained until Retz in 1662 finally agreed to resign the archbishopric in return for the royal abbey of Saint-Denis. Some of his clergy had supported him because they held Jansenist opinions concerning the structure of the church and the autonomy of bishops; others had merely been stubborn about maintaining the rights of the cathedral chapter. Whatever their motives, Mazarin found their agitation very disquieting, remembering how tenaciously devout persons had been seeking to undermine him since he came to power. He had always believed that the devout constituted a political clique, an underground cabal. The ecclesiastical Fronde strengthened his suspicions, and on top of that, his worst fears seemed to be confirmed by the rumors that began to circulate in the late 1650s about a secret society with connections in the highest places.[5]

The secret society in question, the Compagnie du Saint-Sacrament, was indeed well connected, counting among its members curés, bishops, jurists, administrators, and noblemen. The highest ranking among the latter was Mazarin's own nephew-in-law, the prince of Conti, Condé's brother, who had recently married Mazarin's niece Anne Marie Martinozzi and turned pious. The company never acted in its own name; whenever it resolved on a project, such as the prohibition of dueling, encouragement of reverent behavior in Paris churches, curtailment of Huguenot privileges, or the like, those of its members with influence in the appropriate resort would put forward these suggestions as though they came from themselves. They disclaimed any political ambition or involvement and considered themselves unjustly persecuted when Mazarin tried to discover their identity with the intention of prosecuting them for endangering good order in the state. Anne, who was in the secret of the company though not a member, interceded with Mazarin, assuring him that the company did no harm but rather a great deal of good; that, indeed, some of his best friends were members.[6] Mazarin remained unpersuaded. They may not have done anything bad up to now, he said, "but they may do so in future by their great network and the relations they have throughout the kingdom; and as a matter of policy, such a thing should not be tolerated in a state."[7] The king's prosecutor general ultimately obtained a declaration from the Parlement of Paris prohibiting secret assemblies of any sort, and the Compagnie du Saint-Sacrement gradually yielded to the pressure of government hostility and suspended operations.

The clergy in general also gave Mazarin anxiety. Despite, or perhaps because of, his control over the royal ecclesiastical patronage, he continued to have ill-wishers among the bishops. They deplored the continuation of war against Catholic Spain, and the assembly of the clergy in 1656 sent Mazarin memorandums urging him to conclude a peace. He replied that he, for his part, did not need such reminders, that they would do better to address them to the Spanish ministry.[8] Furthermore, the assembly protested against the relatively favorable treatment the government had been giving the Huguenots in recent years. That may have been necessary while times were unsettled and there was danger of spreading civil war, but now, the assembly's speakers maintained, the time had come to return at the very least to a strict observation of the Edict of Nantes. Since Cromwell had signed the Treaty of Westminster with France in 1655 and at that time declared himself satisfied regarding the safety of the French Huguenots, the royal council indeed began to apply a more restricted interpretation of the Edict of Nantes as a concession to the clergy.[9] But then there were protests against the treaty with England, and even more protests after the subsequent military alliance and the occupation by English troops of the fortress of Mardyck and of Dunkirk pending the cession of Calais. In vain Mazarin pointed out that the fortress of Mardyck had no population, Catholic or otherwise, and that the agreement with England specified freedom of worship for Catholics in Dunkirk—a condition the Spaniards had not troubled to make when they were still hoping to conclude their own alliance with Cromwell.[10] It almost seemed as though for the first estate Mazarin could do no right.

As for the second estate, the great nobles were disposed to stand well with the court in hopes of military commands, governorships, offices, and favors. Mazarin secured himself a clientele among the most prominent houses, by marrying his nieces to the duke of Mercoeur of the Vendôme family, to the aforementioned prince of Conti, to the son of Prince Thomas of Savoy-Carignan, to the son of marshall de la Meilleraye. The provincial nobility, however, lacked similar spurs to obedience and remained somewhat behind the times. They were still given to holding assemblies, despite royal prohibitions; and as late as 1658, a delegation of gentlemen from Normandy and central France addressed itself to Gaston of Orléans with the request that he use his influence to get the Estates General to meet as had been promised six years earlier.[11] Gaston was no longer interested in heading a faction, however. He had made his peace with the court in 1656 and was living in retirement at Blois. Accordingly he sent the nobles home. It was suspected at the time that Condé's agents had been stirring them up. Condé himself was fighting in Flanders for Spain, and the war with Spain showed little sign of coming to an end.[12] Although the Spanish military and financial situation was not good, the Spanish court persisted in refusing to yield on anything, apparently hoping, first, that England would prefer a Spanish alliance to the French one, and, when that hope proved vain, that somehow French internal troubles could be revived. Although negotiations between France and Spain went on at intervals from 1656, there were too many obstacles to agreement—not the least of which was the prince of Condé. The Spanish court insisted that in any treaty he be included as an ally and a contracting party, which would have meant according him sovereign status although meanwhile he had been condemned to death as a traitorous subject in France. Consequently the war went on and so did war taxes, accompanied by occasional tax revolts in the provinces. Furthermore, when tax edicts were presented for registration, the Parlement had to be carefully managed lest die-hard activists use the occasion to revive the kind of political discussions that had led to the Fronde. Such discussions had been prohibited since 1652, but in March 1655 the king not only had to forbid them all over again but had himself to take a hand in the enforcement. Contrary to custom he did not let the chancellor of France give the message but spoke it personallly:

> Everyone knows what troubles your meetings have caused in my state and what dangerous effects they produced: I have heard that you still claim to continue them, on the pretext of deliberating on the edicts that were recently read and published in my presence. I have come here expressly to forbid the continuation [of these meetings], and to forbid you, Monsieur, the first president, to tolerate them or to permit them. . . .[13]

Louis was only sixteen, and no doubt Mazarin had coached him in what to say. However, even Mazarin was surprised that Louis chose to appear in hunting clothes with a riding crop in his hand. The Parlement professed to be shocked at such disdain for the dignity to which it felt itself entitled. Even with the display of royal determination, it took several months to overcome the resistance of the activists among the jurists.

Despite such dissonances in the public sector, however, life at the court itself returned to normal. Money, if not plentiful in the war chest, flowed more abundantly into the royal households than it had done in some time. Jewels that had been pawned in the bad years were gradually redeemed, new ones acquired, and, in the course of the decade, Anne was able to indulge her taste for elegant furnishings and sumptuous decoration. This was by no means as frivolous on her part as it seems. The magnificence of the frame in which royalty moved was in itself a show of power; it was both desirable and proper for the queen's manner of living to express confidence in the restored royal authority.

Only one of her household budgets for this entire period has survived: the audited accounts for 1653.[14] Although it is consequently impossible to determine changes in receipts and expenditures over time, even the figures for one year show clearly that the queen's household was the equivalent of a major industry, enriching commoners as well as nobles. Her receipts for 1653 amounted to 3,722,158 livres, and her expenditures totaled 3,255,754 livres.[15] To be sure, these figures included arrears in payments owing to the queen, some going back to 1649, that were carried over from one year to the next. Such sums simply inflated the accounts by about a quarter-million, for they added to the receipts on one hand but on the other, as debts unpaid, they were counted among the expenditures. In addition, more than one-half million in expenditures was applied retroactively to the 1652 budget. Nevertheless, what remained was still a stately amount, about three million in receipts against about two and a half million in expenses.

As it happens, the budget for 1653 is the only such document extant in which the sources of the queen's income are specified. About half a million livres came from the royal treasury, in monthly as well as extraordinary payments.[16] Anne also had considerable income from her domains—some three hundred thousand livres—from Calais, Auvergne, Haute and Basse Marche, and the largest single amount from Brittany, whose titular governor she was.[17] On the other hand, the estates of Brittany owed her one hundred ninety thousand livres for the "free gift" they had voted her in 1651 and 1653.[18] In arrears too were the payments on her holdings in the five great tax farms and the offices of the *gabelle* in Languedoc.[19] The governorship of Brittany, La Rochelle, Aunis, Brouage, Oleron, and Fort Capre brought her more than fifty-thousand livres, but that was the least part among the advantages of her being superintendent general of the navigation and commerce of France: by letters patent in 1651, the king had granted her one-third of the prize money brought in by French privateers. For 1653 that amounted to almost a quarter-million livres, not counting another hundred forty-four thousand or so retroactively credited to her account.[20] Furthermore, she realized, at least on paper, four hundred fifty thousand livres as part of the price for the domains of La Fère, Han, Marle, and the forest of Saint-Gobain, which she had sold to Mazarin.[21] That may have been a somewhat fictitious transaction, for it is possible that she gave him the money to pay her. At any rate, she signed receipts for almost three-quarters of a million livres in cash from the treasury for which no accounting was given and which presumably went into her private purse.[22]

On the expenditure side, the largest single item was six hundred thousand livres for the purchase of *aides* from the elections of Evreux, Pont de L'Arche, and Neufchâtel, with another forty thousand or so to buy offices of the *gabelles* in Languedoc.[23] Like any other person of great wealth, she was investing in taxes, perhaps with the idea of replacing revenues lost by the sale of domains to Mazarin. About one hundred nineteen thousand livres went in salaries and pensions to the staff of her household, music, and stables—the roster comprised almost seven hundred persons eleven years later, though it may not have been quite as large in 1653.[24] Not counting salaries, the ordinary expenses of the household averaged about thirty thousand livres a month.[25] What proportion went for food, drink, candles, and fuel was not specified, but her expense accounts for two days of travel during October of that year give us some idea of what they might have been.[26] On those two days, 447 livres and 477 livres were spent respectively, with the kitchen expenses accounting for about half these amounts. Fifty-three percent and forty-six percent went to the butcher for meats, poultry, and tallow candles, plus another five percent each day for sundries, pastry, and vegetables. The expenses for wine amounted to fourteen and thirteen percent; for bread, eleven and ten percent; and for fruit and wax candles, seven percent. Wood and charcoal for cooking and heating cost nine percent and thirteen percent of the respective daily budgets. No doubt the daily expenses were much larger in Paris, where the queen had more persons in attendance who had the right to be fed and where much larger quarters had to be lit and heated. Allowing for seasonal variations in the use of candles and fuel, however, the proportion allocated for the various items probably approximated the travel budgets.

In addition to the annual household expenses, more than sixty-seven thousand livres went to the queen's silver pantry and chamber for the ordinary provision of tableware, cutlery, linens, and clothing. The needs of the queen's ladies, maids-in-waiting, and personal servants accounted for more than thirty-five thousand livres of that, and her personal allowance was thirty-two thousand livres.[27] Aside from that she made other purchases paid for by special warrants. Thus in January she bought a dressing gown lined with fur for 144 livres, and in December a silk dress of silver and blue with gold flowers for 660 livres.[28] Blue was one of the colors suitable for widows, though she had always liked it in any case. As for jewelry, apart from a diamond ring for some eleven hundred livres,[29] Anne apparently made no important purchases during the year but confined herself to paying off arrears from previous years: 3,600 livres for a pair of diamond drop earrings and 8,000 livres as the balance owing since 1643 on a string of pearls.[30] On the other hand, she did buy furnishings, spending 2,700 livres for wall hangings of Spanish tooled leather and Chinese patterned tapestry, as well as 3,500 livres for a rug and furniture.[31]

As was expected of her, the queen took care of the members of her household. In 1653 that meant she paid 600 livres to replace linen that had been stolen from her pages by soldiers during the annual campaign trip.[32] And in addition to buying coach and saddle horses for her own stables, she reimbursed many of her officers and servants who had lost their horses in her service.[33] Moreover, Anne paid regular pensions to the members of her household from Mazarin, her superintendent, right down to the porters, as supplement to their official salaries or in some cases in lieu of such salary.[34] Old servants were remembered too, as well as arrears in payments—in at least one case going as far back as 1647.[35] Evidently the queen liked to discharge debts as soon as she had the means to do so. The entire list of pensions and gratuities amounted to well over a hundred sixty thousand livres. That sum did not include her donations to religious communities and individuals, some twelve thousand livres, a surprisingly modest amount when compared with the rest of the budget, especially considering her reputation for piety.[36] To be sure, the building of Val-de-Grâce, which she gradually resumed in the following years, never figured in her household accounts.

Among her many expenses in 1653, Anne paid 300 livres to have the malodorous moat of the Louvre cleaned out.[37] The royal family was living in the Louvre again, though Anne had not particularly liked that residence in the past. Mazarin, however, had insisted even from his exile that when the king returned to Paris, it must be to the Louvre.[38] As a royal residence, it could be kept much more secure than the Palais-Royal; and besides, by way of the Great Gallery and the Tuileries palace, it offered an emergency exit beyond the city walls. But the Louvre had not habored the royal family for nine years; repairs and redecoration were needed, not to mention a great general cleaning.

Traditionally the king lived on the floor of honor, the second floor, of the pavilion in the southwest angle of the courtyard. The reigning queen's apartment adjoined his on the same floor, extending along the south or river wing of the palace. Anne did not move into those quarters however, but into the rooms customarily occupied by queen mothers on the floor below. Marie de Medici had had them decorated for herself in 1613, and they had been untenanted since her departure from the kingdom. Remodeling started immediately in 1652.

This part of the Louvre has been so extensively rebuilt that nothing remains of the disposition of Anne's apartment or of the decorations on its walls and ceilings.[39] We know from descriptions, however, that it consisted of a long flight of rooms, each one opening into the next. From the guardroom and the outer reception room on the ground floor of the royal pavilion, one proceeded to the great cabinet, or inner reception room; then to the small cabinet, where the queen usually dined; to the salon, where she gave audiences, held receptions, and balls; then to her bedroom, which was also something of a family living room; her oratory; and her boudoir at the end in approximately the space now devoted to the Venus de Milo. The oratory and the boudoir were the only rooms that did not serve as a passageway to somewhere, and consequently Anne used them as private retreats.

Contemporary accounts combined with clues from the inventory taken at the time of her death give us some idea of how Anne furnished these rooms.[40] Tapestries or leather hangings covered the upper part of the walls beyond the usual wooden paneling, adding warmth to rooms with twenty-foot ceilings where the only sources of heat were fireplaces and braziers. Crystal or silver chandeliers, candelabra, and sconces provided light, which was reflected in the silver ornaments placed on the massive mantelpieces and on the lintels above the doors. In her bed-sitting-room, Anne kept the great silver table she had brought from Spain as a bride, and of her oratory she made a scintillating jewel in itself: chandelier, candelabra, vases, crucifix, and reliquaries of rock crystal ornamented with silver gilt enriched with green enamel and rubies and other jewels dominated the small room. The oratory also housed Anne's collection of relics, which she was constantly enlarging.

Anne's oratory was much admired by contemporaries, but no more so than her boudoir.[41] Travelers who saw it in 1657 while the royal family was absent left a detailed description.[42] The ceiling of the boudoir had been painted by Le Sueur with an assembly of the gods and figures symbolizing the virtues of the queen, the whole framed by gilded stucco ornaments. The upper parts of the walls were black and white marble, and the floor had been laid in aromatic wood. All the furniture—daybed, tables, chairs, standing clocks—was enameled blue with small multicolored flowers, and the daybed and chairs were upholstered in gold and silver brocade and pink satin with embroidery. In this feminine setting, Anne had her dressing table with her gold mirror and matching candelabra, and her toilet case with its gold accessories. Here also she washed in silver basins and had a tub brought in for baths. And because this room was a private retreat, it was here she had hung thirteen portraits of her Spanish family.

Luxurious though it may have been, her suite had one disadvantage: since it had a southern exposure, it was hot in summer. In 1655, therefore, construction began on a summer apartment for her on the ground floor of the little gallery, the present gallery of Apollo, extending at right angles from the south wing of the Louvre to the river.[43] The suite consisted of a large antechamber or reception room, the grand cabinet or workroom, a vestibule at the garden entrance, the queen's bed-sitting-room, and a small cabinet whose balcony overlooked the Seine. The small cabinet no longer exists as a separate room, but in the rest of the apartment most of the original ceiling paintings and decorations have survived to the great interest of art historians, who see this ensemble as a link between Italian baroque style and the later French classicism of Versailles. The special feature as far as Anne herself is concerned, however, lies in the program of the decoration, for it carried a political message. By its means the queen announced to all the world that she and Mazarin were partners in securing the welfare of the kingdom, and that their relationship was above reproach: a triumphant refutation of all the scurrilous charges leveled against both of them at the time of the Fronde.

The designer and painter was Giovanni Francesco Romanelli, a Roman artist who had done work for Mazarin previously.[44] Romanelli

opened the series in the anteroom with a painting of Apollo and Diana
in the center of the ceiling, surrounded by scenes showing the rewards of talent and virtue and the punishment for ill-doing. The decoration of the next room, the grand cabinet, was more specific: this was
the room of the Roman heroes, in tribute to Mazarin. In the center of
the ceiling, Rome is represented majestically in arms, accompanied by
History, Poetry, and Fame, and side panels illustrate Mazarin's ac-
complishments and qualities. Thus the rape of the Sabine women
reminds the beholder that war can be necessry to the growth of states,
and since this particular war had brought about intermarriage and
amity between combatants, it was a clear reference to the results
hoped for from the conflict with Spain. The three other panels illustrate respectively the continence of Scipio, the civic virtue of Cincinna-
tus, and the courage and greatness of soul of Mucius Scaevola. The
vestibule adjoining celebrates France, with three fleur-de-lys upheld
by Mars, Minerva, and Mercury. On two sides, surrounded by gilded
stucco figures of the four chief rivers of France and the attributes of
their provinces, panels show the fertile abundance of the country and
the benefits of peace succeeding war—a further allusion to the French
sincerity in seeking peace that both Spain and the Vatican professed to
doubt.[45]

Beyond the vestibule came the queen's room, on whose ceiling
Religion sits enthroned surrounded by the three cardinal virtues of
Faith, Hope, and Charity. Smaller panels below depict virtuous queens
of antiquity and the allegorical figures of Prudence, Justice, Fortitude,
Temperance, and Chastity as the counterparts of Mazarin's virtues, giving the lie to scandal. In the queen's withdrawing room, her small
cabinet on the water, the theme was the queen's personal triumph.
Although the painting no longer exists, according to description in the
center of the ceiling Minerva, the goddess of wisdom, was seated on a
trophy of arms with a river at her feet, possibly the Seine. Fame and
Victory stood at her side while a child presented her with a fleur-de-
lys.[46] The message was that the queen's wisdom had overcome force,
but not for her own sake: she had done it all for her son, a fact made
unmistakably clear by the seven scenes from the life of Moses that
completed the decoration. Although she had not actually found her
son in the bulrushes, like Moses he was a child of miracle.

Romanelli finished the whole work in 1657, having created a stately
ensemble that nevertheless seemed light and airy enough for summer
living thanks to the colors he used, chiefly cool violets and blues,
greens and yellows. Aside from its immediate purpose, however,

there can be no doubt that it was also meant to serve the needs of diplomacy and public relations, for the king's Italian interpreter published a pamphlet in his native tongue explaining the entire scheme of decoration in detail for an obviously international audience.[47] Painters did not usually invent such programs, so the ideas most probably came from Mazarin although Anne obviously must have approved them. Of the two it was Mazarin who was the connoisseur, the collector and patron of the arts; Anne showed no interest in such pursuits. She cared about content rather than artistic quality, and the pictures she possessed were either portraits or religious subjects. What she collected, aside from relics, were rosaries—she had thirty-seven of them by the end of her life, in everything from diamonds and pearls to paste.[48]

In the minor arts, at least, Anne and Mazarin shared some tastes. Mazarin liked chinoiserie and so evidently did she, for among her suites of furniture, there was one upholstered in Chinese satin worked in "people and grotesques" with matching wall hangings; and she also owned six folding stools and two armchairs covered in Chinese embroidery, twenty pieces of Chinese satin in various colors, seven Chinese screens, and four Chinese cabinets.[49] In her own right, French museum specialists credit Anne with only two direct contributions in the domain of decorative arts: the tooled leather hangings she brought from Spain became fashionable, and the solid silver tables that she also brought were to be the forerunners of the silver furniture that graced Versailles until it had to be sent to the mint in 1689 to meet war costs.[50] Nevertheless her influence, at least on Louis XIV, may have been more pervasive than that. Decorated as they were in the most modern style, with marble, gilded stucco ornaments, and painted ceilings, her apartments were very different from the somber interiors of the previous reign, with their dark wood paneling and heavy beamed ceilings. Spending as much time as he did in his mother's rooms, Louis could not have helped but form his own ideas of the magnificence suitable to royalty, ideas that he expressed on a much grander scale when his time came to build.

Life for Anne in these surroundings took on a comfortable routine.[51] She spent more time in churches and convents than ever, often escorted by her younger son Philippe. She still met in council with Mazarin, now with Louis making a third.[52] Mazarin was apprenticing the king to council work just as he was teaching him the art of managing and supplying armies during their annual campaign tours. Mazarin also confirmed him in social graces by organizing dinners and suppers for him, and usually watched over him when he went hunting—a sport of which Louis was already passionately fond. Sometimes when they were at Vincennes on such an expedition, Anne would join them next day, and after dinner they would all return together to the Louvre, where Mazarin had rooms adjoining Louis's apartment. Indeed, they lived like a family, and a remarkably harmonious family at that. Some few persons in the queen's entourage still resented Mazarin: Madame de Motteville found that he did not treat the queen with enough consideration or gratitude,[53] and La Porte, if his unpublished memoirs are to be believed, accused the cardinal of actual rudeness.[54] These people, however, were too prejudiced where Mazarin was concerned to interpret reliably what they may have seen or heard. Anne and Mazarin best knew what each owed the other. In their letters they still used the same symbols for affection, and if their tone is calmer than it once was, that only reflects the security of long collaboration.[55] The collaboration itself endured. Judging from Anne's two surviving letters to Mazarin from the later 1650s, she continued to rely on his instructions for pending business while she in turn reported on what was being done and with whom she had conferred.[56]

Anne's trust in her minister reflected on his family. For Mazarin's sake she welcomed all his relatives. When the cardinal returned from exile, so did his nieces: Laura Mancini, meanwhile married to the duke of Mercoeur, her sister Olympia, and their cousin Anne Marie Martinozzi. The queen herself welcomed them to the Louvre, where they were immediately included in the entertainments of the carnival season. The following year Mazarin's sisters arrived with three more of his nieces, and the last niece and nephew joined them in 1655. Mazarin as head of the family was doing his duty by them all, but they also served his turn by giving him the means to make marriage alliances with the great houses that now competed for his friendship. In the meantime those girls who were old enough enlarged the court circle, which had become somewhat shrunken with the Fronde.

Apart from her usual ladies and maids of honor, Anne still had her old friends the princess of Carignan and the princess Palatine. Others had been banned from court, however, notably Gaston of Orléans and Mademoiselle; and Anne's sister-in-law Henrietta Maria visited less often since the government had begun diplomatic relations with Cromwell's commonwealth. Even after the king's reconciliation with his uncle, Gaston mostly stayed at Blois with his wife and younger daughters. Only Mademoiselle resumed her old place when the king finally forgave her in 1657.

On their first meeting, Anne kissed her niece cordially, told her she was glad to see her and had always loved her, although admittedly she had been angry with her at times: she had not blamed her for supporting her father Gaston like a filial daughter; but when Mademoiselle had opened Paris to Condé, if she, Anne had been able to lay hands on her, she would have strangled her. And Anne concluded with characteristic bluntness, "I wanted to talk to you about that first off and tell you all that I had on my mind; now I have forgotten it and we need not mention it again."[57] Mademoiselle understood, of course, that there could be no further question of marriage between herself and the king; but she heard rumors of a possible match between herself and Louis's brother Philippe, with whom she had always been a great favorite.[58] She rather liked the idea, until she found him, as she put it, too childish for his seventeen years, still dressing up with the queen's maids of honor.[59] No actual proposal materialized, perhaps because Anne did not quite fancy Mademoiselle as a daughter-in-law after all. But Mademoiselle was no longer a *frondeuse* even at heart. She cultivated good relations with Mazarin, whose qualities she professed to appreciate now that she knew him better,[60] and she readily accepted his nieces. On those terms she had her place with the royal family as well as her share in entertainments and pastimes—and they were many, for the queen liked to see young people enjoying themselves.

Aside from riding, parties, hunts, and visits to pleasant country houses, the court had not lost its fondness for the theater. French and Italian acting troupes frequently gave command performances at the palace, but on occasion the royal family went out also, to the Petit Bourbon or the Hôtel de Bourgogne, for instance, to see some particularly elaborate production with many sets and complex stage machinery. Balls often followed the performances, especially during the winter when they were given by the king, Philippe, Mademoiselle, even Anne herself, not to mention lesser hosts. Although the Compagnie du Saint-Sacrement was trying to substitute pious exercises for the profane amusements of the carnival,[61] its success was limited since the king and his family set a contrary example. The king and his friends, lively young men all, organized and danced not merely the one traditional royal ballet but two or more. They also had masquerade parties when the young men and ladies of the court would dress up in costumes and masks in order to descend on private houses such as the residence of Chancellor Séguier, who ransomed himself by giving the invaders a collation.[62] Piety did not prevent the queen from encouraging such amusements; she gave her opinion on the masqueraders' costumes,[63] applauded the ballets, and turned her salon into a grand ballroom at least once every carnival season. And at any time of year, festivities were multiplied for distinguished foreign visitors, such as Christina of Sweden, for example, who came repeatedly but wore out her welcome when she had one of her gentlemen executed in a gallery at Fontainebleau.

The older ones among Mazarin's nieces were, of course, much in evidence; and one of them, the spirited Olympia Mancini, especially caught the young king's eye. In 1655 even the *Gazette* saw fit to report that the king had danced with Mademoiselle Mancini, had ordered that she be served with food from his own table at this or that dinner, had given her a seat in his carriage.[64] It was apparently only a flirtation, but Mazarin forestalled potentially more serious problems by marrying Olympia to the young count of Soissons, the son of prince and princess Thomas of Carignan-Savoy. As countess of Soissons, Olympia took as lively a part in court doings as ever, and the king still enjoyed her company, though he also seemed taken with other young women.

All that was harmless, for he apparently kept his experiments with sex belowstairs. Tradition has it that Louis was initiated into love at sixteen by his mother's first chambermaid, Madame de Beauvais, who allegedly waylaid him one day in a scantily clad condition.[65] Considering the lack of privacy in all the royal apartments, that sort of ambush seems somewhat improbable. Moreover, Madame de Beauvais was no longer young, having had a daughter married in 1652. Whether the story is actually true or not, it is certain that Louis caught a venereal infection, it was thought from the daughter of some servant.[66] Nevertheless he was not a precocious libertine. He took his religious duties seriously, regularly touched the sick at great holidays, and at eighteen still professed to fear mortal sin.[67] But he was handsome, virile, and women would have been attracted to him even without the magic aura of kingship. While Anne and Mazarin watchfully nipped court flirtations in the bud, they realized it was time to get him married. There seemed to be no hurry about it, however, especially since Anne had always hoped he would marry her niece, the infanta Maria Teresa of Spain. The French diplomats had already introduced the subject long ago, during the negotiations for the Peace of Westphalia,[68] though so far Spain had proved resistant to this as to every other peace overture. The whole matter was thus left suspended in time until, without warning, in 1658 something happened to point up the danger of leaving the royal succession unsecured.

The court had gone on campaign, as it did every year, the queen remaining with Philippe in Calais while Mazarin took Louis to the siege of Dunkirk. In cooperation with their English allies, the French troops earned brilliant victories; on 22 June, Turenne defeated Condé in the Battle of the Dunes, and three days later Dunkirk surrendered. Thanksgiving services were still being held in the churches of the kingdom when the news spread that prayers of another kind were required.[69] The king had fallen ill of a fever, and the usual remedies, bleeding and purges, did not seem to help. For two weeks his doctors considered him critically ill; then in desperation they let a local practitioner prescribe for him. Whether because of their joint efforts or in spite of them, Louis began to improve, but those two weeks had given substance to what before had been only an abstract consideration: if the king died without legitimate issue, his brother Philippe would ascend the throne.

For Anne it was a time of terrible anxiety. It was perhaps the only occasion when she admitted in so many words that she had invested all her deepest love and hope in her firstborn son, for she confided to Madame de Motteville that if she lost Louis she would retire to Val-de-Grâce.[70] Clearly no other attachment, whether to Mazarin or to her younger son, could rival her feeling for Louis. Indeed, she considered Philippe only in relation to his brother: she was pleased because he showed great solicitude for Louis and cried when told he would not be permitted to visit him for fear of infection.[71] But if Philippe showed only the most brotherly feeling at this juncture, other people were not as devoted. Ambitious individuals set out to ingratiate themselves with him and a cabal began to form around the heir apparent.[72]

Anne and Mazarin realized perfectly well that Philippe was not fitted to be king. As Mademoiselle reported, while Louis went to the front, Philippe, although now in his nineteenth year, stayed with the queen like a little boy, went around with her maids of honor, bought English fabrics and ribbons, and played on the beach.[73] When Mademoiselle complained about this behavior to Mazarin one day, Mazarin told her he and the queen were themselves in despair at Philippe's effeminate interests; in fact, they passionately wished that he would ask to go to the army. And Mazarin vehemently rejected Mademoiselle's veiled accusation that they were directly responsible for the way Philippe was turning out.[74] Mazarin may well have been speaking the truth. Although he and Anne had certainly not been raising Philippe as an understudy to Louis, Anne had evidently seen no harm in the boy's amusements when he was younger. Even now she saw nothing wrong in his staying close to her and her women, and took him along so often to churches and convents that the *Gazette* reported he was doing his best "to walk in the footsteps of such a perfect and eminent model of piety."[75] But Anne was not blind to everything. When Philippe began to acquire dissolute friends with a reputation for homosexuality, led on by his favorite companion count de Guiche, she intervened: she gave orders that under no circumstances was Guiche to be allowed to see Philippe alone.[76] Enforcing such an order was another matter, however, and it was precisely these friends who now surrounded Philippe, expecting to dominate him profitably if he rose to power.

Although Louis's recovery put an end to the hopes of Philippe's friends, from then on the question of the king's marriage became Anne's and Mazarin's first concern. Despite the military reverses of the summer, the Spanish court still gave no sign of yielding. In desperation, therefore, Mazarin opened negotiations with Anne's sister-in-law Christine, the dowager duchess of Savoy, for the hand of her daughter, Princess Marguerite. So eagerly did the relatives in Savoy take the bait that they even agreed to the unprecedented concession of letting Louis meet the princess before he actually committed himself. It would be exceedingly humiliating for Savoy if, having seen Marguerite, Louis were to back out; but Christine was encouraged to believe there would be little risk of that.

In November, therefore, Louis set out, accompanied by his mother, brother, Mazarin, and the court, to meet his aunt and cousins. To all appearances they were proceeding in complete good faith. Anne was heard to remark philosophically that since it seemed she could not have the daughter-in-law she preferred, whatever pleased the king would please her too. And on arrival in Lyon, Louis gave every sign of liking Marguerite. The two chatted animatedly while Anne looked gloomier by the hour.[77] But then it turned out that the whole journey had been a gamble to force the hand of Philip IV: while the royal family were still greeting their relations, an envoy arrived from Spain in disguise and great secrecy, since he had been sent off in such a hurry that he had no passports or safe-conducts. That evening Mazarin entered the queen's apartment beaming: "Good news, Madame!" "What," replied the queen, "could it be peace?" "More than that, Madame, I bring your Majesty both peace and the infanta."[78] They told Louis, and, having entertained the Savoyards some days for the sake of decency, lost no time in returning to Paris.

Peace negotiations between France and Spain now began in earnest. There seemed to be no further obstacle to the realization of Anne's hopes, but at this point there arose an unlooked-for complication: on the way home from Lyon, Louis had fallen in love.

The lady in question was another of Mazarin's nieces, Marie Mancini. Marie had begun to appear at court the year before, where she soon gave rise to talk because of her evident feeling for the king.[79] He had not seemed to notice until the return journey from Lyon, which together they proceeded to treat as a long delightful picnic. Things went on the same way in Paris, with Louis spending as much time near Marie as he could and Marie the soul of every outing and every party. She herself later described the following carnival season as a lovers' paradise, recalling that there were other couples in love among their young troop at the Louvre, so that they all moved everywhere in a swirl of high spirits.[80] Marie was of Louis's age, a striking brunette, and well read enough to be able to converse intelligently and amusingly. Unlike her sister Olympia, she was neither ambitious nor calculating, her own defects of character being rather the opposite—temper and wilfulness. Contemporary estimates of her more or less agree with Madame de Motteville's formulation: " . . . This girl was bold and had wit, but a rude and extravagant one."[81] Anne did not like Marie especially well, and she liked her less when the girl, lacking in tact and discretion, began to incite Louis to rebel against his elders. He started to give his mother rude answers, as for example when she opposed his plan to continue dancing his carnival ballet during Lent. If he did such an impious thing, she would move to Val-de-Grâce for the duration, she threatened—and he told her to feel free to go. Mazarin reconciled them; but the next problem was that Marie took every occasion to make derogatory remarks about the infanta, and Louis did not stop her. In Lille she had spoken against Princess Marguerite, asking him if he was not ashamed they were giving him such an ugly wife; now she commented on Marie Teresa, in a similar vein.[82] Report of all this naturally reached the Spanish court. Neither Anne nor Mazarin had been particularly worried by Louis's affair, which they believed to be—correctly, as it happened—quite innocent. Although they were prepared to tolerate youthful amusement, however, they were not about to let the treaty of peace and marriage with Spain be jeopardized. In June 1659, therefore, it was decided that Mazarin, on his way to the Spanish frontier where he would personally conduct the final negotiations, would take along Marie and his other unmarried nieces and stop along the way to establish them in his residence at Brouage.

As it turned out, Anne and Mazarin had underestimated Louis's feelings: far from consenting to letting Marie go, he announced that he wanted to marry her. In the face of their immense consternation and prompt refusal, he pleaded, he wept, and rumor had it that he even went down on his knees.[83] He tried to get around his mother alone, to no avail. She took him into her boudoir for a long talk under four eyes, and when they came out both were seen to have been crying. Anne confided to Madame de Motteville how sorry she felt for the king, though she had told him she was sure he would thank her one day for the pain she was giving him.[84]

Next day Marie left, after a mutually tearful leave-taking from Louis. Absence only fed their love, however, since Anne, against Mazarin's advice, had been tenderhearted enough to permit them to write to each other. The clandestine correspondence went on for several months, and Mazarin took time out from his diplomatic work to send letter after letter to Louis admonishing him to remember his duty to the state and to himself: it was impossible that he should repudiate the infanta and plunge two kingdoms into war again, all for the sake of making a marriage so far beneath him.[85] Indeed, Mazarin wrote in such unvarnished terms that it is a wonder Louis did not afterward hold it against him. But Louis remained stubborn until at last Mazarin threatened to resign and take his whole family back to Italy.

By then the court itself was on the way south, having left Paris at the end of July. Before setting out, Anne had inspected the future queen's rooms, whose remodeling had been taken in hand in good time several years earlier.[86] The Paris city council had received instructions about the decorations and other arrangements it was to get ready for the new queen's formal entry.[87] In fact, everything and everyone was prepared for the king's wedding trip except the king himself, who still seemed unreconciled. His persistent sorrow so moved Anne that she allowed him a last meeting with Marie, on the road as it were.[88] Mazarin reproached Anne for this indulgence, which he considered a dangerous mistake, though his fears proved groundless. Whether his plain speaking had finally reached Louis or whether the meeting with Marie took the bloom off the enchantment, Louis began to recover himself and enter into the spirit of the journey.

Ill-wishers maintained Mazarin had not been averse to seeing his niece a queen, and only turned against the idea when Anne opposed it. Madame de Motteville indeed claimed the queen threatened to raise the kingdom in revolt if he let the king so degrade himself.[89] The lady was not writing from evidence, however, for neither she nor her friends overheard what Mazarin or the queen said to each other on the subject. And in fact Madame de Motteville contradicted herself some pages later when she conceded that Anne herself had never believed Mazarin entertained such a thought.[90] No one can question the sincerity of his monitory letters to the king: it would have gone totally against Mazarin's known character for him to have considered throwing away the culmination of his lifework, the treaty with Spain.

All summer and fall, in twenty-five conferences, Mazarin and the Spanish minister, Don Luiz de Haro, battled out the final points of the treaty and the marriage agreement. At last in mid-November, the essentials were settled: France would keep some of her war gains along the Pyrenees, and in Flanders, Artois, and Lorraine, but agreed to reinstate the prince of Condé in all his estates and honors. To perpetuate the peace, Philip IV's daughter Maria Teresa would marry Louis, although she would have to renounce her right of succession to the Spanish throne for herself and her descendants. The French agreed to that renunciation on condition that her dowry be paid—a matter of five hundred thousand *écus* in gold.[91] Since no one had any serious expectation that the Spanish treasury could raise such a sum and since Maria Teresa's only surviving brother was a sickly child, she would in effect be bringing with her not only peace but great possibilities of eventual inheritance.

Early in February the treaty with Spain was ratified and proclaimed amid universal services of thanksgiving. The war had lasted twenty-four years, but now it was over. Thoughts turned to a happier future as Louis's subjects prepared to welcome the royal bride.

Chapter Nineteen

No Higher Joy

O N THE SPANISH SIDE, PREPA-
ration for the marriage took considerable time. The French court had
months of leisure, which it used to make an extended progress
through the southern provinces. In late spring finally, word came that
Philip IV and his daughter had left Madrid on their way to the frontier.
To coincide with their arrival, the French party came to Saint-Jean-de-
Luz early in May, but as it turned out there was still a month to wait for
the ceremonies. Difficulties arose about the execution of the peace
treaty, giving rise to lengthy discussions between Mazarin and Haro.
Anne took advantage of these weeks to indulge her two greatest pas-
sions: every day she visited churches and afterward saw Spanish plays.[1]
At last on 3 June 1660, at Fuenterrabía just across the border in Spain,
Maria Teresa married Louis by proxy in the presence of Philip IV, just
as Anne herself had been married before leaving her father's kingdom.

Although officially no one of the French family was present, Mademoiselle had arranged to attend the service incognito, accompanied
by Madame de Motteville and other ladies. Still incognito she met the
young queen at dinner, and then hurried back to Saint-Jean-de-Luz to
report her impressions first hand. The queen infanta, she wrote later,
"seemed to me to have a great air, amiable and civil. I did not doubt
she would please every one in France; as for me, I was enchanted with
her."[2] Madame de Motteville in her recollections was more specific,
noting not only the beauty of the queen's silver blonde hair and delicate complexion but also the fact that she was a trifle short and that her
teeth were not as pretty as they might have been.[3] Both ladies agreed
that the Spanish fashions in dress and hair were frightful; much the
same had been said about Anne's turnout forty-five years earlier, but
these were remediable evils.

The following day Anne was able to see for herself. With her ladies
she traveled to the conference island, so called because Mazarin and
Haro had been negotiating there for months. It was a construction in
the middle of the Bidassoa River similar to the divided pavilion that
had been set up for the exchange of brides in 1615. Here, for the first

time since that day, Anne greeted her brother Philip. It was a somewhat disappointing meeting, since Philip behaved with great formality
and would not let his sister kiss him. Nor did they succeed in recapturing the family feeling of their childhood; too much had happened
since then that it was tactful not to recall. "The devil made this war,"
was all Philip had to say about the late unpleasantness.[4] Anne however
insisted on explaining herself: "I think your Majesty will pardon me
for having been such a good Frenchwoman: I owed it to the king, my
son, and to France."[5] Philip assured her he respected her for it and told
her his first wife, the French Princess Elizabeth, had done just the same
in reverse.[6] With her daughter-in-law, on the other hand, Anne felt no
constraint at all; they took to each other immediately. Louis had his
first glimpse of his bride on this occasion and she of him, unofficially
through a doorway and amid the teasing of the company. On 6 June
they all met again, and the two kings swore to uphold the peace. The
day after that, the French party returned to fetch the new queen and
take leave of her father. It was a tearful scene, but Maria Teresa seemed
cheerful enough by the time they reached Saint-Jean-de-Luz, where
she shared Anne's quarters. There Anne presided over a private family
supper, just herself, the young couple, and Philippe, while they all got
better acquainted.[7] It was a far cry from her own formal reception by
Marie de Medici years ago. Maria Teresa found a loving mother, and
one moreover who spoke her language and knew her people.

On 9 June the French marriage ceremony took place in the church
of Saint-Jean. The intervening time had been frantic with the quarrels
over precedence that always plagued the court on ceremonial occasions: who had the right to what length of train, to carry whose train, to
be attended by gentlemen of what rank. Then Anne had to console
Mademoiselle, who was outraged because Louis had forbidden the
queen to kiss any lady except his mother. That was just one of his
notions, said Anne: he wanted his wife to be like no other queen of
France, but he would get over it.[8] In this she was mistaken. Mazarin
managed to resolve the other problems, however, and on the wedding day all was harmony. Anne's face shone with happiness as she
watched her children, Louis resplendent in gold brocade and black
lace, Maria Teresa in her royal velvet and ermine mantle and diamond
crown, and Philippe attending them both.[9] Her dearest wishes had
come true. Fittingly it was Mazarin who after the mass offered the pax
to the married couple and to Anne. Equally fitting was the Latin motto
on the gold medals he tossed among the crowd of onlookers after the
wedding dinner: "No higher joy."[10]

If Anne recalled her own wedding, she did not mention it. Indeed, there was no one around her who remembered her as a bride, for even Gaston had died, early in February 1660. From now on her title was "queen mother," and she wore it with better grace and more generosity than Marie de Medici had done. But Anne, as she herself made plain on numerous occasions, had never craved power.[11] It helped, of course, that Maria Teresa was an affectionate, docile girl who looked up to her aunt with childlike devotion.

Louis seemed well pleased with his wife, and she with him. In their case diplomats did not need to ask anxiously whether the marriage had been consummated or not. The court stayed almost two weeks in Saint-Jean-de-Luz to let Maria Teresa rest and get her bearings before going on to Bordeaux, where a great reception awaited her. From Bordeaux the wedding party proceeded northward in leisurely stages, punctuated by greetings from local dignitaries, visits to churches, and excursions. They reached Fontainebleau on 13 July and stayed some days to refresh themselves. Then on 19 July the young king and queen moved on to Vincennes while Anne and Philippe returned to Paris, where next day Anne promptly went to Val-de-Grâce to give thanks for the happy conclusion of the journey that had lasted a year.[12] Except for occasional short visits, she left the young couple alone at Vincennes, where they spent their honeymoon until the queen's formal entry into the capital on 26 August.

On that day the king and queen, accompanied by the royal cousins and all the crown dignitaries, were met outside the gate of Saint-Antoine by the citizen militia, the city council, the sovereign courts, the officers and the faculty of the university, and delegations from the parishes and the monastic orders of the city.[13] Having paid their respects with elaborate speeches of greeting from their various spokesmen, all these constituted bodies turned back in order of procession to escort the royal pair to the Louvre. The route was a traditional one, through the gate of Saint-Antoine, down the rue Saint-Antoine through the fashionable Marais quarter to the city hall, over the bridge of Notre-Dame to the Ile de la Cité, there from the new market to the Place Dauphine at the tip of the island, and then across the Pont Neuf to the Louvre.

The Parisians had had twelve months to prepare, so that there was no lack of triumphal arches and allegorical tableaus along the way, not to mention the tapestries and conceits that decorated private houses. But the most dazzling sight of all was the young queen, who perhaps for the only time in her married life outshone her husband. He cut a very handsome figure, dressed in silver and red and riding a Spanish bay. Seeing the queen, however, no one could tell what kind of dress she wore for she was covered from head to foot with gold, pearls, and precious stones—in fact, with all the crown jewels. According to reports, her beauty, grace, and visible gentleness and goodness surpassed even this magnificence. The thousands of Parisians who watched from every vantage point had ample opportunity to admire her as she rode past them in an open carriage that itself was a creation in silver and gold, something like a surrey, with jasmine and olive as symbols of love and peace twining around the struts supporting the roof. Not since Anne's entry in 1616 had the citizens enjoyed a sight so promising for future happiness and security; they cheered themselves hoarse, and public rejoicing continued for three days.

The authors of this felicity, Anne and Mazarin, were represented in the procession only by their carriages. They themselves stayed quietly out of the way as spectators from the house of Anne's first chamberwoman, Madame de Beauvais. Whatever else they may have felt, they must have experienced a sense of satisfaction and, more precisely, of vindication. There was no question that Mazarin was the hero of the hour: a delegation from the Parlement—the same Parlement that had put a price on his head a decade earlier—had already come to thank him for having given a glorious peace to France.[14] Old scandals were dead and forgotten. No one thought it even worthy of remark to see Anne and Mazarin together at Madame de Beauvais's windows.

Now that Louis had brought his bride home, the city, the kingdom, and the court settled down to await the realization of everyone's hopes. The municipality had expressed those hopes very explicitly in the fireworks display it put on in front of the Louvre three days after the queen's entry. The chief set piece was a ship, the emblem of Paris, with a figure of Jason and the Golden Fleece: an allusion to Louis returning with his conquest, though perhaps not the most appropriate choice of image, considering the later history of Jason and Medea. More to the point, however, a siren on the prow of the ship carried a dolphin on her head, and on the poop two tritons held up a placard also picturing a dolphin.[15] Dolphin, dauphin—an heir to the throne was what people expected of Maria Teresa, as they had done of Anne more than forty years ago.

Meanwhile the young queen got accustomed to her new surroundings. She shared Anne's taste for visiting convents and churches and was even more punctilious in her piety, since she heard two masses instead of one whenever she took Communion. In October she took the habit of the Third Order of Saint Francis, a perfectly acceptable thing for a lay person to do, though somewhat unusual for a new bride.[16] Her favorite religious, however, were the Discalced Carmelites; in fact, she soon helped found a daughter house of the main Paris convent. This small establishment became for her a more modest version of what Val-de-Grâce meant to her mother-in-law. It reflected the routine she and Anne adopted, for though they sometimes attended sermons or ceremonies together, most often they divided forces and covered twice as much ground.

They enjoyed more worldly pleasures too, of course, promenades and outings to Saint-Germain and to Vincennes, where Mazarin was spending more and more of his time. And the social season was advanced by some months in honor of the king's marriage. Mazarin had commissioned an opera for the occasion from the Italian composer Francesco Cavalli: *Hercules in Love.* The opera was ready, but the new theater in the Tuileries with the required stage machinery was not.[17] In November, therefore, the royal family and the court enjoyed a less elaborate Cavalli production in the Louvre: *Xerxes,* which had had its premiere in Venice some years earlier.[18] The king gave grand balls too, where he and Philippe led out Maria Teresa in turn while Anne watched benignly. Christmas and New Year's interrupted these pastimes with religious observances, but on Twelfth Night eve, Louis treated his wife, his mother, and their ladies to supper and then, dressed in ancient Roman fashion, took the queen not just to one ball but to two. Next day Mazarin entertained the whole family in his palace on the rue de Richelieu,[19] and one evening a week later, the young people trooped off to no fewer than three private parties in succession.[20] It was a great change for Maria Teresa from the solemn ceremonial of the Spanish court, where ladies scarcely met men, and certainly did not mingle with them at informal entertainments.

The king's carnival ballet was to crown all this gaiety, and it was meant to be particularly splendid that year, with sumptuous decorations being set up in the picture gallery off the king's pavilion. At that point, however, the round of pleasure came to an abrupt halt, for on the night of 5 to 6 February 1661, fire broke out in the gallery, presumably owing to the carelessness of workmen. The flames spread rapidly and since the weather was windy, a large part of the palace seemed in imminent danger of catching fire. While a bucket brigade toiled from the courtyard up the stairs, to not much effect, the king and queen had recourse to supernatural aid. They sent for the sacrament from the parish church, and according to pious report no sooner had they received the procession at the entrance to the Louvre than the wind shifted and the fire was brought under control.[21] More likely it was a less miraculous intervention that saved the palace: an Augustinian lay brother had himself hoisted to roof level on an improvised crane and with a wrecking bar pried loose the burning timbers.[22]

For the royal family, it would have meant no more than temporary inconvenience—indeed, the king and queen went to Saint-Germain for a few days to escape the cleanup operations—had it not been for the fire's effect on Mazarin. His quarters were adjacent to the gallery, and he had to be evacuated in a hurry. Almost helpless, whether from shock or smoke inhalation, he was carried down the stairs amid the jostle of the improvised fire brigade and taken to his own palace.[23] From there a few days later, he moved to Vincennes for the sake of better air, but for him the fire turned out to have been the beginning of the end. He died a little more than a month afterward, on 9 March.

Although his rapid decline seems to have been unexpected, Mazarin had suffered increasingly often from kidney stones and gout during the past years. Lately shortness of breath had begun to trouble him, and the months of strain and overwork in the negotiations with Spain had done nothing to improve matters. At Saint-Jean-de-Luz, he had literally worn himself out in the service of the crown; and when Anne and Louis visited him one day when he was indisposed, he told them so, sticking his emaciated leg out of the bed as proof. Anne was touched and wept. On the return trip to Paris, he suffered from such weakness that he traveled much of the way lying on a mattress on the floor of his coach.[24] He continued to attend to business, however, and seemed to be getting along reasonably well during the fall and early winter, with only intermittent bouts of illness, until the night of the fire.

The royal family rallied around Mazarin in an unparalleled display of solicitude. As soon as it became clear that his condition was serious, Louis, his wife, and mother moved to Vincennes and stayed there, except for occasional excursions to the capital for visits to churches and performances of the king's carnival ballet. Both Louis and Anne spent a good deal of time with Mazarin. Louis in particular was in and out of the sickroom at all hours of the day, and Anne actually lived in a room adjacent until Mazarin's cries of pain at night forced her to move upstairs so that she could get some rest.[25] During those weeks Mazarin distilled the political lessons of years into last-minute advice to Louis on how to conduct his government. Although at least some of it was of the variety "do as I say, not as I have done," Louis took pains to have it written out later.[26] But no one recorded what Mazarin and Anne had to say to each other.

Despite occasional mutual exasperation—he deplored her insatiable taste for collecting relics, and she occasionally complained of his avarice and highhanded manner—they had preserved the family idyll they had so carefully constructed. They had exchanged affectionate messages in their old accustomed style whenever they were separated, as happened, for example, in June of the previous year when Mazarin and the king went off on a side excursion while Anne and Maria Teresa journeyed northward to Paris by a more direct route. Anne had evidently written to Mazarin earlier, and he had replied with his usual gallantry, for she answered:

> If I had thought that one of my letters could please you so much, I would have written more: and it is true that to see the transports with which they are received and read, reminded me very much of another time that I recall at almost every moment. Whatever you may believe or doubt, I assure you that all the moments of my life will be used to show you that there has never been truer friendship than mine . . . and if I could show you my heart as clearly as what I am writing on this paper, I am confident that you would be content, or you would be the most ungrateful man in the world, and I do not believe that is the case.[27]

It was a family letter too; Anne mentioned that she was writing at the same table with the young queen, who asked her to thank him for his news of Louis and to assure him, Mazarin, of her affection. Philippe also sent thanks, and for herself Anne concluded: "twenty-two begs me to tell you that until the last breath whatever you believe [four crosshatched vertical lines]."[28]

Whatever they may have said to one another in farewell, Mazarin paid tribute to Anne in his testament for her "incredible steadfastness and fidelity."[29] In gratitude he left her a great diamond, the "Rose of England," as well as several other jewels and some precious furniture, including a pair of inlaid cabinets showing respectively Peace and War. Anne obviously prized these, since she gave them a place of honor in her summer apartment.[30]

Having signed his testament, Mazarin finally turned from business and concentrated on his soul.[31] Although he was attended by his confessor, a priest of the Theatine order, rumor had it that he was dying too much a philosopher and insufficiently a Christian. Besides, the curés of Paris had been contending for years that sick and dying persons must confess to, and receive the sacraments from, their proper parish priests. As a concession to the troublesome clergy of Paris, therefore, as well as to devout opinion in general, Mazarin sent for his parish priest, the curé of Saint-Eustache in Paris. Father Merlin declined the honor and instead delegated a deathbed specialist, Claude Joly of Saint-Nicholas-des-Champs. First Joly tried to get Mazarin to examine his conscience regarding such issues as his treatment of cardinal de Retz or the conduct of state finances. But once Mazarin had headed him off with a diplomatic "let us speak of God," they got along better, and Joly settled down to a course of spiritual exhortation. When Mazarin breathed his last, Joly was able to certify to the skeptics that the cardinal had indeed died like a Christian.

Louis wept copiously and bewailed the loss he had suffered, and Anne too was visibly moved. They left Vincennes with their party the same day and returned to Paris, where they promptly paid condolence visits to all Mazarin's relatives. That much was customary, but Louis went further: he ordered the court into full mourning, a step as unprecedented as his commanding the vigil of forty hours before the exposed Sacrament in all churches during the last days of Mazarin's life. Normally the court only wore full mourning for members of the royal family, and the forty hours were never kept for private subjects.[32] The people who commented on this in astonishment forgot that Mazarin had indeed been a surrogate member of the family, for he was the king's godfather and mentor as well as his first minister. Louis remembered. He seemed so despondent that Anne feared it would make him ill. Everyone around him thought to pay him court by dwelling on Mazarin's merits and on the gap left by his death, until Anne herself discouraged such talk and advised Louis that he should busy himself with something better than useless words of regret. Maternal anxiety may have misled her here.[33] Despondent or not, Louis was keeping busy already, having taken over as his own first minister the day after Mazarin's death. It is true that no one, not even Anne, believed he would persevere in such a routine of hard work.[34]

Not only did Anne discourage sorrowful talk about Mazarin, she also showed herself quite hardheaded in keeping the government of Brittany that Mazarin had asked Louis to confer on his nephew-in-law and chief heir the duke of Mazarin. Anne would not hear of resigning the governorship in the young man's favor; it was too consequential a post, she said, to leave royal hands, and she refused to grant him as much as the expectation of succession to it.[35] Her resistance in this case did not necessarily reflect her feelings about Mazarin, however. Mademoiselle thought indeed that Mazarin was soon forgotten; but

she was not the most acute psychological observer, and in the past
Anne had preserved her secrets from sharper eyes than hers. Unquestionably Anne was a realist. She had watched approvingly while Mazarin took care of his soul and made himself small before God, and
she trusted God would be merciful.[36] Now that Mazarin was committed to the divine keeping, it was time to go on with the living. If she
missed him as a personality, a special part of her life, she did not say.
On the other hand, she continued to receive his nieces, those who
were married in France, just as every Advent she continued to attend
the novena for the Virgin's delivery, a special devotion of the Theatine
fathers, whom Mazarin had brought to France and whose church he
had founded and named in her honor, Sainte-Anne-la-Royale.[37]

Although they had worked together for a long time, she could
scarcely have missed Mazarin as a collaborator, since their joint task
was accomplished. She was the mother of a ruling king, not, as she had
been, a bewildered widow with young children. Moreover, her relationship with Louis was an unusual one for royal families in that it was
both close and direct. She did not interfere in politics and was too well
schooled in respect for kingship to cross him lightly, but whenever
she saw her duty plain to admonish him on a matter of religion or
morals, they talked face to face. After Mazarin's death, there were ambitious souls who urged her to speak for them, promising to use their
good offices with the king on her behalf when they should be in
power. She gave them all short shrift, saying that

> she did not want the good offices of whomsoever with the king; that
> she desired only his glory, and gave him only completely disinterested
> advice; that as long as the king received her advice as he had been
> doing up to the present, she would be pleased with him; but if ever she
> saw herself in need of third parties and good offices with him, she
> would leave him and go to Val-de-Grâce to spend the rest of her days in
> peace.[38]

It never came to that. On the contrary, when Louis had especially serious business, his mother was the person in whom he confided.
When he decided, for example, to proceed against the superintendent
of finance Fouquet on suspicion of treason, Anne was in the secret of
her son's plans, and after Fouquet's arrest they two together read his
captured correspondence.[39]

Meanwhile there were family joys to act as powerful consolation.
Anne and Henrietta Maria had long been at work to arrange a marriage
between Louis's brother, Philippe, and Charles II's sister, Henrietta.

The ceremony took place at the end of March in Henrietta Maria's borrowed apartments in the Palais-Royal, very quietly amid a restricted family circle.[40] Henrietta had grown up in France, so that neither Philippe nor Louis were strangers to her. Philippe liked her well enough and the pair settled down to married life in the Palais-Royal, which Henrietta Maria vacated for them. They were now styled duke and duchess of Orléans, since Philippe had been invested with his late uncle's title to the duchy, though people usually referred to them as Monsieur and Madame.

At the same time that Anne was providing Philippe with a wife, she had the even greater satisfaction of knowing that the young queen was pregnant.[41] Maria Teresa felt unwell enough during her pregnancy to curtail her religious outings, and in order to give her the benefit of fresh air and pleasant surroundings, as soon as the Easter celebrations were over the whole family moved with the court to Fontainebleau. People who were present later recalled the following months as the springtime of youth and enjoyment.[42] The new Madame, vivacious and charming, led the gaiety, surrounded by her own as well as the queen's maids of honor. More often than not, Maria Teresa had to stay in the background because of her condition. There was no question of her dancing at balls or accompanying the king on hunting parties; what was worse, the king's affections seemed to be wandering. It was all very well to be carrying the hopes of France, but Maria Teresa was in love with Louis and resented it bitterly to see him dancing with Madame, riding with Madame, walking with Madame, taking moonlight drives in the park with Madame. At first Anne did not take her daughter-in-law's complaints too seriously. She tried to reason with her, pointing out that the king was his own master and besides was not giving her real cause to be jealous.[43] As the weeks went by, however, and Louis's flirtation with his sister-in-law verged more and more on indiscretion, Philippe also became offended, and Anne judged it necessary to intervene. She asked Madame to moderate her conduct, and she also complained to Henrietta Maria. All to no avail—Madame was having too good a time to stop. As a blind, however, she and Louis agreed that he would seem to be paying attention to one of her maids of honor, Mademoiselle de La Vallière, a stratagem that would explain Louis's constant presence in Madame's company. Anne's appeals to Louis's conscience failed to have any effect, and the round of amusements continued as before.

Meanwhile the time for Maria Teresa's confinement was approaching. By mid-October the ladies of the great nobility were arriving at

Fontainebleau to be with the queen as custom demanded. Relics and prayers for her safe delivery poured in. At last before dawn on 1 November 1661, she went into labor. Louis rose to the occasion, staying with his wife and showing her the tenderest solicitude as though his flirtations of the summer had never happened.[44] For the moment Maria Teresa had every possible happiness: her husband was at her side, and her child was a boy—once more France had a dauphin. Louis ordered public thanksgiving services and, so that his subjects might share his joy, had prisoners freed in Paris and bread and wine distributed to the populace. The governess of the royal children had already been appointed; it was the marquise of Montausier, née Julie d'Angennes, famous daughter of the marquise of Rambouillet, who invented the literary salon.[45] Madame de Montausier took charge of the dauphin and brought him to the Louvre early in December, while his parents and his grandmother went on pilgrimage to the Virgin of Chartres to honor the vows they had made for his birth.[46]

Anne felt boundless satisfaction, the more so because there was another grandchild on the way: Madame was pregnant—with a daughter as it turned out, born in March 1662 and named Marie Louise.[47] Already after the birth of the dauphin, Anne had declared "that God had given her all the blessings she had asked of Him, and that she had nothing more to wish for except her salvation."[48] Of course, that was not quite true. Although she spoke often of retiring to Val-de-Grâce and said the king was so capable that he did not need her any more, she found excellent reasons for continuing to preside over her family and many things to wish for besides her salvation. She considered she had a duty to keep the court respectable and the royal family united, and in particular she claimed to be staying for the sake of Maria Teresa and Philippe.[49] Presumably she enjoyed her role of matriarch, but there is no denying her family sorely tried her patience during these years.

By the summer of 1662, Madame had recovered from childbed, and Maria Teresa was pregnant once more. Madame consequently resumed her sway over the parties and excursions at court, where she and her friends formed a clique that showed scant respect for the queen mother or regard for the feelings of the queen. According to Mademoiselle, in her chagrin one day Anne confided regrets about the match she had made for Philippe; if Mademoiselle had been the one to marry Philippe, "you would have lived on better terms with me, and my son would have been only too fortunate to have a wife as sensible as you are."[50] Louis for his part was pursuing not only Mademoiselle de La Vallière but also one of his wife's maids of honor, in a chase that would have been comic had it not brought unpleasant consequences to innocent parties. Maria Teresa's lady of honor, the duchess of Navailles, who was in charge of the girls, resolutely defended their virtue. She scolded the king roundly to his face and, what was more, had masons block up the secret doorway he was using to enter the girls' quarters. After that he had to converse with the young lady through a keyhole until he began to explore ways of entering the rooms from the roof. The duchess of Navailles put a stop to that with iron grillwork and Louis was irritated beyond measure. Although he abandoned his quest and concentrated on La Vallière, he could not forgive the duchess for having thwarted him. He was only too glad to listen to slander against her, and in the summer of 1664, both she and her husband were banished from court in disgrace.[51]

Since the duchess was a friend of Anne's and had acted with her approval and support, Anne felt this disgrace as a blow against herself. Louis turned a deaf ear to her pleas on behalf of the Navailles couple; for once he seemed to be seriously at odds with his mother. They had nothing to say to each other, speaking in public only to preserve appearances. "You see how he treats me," Anne exclaimed to Philippe and literally cried on his shoulder.[52] She talked of going to Val-de-Grâce and finally one evening stayed away from the usual family supper, which gave Louis pause for thought. Her confessor eventually persuaded her to humble herself and be the first to speak; she was steeling herself to do this when Louis met her halfway. He asked her pardon on his knees, admitted he had not slept all night, and begged her not to go to Val-de-Grâce. Working from such a promising beginning, Anne told him truths about his sins; he was too full of power, she added, and did not curb his desires. He knew what ailed him, he replied, and admitted to feeling distress and shame, but he protested that he could not help himself: his passion was stronger than his reason, and he had lost so much as the wish to struggle against it. Anne observed that his self-knowledge at least showed God had not abandoned him completely, and urged him to pray for better feelings. Moreover, she pointed out to him that his treatment of the duke and duchess of Navailles reflected badly on himself, for it was clear he was banishing them because they were virtuous. In this regard too he claimed to be helpless: he could not overcome his thirst for vengeance on the pair.[53] In short, he was willing to confide in his mother and to face her criticism, but he was not willing to change his conduct to please her. It could have been worse; he might have turned against her. Although Anne had to accept the limits he was setting on her moral authority, she found consolation in his continued trust and affection. Louis on his side considered he had won a point, for one day he took La Vallière to his mother's card circle, which was tantamount to recognition of the young lady's special status. For the sake of her daughter-in-law, Anne felt profoundly embarrassed; but all she did was to take refuge in her oratory: she made no protest.[54] Evidently she feared to push Louis too far lest she lose him.

On one subject Anne and Louis were agreed: no one must tell Maria Teresa about her husband's extramarital affairs.[55] Anne wanted to spare her daughter-in-law pain, whereas Louis preferred to evade face-to-face explanations with his wife. Neither her repeated pregnancies nor shared grief at the death of the infants made Louis more considerate, whatever emotion he showed while she was actually in childbed. She had two daughters in 1662 and 1664, but neither girl lived more than a few weeks.[56] Although she grieved for them, she was more inconsolable over her husband's infidelities. Anne was constantly trying to shield and divert her on the one hand, while on the other assuring her that at heart Louis loved her as his wife and urging her to pay no attention to the rest. Maria Teresa, however, rejected this age-old advice, so that Anne confided to a few close friends that she could wish her daughter-in-law more experience of the world and greater force of mind to make her way in it.[57] It had to be admitted; Maria Teresa was a victim, not a survivor. She desperately wanted to be like her mother-in-law and to succeed to her consequence. It is revealing that eventually she had herself painted in an almost exact copy of one of Anne's portraits, wearing the royal mantle and Anne's pearls. The resemblance was only an illusion: Maria Teresa did not have Anne's spirit. She suffered, wept, and prayed, but she never fought for herself. While Anne lived, Maria Teresa leaned on her. In the nature of things, however, that support could not last forever.

Anne had always enjoyed such robust good health that everyone expected her to have a long and vigorous old age. It came as a shock, therefore, when after Easter 1663 she fell into a prolonged illness. The exact nature of the malady is unclear; she suffered from lassitude in her arms, pain in her legs, nausea, and in particular from fever.[58] Her physicians had her bled repeatedly until one day she fainted from loss of blood. Then they tried quinine, which alleviated the fever but did nothing for her other symptoms, and as a last resort they persuaded her to take a powerful emetic. During all this Philippe hardly left her side, and on the nights when she was especially sick, Louis himself kept the vigil and rested on a mattress at the foot of her bed. As it happened, both Maria Teresa and he came down with measles, and Anne was too ill to be told when the doctors for a few hours thought Louis in danger of death. In June, Anne finally began to improve. She had a slow convalescence, however, for it was 9 August before she went out, and then it was only to Val-de-Grâce to give thanks for her recovery.[59]

Sometimes illness accentuates the passage from one stage of life to another. Louis seems to have noted such a change in his mother. During his bout with measles, when he was thought to be in mortal danger, he had given thought to the question who should be regent if he died. His first choice was his mother, but then he dismissed the idea because he believed she would henceforward be in poor health.[60] This was not immediately apparent, nor did concern for her induce him to change his manner of living. Nevertheless his observation turned out to be correct. In May of the following year, 1664, Anne began to feel pain in her left breast.[61] She had earlier found a nodule there but had paid it no attention, just as she ignored the pain now, being preoccupied with her children's marital problems, court intrigues, and her great quarrel with Louis during the summer. In November she watched day and night over Maria Teresa, who was dangerously ill and had given birth to her second daughter prematurely. By now people remarked how worn and yellow Anne was looking, though they attributed it to worry and exertion.[62]

At this point she must at last have consulted her physician, Séguin, who in turn brought in the king's physician, Vallot; for before the month was out, it was common knowledge among the medical profession in Paris that she had a cancer.[63] Apparently they did not tell her anything so definite, but as her breast got worse she guessed the news from their faces when they examined her. During her annual Christmas visit to Val-de-Grâce, she felt so unwell that her doctors brought in eminent physicians from Paris for a grand consultation. The colleagues only confirmed the original diagnosis: it was cancer and, in their opinion, incurable.[64]

Physicians in the seventeenth century had no concept of cancer as a complex of diseases, nor any clear idea of the process of metastasis.[65] Their knowledge of the subject still corresponded to what Hippocrates and Galen had taught in antiquity. According to those ancient authorities, a cancer was a particular kind of unnatural growth, unnatural as opposed to normal growth or change in body tissue. Practically all the growths so classified were external ones, and mammary tumors were seen as the most common sort. Beyond that all was uncertain; diagnosis could be proved only by time. If a tumor spread and the patient died, it was cancer; if on the other hand the growth did not develop in a malignant way and the patient lived, the physician either could label the tumor as one of the noncancerous growths against nature or could claim a cure. Moreover, if he saw the growth in an early stage, classification was difficult. Thus, for example, the king's physician Vallot held that "in the beginning cancer most often resembles a wart in color and consistency."[66] Such a description was not much help for purposes of identification. In Anne's case, to be sure, this particular problem did not arise. By the time Vallot saw her, her breast was in bad enough condition for there to be no doubt about the diagnosis. Vallot and his colleagues knew this kind of illness was fatal; the only questions were, whether and by what means Anne's life might be prolonged.

There was no generally accepted treatment for breast cancer. Since this like all other diseases was believed to arise from an imbalance of the body's humors—Galen's four humors of blood, phlegm, black and yellow bile—doctors prescribed bleedings and purges in order to restore the balance of the humors as much as possible. Although medical literature included references to simple mastectomy, in the absence of anesthesia and asepsis this was a heroic procedure, performed rarely if at all. In any case no one so much as suggested an operation for Anne. What remained were empirical remedies, ointments or caustics for local application, and in this domain amateur healers competed with physicians. As the news of Anne's illness spread, all sorts of people presented themselves at court with supposedly infallible recipes while Louis himself sent as far afield as Italy for information on experts and medicines. Meantime he put Vallot in charge of his mother's case.

Among his papers, Vallot left a copy of his opinion, although he did not date it and it may refer to November, December, or an even later period.

> The extent of the queen-mother's disease, [he wrote] combined with her advanced age [she was 63] gives great reason to fear an unhappy outcome. Nevertheless if the patient is still able to take treatment, we do not despair of being able to give her relief and keeping her alive for a number of years.[67]

The treatment he prescribed for her consisted of frequent enemas, a little bleeding from the arm, and weekly purges with a concoction whose active ingredients were senna and rhubarb. In addition, during the first weeks she used an ointment based on extract of hemlock, intended to relieve the pain in her breast.[68] When that did not work, her own physician, Séguin, advised her to try a treatment proposed by a village priest from the Orléanais. This man, named Gendron, had no medical training; he gave medical care to the poor on the basis of alleged secret recipes. He promised Anne that his remedy, consisting of belladonna and burnt lime, would harden the afflicted breast like marble so that she could live as though she had never had a cancer.[69] Anne had his mixture applied to her breast until August 1665, by which time her disease had progressed so much that she twice already had been pronounced near death. At everyone's urging she dismissed Gendron and placed herself in the hands of one Alliot, a doctor from Lorraine. His specific was an arsenic paste, a caustic whose effect was to mortify the diseased tissue, which was progressively cut away.[70] She underwent these daily operations from August 1665 to January 1666, and at least for a while, her doctors gave her hope of some success, even to the point of saying that she might after all not die of her cancer.[71] If they actually believed what they said, they were mistaken. Early in January 1666, much weakened by pain and fever, she let herself be persuaded to change Alliot for a doctor from Milan who claimed to have a more efficacious treatment.[72] He kept it a secret, but whatever it was, Anne did not suffer it long, for death released her on 20 January 1666.

Small wonder if preachers likened what she had had to endure to the martyrdom of saints: confinement, pain, razors, knives.[73] They regarded it as good for the health of her soul, however, and she agreed. Once she had heard from the doctors, she said, " . . . What I shall suffer will no doubt help my salvation; I hope that God will give me the strength to endure it with patience."[74] The trouble was that she had only too clear an idea of what awaited her: in the infirmary at Val-de-Grâce, she had seen nuns who were dying of breast cancer and admitted that she had always felt horror at the mere thought of this illness.[75] As her condition grew worse, she had moments of revolt: " . . . Often she said she would never have believed her destiny would be so different from that of other creatures; that people only rotted after death, but as for her, God had condemned her to rot alive."[76] On the whole, though, she took her illness as penance, an opportunity to expiate sins of vanity and self-indulgence: " . . . God wishes to punish me for having loved myself too well and having cared too much about the beauty of my body."[77] She had always been painstakingly fastidious about her person, insistent on cleanliness and so delicate about fabrics that touched her skin that she could not bear ordinary linen. Her shifts and sheets had to be made of the finest batiste, laundered several times to soften them before she would use them. Mazarin used to tease her about this obsession, saying if she were to go to hell she would need no other torment except to sleep in muslin. Although she could not bring herself to change her habits, now she deplored them. She said as much to one of her ladies near the end, "looking fixedly at her and touching the sheet, 'Ah, Countess, batiste sheets! Batiste sheets!' "[78]

It was months before she became bedridden. During the winter of 1664–65, she still went about much as usual, visiting churches on feast days, going to Val-de-Grâce, and attending family parties. The dean of the Paris medical faculty, Gui Patin, saw her in church with the king and queen on Easter Sunday, though he noted that she walked slowly.[79] Shortly thereafter Louis moved the whole court to Saint-Germain for the season, Anne traveling in a sedan chair. She had no pleasure in Saint-Germain; from May on she saw herself growing increasingly infirm. She went through two crises in three months, and though she rallied each time, she felt, "death is so close to me that when I see the end of another day it seems like an unexpected miracle."[80] She made her will, which involved some family unpleasantness. She had wanted to leave her jewelry to her granddaughter Marie Louise, Philippe's and Henrietta's child, because, as she said, the king's children would be well enough provided without any contribution from her, whereas this little girl would be poor.[81] That did not suit Louis, who wanted to add his mother's pearls to the crown jewels. Even Maria Teresa, usually so meek, thought she should have a share.[82] In the end, Anne left her jewelry, valued at more than a million three hundred thousand livres, to be divided between Louis and Philippe, just as they were to divide most of her furniture and other precious objects and some of her relics. The greater number of relics were to go to Val-de-Grâce, along with her own heart and sufficient money to endow a daily mass for her soul. She remembered the people of her household and her friends in a long list of individual bequests, but the rest of her fortune, one million livres, she left to her granddaughter Marie Louise.[83]

In September the court returned to Paris, though Anne had to be transported in a portable bed. She had herself carried to Val-de-Grâce, where she would have liked to stay, but the doctors and the king found the convent too inconvenient. Louis came in person to fetch her home to the Louvre. Her winter apartment had been made cheerful with new furniture, a bed hung with patterned velvet in her favorite color, blue, with a set of chairs and stools to match.[84] To give her as much quiet as possible, carpet was laid in the service passage alongside her room.[85] Her family gathered around her morning and evening while the surgeons attended to her dressings, and they kept her company at other times too. She was concerned lest they be bored waiting on her and was forever urging them to get some fresh air, or go to dinner, or otherwise divert themselves.

While Louis and Philippe indeed gave parties and enjoyed themselves, Anne and Maria Teresa were mourning the death of Philip IV, and Anne remarked that she would soon be following her brother.[86] By mid-January it was plain that this would indeed be the case, so thin and weak had Anne become. For months novenas and forty-hour prayer vigils had been held on her behalf all over France, and she herself had taken to daily confession. These efforts now redoubled. On 19 January her grand almoner told her she had no more time to lose and should prepare to receive the last rites. She spoke at length to her sons and her daughters-in-law, separately and together, and gave them her blessing. After that the clergy took over. Louis, who had fainted, left his mother's room before the end and asked Philippe to follow him. It turned into a contest to show which of them loved Anne best, and for once, Philippe won: he sent word to Louis that he could not obey him in this case, but that he promised him it would be the only disobedience of his life.[87] He was present when Anne died early in the morning of 20 January.

In her last years, Anne had regained all the popularity her regency had cost her. When she no longer had power, people loved her.[88] She herself had never given much sign of caring about public opinion one way or the other: it was the opinion of her son Louis that mattered, and he had a juster appreciation than most people of the way she had acquitted herself. Out of the fullness of his heart on the day of her death, he exclaimed that "the queen, his mother, was not only a great queen but that she deserved to be ranked among the greatest kings."[89] He paid more extensive tribute to her later in his memoirs: he had loved her and spent much time in her company not simply because of the natural tie between them but because he trusted her. She had saved his state for him, and "the vigor with which this princess had upheld my dignity, while I was unable to defend it myself, was the most important and the most useful service I could ever receive."[90] And what was equally remarkable, when he was old enough to act for himself, she had ungrudgingly given up her authority. In Louis's eyes Anne's merit was so great that not even the most eloquent men in the kingdom could do it justice:

> . . . The plain account of [her] actions given by history will always far surpass whatever they have been able to say in her praise.[91]

Few royal mothers have received as feeling an epitaph from their sons, or died as fulfilled.

NOTES

ABREVIATIONS USED

AMRE: Archives du Ministère des Relations Extérieures. (Formerly the Ministère des Affaires Estrangères.)
AN: Archives Nationales, Paris.
BN: Bibliothèque Nationale, Paris. Unless otherwise noted, this reference applies to the Salle des Manuscrits.
Simancas: Archivo General de Simancas.

PREFACE

1. Henri Griffet, *Histoire du règne de Louis XIII, roi de France et de Navarre.*
2. Françoise Bertaut de Motteville, *Mémoires pour servir à l'histoire D'Anne d'Autriche, épouse de Louis XIII, roi de France, par Madame de Motteville, une de ses favorites.*
3. Jules Michelet, *Richelieu et la Fronde,* vol. 12 of *Histoire de France.*
4. Ibid., p. 234.
5. Ibid., pp. 272–87.
6. Ibid., p. 234.
7. Ibid., p. 305.
8. Pierre Adolphe Chéruel, *Histoire de France pendant la minorité de Louis XIV;* and *Histoire de France sous le ministère de Mazarin.*
9. Jean Baptiste Honoré Raymond Capefigue, *Anne d'Autriche, reine-régente, et la minorité de Louis XIV.*
10. Jean Baptiste Honoré Raymond Capefigue, *Richelieu, Mazarin, la Fronde et le règne de Louis XIV.*
11. Martha Walker Freer, *The Regency of Anne of Austria.*
12. Alexandre Dumas, père, *Les Trois Mousquetaires.* See also *Vingt ans après: suite des "Trois Mousquetaires."*
13. François, prince de Marsillac, baron de Verteuil, duc de La Rochefoucauld, *Mémoires de La Rochefoucauld,* Collection des mémoires relatifs à l'histoire de France, 2e série, vols. 51–52, 51:343–44.
14. Meriel Buchanan, *Anne of Austria, the Infanta Queen.*
15. Paul Robiquet, *Le Coeur d'une reine: Anne d'Autriche, Louis XIII, et Mazarin.*
16. Jean de la Varende, *Anne d'Autriche, femme de Louis XIII, 1601–1666.*
17. Emile Emmanuel Herbillon, *Anne d'Autriche, reine, mère, régente.*
18. Tomy Saint-Félix, *La Reine stérile.*
19. Claude Dulong, *Anne d'Autriche, mère de Louis XIV.*

CHAPTER ONE

1. The details of Anne's embarkation come from an eyewitness report, BN, Fonds Français 16631, fol. 328.

2. María Jesús Perez-Martin, *Margarita de Austria*, p. 111.

3. Armand Baschet, *Histoire secrète du mariage de Louis XIII et d'Anne d'Autriche: le roi chez la reine*, pp. 100–101, 105.

4. Louis Vaunois, *Vie de Louis XIII*, p. 44.

5. There is very little information on Anne's early years. The meager sources have been used by Perez-Martin, *Margarita de Austria*, and by Baschet, *Histoire secrète*, pp. 100–107.

6. Perez-Martin, *Margarita de Austria*, p. 120.

7. Felipe III, *Cartas de Felipe III a su hija Ana, reina de Francia, 1616–1618*, p. 56; from Madrid, 3 October 1618.

8. Baschet, *Histoire secrète*, p. 103.

9. The reports of the French ambassadors are to be found in BN, Fonds Français 16115 and 16116.

10. Vaucelas from Madrid, 2 January 1614, 29 January 1614, 9 July 1614; BN, Fonds Français 16116, fols. 1–2, 3–4, 21–21v, 25v–27, 142.

11. Felipe III, *Cartas*, pp. 31–32; from San Lorenzo, 21 August 1617.

12. Felipe III, *Cartas*, passim.

13. Vaucelas from Madrid, 15 November 1613; BN, Fonds Français 16115, fol. 506.

14. Jean Héroard, "Journal de la vie active du roy Louis exactement descrit depuis le premier janvier 1605 jusqu'au xxx . . . janvier . . . 1628 par messire Jehan Hérouard, seigneur de Vaugrigneuse, son premier medecin," BN, Fonds Français 4022–27. Citations will be from this manuscript, although there is also a contemporary abridgement in BN, Nouvelles Acquisition Françaises 13008–11; and a not completely reliable printed edition, *Journal de Jean Héroard sur l'enfance et la jeunesse de Louis XIII*. See also the standard biographies, Pierre Chevallier, *Louis XIII: le roi cornélien*, and Vaunois, *Vie*.

15. Louis Batiffol, *Le Roi Louis XIII à vingt ans*, p. 23; *Le Louvre sous Henri IV et Louis XIII: la vie de la cour en France au XVIIe siècle*, pp. 161, 165.

16. A scholarly appraisal of Marie de Medici remains to be written. Meanwhile see Louis Batiffol, *La Vie intime d'une reine de France au XVIIe siècle*; Françoise Kermina, *Marie de Médicis: reine, régente et rebelle*; and Michel Carmona, *Marie de Médicis*.

17. Batiffol, *La Vie intime*, pp. 467–537.

18. Dr. Elizabeth W. Marvick has called to the attention of the author several extant paintings by Louis.

19. Elizabeth Wirth Marvick, "The Character of Louis XIII: The Role of His Physician," *Journal of Interdisciplinary History* 4 (Winter 1974): 347–74. This article corrects some of the conclusions drawn by David Hunt, *Parents and Children in History: The Psychology of Family Life in Early Modern France*, pp. 113–86 passim.

20. Marvick, "The Character," pp. 369–74; and Elizabeth Wirth Marvick, "Childhood History and Decisions of State," *History of Childhood Quarterly: Journal of Psychohistory* 2 (Fall 1974): 177.

21. François Tommy Perrens, *Les Mariages espagnols sous le règne de Henri IV et la régence de Marie de Médicis, 1602–1615*, pp. 261–62.

22. Ibid., p. 212. Nevertheless, in the dauphin's nursery the infanta continued to be the only marriage candidate mentioned.

23. Based on their retrospective perception of French national interests, nineteenth-century French historians generally deplored the Spanish marriages. Thus Perrens thought it necessary to mention that the "mistake" of the Spanish marriages was "repaired" by Luynes and Richelieu (ibid., pp. 563–67).

24. For the feelings of the Catholic party, and for religious tensions in general at this point, see Roland Mousnier, *L'Assassinat de Henri IV, 14 mai 1610: le problème du tyrannicide et l'affermissement de la monarchie absolue*, pp. 122–42.

25. Perrens, *Les Mariages*, p. 484; Maurice Lee, Jr., *James I and Henri IV: An Essay in English Foreign Policy, 1603–1610*, pp. 170–73.

26. Baschet, *Histoire secrète*, pp. 104–5.

27. BN, Fonds Français 2748, fols. 207–12v., "Triomphe royal."

28. Baschet, *Histoire secrète*, pp. 110–18; the reports of the extraordinary ambassadors, the duke of Mayenne and Puysieux, are in BN, Fond Français 16115, fols. 113–14 v., 118–20, 126–28, 130–32.

29. For a brief summary of the contract provisions, see Perrens, *Les Mariages*, p. 350. There are numerous copies of the documents pertaining to the marriage; see, for example, AN, Fonds dit de Simancas, K1617, C 4, Nos. 1–37; BN, Fonds Francais 4330, fol. 90; 4643, No. 19 fol. 114; No. 20, fol. 124; 4648, Nos. 16–50, fols. 232ff.; 4895, No. 116, fol. 94; 5174, No. 1, fols. 1–9; AMRE, Correspondance Politique: Espagne, 12 (1600–1620), fols. 321–62v.; fols. 321–28 contain a French text of the marriage contract. In theory the gold écu at the time was worth three livres tournois, the money of account; since each livre tournois supposedly had the value of 10.98 grams of silver, the gold écu was the equivalent of 32.94 grams of silver. See Richard Bonney, *The King's Debts: Finance and Politics in France, 1589–1661*, p. x. Counting this amount of silver according to its present value would not necessarily give a useful idea of its purchasing power in the early seventeenth century. It may be helpful to consider that in 1612 about ten livres tournois bought a *setier* (156 liters, or 4.4 bushels) of wheat in Paris; see Richard Bonney, *Political Change in France under Richelieu and Mazarin, 1624–1661*, p. 177.

CHAPTER TWO

1. Desiderius Erasmus, *The Education of a Christian Prince*, p. 243.

2. Paula Sutter Fichtner, "Dynastic Marriage in Sixteenth-Century Habsburg Diplomacy and Statecraft: An Interdisciplinary Approach," *American Historical Review*, 81 (April 1976): 243–65.

3. AMRE, Mémoires et Documents: Espagne, 138, fols. 257–63v. This is a copy. The text has been published in Matéas de Novoa, *Primera parte de las memorias de Matéas de Novoa, conocida haste ahora bajo el titulo de "Historia de Felipe III, por Bernabé de Vibanco,"* vols. 60–61, Colección de documentos ineditos para la historia de Espagna, 61:15–21.

4. AMRE, Mémoires et Documents: Espagne, 138, fols. 259–61v.

5. Ibid., fol. 258.

6. Ibid., fols. 262–63.

7. Perrens, *Les Mariages*, pp. 521–26.

8. For a sampling of pamphlets supporting Marie de Medici, see BN, Fonds Francais 3806, fols. 155–72v.

9. Perrens, *Les Mariages*, pp. 490–96.

10. This bracelet did not, however, become Anne's personal property. The diamonds in it belonged to the French crown jewels, and upon the death of Louis XIII, she surrendered them to the crown in return for compensation. BN, Fonds Français 18552, fols. 59–59v.

11. *Le Mercure françois, ou les mémoires de la suitte de l'histoire de nostre temps, sous le règne du très chrestien roy de France et de Navarre Louys XIII*, 4 (1617): 282–83.

12. Novoa, *Prima parte*, 60:535. For a complete list of Anne's trousseau, see AN, Fonds dit de Simancas, K1617, C 4 (1616–20), No. 39; and No. 40 for the dowry jewels specified in her marriage contract. For these jewels see also AMRE, Correspondance Politique: Espagne, 12, fols, 354–56v.; and fols. 356v–57v for the jewels presented to her by Louis in accordance with the marriage contract.

13. AMRE, Correspondance Politique: Espagne, 12, fols. 358–62v. See also a copy of this in BN, Fonds Français 15515, fol. 178.

14. AN, Fonds dit de Simancas, K1617, C 4 (1616–20), No. 38, contains a list of the extensive Spanish household that accompanied Anne to the frontier. It contrasts sharply with the much smaller number of Spaniards that Marie and Louis proposed to let her keep; see BN, Fonds Français 16115, fols. 437–38v. Comments in this document also indicate some of the negotiations around this issue. See also BN, Fonds Français 16116, fols. 465–66 for the end result.

15. AN, Fonds dit de Simancas, K 1617, C 4 (1616–20), No. 38.

16. BN, Fonds Français 16116, fol. 446; Vaucelas from Burgos, 19 October 1615.

17. *Le Mercure*, 4 (1617): 287–301.

18. Cárlos de Arellano, *Cartas originales de don Cárlos de Arellano al gran duque de Lerma*, pp. 445–49.

19. BN, Fonds Français 16631, fols. 314–24 *bis*.

20. Ibid., fol. 329; *Le Mercure*, 4 (1617): 312–13.

21. Arellano, *Cartas*, p. 450.

22. Ibid., p. 459.

23. Ibid., p. 456; BN, Fonds Français 16631, fol. 338.

24. BN, Fonds Français 16631, fols. 341–43. Translations of quotations are the author's own.

25. Arellano, *Cartas*, p. 457.

26. Ibid., pp. 458–59; *Le Mercure*, 4 (1617), 337–41.

27. *Le Mercure*, 4 (1617): 340.

28. BN, Fonds Français 16631, fols. 453–53 v. Louis's nursery staff had rehearsed him practically from infancy for his wedding night; see Elizabeth W. Marvick, "Nature versus Nurture: Patterns and Trends in Seventeenth Century French Child-Rearing," in Lloyd DeMause, ed., *The History of Childhood*, pp. 262–63; "Childhood History," p. 175.

29. Baschet, *Histoire secrète*, p. 168; Chevallier, *Louis XIII*, pp. 101-2.

30. Vaunois, *Vie*, pp. 196–98.

31. Héroard. "Journal," 4025, fol. 224.

32. Arellano, *Cartas*, p. 459. Medical opinion would in any case have kept Louis and Anne separated for some time.

33. Héroard, "Journal," 4025, fol. 224.

CHAPTER THREE

1. Jean Philippe Varin, *Le Grand Jubilé de joye donné à la France pour le très-heureux mariage et arrivée de Louis XIII avec la serenissime princesse infante d'Espagne, Anne d'Autriche* (Paris: N. Alexandre, 1616), p. 9.

2. BN, Cabinet des Estampes, Série Q bl: Histoire de France, Louis XIII (1615-1617), fols. 5-25.

3. Arellano, *Cartas*, p. 453.

4. Perrens, *Les Mariages*, p. 558.

5. Françoise Bertaut de Motteville, *Mémoires*, 36:336-37.

6. AMRE, Correspondance Politique: Espagne, 12, fols. 356v-57v; Germain Bapst, *Histoire des joyaux de la couronne*, pp. 304-5.

7. *Le Mercure*, 4 (1617): 341-42, 362; Arellano, *Cartas*, p. 461.

8. BN, Fonds Français 16631, fol. 457; Arellano, *Cartas*, p. 462.

9. *Le Mercure*, 4 (1617): 353.

10. *Registres des délibérations du bureau de la ville de Paris*, 16, fasc. 2, pp. 339-40, 402-13.

11. Ibid., p. 412.

12. Batiffol, *Le Louvre*, pp. 11-14.

13. AMRE, Mémoires et Documents: France, 35 (1560-1628), fols. 61-61v., 126-26v.

14. Ibid., fols. 54-60v. 122-31v.

15. BN, Fonds Français 15597, fols. 279-83v.

16. The cumulative listing of Anne's household personnel until 1666 is to be found in BN, Nouvelles Acquisitions Françaises 9175, fols. 425-45. It was published in Eugène Griselle, ed., *Etat de la maison du roi Louis XIII . . . comprenant les années 1601 à 1665*, pp. 89-133.

17. On Marie's household, see Batiffol, *La Vie intime*, pp. 103-44.

18. Louis Batiffol, "Un Jeune Ménage royal," *Revue de Paris* 16 (Nov.-Dec. 1909): 108; *Le Roi Louis XIII à vingt ans*, pp. 389-90.

19. Felipe III, *Cartas*, p. 30.

20. AMRE, Mémoires et Documents: Espagne, 138, fol. 261v.

21. Ibid., fol. 261.

22. *Registres*, 17 (1616-20): 87.

23. Ibid., pp. 169-171.

24. Felipe III, *Cartas*, p. 37.

25. Batiffol, *La Vie intime*, pp. 122-29.

26. For a full account of the French court ballets and their uses, see Margaret M. McGowan, *L'Art du ballet de cour en France, 1581-1643.*

27. Paula Sutter Fichtner, *Ferdinand I of Austria: The Politics of Dynasticism in the Age of the Reformation*, p. 237.

28. Felipe III, *Cartas*, passim. Anne's letters to her father are not extant, but an impression of her side of the correspondence may be gathered from her father's replies.

29. Ibid., pp. 9-10.

30. It seems Marie de Medici had feared from the outset that Anne would consider herself more highly born than her mother-in-law and therefore would not respect her sufficiently. Having been made aware of Marie's concern, the Spaniards had taken pains to reassure the French ambassador that Anne's sentiments were everything that

could be wished (BN, Fonds Français 16115, fol. 506, Vaucelas from Madrid, 15 November 1613; and BN, Fonds Français 16116, fol. 1v, Vaucelas from Madrid, 2 January 1614).

31. Felipe III, *Cartas*, p. 29.

32. Sometimes he did not except even the infanta from his hostility against Spaniards; see Chevallier, *Louis XIII*, p. 248.

33. Simancas, Secretaria de Estado: Capitulaciones con Francia y negociaciones diplomáticos de los embajadores de España en aquela corte, serie K, legajo 1473, fols. 14, 15, 16, letters from the ambassador Monteléon, 2, 12, 14 March 1617.

34. Felipe III, *Cartas*, pp. 10, 14, 37, 44, 46.

35. Guido Cardinal Bentivoglio, *La Nunziatura di Francia del cardinale Guido Bentivoglio: Lettere a Scipione Borghese, cardinal nipote e segretario de stato di Paolo V,* 2:520.

36. Felipe III, *Cartas*, p. 15.

37. The best and fullest account of the French situation in foreign policy during these years is Victor-L. Tapié, *La Politique étrangère de la France et le début de la guerre de trente ans, 1616–1621.*

38. Felipe III, *Cartas*, pp. 9, 14, 31; Simancas, Estado: Capitulaciones con Francia, serie K, legajo 1473, fol. 35, Monteléon to Philip III, 1 July 1617. Monteléon was suggesting ways for Anne to promote Spanish diplomatic interests with her husband while avoiding any jeopardy to herself, in accordance with Philip's intentions.

39. Simancas, Estado: Capitulaciones con Francia, serie K, legajo 1473, fol. 51, the duke of Uceda to Juan de Cirica, 22 July 1617.

40. Batiffol, "Un Jeune Ménage royal," p. 110; Chevallier, *Louis XIII*, p. 252.

41. Bentivoglio, *La Nunziatura*, 2:176.

42. Ibid., 3: 173.

43. Héroard, "Journal," 4025, fol. 224.

44. Bentivoglio, *La Nunziatura*, 2:409.

45. Simancas, Estado: Capitulaciones con Francia, serie K, legajo 1475, fol. 94, Ambassador Fernando Giron to Philip III, 21st October 1618.

46. Felipe III, *Cartas*, p. 55.

47. BN, Fonds Français 24979, fols. 270–71.

48. Felipe III, *Cartas*, pp. 13, 20, 22, 36, 51.

49. Bentivoglio, *La Nunziatura*, 2:394.

50. Ibid., 3:165.

51. BN, Fonds Italien 1772, filza 51, p. 303.

52. Héroard, "Journal," 4026, fol. 131v.

53. Ibid., fol. 133v.; *Le Mercure* 5 (1619):85; BN, Fonds Italien 1772, filza 51, p. 303.

54. Batiffol, "Un Jeune Ménage royal," p. 117; *Le Roi Louis XIII à vingt ans*, p. 407.

55. Bentivoglio, *La Nunziatura*, 3:173.

56. *Le Mercure,* 5 (1619): 88.

CHAPTER FOUR

1. BN, Fonds Italien 1772, filza 51, p. 304; report of the Venetian ambassador Anzolo Contarini, 27 January 1619. Contarini had informers among the royal servants.

2. Héroard, "Journal," 4026, fols. 134–86, for example.

3. Batiffol, "Un Jeune Ménage royal," p. 120; *Le Roi Louis XIII à vingt ans*, p. 411; Bentivoglio, *La Nunziatura* 4: 18.

4. *Récit de la maladie de la reyne, fait le sixiesme fevrier 1620*; BN, Fonds Italien 1773, filza 52, p. 416, Anzolo Contarini, 18 February 1620. See also Louis XIII, *Lettres de la main de Louis*, 1:46–47, to Philip III, 13 February 1620.

5. As quoted in Vaunois, *Vie*, p. 273.

6. Batiffol, "Un Jeune Ménage royal," pp. 122–23; *Le Roi Louis XIII à vingt ans*, pp. 415–16; BN, Fonds Italien 1774, filza 53, fols. 89–91, Anzolo Contarini 26 May 1620.

7. *Registres*, 17:352–55.

8. Ibid., pp. 360–64.

9. Ibid., pp. 365, 371, 386–88, 388–89; 18:8–10.

10. Louis XIII, *Lettres*, 1:63–64. Griselle wrongly identified this note as addressed to the queen mother.

11. BN, Cabinet des Estampes, Portraits B 134, Na 24 bis, fol. 4. See the Frontispiece.

12. On the career of Marie de Rohan, see Victor Cousin, *Madame de Chevreuse: nouvelles études sur les femmes illustres et la société du XVIIe siècle*; and especially Louis Batiffol, *La Duchesse de Chevreuse: une vie d'aventures et d'intrigues sous Louis XIII*.

13. Simancas, Estado: Capitulaciones con Francia, serie K, legajo 1476, fol. 79; Fernando Giron to Philip III, 17 May 1620.

14. Bentivoglio, *La Nunziatura*, 3:450.

15. Ibid., p. 513.

16. Motteville, *Mémoires*, 36:339.

17. *Registres*, 18:70–74.

18. Simancas, Estado: Capitulaciones con Francia, serie K, legajo 1476, fol. 79; Fernando Giron to Philip III, 17 May 1620.

19. Héroard, "Journal," 4026–27 passim.

20. About the 1621 campaign, aside from standard histories of the period such as Jean-H. Mariéjol, *Henri IV et Louis XIII*, see Vaunois, *Vie*, pp. 287–300.

21. BN, Fonds Français 3818, fol. 20.

22. Vaunois, *Vie*, p. 289. Whatever the source of these rumors, Héroard does not mention any pregnancy, or abortion, or miscarriage.

23. BN, Fonds Français 3687, fols. 17v–19, instructions to Marshall Bassompierre going to Spain, 1621; see also 4149, fols. 150–51v for an undated memorandum with essentially the same contents.

24. Simancas, Estado: Capitulaciones con Francia, serie K, legajo 1473, fol. 35, Monteléon to Philip III, 1 July 1617.

25. See Philip III's instructions, AMRE, Mémoires et Documents: Espagne, 138, fols. 259v–60. For Anne's charities during her early years in France, see Motteville, *Mémoires*, 37:443–44.

26. Janvier-J.-J. Servier, *Le Val-de-Grâce: histoire du monastère et de l'hôpital militaire*, pp. 5–10.

27. Motteville, *Mémoires*, 36:349; see pp. 339–51 and 366–70 on the queen's admirers and the court beauties of the day.

28. Ibid., pp. 342–43.

29. These collections appeared annually at the time; see, for example, *Le Cabinet satyrique: première édition complète et critique d'après l'édition originale de 1618*.

30. Batiffol, *La Duchesse de Chevreuse*, pp. 15–16.

31. *Le Cabinet satyrique*, 1:48.

32. Batiffol, *La Duchesse de Chevreuse*, pp. 19–20.

33. Héroard, "Journal," 4027, fols. 26, 27.

34. Vaunois, *Vie*, pp. 305–6; Batiffol, "Un Jeune Ménage royal," p. 126.

35. Motteville, *Mémoires*, 36:338–39.

36. Louise Bourgeois, *Observations diverses sur la stérilité, perte de fruict, fécondité, accouchements et maladies des femmes et enfans nouveau naiz*, 1:25–37.

37. Héroard, "Journal," 4027, fol. 27.

CHAPTER FIVE

1. Motteville, *Mémoires*, 36:350–51.

2. Louis XIII, *Lettres*, 1:178–79, 25 March 1622.

3. Anne's defense of her friend can be gathered from Louis's replies; see Louis XIII, *Lettres*, 1:182, 190; Batiffol, *La Duchesse de Chevreuse*, pp. 23–24.

4. Louis XIII, *Lettres*, 1:190, 12 April 1622.

5. Ibid., p. 191, 15 April 1622.

6. *Registres*, 18:270–71; for her arrest of the supposed spy, see Louis XIII, *Lettres*, 1:205–6, end of April 1622.

7. Louis XIII, *Lettres*, 1:213, 11 May 1622.

8. Ibid., p. 230, 4 July 1622.

9. Ibid., p. 231, 4 July 1622.

10. Batiffol, *La Duchesse de Chevreuse*, pp. 25–34.

11. Louis XIII, *Lettres*, 1:260, no date.

12. Batiffol, "Un Jeune Ménage royal," p. 130; *Le Roi Louis XIII à vingt ans*, p. 429.

13. *Le Mercure*, 9 (1624): 406.

14. *Récit véritable de la magnifique entrée de la reyne de France en la ville de Lyon, avec l'ordre des préparatifs, triomphes et magnificences faictes à sa majesté.* See also BN, Cabinet des Estampes, Série Q^b1, Histoire de France: Louis XIII (1622), pictures relating to the 11 December entry, no foliation or pagination.

15. *Le Mercure*, 9 (1624): 430, 472; Roger Lockyer, *Buckingham: The Life and Political Career of George Villiers, First Duke of Buckingham, 1592–1628*, p. 139.

16. Lockyer, *Buckingham*, p. 139. Batiffol, *Le Roi Louis XIII à vingt ans*, p. 430, made a connection between this incident and an order by Louis forbidding men to enter the queen's cabinet in his absence. Any such connection is purely speculative however, since there is no evidence that Anne actually met, or even saw, Buckingham on this occasion.

17. AMRE, Mémoires et Documents: France, 35, fols. 249–49v.

18. Vaunois, *Vie*, p. 328, does not venture an explanation.

19. The specialized literature on Richelieu is extensive, and there are various editions of his letters and papers, although the best and most complete is still in progress: Armand Jean du Plessis, cardinal, duc de Richelieu, *Papiers . . .* , éd. Pierre Grillon. For general references see the classic Gabriel Hanotaux and A. de La Force, *Histoire du cardinal de Richelieu*; and Armand Jean du Plessis, cardinal, duc de Richelieu, *Les*

Mémoires du cardinal de Richelieu. For an interesting examination of his leadership qualities, see Elizabeth Wirth Marvick, *The Young Richelieu: a Psychoanalytic Approach to Leadership.*

20. Richelieu, Mémoires, vol. 22, 2e partie, pp. 292–302.

21. Motteville, *Mémoires*, 36:348–49.

22. Aside from Lockyer, *Buckingham*, see also Hugh R. Williamson, *George Villiers: First Duke of Buckingham.*

23. Tanneguy Leveneur, comte de Tillières, *Mémoires inédits du comte Leveneur de Tillières, ambassadeur en Angleterre, sur la cour de Charles I, et son mariage avec Henriette de France.* p. 60.

24. Williamson, *George Villiers*, pp. 161–62.

25. *Le Mercure,* 11 (1626): 353, 365–67.

26. Pierre de La Porte, *Mémoires de P. de La Porte, premier valet de chambre de Louis XIV, contenant plusieurs particularités des règnes de Louis XIII et de Louis XIV,* p. 296.

27. Tillières, *Mémoires,* p. 61.

28. Ibid., pp. 61–62.

29. Batiffol, *La Duchesse de Chevreuse,* pp. 59, 61.

30. La Porte, *Mémoires,* pp. 296–97.

31. Motteville, *Mémoires,* 36:343–44.

32. Ibid., p. 345.

33. Ibid., pp. 345–46.

34. La Porte, *Mémoires,* p. 299.

35. Motteville, *Mémoires,* 36:347; La Porte, *Mémoires,* pp. 299–301.

36. Motteville, *Mémoires,* 36: 348; Tillières, *Mémoires,* pp. 63–68.

37. Lockyer, Buckingham, pp. 293–94.

38. Ibid., p. 294.

39. As quoted ibid., pp. 295–96.

40. Ibid., p. 296.

41. Ibid.

42. Richelieu, *Mémoires,* 23:183.

43. Batiffol, *La Duchesse de Chevreuse,* p. 72.

44. Motteville, *Mémoires,* 36: 342 n. 1.

45. The story of the diamond *ferrets,* or lace points, comes from La Rochefoucauld, *Mémoires,* 51:343–44. La Rochefoucauld could not have had direct knowledge of events at court. His aunt, Madame de Sénécey, whom he claimed as a witness, did not enter Anne's service until the following year. Since no one else mentioned this incident, it seems most likely that La Rochefoucauld invented it.

46. Concerning the complications of Gaston's marriage, see Georges Dethan, *Gaston d'Orléans: conspirateur et prince charmant,* pp. 62–63; Batiffol, *La Duchesse de Chevreuse,* pp. 80–83.

47. Motteville, *Mémoires,* 36:352.

48. Batiffol, *La Duchesse de Chevreuse,* pp. 83–101.

49. Motteville, *Mémoires,* 36:353; La Porte, *Mémoires,* pp. 302–3.

50. M. Devèze, *L'Espagne de Philippe IV, 1621–1665,* 1:134. This title was communicated to the author by the courtesy of Professor John H. Elliot, of the Institute for Advanced Study, Princeton University.

CHAPTER SIX

1. For Richelieu's career at this point, aside from the reference in chapter 5, note 19, above, see also Louis Batiffol, *Richelieu et le roi Louis XIII: les véritables rapports du souverain et de son ministre*; and Victor-L. Tapié, *La France de Louis XIII et de Richelieu.*

2. Français de Paule de Clermont, marquis de Montglat, *Mémoires*, 49:40; Motteville, *Mémoires*, 36:357; Tillières, *Mémoires*, p. 65; Gédéon Tallemant des Réaux, *Historiettes*, 2:9–10.

3. Motteville, *Mémoires*, 36:357.

4. AMRE, Mémoires et Documents: France, 795 bis, fol. 358 v. Richelieu's journal for this period can also be found published in *Archives curieuses de l'histoire de France . . .* , 2e série, vol. 5.

5. AMRE, Mémoires et Documents: France, *passim.*

6. Tallement des Réaux, *Historiettes*, 2:81–85.

7. Batiffol, *La Duchesse de Chevreuse*, pp. 105–37.

8. La Porte, *Mémoires*, pp. 304–8. La Porte's testimony seems plausible. Montague was certainly seized while carrying numerous documents relating to the alliance project; see Batiffol, *La Duchesse de Chevreuse*, p. 113.

9. Kermina, *Marie de Médicis*, p. 322; Dethan, *Gaston d'Orléans*, p. 84; Nicolas Goulas, sieur de la Mothe, *Mémoires de Nicolas Goulas, gentilhomme ordinaire de la chambre du duc d'Orléans . . .* , 1:61–66.

10. There is no comprehensive work on the role of the devout in seventeenth-century French political life. On Marillac, however, see Georges Pagès, "Autour du 'grand orage': Richelieu et Marillac, deux politiques," *Revue Historique* 179 (jan.–juin 1937): 63–97. For a recent reassessment of Marillac's and the *dévots'* desire for peace with the Habsburgs as not anachronistic but rather more realistic than Richelieu's war policy, see J. Russell Major, *Representative Government in Early Modern France*, p. 573.

11. For a complete account, see Georges Mongrédien, *La Journée des dupes: 10 novembre 1630.* Chevallier, *Louis XIII*, pp. 379–99 is, however, better informed.

12. Mongrédien, *La Journée*, pp. 74–76, 83–84; Chevallier, *Louis XIII*, pp. 389–90.

13. Mongrédien, *La Journée*, pp. 84–87; Chevallier, *Louis XIII*, pp. 393–99. For a psychological analysis of the relationship between Richelieu and Louis, see Marvick, "The Character of Louis XIII," pp. 371–73; "Childhood History," pp. 174–75, 177; "Favorites in Early Modern Europe: A Recurring Psychopolitical Role," *Journal of Psychohistory*, 10 (Spring 1983):468–70.

14. AMRE, Mémoires et Documents: France, 795 bis, fol. 355 v.

15. Ibid., fol. 356.

16. Ibid., 795 bis, fol. 355v–58.

17. Motteville, *Mémoires*, 36:361–62.

18. AMRE, Mémoires et Documents: France, 795 bis, fols. 356–56v.

19. Ibid., fol. 357v.

20. Ibid.

21. Motteville, *Mémoires*, 36:375–77.

22. Ibid., p. 377.

23. For Marie's wanderings in her last years, see Kermina, *Marie de Médicis*, pp. 353–405. Tapié, *La France*, p. 295, has written a terrible indictment of her:

"Greedy and small-minded, loving France only as a source of power and wealth, Marie de Medici left behind no work, no grounds for fame, so that today it takes an effort of mind to understand the extent and the duration of her power."

24. AMRE, Mémoires et Documents: France, 795 bis, fols. 359v–360; Motteville, *Mémoires*, 36:379–80.

25. AMRE, Mémoires et Documents: France, 795 bis, fol. 354v.

26. Ibid.

27. Ibid., fols. 354v–55.

28. Ibid., fol. 359 v.

29. Batiffol, *La Duchesse de Chevreuse*, pp. 124–35.

30. AMRE, Mémoires et Documents: France, 795 bis, fol. 357; Motteville, *Mémoires*, 36:360, 375.

31. AMRE, Mémoires et Documents: France, 795 bis, fols. 357v–58, 359.

32. BN, Fonds Français 3747, fols. 1–44; these are copies, sometimes translated and decoded where necessary, of the intercepted correspondence from 1634 to 1637. AMRE, Mémoires et Documents: France, 255, fols. 205–12, 348–51, includes most of this correspondence in each of two separate lists of letters intercepted 1634–37.

33. BN, Fonds Français 3747, fol. 3 v, 11 January 1635.

34. Ibid., 26 January 1635.

35. Ibid.

36. Ibid., fol. 36, 2 May 1637.

37. Ibid., fols. 22–22v, no date; probably December 1636.

CHAPTER SEVEN

1. AMRE, Mémoires et Documents: France, 795 bis, fols. 358v–59.

2. Bourgeois, *Observations diverses*, pp. 39–42.

3. For Louis's itinerary year by year, see Vaunois, *Vie*, pp. 435–577, covering 1631–37.

4. BN, Fonds Français 4027, fols. 378v and 384v, for example, for the last two incidents in 1627.

5. The romantic tradition that Anne was the victim of Richelieu's deliberate persecution may have started with La Rochefoucauld, *Mémoires*, 51:338–39; and Montglat, *Mémoires*, 49:40, 178. La Rochefoucauld would have had it from Madame de Chevreuse.

6. The view that Anne obstructed the French path to greatness persists to this day; see Chevallier, *Louis XIII*, p. 530.

7. Motteville, *Mémoires*, 36:356–57. It is interesting to note that Philip IV's minister, Olivares, kept informed of Anne's problems in 1626 by the Spanish ambassador, Mirabel, gave the very same opinion concerning a wife's duty (British Museum, British Library, Additional Manuscripts 14000, fols. 731–36; communicated to the author by the courtesy of Professor John H. Elliott, of the Institute for Advanced Study, Princeton University).

8. Marvick, "The Character of Louis XIII," pp. 369–73; "Childhood History," pp. 176–77. It would seem that, for Louis, Anne took the place of his sister Elizabeth. This did not give as much advantage to Anne as might be supposed, however, since

Louis had always treated Elizabeth as a narcissistic object; see Marvick, "Childhood History," p. 175.

9. Motteville, *Mémoires*, 36:359.

10. Ibid., pp. 359–60.

11. Lawrence Stone, *The Family, Sex, and Marriage in England, 1500–1800,* pp. 195–99, 493–501; Hunt, *Parents and Children,* pp. 78–81. These are the two most notable examples.

12. *La Gazette de France,* 29 August 1631, p. 4 (hereafter cited as *Gazette*). About the *Gazette* and its editor, see Howard M. Solomon, *Public Welfare, Science, and Propaganda: The Innovations of Théophraste Renaudot.*

13. *Gazette,* 11 July 1962, p. 276.

14. Ibid., 22 July 1632, p. 284.

15. Ibid., 1 October 1632, p. 403.

16. Ibid., 17 December 1632, p. 509.

17. AMRE, Mémoires et Documents: France, 795 bis, fol. 361, 27 September 1631.

18. On the career of Marie de Hautefort, the only full narrative is in Victor Cousin, *Madame de Hautefort: nouvelles études sur les femmes illustres et la société du XVIIe siècle.*

19. Motteville, *Mémoires*, 36:378–79.

20. Henri-Auguste de Loménie, comte de Brienne, *Mémoires,* 36:3.

21. Motteville, *Mémoires*, 36:370.

22. Cousin, *Madame de Hautefort,* pp. 12–13.

23. Montglat, *Mémoires,* 49:237.

24. Anne Marie Louise d'Orléans, duchesse de Monpensier, *Mémoires de Mlle de Montpensier, fille de Gaston d'Orléans, frère de Louis XIII,* 40:398–400.

25. BN, Nouvelles Acquisitions Françaises 9175, fol. 427; and Griselle, *Etat de la maison,* p. 93. A brief account of her career is to be found in Cousin, *Madame de Hautefort,* pp. 251–351.

26. La Porte, *Mémoires,* pp. 333–34.

27. BN, Nouvelles Acquisitions Françaises 9175 passim; and Griselle, *Etat de la maison,* pp. 89–133 passim.

28. AMRE, Mémoires et Documents: France, 244, fol. 92.

29. Ibid., fol. 93.

30. La Porte, *Mémoires,* pp. 329–30.

31. Tapié, *La France de Louis XIII,* pp. 288–89; see also Batiffol, *Richelieu et le roi,* pp. 83, 291 ff.

32. Perrens, *Les Mariages,* pp. 563–67.

33. Simancas, Estado: Capitulaciones con Francia, serie K, legajo 1416, fol. 20, 27 May 1633.

34. Ibid., fol. 63, 29 October 1633.

35. *Gazette,* 4 June 1633, p. 236; second version.

36. Issue no. 54 of the *Gazette* (1633) came out twice, with the same page numbers each time; but the second version has an addition to the report from Fontainebleau, 3 June, that relates the rumor, traces it to its supposed origin, and denies it.

37. Richelieu in 1626 and Louis XIII in 1642 and perhaps also earlier. See J. H. Elliott, *Richelieu and Olivares,* pp. 87–88, 147–48.

38. According to a summary attributed to Richelieu, the letter was addressed to

Madame de Chevreuse (BN, Nouvelles Acquisitions Françaises 4334, fol. 2). The same version appears in Motteville, *Mémoires*, 36:395; and La Porte, *Mémoires*, p. 345. But on pp. 357 and 369, La Porte also mentioned the interception of a letter from the queen to Mirabel, but Brienne, *Mémoires*, 36:62, stated the letter came from Mirabel to the queen.

39. AMRE, Mémoires et Documents: France, 255, fols. 205–12, 348–51; BN, Fonds Français 3747, fols. 2–43v.

40. Chevallier, *Louis XIII*, p. 536. If it was indeed Louis who initiated the investigation, it would have been awkward for Richelieu to produce a long file of intercepted letters; consequently Louis may never have known of its existence. During the proceedings, however, Richelieu certainly used his own knowledge to extract a confession from the queen.

41. Cousin, *Madame de Hautefort*, pp. 251–332; Henri Griffet, S.J., *Histoire du règne de Louis XIII, roi de France et de Navarre*, vols. 13–15, *Histoire de la France depuis l'établissement de la monarchie françoise dans les Gaules*, 15:93–102.

42. P. 308.

43. *Gazette*, 26 December 1637, p. 804.

44. BN, Fonds Français 3747, fols. 32–32v, 6 March 1637.

45. Ibid., fol. 38, Mme du Fargis to the queen, 23 May 1637.

46. Ibid., fol. 41, 9 July 1637; 42v–43, 23 July 1637.

47. Ibid., fols. 41v–42, 28 May 1637.

48. Ibid., fol. 41v, Mirabel to Olivares, forwarding the queen's letter, 25 June 1637.

49. Richelieu, *Mémoires*, 30:195. This corresponds to the text in BN, Nouvelles Acquisitions Françaises 4334, fol. 2.

50. BN, Fonds Français 3747, fols. 42v–43, 23 July 1637.

51. BN, Nouvelles Acquisitions Françaises 4334, fols. 1–31v, is a manuscript copy of a memorandum summarizing the events and interrogations. Though the original is not extant, the text evidently served as the basis for Richelieu, *Mémoires*, 30:195–205.

52. La Porte, *Mémoires*, pp. 367–73.

53. Montglat, *Mémoires*, 49:179. No one else mentioned this alleged incident, and indeed the queen's interrogation took place at Chantilly, not at Val-de-Grâce.

54. BN, Nouvelles Acquisitions Françaises 4334, fol. 2.

55. Ibid., fol. 2v. For her state at Chantilly during these days, see La Porte, *Mémoires*, p. 358.

56. BN, Nouvelles Acquisitions Françaises 4334, fols. 2v–3.

57. Ibid., fol. 3.

CHAPTER EIGHT

1. BN, Nouvelles Acquisitions Françaises 4334, fols. 4–4v, 5–5v.

2. Ibid., fols. 4v, 6.

3. Ibid., fols. 6v–7.

4. Ibid., fol. 7.

5. Montpensier, *Mémoires*, 40:400; Cousin, *Madame de Hautefort*, p. 41 n. 2.

6. Griffet, *Histoire*, 15:54.

7. The expression was used by the English resident in Brussels, writing to the

secretary of the English embassy in Paris (BN, Fonds Français 3747, fol. 43v, 26 September 1637).

8. Griffet, *Histoire*, 15:54.

9. AMRE, Mémoires et Documents: France, 830, fol. 170.

10. Simancas, Estado: Capitulaciones con Francia, serie K, legajo 1419, fol. 23.

11. Brienne, *Mémoires*, 36:64.

12. Georges Dethan, *Mazarin: un homme de paix à l'âge baroque, 1602–1661*, p. 185, gives the quotation from Walter Montague.

13. *Les Amours d'Anne d'Autriche . . . avec Monsieur . . . le C D R le véritable père de Louis XIV. . . .*

14. Dethan, *Mazarin*, pp. 184–85.

15. *Gazette*, 5 September 1638, p. 503.

16. Ibid., 28 April 1638, p. 200.

17. Motteville, *Mémoires*, 36:393; Griffet, *Histoire*, 15:101–2.

18 Montglat, *Mémoires*, 49:180–81; Motteville, *Mémoires*, 36:393–94. But La Porte, *Mémoires*, p. 381, claimed it happened after both Louis and Anne had returned from St. Maur, and he called the result "the child of his silence."

19. *Gazette*, 5 December 1637, p. 768.

20. Vaunois, *Vie*, p. 585.

21. Cousin, *Madame de Hautefort*, p. 165.

22. Ibid., pp. 117 n. 1, 160.

23. Montglat, *Mémoires*, 49:177; Cousin, *Madame de Hautefort*, p. 37.

24. Marvick, "Childhood History of Louis XIII," pp. 175–76.

25. See, for example, *Action de grace et resiouissance de la France sur l'heureuse grossesse asseurée de la reyne*; and *Gazette*, 6 March 1638, p. 116; 28 April 1638, p. 200.

26. *Gazette*, 6 February 1638, p. 60.

27. Ibid., 27 March 1638, p. 156.

28. AMRE, Mémoires et Documents: France, 830, fols. 247–247v.

29. Ibid., 831, fol. 27.

30. Ibid., fol. 90.

31. *Gazette*, extra issue no. 122, no date but published between 5 and 11 September 1638, p. 506.

32. AMRE, Mémoires et Documents: France, 831, fol. 160.

33. Bourgeois, *Observations diverses*, pp. 97–106.

34. *Gazette*, extra issue no. 122, p. 508. See also Alfred Franklin, *L'Enfant, la naissance, le baptême*, vol. 17, *La Vie privée d'autrefois*, p. 82.

35. Brienne, *Mémoires*, 36:65.

36. AMRE, Mémoires et Documents: France, 831, fol. 27.

37. Ibid., 2164, fol. 89v, 19 August 1638.

38. Ibid., 831, fols. 61v, 62, 65, 89–90, 104; and 2164, fols. 95v, 96, for quarrels in September.

39. Ibid., fols. 90, 113; see also Cousin, *Madame de Hautefort*, pp. 378–79.

40. *Gazette*, comprising the two extra issues nos. 121 and 122, pp. 501–8.

41. AMRE, Mémoires et Documents: France, 831, fol. 195, Chavigny to Richelieu, 6 September 1638.

42. Ibid.

43. Motteville, *Mémoires*, 36:398.

44. *Gazette,* pp. 504, 507–8.

45. AMRE, Mémoires et Documents: France, 2164, fol. 90, 24 August 1638.

46. *Gazette,* p. 501.

47. *Gazette,* 2 October 1638, pp. 579–80; see also Franklin, *L'Enfant, la naissance,* p. 83.

48. Griselle, *Etat de la maison,* p. 166.

49. For discussion of the practice of wet-nursing, see Alfred Franklin, *L'Enfant, la layette, la nourrice, la vie de famille, les jouets et les jeux,* vol. 19, *La Vie privée d'autrefois,* pp. 37–117; Hunt, *Parents and Children,* pp. 100– 102, 106–7, 120; Elizabeth Wirth Marvick, "Nature versus Nurture: Patterns and Trends in Seventeenth-Century French Child-Rearing," pp. 259–301, in *The History of Childhood,* pp. 263–69.

50. Stone, *The Family,* pp. 100–101.

51. For a discussion of swaddling, see Franklin, *L'Enfant, la layette,* pp. 8–10; Hunt, *Parents and Children,* pp. 126–30; Marvick, "Nature versus Nurture," pp. 269–70.

52. On the possible psychological effects or lack of them, see Hunt, *Parents and Children,* p. 132; Stone, *The Family,* p. 162.

53. According to one of Anne's attendants, Mlle Andrieu, in a letter to the exiled lady of honor Mme de Sénécey, as cited in Cousin, *Madame de Hautefort,* p. 348.

54. Ibid., pp. 347–48.

55. Cousin, *Madame de Hautefort,* pp. 85–96, 339–40. The regular reports of M. de Brassac to Chavigny and to Richelieu are to be found in AMRE, Mémoires et Documents: France, for the relevant years.

56. See, for example, AMRE, Mémoires et Documents: France, 835, fol. 140, Brassac to Richelieu, 22 May 1640.

57. For the career of Cinq-Mars, the most complete account is Philippe Erlanger, *The King's Minion: Richelieu, Louis XIII, and the Affair of Cinq-Mars.*

58. *Gazette,* 4 February 1640, p. 84.

59. AMRE, Mémoires et Documents: France, 836, fols. 7–8, 31, 39–39v, 52–52v; lying-in queens had the right to a special allowance, the *compte de gésine*; see Franklin, *L'Enfant, la naissance,* p. 84.

60. AMRE, Mémoires et Documents: France, 836, fol. 80, Brassac to Richelieu, 10 September 1640.

61. Ibid., fol. 80v.

62. Ibid.

63. Ibid., fol. 83, Le Gras to Richelieu, 13 September 1640.

CHAPTER NINE

1. *Gazette,* 24 September 1640, p. 675.

2. Motteville, *Mémoires,* 36:398.

3. Montpensier, *Mémoires,* 40:416.

4. See Erlanger, *The King's Minion.*

5. *Gazette,* 19 January 1641, pp. 35–36. The report included a complete description of the production.

6. Jean Desmarets de Saint-Sorlin, *Mirame, tragicomédie.* The heading reads: "Ouverture du théâtre de la grande salle du Palais-Cardinal"; the play was the first production in Richelieu's theater. See also Emile Henriot, *Courrier littéraire: XVIIe*

siècle, 1:46–52 for a critical discussion of the rumor that Richelieu meant to humiliate Anne.

7. Desmarets, *Mirame,* p. 2; act 1, scene 1.

8. Ibid.

9. *Gazette,* 19 January 1641; p. 36.

10. See, for example, AMRE, Mèmoires et Documents: France, 836, fols. 80–81, 108–9, 10 and 24 September 1640, respectively.

11. BN, Nouvelles Acquisitions Françaises 9175, fols. 425–26; and Griselle, *Etat de la maison,* pp. 90–92.

12. AN, série KK, 203; comptes de la maison d'Anne d'Autriche en 1642. The tradesmen on retainer are listed on fols. 26–29, and the extraordinary expenses on fols. 44–131v.

13. Robert Arnauld d'Andilly, *Mémoires,* 34:75.

14. BN, Fonds Français 19043, "Maximes d'education et direction puerile. Des devotions, meurs, actions et petite etude de Monseigneur le Dauphin jusques a l'aage de sept ans, avec un abrege des principes et termes generaux des vertus theologales et cardinales qu'on commencera d'enseigner a Son Altesse Royale en ce bas aage et luy faire pratiquer par les soings et adresse de ceux qui auront l'honneur d'estre pres de luy." Georges Lacour-Gayet, *L'Education politique de Louis XIV,* pp. 60–64, describes this work, but it has never been published. Not much has been written about primary education in mid-seventeenth-century France; Georges Snyders, *La Pédagogie en France aux XVIIe et XVIII siècles,* does not really cover the subject. But Philippe Ariès, *Centuries of Childhood: A Social History of Family Life,* proposes that attitudes toward small children and childhood underwent a marked change in the course of the seventeenth century, and the "Maximes" are an example of that.

15. "Maximes," p. 5.

16. Ibid., p. 112.

17. Ibid.

18. Ibid., p. 114v.

19. Ibid., p. 132v.

20. Ibid., p. 123v.

21. Ibid., pp. 147v–49.

22. Ibid., pp. 35–36.

23. Ibid., p. 47.

24. Ibid., pp. 46–46v.

25. Ibid., pp. 169v–170.

26. Ibid., p. 163v.

27. Ibid., pp. 76–77v.

28. Ibid., pp. 38, 51v. Contemporaries thought a taste for solitude and solitary pursuits very undesirable, especially in a prince; Motteville, *Mémoires,* 36:427, commented that Louis XIII knew a thousand things with which melancholy spirits usually occupy themselves, such as music and all the mechanical arts. The author of the "Maximes" urged that the dauphin not be encouraged along any of those lines.

29. "Maximes," p. 105v.

30. Ibid., pp. 38v–39.

31. Ibid., p. 26.

32. Ibid., pp. 61v–64.

33. Ibid., pp. 67v–69, 69v–70.

34. For an overview of the political and economic situation in 1641–42, see Tapié, *La France de Louis XIII*, pp. 483–518.

35. Erlanger, *The King's Minion*, pp. 84–89, 99.

36. Ibid., pp. 119–21; Chevallier, *Louis XIII*, pp. 583–86.

37. La Rochefoucauld, *Mémoires*, 51:362–63; Montpensier, *Mémoires*, 40:410.

38. Brienne, *Mémoires*, 36:75–76.

39. Motteville, *Mémoires*, 36:408–9; Dethan, *Gaston*, p. 268.

40. AMRE, Mémoires et Documents: France, 842, fols. 82–90; fols. 90–105v, give a summary of the interrogations and the list of judges at the trial of Cinq-Mars and de Thou.

41. Ibid., fol. 83.

42. La Rochefoucauld, *Mémoires*, 51:363; Tallemant, *Les Historiettes*, 2:61.

43. Goulas, *Mémoires*, 1:391–92, 438–39; Tallemant, *Les Historiettes*, 2:61–64; Montglat, *Mémoires*, 49:385; Griffet, *Histoire*, 15:460–62. Dethan, *Gaston*, pp. 271–73, is the first among modern historians to suggest, on the basis of surviving correspondence in the AMRE, that the rumors may have had substance.

44. Montpensier, *Mémoires*, 40:410.

45. Ibid., pp. 409–10.

46. La Porte, *Mémoires*, 59:391; Motteville, *Mémoires*, 36:403; Montpensier, *Mémoires*, 40:410, referred to repeated such orders. See also AMRE, Mémoires et Documents: France, 842, fol. 185, Le Gras to Richelieu, 30 April 1642.

47. AMRE, Mémoires et Documents: France, 842, fol. 185.

48. Ibid., fols. 185–85v; fols. 188–88v, Brassac to Chavigny, 30 April 1642.

49. Ibid., 845, fols. 68–68v, Brassac to Richelieu, 3 May 1642; communicated to the author by the courtesy of M. Georges Dethan, Conservateur en Chef de la Bibliothèque, Ministère des Relations Extérieures. Anne's message was probably the letter she sent to Richelieu, apparently in her own hand, on 30 April 1642; Archives de la famille Richelieu, Bibliothèque Victor Cousin, tôme 18; communicated to the author by the courtesy of Dr. Elizabeth W. Marvick.

50. AMRE, Mémoires et Documents: France, 842, fols. 304–4v, Brassac to Chavigny, 26 May 1642.

51. Ibid., fols. 304–5, Brassac to Chavigny, 26 May 1642; fols. 307–7v, Le Gras to Chavigny, 26 May 1642.

52. Ibid., 845, fol. 68, Brassac to Richelieu, 3 May 1642; courtesy of M. Georges Dethan.

53. Ibid., fol. 103, Brassac to Richelieu, 8 June 1642; courtesy of M. Georges Dethan.

54. Ibid., fol. 104, Brassac to Chavigny, 15 June 1642; courtesy of M. Georges Dethan.

55. Ibid.

56. Ibid.

57. Erlanger, *The King's Minion*, pp. 166–67; Chevallier, *Louis XIII*, pp. 597–98.

58. Goulas, *Mémoires*, 1:438–39.

59. AMRE, Mémoires et Documents: France, 843, fol. 36, Le Gras to Richelieu, 2 July 1642.

60. Ibid., fols. 37–37v, Brassac to Chavigny, 2 July 1642.

61. Dethan, *Gaston*, pp. 272–73; Erlanger, *The King's Minion*, pp. 162–63; but Chevallier, *Louis XIII*, while citing Dethan, does not commit himself (pp. 596–97).

62. Claude Dulong, *Anne d'Autriche, mère de Louis XIV*, p. 188.

63. Griffet, *Histoire*, 15:462.

64. Montglat, *Mémoires*, 49:395.

CHAPTER TEN

1. Chevallier, *Louis XIII*, pp. 622–27; Erlanger, *The King's Minion*, pp. 229–33.

2. AMRE, Mémoires et Documents: France, 846, fols. 97–98, 99, 100–100v.

3. Chevallier, *Louis XIII*, p. 630; Erlanger, *The King's Minion*, pp. 234–35.

4. Motteville, *Mémoires*, 36:419.

5. Edmé de La Châtre, *Memoires contenant la fin du règne de Louis XIII et le commencement de celui de Louis XIV*, pp. 171–72, 184.

6. Brienne, *Mémoires*, 36:78–79.

7. La Châtre, *Mémoires*, p. 183; La Rochefoucauld, *Mémoires*, 51:367–68.

8. Vaunois, *Vie*, p. 667; Chevallier, *Louis XIII*, pp. 649–51.

9. *Gazette*, 10 April 1643, p. 300.

10. Vaunois, *Vie*, p. 661; La Rochefoucauld, *Mémoires*, 51:366; Montglat, *Mémoires*, 49:404.

11. La Rochefoucauld, *Mémoires*, 51:366; Montglat, *Mémoires*, 49:404.

12. For the early part of Chavigny's career, and his importance, see Orest Ranum, *Richelieu and the Councillors of Louis XIII: A Study of the Secretaries of State and Superintendents of Finance in the Ministry of Richelieu, 1635–1642*; Dethan, *Mazarin*, pp. 128–35.

13. As yet there is no truly comprehensive biography of Mazarin that treats all aspects of his personality and career, based on the voluminous sources available. The best and most recent study is Dethan, *Mazarin: un homme de paix à l'âge baroque, 1602–1661*, the first part of which includes the author's earlier *Mazarin et ses amis*. On pp. 385–87 Dethan lists the biographical materials published on Mazarin from the seventeenth century to 1980. For the most complete narrative of Mazarin's political activities and diplomacy, see Chéruel, *Histoire de France pendant la minorité de Louis XIV*, and *Histoire de France sous le ministère de Mazarin*.

14. Dethan, *Mazarin*, pp. 106–10.

15. Tallemant des Réaux, *Historiettes*, 2:68.

16. Dethan, *Mazarin*, pp. 182–83.

17. Ibid., pp. 182, 185.

18. Ibid., pp. 135–38.

19. Ibid., pp. 136–37; AN, série K 118 B$_1$, no. 69, is a document, dated 30 March 1654, confirming Mazarin's naturalization.

20. Dethan, *Mazarin*, pp. 140, 144–46.

21. Goulas, *Mémoires*, 1:438–39.

22. Dethan, *Mazarin*, pp. 147–48; Tallemant des Réaux, *Historiettes*, 2:68, reported that Richelieu had been heard to speak of Mazarin as his successor.

23. Dethan, *Mazarin*, p. 148.

24. Victor Cousin, "Des carnets autographes du cardinal Mazarin conservés à la Bibliothèque Impériale: deuxième article," *Journal des Savants*, September 1854, pp. 526–27.

25. BN, Fonds Français 2748, fol. 211. The metaphor was still current in 1643, judging by a sermon preached on 29 July of that year and reported in the *Gazette*, 1 August 1643, pp. 651–52. For a comprehensive survey of legal issues and controversies raised over French regencies in the sixteenth and seventeenth centuries, see Harriet L. Lightman, "Sons and Mothers: Queens and Minor Kings in French Constitutional Law," University Microfilms International, (1981), 8220695 (Bryn Mawr).

26. La Rochefoucauld, *Mémoires*, 51:367.

27. Dethan, *Mazarin*, p. 187; Cousin, "Des carnets autographes: deuxième article," pp. 531–32. See also La Rochefoucauld, *Mémoires*, 51:368–69; Brienne, *Mémoires*, 36:80.

28. Brienne, *Mémoires*, 36:81.

29. La Rochefoucauld, *Mémoires*, 51:368–69.

30. AMRE, Mémoires et Documents: France, 848, fols. 31–44v; Marie Dubois de Lestourmière, "Mémoire fidèle des choses qui se sont passées à la mort de Louis XIII, fait par Dubois, l'un des valets de chambre de Sa Majesté." Dubois's memoir was published in *Nouvelle collection des mémoires pour servir à l'histoire de France depuis le XIIIe siècle jusqu'à la fin du XVIIIe*, 11:521–31.

31. Montpensier, *Mémoires*, 40:425.

32. AMRE, Mémoires et Documents: France, 846, fols. 153–62v. See also Cousin, "Des carnets autographes: deuxième article," pp. 527–30.

33. Ibid.

34. Dubois, "Mémoire fidele," fol. 33.

35. *Gazette* 24 April 1634, pp. 324–28; the baptism had taken place on 21st April. See also Dubois, "Mémoire fidèle," fol. 41.

36. John B. Wolf, *Louis XIV*, p. 11.

37. La Porte, *Mémoires*, 59:394–95.

38. Dubois, "Mémoire fidèle," fols. 37, 38v–39, 40–40v, 42–42v; see also *Gazette*, 1 May 1643, pp. 359–60; 16 May 1643, pp. 400, 401–8.

39. Motteville, *Mémoires*, 36:424–25.

40. Goulas, *Mémoires*, 1:438.

41. La Rochefoucauld, *Mémoires*, 51:372; Motteville, *Mémoires*, 37:9, 23–24.

42. La Châtre, *Mémoires*, pp. 184, 197; La Rochefoucauld, *Mémoires*, 51:372.

43. Motteville, *Mémoires*, 37:10–11, 54–55; Jean Français Paul de Gondi, cardinal de Retz, *Mémoires*, pp. 44, 50.

44. La Rochefoucauld, *Mémoires*, 51:370–71.

45. Omer Talon, *Memoires de feu M Omer Talon*, 3:11.

46. Ibid.

47. Ibid., 3:11–12. Concerning the role of the Parlement at this juncture, and Anne's supporters, see Cousin, "Des carnets autographes: cinquième article," *Journal des Savants*, December 1854, pp. 754–73.

48. Cousin, "Des carnets autographes: deuxième article," p. 532. According to Motteville, *Mémoires*, 37:6–7, Mazarin, however, had misgivings about the queen's using the Parlement to have herself declared sole regent, lest she seemed to be conceding too much power to that body.

49. Motteville, *Mémoires*, 37:11–12.

50. La Châtre, *Mémoires*, p. 200.

51. Ibid., Montglat, *Mémoires*, 49:418; Motteville, *Mémoires*, 37:11–12, 17.

52. Brienne, *Mémoires*, 36:81.

53. Ibid., 36:85–86. Brienne's son recounted the same incident in more detail, as having heard it from his father; see Louis-Henri de Lomémie, comte de Brienne (le jeune), *Mémoires inédits,* 1:296–308.

54. *Gazette,* extra no. 161, "La France en deuil," n.d. (1643), p. 407; see also Motteville, *Mémoires,* 36:425.

CHAPTER ELEVEN

1. *Gazette,* 21 May 1643, p. 425.

2. Ibid., n.d. (1643), pp. 473–80.

3. Cousin, "Des carnets autographes: douzième article," *Journal des Savants,* September 1855, pp. 523–45; "Des carnets autographes: troizième article," *Journal des Savants,* October 1855, pp. 622–37, describes the *Importants* and their efforts.

4. *Gazette,* 23 May 1643, pp. 425–27.

5. Cousin, "Des carnets autographes: deuxième article," pp. 533, 542.

6. La Châtre, *Mémoires,* pp. 202, 209. Mazarin heard about these remarks, as quoted in Cousin, "Des carnets autographes: troisième article," p. 603.

7. La Châtre, *Mémoires,* p. 211; Motteville, *Mémoires,* 37:8.

8. For a standard narrative of events during this period, see Chéruel, *Histoire de France pendant la minorité de Louis XIV,* vol. 1. For the most detailed analysis of the problems of the regency in 1643, see Cousin, "Des carnets autographes," published in sixteen parts altogether, in the *Journal des Savants,* August 1854–February 1856.

9. Cousin, "Des carnets autographes: troisième article," pp. 609–10.

10. BN, Nouvelles Acquisitions Françaises 4334, fol. 6, bears a copyist's note to that effect.

11. For the date and duration of all household appointments, see BN, Nouvelles Acquisitions Françaises 9175, fols. 425–45; or Griselle, *Etat de la maison.*

12. La Rochefoucauld, *Mémoires,* 51:379.

13. *Gazette,* n.d. (1643), p. 559.

14. Ibid., 24 August 1643, p. 728.

15. Ibid., 29 August 1643, p. 748.

16. La Châtre, *Mémoires,* pp. 221–23; La Rochefoucauld, *Mémoires,* 51:373–74.

17. BN, Fonds Baluze 174, 15 vols., 1642–50. A sixteenth volume, apparently genuine, was published as Jules cardinal Mazarin, *Carnet 16.* Because of Mazarin's crabbed handwriting and the elliptic sentences he used, the material in the fifteen manuscript notebooks is practically inaccessible to all but experts. The Sorbonne has the transcripts of these volumes made by and for Victor Cousin; see Manuscrits de la bibliothèque Victor Cousin à la Sorbonne, III, nos. 37–41. Cousin cited long excerpts from these transcripts in his series of articles "Des carnets autographes," but to date there is no edition, critical or otherwise, of Mazarin's notebooks as a whole.

18. Cousin, "Des carnets autographes: deuxième article," pp. 544–45.

19. Ibid., pp. 546–47; "Des carnets autographes: troisième article," pp. 601–2.

20. Mazarin repeatedly offered to withdraw if she had any doubts concerning his superiority over his rivals, and he painted an affecting picture of the comfortable life he could be leading in Rome (as quoted in Cousin, "Des carnets autographes: deuxième article," p. 547).

21. Jules, cardinal Mazarin, *Lettres du cardinal Mazarin à la reine, à la princesse Palatine, etc., écrites pendant sa retraite hors de France en 1651 et 1652,* p. 257, 12 September 1651.

22. Motteville, *Mémoires,* 37:68, 72. Motteville's judgment seems trustworthy, since she did not hesitate to attribute less desirable characteristics to the queen, notably laziness.

23. Ibid., pp. 13, 17.

24. La Châtre, *Mémoires,* p. 216.

25. References in Motteville, *Mémoires,* passim, attest to this, for example, as do frequent reports in the *Gazette* about Anne's activities and companions. Probably less indicative are the quantities of official letters that went out over her signature, to which secretaries attended and which most likely she never saw.

26. Retz, *Mémoires,* p. 44; Motteville, *Mémoires,* 37:3.

27. Olivier d'Ormesson, *Journal* . . . , 1:100; Chéruel, *Histoire de France pendant la minorité,* 1:121. See also BN, Fonds Français 17470, fols. 43v–44.

28. Cousin, "Des carnets autographes: deuxième article," pp. 543–545; "Des carnets autographes: troisième article," pp. 602, 604.

29. Cousin, "Des carnets autographes: troisième article," pp. 602, 604.

30. Cousin, "Des carnets autographes: deuxième article," pp. 543–45.

31. Ibid., pp. 544–45.

32. Ibid., pp. 544–45, 546.

33. Ibid., p. 545.

34. Cousin, "Des carnets autographes: troisième article," p. 605; "Des carnets autographes: quatrième article," *Journal des Savants,* November 1854, pp. 687–93.

35. Cousin, "Des carnets autographes: troisième article," p. 606.

36. Ibid.

37. Mazarin, Carnet 3:32, as quoted in Cousin, "Des carnets autographes: troisième article," p. 606 n. 2.

38. Cousin, "Des carnets autographes: troisième article," pp. 601–5, 607.

39. Ibid., p. 607; Motteville, *Mémoires,* 37:19.

40. Chéruel, *Histoire de France pendant la minorité,* 1:154–55; Cousin, "Des carnets autographes: deuxième article," p. 546.

41. Cousin, "Des carnets autographes: troisième article," pp. 607–8.

42. AMRE, Mémoires et Documents: France, 855, fols. 220–23.

43. Cousin, "Des carnets autographes: deuxième article," pp. 543, 546–47.

44. Mazarin, Carnet 2:44, as quoted in Cousin, "Des carnets autographes: deuxième article," p. 547.

45. Cousin, "Des carnets autographes: deuxième article," p. 547.

46. The words are Victor Cousin's, ibid., p. 545.

47. See, for example, Ernest Lavisse, *Louis XIV, de 1643 à 1685,* vol. 7 of *Histoire de France depuis les origines jusqu'à la révolution française,* pp. 8, 77.

48. La Rochefoucauld, *Mémoires,* 51:380. See also BN, Fonds Français 17470, fol. 43v.

49. Mazarin, Carnet 2:54, as quoted in Cousin "Des carnets autographes: deuxième article," p. 547.

50. *Gazette,* 23 May, 1643, p. 427.

51. Cousin, "Des carnets autographes: neuvième article," *Journal des Savants,*

April 1855, p. 227; "Des carnets autographes: onzième article," *Journal des Savants,* July 1855, pp. 442–43.

52. Cousin, "Des carnets autographes: troisième article," p. 611; "Des carnets autographes: onzième article," pp. 433–444.

53. Cousin, "Des carnets autographes: deuxième article," p. 543.

54. Ibid.

55. Mazarin, Carnet 1:89, as quoted in Cousin, "Des carnets autographes: deuxième article," p. 543.

56. Motteville, *Mémoires,* 37:31.

57. Chéruel, *Histoire de France pendant la minorité,* 1:161–62.

CHAPTER TWELVE

1. Simancas, Estado: Capitulaciones con Francia, serie K, legajo 1420, fol. 88, 28 May 1643.

2. Ibid.

3. Ibid.

4. Ibid., fol. 89, 31 May 1643.

5. Ibid.

6. Ibid., fol. 92, 10 June 1643.

7. Ibid., fol. 94, 14 June 1643.

8. Riqueti served on other delicate missions; in 1644 Anne sent him to Madame de Chevreuse with orders to escort the lady farther away from the court; see Cousin, "Des carnets autographes: quatorzième article," *Journal des Savants,* November 1855, pp. 714–16.

9. Simancas, Estado: Capitulaciones con Francia, serie K, legajo 1420, fol. 101, 29 July 1643.

10. Ibid.

11. Ibid.

12. Ibid.

13. Ibid., fol. 102, 29 July 1643.

14. Ibid., fol. 103, 17 August 1643. Sarmiento already had more than a decade's experience in negotiating with French malcontents.

15. Ibid.

16. Ibid. These remarks are echoed in Mazarin's notebooks for the period; see Cousin, "Des carnets autographes: deuxième article," pp. 543, 545; "Des carnets autographes: onzième article," pp. 442–43.

17. Simancas, Estado: Capitulaciones con Francia, serie K, legajo 1420, fol. 103.

18. Ibid.

19. Ibid.

20. Ibid., fol. 105, 18 September 1643.

21. Motteville, *Mémoires,* 37:31.

22. Ibid., pp. 37–45.

23. Ibid., p. 30.

24. René de Voyer, comte d'Argenson, *Annales de la compagnie du Saint-Sacrement.* See also Raoul Allier, *La Cabale des dévots, 1627–1666.*

25. As already indicated in chapter 6, note 10, there is no comprehensive study of the *dévots* in all their variety. Allier, *La Cabale*, cannot count as such, since not all *dévots* necessarily belonged to the Compagnie du Saint-Sacrement. For the spiritual content of the Catholic revival in France, see the encyclopedic Henri Bremond, *Histoire littéraire du sentiment religieux en France depuis les guerres de religion jusqu'à nos jours*, which, despite the title, hardly goes beyond the eighteenth century. There are also more modern works, such as Henri Busson, *La Pensée religieuse française de Charron à Pascal*, and *La Religion des classiques, 1660–1685*. For a general summary, however, of the activities of the *dévots* and the context within which they operated, see Orest Ranum, *Paris in the Age of Absolutism: An Essay*, pp. 109–31, 229–51.

26. Mazarin, Carnet 2:32–33, as quoted in Cousin, "Des carnets autographes: troisième article," p. 606.

27. Cousin, "Des carnets autographes: sixième article," *Journal des Savants*, January 1855, pp. 19–42.

28. Arnauld d'Andilly, *Mémoires*, 34:75–76; Antoine Arnauld, *Mémoires*, p. 214.

29. The *Gazette* in its weekly reports carried increasingly detailed accounts of the queen's public devotions and visits to churches and convents from 1643 to her final illness in 1665.

30. Motteville, *Mémoires*, 37:75.

31. Ibid. The *Gazette*, passim, confirms this.

32. Jean Cordey, "L'Inventaire après décès d'Anne d'Autriche et le mobilier du Louvre," *Bulletin de la Société de l' Histoire de l'Art Francais* (1930), pp. 228–31, 261–66, 272–73.

33. BN, Fonds Français 20866, fols. 46–47; *Gazette*, 12 September 1643, p. 796; 24 October 1643, p. 920.

34. Griffet, *Histoire*, 15:54.

35. Cousin, "Des carnets autographes: sixième article," pp. 29, 32–33; La Châtre, *Mémoires*, p. 203.

36. Pierre Coste, *Le Grand Saint du grand siècle: Monsieur Vincent*, 2:98–99.

37. Chéruel, *Histoire de France sous la minorité*, 1:93–94, 105–6; Simancas, Estado: Capitulaciones con Francia, serie K, legajo 1420, fol. 104, Sarmiento to Philip IV, 14 September 1643.

38. Cousin, "Des carnets autographes: sixième article," pp. 29–32.

39. Mazarin, Carnet 3:23, 89, as quoted in Cousin, "Des carnets autographes: sixième article," p. 30 n. 3.

40. Mazarin, Carnet 2:62; Carnet 4:77, and quoted in Cousin, "Des carnets autographes: sixième article," p. 32 n. 2.

41. Mazarin, Carnet 3:6, as quoted in Cousin, "Des carnets autographes: sixième article," p. 38 n. 3.

42. La Porte, *Mémoires*, pp. 400–401.

43. Ibid., p. 404. La Porte was observed in the act; see Mazarin, Carnet 4:21, as quoted in Cousin, "Des carnets autographes: septième article," *Journal des Savants*, February 1855, p. 96 n. 3.

44. Brienne (le jeune), *Mémoires*, 1:41–44. Mazarin complained about the fact that the queen would speak to him only concerning affairs of state (Carnet 3:52, as quoted in Cousin, "Des carnets autographes: troisième article," p. 603 n. 1). Mazarin also knew Madame de Brienne was admonishing the queen (Carnet 4:59, as quoted in Cousin, "des carnets autographes: sixième article," p. 33 n. 3).

45. La Porte, *Mémoires*, p. 402.

46. Ibid., p. 337.

47. Mazarin, Carnet 3:5, 52, as quoted in Cousin, "Des carnets autographes: troisième article," p. 603 n. 1; see also Cousin, "Des carnets autographes: douzième article," pp. 527-29.

48. Mazarin, Carnet 3:68, as quoted in Cousin, "Des carnets autographes: sixième article," p. 40 n. 2.

49. Mazarin, Carnet 2:3, 20, 21; Carnet 3:25, 29, 46, as quoted in Cousin, "Des carnets autographes: troisième article," p. 603 n. 1.

50. Orest Ranum, "The French Ritual of Tyrannicide in the Late Sixteenth Cenury," *Sixteenth Century Journal*, vol. 11, no. 1 (1980), pp. 63-81.

51. La Porte, *Mémoires*, pp. 402-3. See also Mazarin, Carnet 3:23, as quoted in Cousin, "Des carnets autographes: sixième article," p. 30 n. 3.

52. Mazarin, Carnet 4:3, as quoted in Cousin, "Des carnets autographes: sixième article," p. 31 n. 3.

53. Cousin, "Des carnets autographes: douzième article," pp. 524-45; "Des carnets autographes: treizième article," pp. 622-37; "Des carnets autographes: quatorzième article," pp. 703-19.

54. *Gazette*, 5 September 1643, p. 776.

55. For the subsequent events of Madame de Chevreuse's life, see Batiffol, *La Duchesse de Chevreuse*, pp. 221-99.

56. Motteville, *Mémoires*, 37:57-58.

57. Cousin, "Des carnets autographes: quatorzième article," p. 705.

58. Cousin, "Des carnets autographes: neuvième article," pp. 228-29; *Madame de Hautefort*, pp. 76-77.

59. Brienne, (le jeune), *Mémoires*, 2:42-43.

60. For her portrait at this time, see Motteville, *Mémoires*, 37:71-78. BN, Cabinet des Estampes, has prints that are not as flattering, but they are not particularly good likenesses either. On medals struck during these years, Anne appears quite heavy-set.

61. Dethan, *Mazarin*, pp. 149-75. See also the anonymous piece in BN, Fonds Français 17470, fols. 288 ff., "Amours de Madame Christine, duchesse de Savoye, traduittes d' italien en françois par l'autheur."

62. *Gazette*, 26 September 1643, p. 832.

63. Motteville, *Mémoires*, 37:61-62.

64. BN, Nouvelles Acquisitions Françaises 14286, 1ère partie, p. 296. This manuscript came from the library of Victor Cousin and is identified as the memoirs of La Porte, followed by thirty-four unpublished anecdotes. The second part of the manuscript contains a number of documents related to the memoirs, with the notation that they appear to be authentic. The citation above comes from one of the unpublished anecdotes. It should be pointed out that not everyone accepts the authenticity of the anecdotes; they must be treated with caution.

65. Mazarin, Carnet 4:3, as quoted in Cousin, "Des carnets autographes: quatorzième article," p. 706 n. 2.

66. See particularly Victor Molinier, *Notice sur cette question historique: Anne d'Autriche et Mazarin étaient-ils secrètement mariés?* p. 15.

67. Mazarin, Carnet 3:10, as quoted in Cousin, "Des carnets autographes: quatorzième article," p. 704 n. 1.

68. Simancas, Estado: Capitulaciones con Francia, serie K, legajo 1420, fol. 101, 29 July 1643.

69. Motteville, *Mémoires*, 37:315, 332, 349, 411; 39:408-9; Cousin, "Des carnets autographes: deuxième article," pp. 543-45.

70. BN, Fonds Clairembault 1144, fols. 88, n.d.; 91–92v, 28? January 1653; 95–95v, 12 August 1653.

71. Ibid., fols. 91–92v, 28? January 1653; 98–99v, 3 August 1658.

72. Ibid., fols. 91–91v, 28? January 1653, 94–94v, 29 January 1653.

73. Ibid., fols. 91–91v, 28? January 1653.

74. Chéruel, *Histoire de France sous le ministère*, 1:427–32.

75. Elliott, *Richelieu and Olivares*, p. 41.

CHAPTER THIRTEEN

1. BN, Fonds Français 15597, fols. 277–92. See also BN, Fonds Français 4643, fol. 124; and 18552, fol. 49.

2. AMRE, Mémoires et Documents: France, 855, fols. 200–23. These letters patent were issued on 4 July 1646, and were registered by the Parlement on 16 July and by the Chambre des Comptes on 31 July.

3. BN, Fonds Français 18552, fols. 56–61. In these proceedings the inventory of 1631 was verified by the king in the presence of Condé and Chancellor Séguier on 24 July 1644.

4. *Gazette*, 10 October 1643, p. 884.

5. Batiffol, *Le Louvre*, pp. 13–14.

6. *Gazette*, 8 June 1647, p. 420, reported the outcome of the lawsuit.

7. Victor Champier and G. R. Sandoz, *Le Palais-Royal d'après des documents inédits, 1629-1900*, 1:108–15.

8. The queen's remarks to the council were reported in a dispatch, quoted by Chéruel, *Histoire de France pendant la minorité*, 1:182 n. 1.

9. Henri Sauval, *Histoire et recherches des antiquités de la ville de Paris*, 2:169. See also Daniel Alcouffe, "Les Macé, ébénistes et peintres," *Bulletin de la Société de l'Art Français*, 1971, p. 64.

10. Roger-Armand Weigert, "Deux marchés passés par Simon Vouet pour les décorations de l'appartement d'Anne d'Autriche au Palais-Royal, 1645," *Bulletin de la Société de l'Histoire de l'Art Français*, 1951, pp. 101–5. How much it all cost is not clear; the queen's accounts 1645–48, insofar as they survive, mention 20,000 livres for the cabinetwork, paintings, and gilding of her gallery; see BN, Fonds Français 10413, fol. 13v.

11. No one called Madame's condition agoraphobia at the time. The term had not yet been invented, but the description of Madame's symptoms leaves little doubt that agoraphobia was her problem. See Mottevile, *Mémoires*, 37:230.

12. Montpensier, *Mémoires*, 40:426, 472–73.

13. Ibid., pp. 433; 41:2–3.

14. Ibid., 40:433.

15. Ibid., p. 372.

16. Ibid., 41:84.

17. Ibid., 40:398, 401.

18. Ibid., 41:18–20.

19. The *Gazette* over the years provides a chronicle of Henrietta-Maria's activities.

20. Motteville, *Mémoires*, 37:198–200. For the memorial service, see *Gazette*, n.d. (1644), pp. 1013–20.

21. For a roster of Anne's usual companions, see especially Motteville, *Mémoires*, 37:1–311 passim; see also *Gazette*, 1644–48, passim.

22. Motteville, *Mémoires*, 37:77–78, 164–65.

23. Madame de Hautefort's remarks were reported by La Porte, *Mémoires*, p. 406; and Motteville, *Mémoires*, 37:31–32, 33–34, 62. See also Cousin, "Des carnets autographes: neuvième article," pp. 235–36, and *Madame de Hautefort*, p. 83. According to Ormesson, *Journal*, 1:177, she advised her friends to address themselves to Mazarin with their requests because the queen refused Mazarin nothing.

24. Cousin, "Des carnets autographes: neuvième article," pp. 238–39.

25. Motteville, *Mémoires*, 37:34.

26. Mazarin, Carnet 2:12, 39; Carnet 3:83, 92–93, as quoted in Cousin, "Des carnets autographes: neuvième article," p. 236 n. 2; see also La Porte, *Mémoires*, p. 406.

27. Motteville, *Mémoires*, 37:35–36.

28. Cousin, "Des carnets autographes: neuvième article," p. 237.

29. AMRE, Mémoires et Documents: France, 849, fols. 177–78, newsletter of 23 April 1644.

30. Motteville, *Mémoires*, 37:62–65.

31. *Gazette*, 29 September 1646, p. 854. For the lady's subsequent life, see Cousin, *Madame de Hautefort*, pp. 116–21.

32. Mazarin, Carnet 4:67, as quoted in Cousin, "Des carnets autographes: neuvième article," p. 238 n. 3.

33. Motteville, *Mémoires*, 37:34–35, 172–79.

34. Georges Dethan, "Madame de Motteville et Mazarin, ou le complexe d'Oenone," *Les Valeurs chez les mémorialistes français du XVIIe siècle avant la Fronde, Actes et colloques*, No. 22, Société d'Etude du XVIIe Siècle, Colloque de Strasbourg et Metz, 18–20 mai 1978, pp. 103–10.

35. Motteville, *Mémoires*, 40:305–6.

36. Mazarin proceeded this way not only with Madame de Hautefort but with every enemy throughout his career.

37. See, for example, AMRE, Mémoires et Documents: France, 849, fol. 272 v, newsletter to the Netherlands, 12 June 1644.

38. The *Gazette* reported the royal outings every year; see also Motteville, *Mémoires*, 37:182–83.

39. Motteville, *Mémoires*, 37:76.

40. Ibid., pp. 207–9. Courtiers said Vincent de Paul was involved in this proceeding, but Anne did not believe it.

41. Coste, *Le Grand Saint*, 3:103.

42. See, for example, Eugène François Léon Lintilhac, *Histoire générale du théâtre en France*, vol. 3; and Antoine Adam, *Histoire de la littérature française au XVIIe siècle*, vols. 1–2; and Henriot, *Courrier littéraire*, vol. 1.

43. Bibliothèque Nationale, *Mazarin: homme d'état et collectionneur, 1602–1661*, pp. xxiii, 201–2; for the review see *Gazette*, 16 December 1645, p. 1180.

44. Bibliothèque Nationale, *Mazarin*, p. xxxiii; *Gazette*, n.d. (1647), pp. 201–12.

45. *Gazette*, 2 November 1647, p. 1016.

46. Ibid., 11 February and 4 March 1645, pp. 124, 180, respectively.

47. Motteville, *Mémoires*, 37:75–76.

48. The *Gazette* carried regular reports of these activities over the years.

49. Mazarin, Carnet 5:24–28, as quoted in Cousin, "Des carnets autographes: six-ième article," p. 42 n. 1.

50. Cousin, "Des carnets autographes: sixième article," pp. 36–40, offers many examples of Mazarin's knowledge.

51. Ibid., p. 40.

52. Mazarin, Carnet 5:24–28, as quoted in Cousin, "Des carnets autographes: six-ième article," pp. 41, 42 n. 1.

53. Ibid.

54. *Gazette*, 9 January 1644, p. 36.

55. The *Gazette* steadily repeated this theme during the rest of her life.

56. For the building of Val-de-Grâce, see Victor Ruprich-Robert, *L'Eglise et le monastère du Val-de-Grâce, 1645–1665*; and Janvier Joseph Jules Servier, *Le Val-de-Grâce: histoire du monastère et de l'hôpital militaire.* Anne's letters patent beginning construction are in BN, Fonds Français 10413, fols. 1–2v, and fols. 3–321v contain the accounts until the Fronde.

57. BN, Fonds Français 10413, fols. 3–321v.

58. Ibid., fols. 256–63v.

59. Ibid., fol. 281v.

60. Saint Vincent de Paul, *Correspondance, entretiens, documents*, 13:821. See also Coste, *Le Grand Saint*, 1:313–14.

61. On Mazarin's ecclesiastical policy, see Cousin, "Des carnets autographes: six-ième article," pp. 19–27.

62. These minutes are to be found in AMRE, Mémoires et Documents: France; see, for example, 849, fols. 6–7, 36–37, 45–45v, 50–50v, 70, 77, 82, 103–4, 121–21v, 141, 161, 172–72v, 216–17, 235, 244, 264–64v, 343–44. This volume covers the period January–August 1644; many other reports are included in the preceding and subsequent volumes.

63. AMRE, Mémoires et Documents: France, 849, fol. 319v, newsletter to the Netherlands, n.d. but probably June 1644.

64. Motteville, *Mémoires*, 37:67–68.

CHAPTER FOURTEEN

1. La Porte, *Mémoires*, p. 419. See also Léon Aubineau, ed., "Fragments des mémoires inédites de Dubois, gentilhomme servant du roi, valet de chambre de Louis XIII et de Louis XIV," *Bibliothèque de l'Ecole des Chartes*, 2e série (1847–48), 4:18–20. Motteville, *Mémoires*, 37:70, reported that the boys spent most of the day with the queen, though they had their meals apart until they grew older. On Louis's early childhood, there are several books, which do not, however, add much to our knowledge: Henri Carré, *L'Enfance et la première jeunesse de Louis XIV*; Madeleine M. L. Saint-René Taillandier, *La Jeunesse du Grand Roi: Louis XIV et Anne d'Autriche.*

2. Motteville, *Mémoires*, 37:297–98, 299.

3. *Gazette*, 24 December 1649, p. 1200; Montpensier, *Mémoires*, 41:76.

4. *Gazette*, 24 December 1649, p. 1272; extra no. 160, n.d. (1649), pp. 1273–80, for the full account of the proceedings.

5. *Gazette*, extra no. 160, p. 1276.

6. La Porte, *Mémoires,* pp. 419–20.

7. Montpensier, *Mémoires,* 41:141.

8. Brienne (le jeune), *Mémoires,* 1:218–20.

9. Ibid., pp. 226, 241–42. See also *Gazette,* 24 November 1652, p. 1116, for an account of one of the king's mock attacks.

10. Franklin, *L'Enfant,* 19:276.

11. Brienne (le jeune), *Mémoires,* 1:222–23.

12. *Gazette,* 13 April 1644, p. 244.

13. Ibid., covering May–June 1646, pp. 276, 328, 348, 392, 456, 491.

14. Ibid., n.d. (1646), p. 492.

15. Ibid., covering May–August 1647, pp. 372, 383, 395–96, 408, 656, 679–80.

16. Ibid., passim, over subsequent years for the campaign routine.

17. See, for example, Wolf, *Louis XIV,* pp. 25, 61–62.

18. Bremond, *Histoire littéraire,* takes this as one of its main themes.

19. Motteville, *Mémoires,* 37:227. When people reproached Anne for having accepted and enjoyed a gift of fruit from Arnauld, she was said to have replied, "Monsieur Arnauld's peaches are not Jansenist" (Lacour-Gayet, *L'Education politique,* p. 15).

20. The *Gazette* reported all these observances over the years. See also Henri Chérot, *La Première Jeunesse de Louis XIV, 1649–1653, d'après la correspondance inédite du P. Charles Paulin, son premier confesseur.*

21. *Gazette,* 26 March 1644, p. 200.

22. Ibid., 24 October 1643, p. 920.

23. Ibid., 22 April 1645, p. 320; 5 December 1648, p. 1668.

24. Reports of this are to be found in the *Gazette* over the years. Philippe was by no means coerced; he actually begged his mother to take him with her (Motteville, *Mémoires,* 38:135–36).

25. La Porte, *Mémoires,* p. 428; Montpensier, *Mémoires,* 42:291–92.

26. Motteville, *Mémoires,* 37:266–67.

27. Ibid., pp. 285–88; *Gazette,* 5 October 1647, p. 884.

28. Montpensier, *Mémoires,* 42:300.

29. Motteville, *Mémoires,* 37:267.

30. Lacour-Gayet, *L'Education politique,* pp. 6–7.

31. *Gazette,* 10 March 1646, p. 168.

32. AMRE, Mémoires et Documents: France, 855, fols. 55–56, 15 March 1646.

33. Elisabeth Charlotte, duchesse d'Orléans, *Correspondance de Madame duchesse d'Orléans, née princess Palatine,* 1:273, 19 October 1716. Louis de Rouvroy, duc de Saint-Simon, *Mémoires de Saint-Simon,* 28:25–30; Michelet, *Histoire,* 12:304–5; Chéruel, *Histoire de France pendant la minorité,* 2:115–18; Lavisse, *Histoire,* vol. 7, part 1, pp. 112–13, 124–26. A notable exception to this tradition is Wolf, *Louis XIV,* pp. 56–57.

34. He called Louis "the child of his silence" (La Porte, *Mémoires,* p. 381).

35. Ibid., pp. 414, 415, 423.

36. Ibid., p. 419.

37. Ibid., p. 418.

38. Ibid., p. 416.

39. Ibid., 433.

40. Ibid., p. 415; as opposed to Brienne, *Mémoires, inédits*, 1:217–18.

41. Louis entered the queen's small council in September 1649, and the council of finance in October. On the occasion the *Gazette,* 11 September 1649, p. 791, editorialized: "This way of giving him early knowledge of affairs of state, following the example of the greatest kings, shows everyone what care the queen regent his mother takes with his royal education." However, according to Motteville, *Mémoires,* 39:408, during these meetings the boy used to fidget and try to sneak out. For an appreciation of the practical political education Mazarin gave Louis, see John B. Wolf, "The Formation of a King," in *Louis XIV and the Craft of Kingship,* pp. 113–19; Wolf, *Louis XIV,* pp. 68–73; Dethan, *Mazarin,* pp. 209–11.

42. *Gazette,* 6 November 1654, p. 1207; 6 November 1655, p. 1248; 4 November 1656, p. 1320.

43. Ibid., 28 May 1644, p. 380; on 4 June 1644, p. 407, it reported that Péréfixe had started to give Louis lessons twice a day. On the unsuccessful competitors, see Lacour-Gayet, *L'Education politique,* pp. 6, 11–13.

44. As cited in Lacour-Gayet, *L'Education politique,* pp. 14, 51.

45. Arnauld, *Mémoires,* 34:75.

46. Lacour-Gayet, *L'Education politique,* pp. 16–17, 72–76.

47. See, for example, Lavisse, *Histoire,* vol. 7, part 1, pp. 124–25.

48. *Gazette,* 9 May 1648, p. 588.

49. La Porte, *Mémoires,* pp. 413, 420.

50. See chapter 9, notes 27, 28, above.

51. For Vauquelin's career, see George Mongrédien, *Etude sur la vie et l'oeuvre de Nicolas Vauquelin, seigneur des Yvetaux, précepteur de Louis XIII, 1567–1649.*

52. Nicolas Vauquelin des Yvetaux, *Oeuvres complètes,* pp. 48–59.

53. Vauquelin, "L'Institution du prince," in *Oeuvres,* pp. 158–77.

54. Ibid., p. 159.

55. Ibid., p. 161.

56. Ibid., pp. 172–73.

57. Ibid., pp. 160–61.

58. Ibid., p. 167; compare with BN, Fonds Français 19043, "Maximes," pp. 76–78v.

59. Vauquelin, "L'Institution," p. 165.

60. Ibid., p. 171.

61. For detailed reports on the course of the king's illness, see *Gazette,* 16 November 1647, p. 1088; 23 November 1647, p. 1124; 29 November 1647, pp. 1137–48. See also Motteville, *Mémoires,* 37:296–301.

62. Motteville, *Mémoires,* 37:310.

63. *Gazette,* 7 December 1647, p. 1196; 21 December 1647, p. 1244.

64. Ibid., 7 December 1647, p. 1196.

65. Ibid., 18 January 1648, p. 96; 25 January 1648, p. 132; 28 March 1648, p. 412; extra no. 48, n.d., pp. 413–24.

66. Motteville, *Mémoires,* 37:310.

CHAPTER FIFTEEN

1. Some of the best-known short histories of the Fronde are Ernst H. Kossmann, *La Fronde*; Pierre-Georges Loris, *La Fronde*; and Louis Madelin, *Une Révolution manquée: la Fronde*. Among longer histories, Louis-Clair de Beaupoil de Sainte-Aulaire, *Histoire de la Fronde*, was superseded by Chéruel, *Histoire de France pendant la minorité*, and *Histoire de France sous le ministère*. For the most lucid and concise treatment of the financial and political issues, see the pertinent chapters in Bonney, *The King's Debts*, and *Political Change*. For some of the highlights of the controversy concerning social and economic aspects of the Fronde, see Boris F. Porchnev, *Les Soulèvements populaires en France de 1623 à 1648*; Roland E. Mousnier, *Fureurs paysannes: les paysans dans les révoltes du XVIIe siècle, France, Russie, Chine*; Roland E. Mousnier, ed., *Lettres et mémoires adressés au chancelier Séguier, 1633–1649*; and Roland E. Mousnier, J. P. Labatut, and Y. P. Durand, eds., *Problèmes de stratification sociale: deux cahiers de la noblesse pour les états-généraux de 1649–1651*. See also Trevor Aston, ed., *Crisis in Europe, 1560–1660*, pp. 63–123. The primary literature of the Fronde period is very rich also, since almost everyone connected with events wrote memoirs. The memoirs of La Châtre, La Rochefoucauld, Mademoiselle, Madame de Motteville, and Talon, are notable examples, and have already been cited. With the qualified exception of Madame de Motteville, these authors favored the *frondeurs*, but that attitude was not shared by other observers. See, for example, BN, Fonds Français 20858–61, "Histoire de la régence de la reine Anne d'Autriche, ou mémoires de Mre Robert Aubery, seigneur de Sully"; or BN, Fonds Français 17470, fols. 40–191v, "Troubles de France sous la régence de la reyne Anne d'Autriche," whose anonymous author noted regretfully on fol. 41 that "it is almost impossible to write an accurate account of what happened because those who caused the troubles acted from bad principles and hid the knowledge of their actions carefully so that posterity would not accuse them of having risked their country's welfare for their own interests."

2. For the role of the Parlement, see A. Lloyd Moote, *The Revolt of the Judges: The Parlement of Paris and the Fronde*.

3. So at least Madame de Motteville claimed (*Mémoires*, 37:6–7). For Mazarin's subsequent warnings, see Cousin, "Des carnets autographes: cinquième article," pp. 753–73.

4. Cousin, "Des carnets autographes: cinquième article," pp. 772 n. 1; Talon *Mémoires*, 1:247.

5. Mazarin, Carnet 3:12, as quoted in Cousin, "Des carnets autographes: cinquième article," p. 768 n. 2.

6. BN, Nouvelles Acquisitions Françaises 4197, fols. 82–85, "Harangue au lit de justice du Roy tenu au Parlement de Paris le 15e janvier 1648."

7. Mazarin, Carnet 1:87; 2:10, 15; as quoted in Cousin, "Des carnets autographes: cinquième article," p. 772 n. 3.

8. Motteville, *Mémoires*, 37:359.

9. Ibid., p. 386.

10. Chéruel, *Histoire de France pendant la minorité*, 3:516–17.

11. *Gazette*, 25 July 1648, p. 960.

12. Ibid., 1 August 1648, p. 999; extra no. 116, n.d. (1648), pp. 1005–10.

13. Motteville, *Mémoires*, 37:427.

14. Ibid.

15. Pierre Adolphe Chéruel, "Les Carnets de Mazarin pendant la Fronde, septem-

bre–octobre 1648," *Revue Historique* 15 (May–Aug. 1877): 113–16. Chavigny remained a minister of state without portfolio until the summer of 1651.

16. Motteville, *Mémoires*, 38:30–32; La Rochefoucauld, *Mémoires*, 51:437.

17. For a full account of the life and career of Retz, see J. H. M. Salmon, *Cardinal de Retz: The Anatomy of a Conspirator.*

18. Retz, *Mémoires*, pp. 28–29.

19. He claimed to have been involved in plots against Richelieu (*Mémoires*, pp. 18–20; Salmon, *Cardinal de Retz*, pp. 45–52).

20. Chéruel, "Les Carnets de Mazarin," p. 123; Motteville, *Mémoires*, 38:125. Salmon, *Cardinal de Retz*, pp. 105–6, contends it was the other way around: that Mazarin offered Retz the governorship in order to discredit him; however, on p. 105, in note 1, the author admits that this is not the only version of the story.

21. Retz, *Mémoires*, pp. 120–21.

22. Montpensier, *Mémoires*, 41:31–32.

23. Chéruel, "Les Carnets de Mazarin," pp. 107–10.

24. *Gazette*, 19 September 1648, p. 1292; 26 September 1648, p. 1328.

25. Motteville, *Mémoires*, 38:57–58.

26. Ibid., p. 79. For the text of the declaration, see F. A. Isambert et. al., eds., *Receuil général des anciennes lois francaises depuis l'an 420 jusqu'à la révolution de 1789*, 17:72–84.

27. Chéruel, "Les Carnets de Mazarin," p. 135.

28. Ibid., pp. 125–27, 129.

29. Ibid., p. 136. Similar stratagems were used on more than one occasion; see Motteville, *Mémoires*, 38:79–80.

30. Motteville, *Mémoires*, 38:96.

31. *Gazette*, 28 November 1648, p. 1628; 2 January 1649, p. 14; Motteville, *Mémoires*, 38:109–10, 114.

32. In letters of explanation to the archbishop of Paris and other notables, the queen claimed that her flight had been made necessary by the existence of plots to seize the person of the king (AMRE, Mémoires et Documents: France, 865, fols. 3–6).

33. Motteville, *Mémoires*, 38:134–39.

34. Montpensier, *Mémoires*, 41:43.

35. Ibid., p. 48; see pp. 40–53 for the complete account of the miseries the court suffered. See also Motteville, *Mémoires*, 38:141–42.

36. *Gazette*, 20 February 1649, p. 128. The message, however, had been composed by some of the *frondeur* nobles, and the messenger was a monk without diplomatic status, though a more official envoy followed him in March (Salmon, *Cardinal de Retz*, pp. 124–25, 128). For Mazarin's contacts with the Spanish agent, see Chéruel, *Histoire de France pendant la minorité*, 3:254–57.

37. For the text of the treaty, see Isambert, *Recueil*, 17:161–63.

38. *Gazette*, 1 May 1649, p. 159.

39. Ibid., extra no. 93, 20 August 1649, pp. 661–72.

40. Ibid., extra no. 104, n.d. (1649), pp. 760–67.

41. Chéruel, *Histoire de France pendant la minorité*, 3:285–87. Compare this with the account sympathetic to Condé in Pierre Lenet, *Mémoires inédits concernant l'histoire du prince de Condé depuis sa naissance, en 1621, jusqu'au traité des Pyrénées, en 1659*, pp. 209–15; and Henri d'Orléans, duc d'Aumale, *Histoire des princes de Condé, pendant les XVIe et XVIIe siècles*, 5:357–77.

42. Chéruel, *Histoire de France pendant la minorité*, 3:298–300.

43. Ibid., 3:297–98; Mazarin had Anne write him a letter, ordering him to submit to Condé.

44. Mazarin, Carnet 16:17; Chéruel, *Histoire de France pendant la minorité*, 3:301–3.

45. For details see Batiffol, *Madame de Chevreuse*, pp. 245–53.

46. Salmon, *Cardinal de Retz*, pp. 149–50.

47. AMRE, Mémoires et Documents: France, 870, fol. 19. The text was published in Chéruel, *Histoire de France pendant la minorité*, 3:357–58.

48. AMRE, Mémoires et Documents: France, 870, fol. 19.

49. Motteville, *Mémoires*, 38:438–39.

50. Ibid., pp. 443–44.

51. Aumale, *Histoire des princes de Condé*, 5:374.

52. For these and subsequent events until the fall of 1650, see Chéruel, *Histoire de France pendant la minorité*, 3:376–87; 4:3–290. The *Gazette* as usual gave the itinerary of the royal family.

53. Dethan, *Gaston d'Orléans*, pp. 376–79.

54. AMRE, Mémoires et Documents: France, 872, fols. 338–38v; fols. 374–74v.

55. Ibid., fols. 339, 349–50, 370–71, 378, 381, 386, 397–98, 420–21, 433–33v, in addition to the folios cited above.

56. Chéruel, *Histoire de France pendant la minorité*, 4:223–25.

CHAPTER SIXTEEN

1. Chéruel, *Histoire de France pendant la minorité*, 4:248–53.

2. Dethan, *Gaston d'Orléans*, pp. 385–89.

3. *Gazette*, 11 February 1651, p. 171; Marie d'Orléans, duchesse de Nemours, *Mémoires de la duchesse de Nemours*, p. 468.

4. Motteville, *Mémoires*, 39:137–38.

5. Nemours, *Mémoires*, pp. 471–72.

6. Chéruel, *Histoire de France pendant la minorité*, 4:263–66.

7. Motteville, *Mémoires*, 39:139–40.

8. Ibid., p. 155; Madame de Motteville reports that she was present all night.

9. Ibid., pp. 154, 155–56.

10. Ibid., 156–58; according to Mademoiselle, the queen never forgot that night (Montpensier, *Mémoires*, 41:128–29).

11. Motteville, *Mémoires*, 39:158–59.

12. Ibid., pp. 159–61.

13. *Gazette*, 18 March 1651, pp. 294–95.

14. The charges were summed up on 11 March (ibid., 18 March 1651, p. 294).

15. Bonney, *The King's Debts*, pp. 193–241; *Political Change*, pp. 443–51.

16. For Colbert's management of Mazarin's affairs, at least from 1651 on, see Inès Murat, *Colbert*, pp. 31–51.

17. Chéruel, *Histoire de France pendant la minorité*, 2:479–81.

18. Ibid., pp. 475–89.

19. Montpensier, *Mémoires*, 41:99.

20. Société de l'Histoire de France, *Bibliographie des mazarinades*, 1:174.

21. *Ballet dansé devant le roi et la reine régente sa mère, par le trio mazarinique, pour dire adieu à la France, en vers burlesques.*

22. Philip A. Knachel, *England and the Fronde: The Impact of the English Civil War and Revolution on France*, pp. 78–111.

23. Claude Joly, *Recueil de maximes véritables et importantes pour l'institution du roy, contre la fausse et pernicieuse politique du cardinal Mazarin, prétendu surintendant de l'éducation de sa majesté*. The book had been published first in 1652, and that edition was ordered to be burned.

24. Ibid., pp. 514–15.

25. Ibid., pp. 411–12.

26. *Advis, remonstrance et requeste, par huict paysans de huict provinces, deputés par les autres du royaume, sur les miseres et affaires du temps present, 1649, au parlement de Paris, et de ceux deputez et assemblez à Ruë pour la conferance.*

27. *Le Chevalier chrétien parlant des misères du temps, à la royne régente.*

28. *La Vérité parlant à la reyne.*

29. *Les Ris et les pleurs de la France sur la conduite de la reyne et du conseil d'état, découvrant l'origine de nos misères et des calamitez publiques.*

30. *Le Miroüer de la reyne, luy representant tous les desordres de sa régence, et luy donnant d'infaillibles moyens pour les réparer.*

31. *L'Esprit de feue la reyne-mère, parlant à la reyne, sur l'estat de la régence.*

32. *L'Ombre du roy d'Angleterre apparue à la reyne de France.*

33. *Chronologie des reynes malheureuses par l'insolence de leurs favoris, dediée à la reyne regente pour luy servir d'exemple et de miroir.*

34. Montpensier, *Mémoires*, 41:113–15.

35. Ibid., p. 101.

36. Motteville, *Mémoires*, 39:143.

37. As quoted in Paul Guth, *Mazarin*, p. 519.

38. *La Custode de la reyne, qui dit tout.*

39. *Bibliothèque des mazarinades*, 1:256–57; *Gazette*, 24 July 1649, p. 528.

40. As quoted in Guth, *Mazarin*, p. 525.

41. *Les Convulsions de la reyne la nuit de devant le départ de Mazarin, avec la consolation qu'elle receut par l'apparition d'une bonne sainte.*

42. *Les Convulsions*, p. 5.

43. BN, Fonds Clairembault 1144, fols. 88–101v. There are no letters, however, before 1653.

44. Cousin, *Madame de Hautefort*, pp. 392–404, though there is an error in the chronology. The twelfth letter had been published earlier in Charles Athanase, baron Walckenaer, *Mémoires touchant la vie et les écrits de Marie de Rabutin-Chantal, dame de Bourbilly, marquise de Sévigné, durant la régence et la Fronde*, 3:471–72.

45. Mazarin had to go into exile twice, and this letter was written near the end of his second exile. On his way back to court, he was making a lengthy detour in Champagne where an army he had raised, under the command of Turenne, was recapturing places that had been taken by Condé. Mazarin's actual arrival at court, therefore, was put off several times.

46. BN, Fonds Clairembault 1144, fol. 90, 26 January 1653.

47. Ibid., fols. 91–92, 28? January 1653.

48. Ibid., fols. 94–94v, 29 January 1653.

49. Mazarin, *Lettres à la reine* pp. 30–31, 11 May 1651.

50. Ibid., p. 36, 11 May 1651. Balzac and Voiture were contemporary authors famous for elegant style.

51. Ibid., p. 170, 7 July 1651.

52. Ibid., p. 192, 18 July 1651.

53. For the view that Anne and Mazarin were lovers, see Michelet, *Histoire de France*, 12:233–34, 286–87; Mazarin, *Lettres à la reine*, pp. ix–x. For supporters of the marriage theory, see Molinier, *Notice sur cette question*, pp. 12–21, 28; Robiquet, *Le Coeur d'une reine*, pp. 4–10; Herbillon, *Anne d'Autriche*, p. 221. Some authors, however, considered the question unanswerable; see Walckenaer, *Mémoires touchant la vie . . . ,* 1:213–15; Cousin, *Madame de Hautefort*, pp. 77–82.

54. Mazarin, *Lettres à la reine*, p. 339, 27 October 1651.

55. Coste, *Le Grand Saint,* 3:101.

56. Orléans, *Correspondance,* 2:3, 27 September 1718; 2:373, 2 July 1722.

57. See, for example, Molinier, *Notice sur cette question,* pp. 22–27.

58. Wolf, *Louis XIV,* pp. 84–87.

59. Mazarin, *Lettres à la reine,* p. 36, 11 May 1651.

60. Ibid., p. 210, 27 July 1651.

61. Ibid., p. 374, 17 November 1651.

62. BN, Fonds Clairembault 1144, fol. 99, 3 August 1658.

63. Madeleine Laurain-Portemer, "Le Statut de Mazarin dans l'église: apercus sur le haut clergé de la contre-réforme, *Bibliothèque de l'Ecole des Chartes* 128 (1970): 8–9, 55–56; *Etudes mazarines,* 1:83–84, 128. Her conviction is shared by Dethan, *Mazarin,* pp. 189–90.

64. BN, Fonds Clairembault 1144, fol. 90, 26 January 1653.

65. Mazarin, *Lettres à la reine,* p. 222, 8 August 1651.

66. Ibid., p. 467, 26 December 1651.

67. Ibid., p. 483, 17 January 1652.

68. Motteville, *Mémoires,* 36:342–43.

69. Retz, *Mémoires,* pp. 566–67.

70. Brienne (le jeune), *Mémoires,* 2:306.

71. Mazarin, *Lettres à la reine,* pp. 291–300, 26 September 1651.

72. Ibid., pp. 301–12, 27 September 1651. See p. 303 for his statement concerning Louis XIII's intentions in choosing him as the godfather of his eldest son.

73. Dethan, *Mazarin,* p. 190.

CHAPTER SEVENTEEN

1. Jules cardinal Mazarin, *Lettres du cardinal Mazarin pendant son ministère,* 27:111, to Lionne, 31 March 1651.

2. Mazarin, *Lettres à la reine,* p. 83, to Lionne, May 1651.

3. Ibid., pp. 41–64, 12 May 1651.

4. Ibid., pp. 38–41, 12 May 1651.

5. Ibid., p. 38, 12 May 1651.

6. Ibid., p. 340, 29 October 1651; p. 469, 29 December 1651. Madame de Chevreuse was not the only one to be deceived; see Nemours, *Mémoires*, pp. 472–74.

7. Mazarin, *Lettres à la reine*, p. 473, 29 December 1651.

8. Ibid., passim. It had been Mazarin's goal from the outset that a party be formed for the queen; see Mazarin, *Lettres pendant son ministrère*, 4:43, to Servien, 1 March 1651; p. 63, to Servien, 9 March 1651.

9. Chéruel, *Histoire de France pendant la minorité*, 4:325–26.

10. Mazarin, *Lettres à la reine*, p. 207, 27 July 1651. In the winter of 1648–49, there had already been demands for a meeting of the Estates-General; and indeed, in January 1649 a royal circular letter had gone out to provincial officials with orders to prepare for such a meeting (see Isambert, *Recueil*, 17:144–46). The letter never reached the status of letters-patent, however, and was ignored by the parlements. For the 1651 assembly of the nobility, see *Journal de l'assemblée de la noblesse tenue à Paris en l'année mil six cens cinquante-un.*

11. Chéruel, *Histoire de France pendant la minorité*, 1:62 n. 2; 4:299.

12. Mazarin, *Lettres pendant son ministère*, 4:73, to Lionne, 14 March 1651.

13. Chéruel, *Histoire de France pendant la minorité*, 4:295–96. Very similar projects had been aired in 1559 when anti-Guise pamphleteers called for a *curatelle*, or caretaker, council under the authority of the Estates-General to supervise the king until the age of 21 or 25 (see Lightman, *Sons and Mothers*, pp. 106–8, 120–28). There is no evidence, however, that the alleged scheme of 1651 was based on this historical precedent.

14. For the royal letters to governors and *baillis*, see Isambert, *Recueil*, 17:235–37. For the (unauthorized) election meetings in Paris, see *Gazette*, 2 September 1651, p. 935; 9 September 1651, p. 971; 16 September 1651, p. 998.

15. Brief summaries or notations of these, with reference numbers, are to be found in AN, Inventaire 50: "Répertoire chronologique et analytique des arrêts du conseil des dépêches, 1611–1710," 6:117, 180, for the Huguenot *cahier*; 145–53 for the *cahier* of the Estates of Languedoc. See also *Gazette*, 23 August 1653, p. 899, for the report that bourgeois notables of Paris had been named receivers of complaints, or grievances, for a *cahier*. See also Mousnier, Labatut, Durand, eds., *Problèmes de stratification sociale* for two *cahiers* of the nobility.

16. AN, Inventaire 50, 6:115, 119, 127, 129–30, 138–39, 154, 157, 159–62, 169–70, 175–79, 185.

17. That is the report Mazarin heard (Chéruel, *Histoire de France pendant la minorité*, 4:378). Motteville, *Mémoires*, 39:232–33, recorded Anne's feelings about Chavigny at this time, though she did not cite this particular incident.

18. See, for example, Mazarin, *Lettres pendant son ministère*, 4:43, to Servien, 1 March 1651; p. 63, to Servien, 9 March 1651.

19. Motteville, *Mémoires*, 39:273–77; Chéruel, *Histoire de France pendant la minorité*, 4:387–90.

20. Motteville, *Mémoires*, 39:230, 245; see also *Gazette*, 19 August 1651, p. 864.

21. Isambert, *Recueil*, 17:249–50. The Parlement registered the declaration on its own initiative on 29 December (see *Gazette*, 30 December 1651, p. 1515).

22. Mazarin, *Lettres à la reine*, p. 257, 12 September 1651; see also pp. 249–50, 5 September 1651.

23. Secretly, through intermediaries, Anne had been trying to make sure of Mazarin's safety in Rome, and perhaps also to discourage any attempt to put him on trial there (Laurain-Portemer, "Le Statut de Mazarin," pp. 62–63; *Etudes mazarines*, 1:134–35).

24. Mazarin, *Lettres à la reine*, p. 292, to the queen, 26 September 1651.

25. Ibid.

26. Ibid., pp. 300–301, to Louis XIV, 26 September 1651.

27. Chéruel, *Histoire de France pendant la minorité*, 4:405–6.

28. Mazarin, *Lettres pendant son ministère*, 4:322:35, to Zongo Ondedei from Brühl, 14 July 1651, for example; see also editors note, p. 332.

29. Mararin, *Lettres à la reine*, pp. 301–12, to Bartet, 27 September 1651.

30. *Gazette*, 7 September 1651, p. 969.

31. For the report of the proceedings, see *Gazette*, extra no. 119, n.d. (1651), pp. 973–88; see also Motteville, *Mémoires*, 39:278–93.

32. *Gazette*, extra no. 119, n.d. (1651), p. 985; Motteville, *Mémoires*, 39:289.

33. *Gazette*, extra no. 119, n.d. (1651), pp. 985–86; Motteville, *Mémoires*, 39:290.

34. *Gazette*, extra no. 119, n.d. (1651), p. 986; Motteville, *Mémoires*, 39:290–91.

35. *Gazette*, 23 September 1651, p. 1048.

36. Ibid., 30 September 1651, p. 1084.

37. Ibid., 27 January 1652, p. 108.

38. Isambert, *Recueil*, 17:280.

39. See, for example, Mazarin, *Lettres à la reine*, pp. 480–83, to the queen, 11 January 1652; pp. 483–84, to the queen, 17 January 1652.

40. *Gazette*, 31 January 1652, p. 131.

41. Ruth Kleinman, "Gratitude Revisited: The Declaration of Saint-Germain, 1652," *French Historical Studies* 5 (Spring 1968): 249–62; "Belated Crusaders: Religious Fears in Anglo-French Diplomacy, 1654–1655," *Church History* 44 (March 1975): 1–13.

42. For Mazarin's desire to reassure the Huguenots as early as the 1640s, see, for example, BN, Fonds Baluze, 174, Carnet 4:89. See also Cousin, "Des carnets autographes: quatrième article," pp. 708–19; "Des carnets autographes: quinzième article," pp. 48–55; Ruth Kleinman, "Changing Interpretations of the Edict of Nantes: The Administrative Aspect, 1643–1661," *French Historical Studies* 10 (Fall 1978): 541–71.

43. Motteville, *Mémoires*, 39:338–39.

44. Montpensier, *Mémoires*, 41:139–42.

45. Mazarin, *Lettres à la reine*, p. 478, to the queen, 7 January 1652. For Gaston's attitude, see Chéruel, *Histoire de France sous ministère*, 1:117–18.

46. Montpensier, *Mémoires*, 41:141.

47. Ibid., p. 142.

48. Motteville, *Mémoires*, 39:341–42, reported that Mademoiselle told her the Bastille cannon had not been fired at her order; the king and queen, however, believed Mademoiselle had been responsible for the action, and Madame de Motteville thought they might have been right.

49. Chéruel, *Histoire de France sous le ministère*, 1:245.

50. Ibid., p. 345.

51. *Gazette*, extra no. 125, n.d. (1652), pp. 985–96.

52. Ibid., p. 987.

53. Ibid., p. 988.

54. BN, Fonds Clairembault 1144, fol. 89.

55. Ibid., fol. 94v.

56. *Gazette*, 8 February 1653, pp. 139–40.

57. For a report of all ceremonies, see *Gazette*, 10 June 1654, pp. 574–76; extra no. 73, n.d. (1654), pp. 577–88. A multitude of pamphlets also appeared, with the same information.

58. Ibid., 17 June 1654, p. 600.

59. Ibid., extra no. 73, p. 588.

CHAPTER EIGHTEEN

1. Motteville, *Mémoires*, 39:293–94.

2. *Gazette*, 5 April 1653, p. 339.

3. Chéruel, *Histoire de France sous le ministère*, 2:3–50.

4. Richard M. Golden, *The Godly Rebellion: Parisian Curés and the Religious Fronde, 1652–1662*. See also Madeleine Laurain-Portemer, "Opposition et propagande à Paris au temps du sacre de Louis XIV," *Etudes mazarines*, 1:155–74.

5. Allier, *La Compagnie*, p. 361; Argenson, *Annales*, pp. 263–64.

6. Argenson, *Annales*, pp. 179, 205.

7. Allier, *La Compagnie*, p. 361; see also Argenson, *Annales*, p. 205.

8. *Gazette*, 27 May, 1656, p. 539.

9. Kleinman, "Changing Interpretations," pp. 561–63.

10. As Mazarin wrote to Colbert, cited in Chéruel, *Histoire de France sous le ministère*, 3:72–73.

11. Dethan, *Gaston*, pp. 424–28. Gaston was also helpful to the government in quieting peasant rebels in Orléanais (see *Gazette*, 9 July 1658, p. 639).

12. For the course of war and diplomacy during these years, see Chéruel, *Histoire de France sous le ministère*, vols. 2–3; and Mazarin, *Lettres pendant son ministère*, vols. 6–9.

13. Chéruel, *Histoire de France sous le ministère*, 2:254–55, gives the quotation.

14. BN, Fonds Français 23945, fols. 1–104v.

15. Ibid., fol. 104.

16. Ibid., fols. 3–5.

17. Ibid., fols. 6–6v, 8–8v.

18. Ibid., fols. 10v–12.

19. Ibid., fols. 9v–10. The *gabelle* was the salt tax, and the five great tax farms were districts of internal taxation.

20. Ibid., fols. 14–21v.

21. Ibid., fols. 12v–13.

22. Ibid., fol. 97 v.

23. Ibid., fol. 13 v.

24. Ibid., fols. 32v–33. For the roster of 1664, see AN, Série Z[1A], 512, which shows 687 persons on salary, plus 25 nonsalaried ladies.

25. BN, Fonds Français 23945, fols. 27–28v.

26. AN, Série K, 118[B], 64, 6 October 1653 at Laon; 64 bis, 28 October 1653 at Châlons.

27. BN, Fonds Français 23945, fols. 29–30.

28. Ibid., fols. 38v and 62, respectively.

29. Ibid., fol. 39 v.

30. Ibid., fols. 52, 70–70v, respectively.

31. Ibid., fols. 43, 50, respectively.

32. Ibid., fols. 47v, 57.

33. These items were spread out over the year and are scattered in the manuscript.

34. BN, Fonds Français 23945, fols. 34v–37v.

35. Ibid., fols. 71 ff.

36. These items were spread out over the year and are scattered in the manuscript.

37. BN, Fonds Français 23945, fol. 66.

38. Mazarin, *Lettres pendant son ministère,* 4:10, to Le Tellier, 8 February 1651.

39. Christiane Aulanier, *Histoire du palais et du musée du Louvre,* 8:20–24.

40. Jean Cordey, "L'Inventaire après décès d'Anne d'Autriche et le mobilier du Louvre," *Bulletin de la Société de l'Histoire de l'Art Francais,* 1930, pp. 209–75. Cordey is more complete than Vicomte de Grouchy, *Inventaire après décès de la reine Anne d'Autriche, 1666.*

41. The duke of Modena saw and admired both rooms (*Gazette,* 15 January 1656, p. 59); and so did Queen Christina of Sweden (ibid., 16 September 1656, p. 1028).

42. Cordey, "L'Inventaire," pp. 221–22.

43. Christiane Aulanier, *Histoire du palais et du musée du Louvre,* 5:16–30; Cordey, "L'Inventaire," pp. 223–25.

44. Madeleine Laurain-Portemer, "La Politique artistique de Mazarin," pp. 65–68; *Etudes mazarines,* 1:385–90. I am grateful to M. Daniel Alcouffe, of the curatorial staff of the Louvre, for the opportunity to see these rooms, which were closed to the public for some time.

45. Laurain-Portemer, "La Politique artistique," p. 68; *Etudes mazarines,* 1:389.

46. Aulanier, *Histoire du palais,* 5:28–29.

47. Laurain-Portemer, "La Politique artistique," p. 66; *Etudes mazarines,* 1:386–87.

48. Cordey, "L'Inventaire," pp. 261–65, 272–73. There is a partial listing of them in a manuscript excerpt of the inventory that shows her more important jewelry and furnishings that Louis and Philippe divided between them: BN, Nouvelles Acquisitions Françaises 9560, fols. 23–27, 60–64.

49. Cordey, "L'Inventaire," pp. 243–44, 245, 247, 259, 267. For Mazarin's taste for chinoiserie, see Laurain-Portemer, "La Politique artistique," pp. 64–65.

50. Personal interview with M. Daniel Alcouffe, of the curatorial staff of the Louvre, 7 November 1977.

51. The *Gazette* for these years recorded her visits to churches and convents and her excursions and parties. We may note here that Anne's activities and social circle were not characterized by *préciosité,* even though her contemporary, Somaize, listed her among the *précieuses;* see Carolyn C. Lougee, *Le Paradis des Femmes: Women, Salons, and Social Stratification in Seventeenth-Century France,* p. 215. Anne's afternoon circle was a polite social gathering, but by no means a literary salon.

52. Motteville, *Mémoires,* 39:408–9.

53. Ibid., pp. 409–10, 450–51.

54. BN, Nouvelles Acquisitions Françaises 14286, 1ère partie, p. 308. Even if these unpublished memoirs are authentic, however, La Porte may have invented the incident to which he referred.

55. Aside from Anne's letters, previously cited, see Mazarin's letters to her, for example, in AMRE, Mémoires et Documents: France, 891–96 passim., for the years 1653–56.

56. BN, Fonds Clairembault 1144, fols. 98–99v, from Compiègne, 3 August 1658; fol. 100, from Compiègne, 5 August 1658.

57. Montpensier, *Mémoires*, 42:198.

58. Ibid., p. 202.

59. Ibid., pp. 270, 285, 316–17.

60. Ibid., p. 273.

61. Argenson, *Annales*, p. 252.

62. *Gazette*, 30 January 1655, p. 126.

63. Montpensier, *Mémoires*, 42:407.

64. *Gazette*, 18 September 1655, p. 1068; 30 September 1655, pp. 1126, 1128; 21 October 1655, p. 1200.

65. Wolf, *Louis XIV*, p. 94. The story, though unproved, has been repeated by everyone who has written about the youth of Louis XIV.

66. Wolf, *Louis XIV*, p. 95.

67. The *Gazette* regularly reported how many sick the king touched on religious holidays. For his fear of mortal sin, see Chérot, *La Première Jeunesse*, p. 183.

68. Chéruel, *Histoire de France pendant la minorité*, 2:275–76; *Histoire de France sous le ministère*, 3:209.

69. There were reports, though not in detail, in *Gazette*, 9 July 1658, pp. 638–39; 13 July 1658, pp. 639–40; 15 July 1658, pp. 662–63; 23 July 1658, p. 686. According to Motteville, *Mémoires*, 39:430, the king had scarlet fever.

70. Motteville, *Mémoires*, 39:430.

71. Ibid., pp. 430–31.

72. Montpensier, *Mémoires*, 42:317.

73. Ibid., p. 316.

74. Ibid., pp. 300–301.

75. *Gazette*, 23 December 1656, p. 1500.

76. Motteville, *Mémoires*, 39:379.

77. Montpensier, *Mémoires*, 42:360–61.

78. Motteville, *Mémoires*, 39:452; Montpensier, *Mémoires*, 42:362–63.

79. Montpensier, *Mémoires*, 42:332.

80. Wolf, *Louis XIV*, p. 105, cites her unpublished memoirs.

81. Motteville, *Mémoires*, 39:435.

82. Montpensier, *Mémoires*, 42:414–15.

83. Ibid., p. 425. The whole crisis is discussed at length in Chéruel, *Histoire de France sous le ministère*, 3:223–46.

84. Motteville, *Mémoires*, 40:12–13.

85. See, for example, Jules cardinal Mazarin, *Lettres du cardinal Mazarin, où l'on voit le secret de la négotiation de la paix des Pyrénées . . .* , pp. 14–27, 16 July 1659; pp. 27–33, 22 July 1659; pp. 179–202, 28 August 1659. See also Chéruel, *Histoire de France sous le ministère*, 3:236–45.

86. Motteville, *Mémoires*, 40:18–19.

87. *Gazette*, 31 July 1659, p. 738.

88. Motteville, *Mémoires*, 40:23.

89. Ibid., p. 3. Chéruel, *Histoire de France sous le ministère*, 3:223–45, canvasses the arguments for and against the allegations that Mazarin would have liked to marry his niece to the king, and shows the allegations unfounded. Mademoiselle in her time

must have come to the same conclusion, for she cited the parellel example of Mazarin's refusal to accept Charles II of England's proposal for Mazarin's niece Hortensia (Montpensier, *Mémoires*, 42:434–35).

90. Motteville, *Mémoires*, 40:16–17.

91. For the marriage treaty, religious dispensations, and other documents, see AN 21 MI 204, série K, 1625, C 16–27; see also Chéruel, *Histoire de France sous le ministère*, 3:246–54.

CHAPTER NINETEEN

1. Montpensier, *Mémoires*, 42: 489–90.

2. Ibid., p. 500.

3. Motteville, *Mémoires*, 40:50–56.

4. Ibid., pp. 58–59.

5. Ibid., pp. 59–60.

6. Ibid.

7. Ibid., pp. 66–67.

8. Montpensier, *Mémoires*, 42:509; see also pp. 503–4, 512.

9. Motteville, *Mémoires*, 40:71.

10. *Gazette*, extra no. 73, n.d. (1660), pp. 565–75.

11. Motteville, *Mémoires*, , 39:294; 40:19–20, 97–98, 113, 137–38.

12. The *Gazette* reported the court's itinerary.

13. *Gazette*, extra no. 103, n.d. (1660), pp. 785–816 [*sic;* should be paginated 805–36].

14. Chéruel, *Histoire de France sous le ministère*, 3:314–15.

15. *Gazette*, 4 September 1660, pp. 826–27 [should be 846–47].

16. Ibid., 30 October 1660, p. 1089 [should be 1031]. The *Gazette* reported both queens' church and convent visits.

17. Bibliothèque Nationale, *Mazarin*, p. 209.

18. *Gazette*, 27 November 1660, p. 1177 [should be 1119]. See subsequent issues for other amusements.

19. *Gazette*, 8 January 1661, p. 36.

20. Ibid., 22 January 1661, p. 83.

21. Ibid., 12 February 1661, pp. 151–52 [*sic;* should be 155–56].

22. Brienne (le jeune), *Mémoires*, 2:111.

23. Ibid., pp. 112–13.

24. The details are given ibid., pp. 108–10.

25. Motteville, *Mémoires*, 40:90, 98.

26. Jean-Baptiste Colbert, *Lettres, instructions et mémoires de Colbert*, 1:535–36.

27. Cousin, *Madame de Hautefort*, pp. 403–4. For an earlier but relatively inaccessible publication, see Walckenaer, *Mémoires touchant*, 3:471–72. The original of the letter has been lost.

28. Cousin, *Madame de Hautefort*, p. 404.

29. BN, Fonds Français 4332, fol. 233.

30. Cordey, "L'Inventaire," p. 224.

31. Raymond Darricau et Madeleine Laurain, "La Mort du cardinal Mazarin," *Annuaire-Bulletin de la Société de l'Histoire de France*, 1960, pp. 59–120.

32. Motteville, *Mémoires*, 40:91, 105.

33. Ibid., pp. 100–101. According to Mademoiselle, the king and his mother were distressed only a few days (Montpensier, *Mémoires*, 43:4.

34. As she was reported to have remarked to secretary of state Le Tellier (Brienne [le jeune], *Mémoires*, 2:158, editor's note 1).

35. Brienne (le jeune), *Mémoires*, 2:150–60.

36. Anne said this to Madame de Motteville after Mazarin had taken communion on 3 March (Motteville, *Mémoires*, 40:93).

37. The *Gazette* reported this devotion every year.

38. Motteville, *Mémoires*, 40:137–38.

39. Ibid., pp. 138, 144–45.

40. *Gazette*, 2 April 1661, p. 308 [should be 312].

41. The announcement was made in late March (*Gazette*, 26 March 1661, p. 283 [should be 287]).

42. Motteville, *Mémoires*, 40:111.

43. For all the complications, see ibid., pp. 116–37.

44. Ibid., pp. 154–55; *Gazette*, 3 November 1661, pp. 1178–80.

45. Anne did not care for the lady and refused her thanks on the occasion, telling her that she, the queen mother, had contributed nothing to the appointment (Motteville, *Mémoires*, 40:157.

46. *Gazette*, 13 December 1661, pp. 1324–25.

47. Ibid., 1 April 1662, p. 307.

48. Motteville, *Mémoires*, 40:157.

49. Ibid., pp. 161, 164.

50. Montpensier, *Mémoires*, 43:26; Anne may have said this, but whether she meant it sincerely is another matter.

51. For the Navailles story, see Motteville, *Mémoires*, 40:168–74, 192–200.

52. Ibid., pp. 202–3.

53. Ibid., pp. 203–7.

54. Ibid., p. 213.

55. Ibid., pp. 135–36, 175. Nevertheless, the queen got the whole story from the countess of Soissons in 1663 (see p. 192).

56. Anne took their hearts to Val-de-Grâce, though the bodies were buried in the royal crypt at Saint-Denis; for the orders, see AN, série K 118^{B}2, nos. 118^2, 118^3, 118^4, 118^5.

57. Motteville, *Mémoires*, 40:217.

58. For the course of the illness, see ibid., pp. 183–88.

59. *Gazette*, 18 August 1663, p. 798.

60. Madame de Motteville had it from Le Tellier, whom she knew well (Motteville, *Mémoires*, 40:187).

61. Ibid., p. 198.

62. Ibid., p. 218.

63. Gui Patin, *Lettres de Gui Patin à Charles Spon, médecin à Lyon*, 3:493, 494. Madame de Motteville recorded the progress of Anne's illness, as well as her remarks and reactions (Motteville, *Mémoires*, 40:212–304).

64. Motteville, *Mémoires*, 40:221.

65. Ruth Kleinman, "Facing Cancer in the Seventeenth Century: The Last Illness of Anne of Austria, 1664–1666," *Advances in Thanatology*, vol. 4, no. 1 (1977), pp. 41–44.

66. BN, Fonds Français 17055, fol. 389.

67. Ibid., fols. 231–231v.

68. Motteville, *Mémoires*, 40:219.

69. Ibid., p. 222.

70. Ibid., p. 223. Gui Patin, the dean of the Paris medical faculty, had a low opinion of Alliot because Alliot prescribed drugs instead of confining treatment to bleedings and purges (Patin, *Lettres*, 3:513).

71. Motteville, *Mémoires*, 40:261, 263.

72. Ibid., pp. 273–74.

73. See the funeral sermon preached by the bishop of Mende at the Grands Augustins in Paris, 13 March 1666 (BN, Fonds Français 15604, fols. 384–99v); or the funeral sermon by the bishop of Amiens preached at Saint-Denis on 12 February 1666 (BN, Fonds Français 15604, fols. 400–422v).

74. Motteville, *Mémoires*, 40:220.

75. Ibid.; for Anne's visit to an afflicted nun in 1647, see ibid., 37:237.

76. Ibid., 40:262.

77. Ibid., p. 277; Anne reiterated these sentiments frequently (see also p. 221).

78. Ibid., p. 284.

79. Patin, *Lettres*, 3:523; this was on 5 April 1665.

80. Motteville, *Mémoires*, 40:242–43.

81. Ibid., p. 235.

82. Ibid., pp. 235–36.

83. For Anne's testament, made 3 August 1665, see BN, Nouvelles Acquisitions Françaises 4385, fols. 270–76. There are other copies; BN, Fonds Français 4332, fols. 242–43; BN, Fonds Français 7605, fols. 475–78. It was published in Motteville, *Mémoires*, 40:310–15. For the valuation of Anne's jewelry, see Cordey, "L'Inventaire," p. 274.

84. Cordey, "L'Inventaire," pp. 219–20, 247–48. After Anne's death, the king gave this furniture to her first chamberwoman, Madame de Beauvais.

85. AN, série 0¹ 3304, "Journal du garde-meuble; Journal concernant le garde-meuble de la couronne et maisons royalles commencant le 2 janvier 1666 et finissant le 11 août 1672," fol. 10v, 12 February 1666.

86. Motteville, *Mémoires*, 40:270.

87. Ibid., p. 303; for the deathbed scene, see also pp. 286–304, and Montpensier, *Mémoires*, 43:92–95. Contemporary pamphlets and newsletters gave extensive accounts of Anne's death and funeral services and ceremonies; see, for example, BN, Fonds Francais 18538, fols. 399–406v, 407–12, 413–18v, to mention only a few. See also AN, série K 118ᴮ2, 131: 131¹–131⁶.

88. Montglat, *Mémoires*, 3:136–37. Already during Anne's illness in 1663, on Sundays and holidays Parisian artisans and humble folk, instead of taking their usual walks and outings, would come to the queen mother's guardroom to ask after her progress (Motteville, *Mémoires*, 40:188).

89. Motteville, *Mémoires*, 40:305; Louis made the remark to his son's governess, the duchess of Montausier.

90. Louis XIV, *Oeuvres*, 1:50.

91. Ibid.

BIBLIOGRAPHY

MANUSCRIPT SOURCES

Archives du Ministère des Relations Extérieures, Correspondance Politique: Espagne, 12; Mémoires et Documents: Espagne, 138; Mémoires et Documents: France, 35, 255, 795 bis, 830, 831, 836, 842, 843, 846, 848, 849, 855, 865, 870, 872, 891, 892, 893, 894, 895, 896, 2164.

Archives Nationales, Fonds dit de Simancas, K 1617, C 4, Nos. 1–40; K 1625, C 16–27; Série K, 118^B, 64, 64 bis; 118^{B1}, No. 69; 118^{B2}, No. 131; Série KK, 203; Série 0^1, 3304; Série Z^{1A}, 511, 512; Inventaire 50: "Répertoire chronologique et analytique des arrêts du conseil des dépêches, 1611–1712," vol. 7.

Archivo General de Simancas, Secretaria de Estado, Capitulaciones con Francia y negociaciones diplomáticos de los embajadores de España en aquela corte, Serie K, legajos 1416, 1419, 1420, 1473, 1475, 1476.

Bibliothèque Nationale, Salle des Manuscrits, Fonds Français 2748, 3687, 3747, 3806, 3818, 4022–27, 4149, 4330, 4332, 4643, 4648, 4895, 5174, 7605, 10412–14, 15397, 15515, 15597, 15604, 16115–16, 16631, 17055, 17470, 18538, 18552, 19043, 20858–61, 20866, 23945, 24979; Nouvelles Acquisitions Françaises 4334, 4385, 9175, 9560, 13008–11, 14286; Fonds de Baluze 174; Fonds Clairembault 1144; Fonds Italien 1772; Mélanges Colbert 75.

Bibliothèque Victor Cousin à la Sorbonne, Manuscrits, III: Documents Historiques, 37–41.

PRINTED SOURCES

Action de grace et resiouissance de la France sur l'heureuse grossesse asseurée de la reyne. Paris: Jean Brunet, 1638.

Les Amours d'Anne d'Autriche . . . avec Monsieur . . . le C D R le véritable père de Louis XIV. Cologne: n.p., 1693.

Archives curieuses de l'histoire de France depuis Louis XI jusqu'à Louis XVIII, ou collection de pièces rares et intéressantes. 2e sér. Ed. M. L. Cimber (pseud.) et. al. Paris: Beauvais, 1834–40. Vol. 5.

Arellano, Cárlos de. *Cartas originales de don Cárlos de Arellano al Gran Duque de Lerma.* Ed. el marqués de la Fuensantana del Valle. Colección de documentos inéditos para la historia de España, Vol. 112. Madrid: Imprenta de José Perales y Martinez, 1895.

Argenson II, René de Voyer, comte d'. *Annales de la Compagnie du Saint-Sacrement.* Ed. Dom H. Beauchet-Filleau. Marseille: St.-Léon, 1900.

Arnauld, abbé Antoine. *Mémoires.* Collection des mémoires relatifs à l'histoire de France, 2e ser. Vol. 34. Ed. C. B. Petitot. Paris: Foucault, 1824).

Arnauld d'Andilly, Robert. *Mémoires.* Collection des mémoires relatifs à l'histoire de France. 2e sér. Vols 33–34. Ed. C. B. Petitot. Paris: Foucault, 1824.

Bentivoglio, Guido, cardinal. *La Nunziatura di Francia del cardinale Guido Benti-*

voglio: lettere a Scipione Borghese, cardinal nipote e segretario di stato di Paolo V.
4 vols. Ed. Luigi de Steffani. Firenze: Felice Le Monnier, 1863–70.

Bourgeois, Louise. *Observations diverses sur la stérilité, perte de fruict, fécondité, accouchements et maladies des femmes et enfans nouveau naiz.* 3 vols. in 1. Paris: Melchior Mondière, 1626.

Brienne, Henri-Auguste de Loménie, comte de. *Mémoires.* Collection des mémoires relatifs à l'histoire de France. 2e sér. Vols 35–36. Ed. C. B. Petitot. Paris: Foucault, 1824.

Brienne, Louis-Henri de Loménie, comte de (le jeune). *Mémoires inédits.* 2 vols. Ed. F. Barrière. Paris: Ponthieu et Cie., 1828.

Le Cabinet satyrique: première édition complète et critique d'après l'édition originale de 1618, augmentée des éditions suivantes, avec une notice, une bibliographie, un glossaire, des variantes et des notes. 2 vols. Ed. F. Fleuret et L. Perceau. Paris: J. Fort, 1924.

Colbert, Jean-Baptiste. *Lettres, instructions et mémoires de Colbert.* Ed Pierre Clément. Paris: Imprimerie Impériale, 1861–73. Vol. I.

Desmarets de Saint-Sorlin, Jean. *Mirame, tragicomédie.* Paris: Henri Le Gras, 1641.

Dubois de Lestourmière, Marie. *Mémoire fidèle des choses qui se sont passées à la mort de Louis XIII, fait par Dubois, l'un des valets de chambre de sa majesté.* Nouvelle collection des mémoires pour servir à l'histoire de France depuis le XIIIe siècle jusqu'à la fin du XVIIIe. 1ere sér. Vol 11. Ed. J.-F. Michaud et J.-J. F. Poujoulat. Paris: Editeur du Commentaire Analytique du Code Civil, 1836–39.

———. "Fragments des mémoires inédites de Dubois, gentilhomme servant du roi, valet de chambre de Louis XIII et de Louis XIV." Ed. Léon Aubineau. *Bibliothèque de l'Ecole des Chartes,* 2e série, 4 (1847–48): 1–45.

Erasmus, Desiderius. *The Education of a Christian Prince.* Trans. and ed. Lester K. Born. New York: Norton, 1968.

Felipe III. *Cartas de Felipe III a su hija Ana, reina de Francia, 1616–1618.* Ed. R. Martorell Tellez-Girón. Madrid: Imprenta Helénica, 1929.

Fénelon, François de Salignac de la Mothe. *Ecrits et lettres politiques, publiés sur les manuscrits autographes.* Ed. Ch. Urbain. Paris: Editions Bossard, 1921.

La Gazette de France. 1631–66.

Goulas, Nicolas, sieur de la Mothe. *Mémoires de Nicolas Goulas, gentilhomme ordinaire de la chambre du duc d'Orléans, publiès pour la première fois d'après le manuscrit original de la Bibliothèque Nationale.* Vol. I. Ed. Charles Constant. Paris: Société de l'Histoire de France, 1879.

Griselle, Eugène, éd. *Etat de la maison du roi Louis XIII, de celles de sa mère, Marie de Médicis, de ses soeurs, Chrestienne, Elisabeth et Henriette de France, de son frère, Gaston d'Orléans, de sa femme, Anne d'Autriche, de ses fils, le dauphin (Louis XIV) et Philippe d'Orléans, comprenant les années 1601 à 1665.* Paris: P. Catin, 1912.

Héroard, Jean. *Journal de Jean Héroard sur l'enfance et la jeunesse de Louis XIII.* 2 vols. Ed. E. Soulié et E. de Barthélemy. Paris: Firmin-Didot, 1868.

Isambert, François André, et. al., éds. *Receuil général des anciennes lois françaises depuis l'an 420 jusqu'à la révolution de 1789.* Paris: Belin, Le Prieur, et. al., 1821–33. Vol. 17.

Joly, Claude. *Recuil de maximes véritables et importantes pour l'institution du roy, contre la fausse et pernicieuse politique du cardinal Mazarin, prétendu surintendant de l'éducation de sa majesté.* Paris: n.p., 1663.

Journal de l'assemblée de la noblesse tenue à Paris en l'année mil six cens cinquante-un. N.p.: n.p., n.d.

La Châtre, Edmé comte de. *Mémoires contenant la fin du règne de Louis XIII et le commencement de celui de Louis XIV.* Collection des mémoires relatifs à l'histoire de France. 2e sér. Vol. 51. Ed. A. Petitot et L.-J.-N. de Monmerqué. Paris: Foucault, 1826.

La Porte, Pierre de. *Mémoires de P. de La Porte, premier valet de chambre de Louis XIV, contenant plusieurs particularités des règnes de Louis XIII et de Louis XIV.* Collection des mémoires relatifs à l'histoire de France. 2e sér. Vol. 59. Ed. A. Petitot et L.-J.-N. de Monmerqué. Paris: Foucault, 1827.

La Rochefoucauld, Francois prince de Marsillac, baron de Verteuil et duc de. *Mémoires de La Rochefoucauld.* Vols. LI–LII of Collection des mémoires relatifs à l'histoire de France. 2e sér. Vols. 51–52. Ed. A. Petitot et L.-J.-N. de Monmerqué. Paris: Foucault, 1826.

Lenet, Pierre. *Mémoires inédits concernant l'histoire du prince de Condé depuis sa naissance, en 1621, jusqu'au traité des Pyrénées, en 1659.* Nouvelle collection des mémoires pour servir à l'histoire de France. 3e sér. Vol. 2. J.-F. Michaud et J.-J. F. Poujoulat. Paris: Editeur du Commentaire Analytique du Code Civil, 1838.

Louis XIII. *Lettres de la main de Louis XIII.* Ed. E. Griselle. 2 vols. Paris: Société des Bibliophiles François chez E. Rahir, 1914.

Louis XIV. *Oeuvres.* Ed. P. H. Grimoard et P. A. Grouvelle. Paris-Strasbourg: Treuttel et Würtz, 1806. Vo. 2.

Mazarin, Jules, cardinal. *Carnet 16.* Ed. Victor Luzarche. Tours: Péricat, 1893.

———. *Lettres du cardinal Mazarin à la reine, à la princesse Palatine, etc., écrites pendant sa retraite hors de France entre 1651 et 1652.* Ed. J. A. D. Ravenel. Paris: Société de l'Histoire de France, 1836.

———. *Lettres du cardinal Mazarin où l'on voit le secret de la négotiation de la paix des Pyrénées, et la relation des conférences qu'il a eües pour ce sujet avec D. Louis de Haro, ministre d'Espagne, avec d'autres lettres très-curieuses écrites au roi et à la reine, par le même cardinal, pendant son voyage.* Nouv. éd. augmentée. Amsterdam: Henri Wetstein, 1693.

———. *Lettres du cardinal Mazarin pendant son ministère.* Eds. P. A. Chéruel et G. d'Avenel. 9 vols. Paris: Imprimerie Nationale, 1872–1906.

"Mazarinades"

Advis, remonstrance et requeste par huict paysans de huict provinces, deputés par les autres du royaume, sur les miseres et affaires du temps present, 1649, au parlement de Paris, et de ceux deputez et assemblez à Ruël pour la conferance. Paris: Composé par Misere et imprimé en Calamité, 1649.

Ballet dansé devant le roi et la reine-régente sa mère, par le trio mazarinique, pour dire adieu à la France, en vers burlesques. Paris: Claude Morlot, 1649.

Le Chevalier chrétien parlant des misères du temps, à la royne régente. Paris: n.p., 1649.

Chronologie des reynes malheureuses par l'insolence de leurs favoris, dediée à la reyne regente pour luy servir d'exemple et de miroir. Paris: Claude Morlot, 1649.

Les Convulsions de la reyne la nuit de devant le départ de Mazarin, avec la consolation qu'elle receut par l'apparition d'une bonne sainte. Paris: n.p., 1652.

La Custode de la reyne, qui dit tout. N.p.: Claude Morlot, 1649.

L'Esprit de feue la reyne-mère, parlant à la reyne, sur l'estat de la régence. Paris: n.p., 1652.

Le Miroüer de la reyne, luy représentant tous les desordres de sa régence, et luy donnant d'infaillibles moyens pour les réparer. Paris: n.p., 1652.

L'Ombre du roy d'Angleterre apparue à la reyne de France. N.p.: n.p., n.d.

Les Ris et les pleurs de la France sur la conduite de la reyne et du conseil d'état, découvrant l'origine de nos misères et des calamitez publiques. Paris: n.p., 1652.

La Vérité parlant à la reyne. N.p.: n.p., 1649.

Le Mercure françois, ou, les memoires de la suitte de l'histoire de nostre temps, sous le regne du très-chrestien roy de France et de Navarre, Louis XIII. Vols. 4–11 (1615–26).

Montglat, François de Paule de Clermont, marquis de. *Mémoires.* Collection des mémoires relatifs à l'histoire de France. 2e sér. Vols. 49–51. Ed. A. Petitot et L.-J.-N. de Monmerqué. Paris: Foucault, 1825–26.

Montpensier, Anne Marie Louise d'Orléans, duchesse de. *Mémoires de Mlle de Montpensier, fille de Gaston d'Orléans, frère de Louis XIII.* Collection des mémoires relatifs à l'histoire de France. 2e sér. Vols. 40–43. Ed. M. Petitot. Paris: Foucault, 1824–25.

Motteville, Françoise Bertaut de. *Mémoires pour servir à l'histoire d'Anne d'Autriche, épouse de Louis XIII, roi de France, par Madame de Motteville, une de ses favorites.* 5 vols. Amsterdam: Francois Changuion, 1723.

————. *Mémoires.* Collection des mémoires relatifs à l'histoire de France. 2e sér. Vols. 36–40. Ed. C. B. Petitot. Paris: Foucault, 1824.

Nemours, Marie d'Orléans, duchesse de. *Mémoires de la duchesse de Nemours.* Collection des mémoires relatifs à l'histoire de France. 2e série. Vol. 34. Ed. A. Petitot et L.-J.-N. de Monmerqué. Paris: Foucault, 1824.

Novoa, Matéas de. *Primera parte de las memorias de Matéas de Novoa, conocida hasta ahora bajo el titulo de "Historia de Felipe III, por Bernabé de Vibanco," precedida de un prólogo escrito por el Excmo. Sr. D. Antonio Cánovas del Castillo.* Colección de documentos ineditos para la historia de España. Vols. 60–61. Ed. el Marqués de la Fuensantana del Valle y J. S. Rayon. Madrid: Imprenta de Miguel Ginesta, 1875.

Orléans, Elisabeth Charlotte, duchesse d'. *Correspondance complète de Madame duchesse d'Orléans née princesse Palatine, mère du régent.* Trad. et éd. G. Brunet. 2 vols. Paris: Charpentier, 1857.

Ormesson, Olivier Lefèvre d'. *Journal d'Olivier Lefèvre d'Ormesson et extraits des mémoires d'André Lefèvre d'Ormesson.* Ed. P. A. Chéruel. 2 vols. Paris: Imprimerie Impériale, 1860–61.

Patin, Gui. *Lettres de Gui Patin à Charles Spon, médecin à Lyon.* Nouv. éd. Ed. J. H. Réveillé-Parise. Paris: J.-B. Baillière, 1846, Vol. 3.

Rapport fidèle de tout ce qui s'est passé aux voyages, tant de Madame Anne d'Autriche, royne de France et de Navarre, que de Madame Isabel de Bourbon, princesse d'Espagne. Lyon: Simon Millanges, 1616.

Récit de la maladie de la reyne, fait le sixiesme fevrier 1620. Paris: F. Bourriquant, n.d.

Récit véritable de la magnifique entrée de la reyne de France en la ville de Lyon, avec l'ordre des préparatifs, triomphes et magnificences faictes à sa majesté. Paris: n.p., 1622.

Registres des délibérations du bureau de la ville de Paris. Eds. Henry de Suriray de Saint Rémy, et. al. Paris: Imprimerie Nationale, 1883–1953. Vols. 16–18.

Retz, Jean François Paul de Gondi, cardinal de. *Mémoires.* Ed. M. Allen et E. Thomas. Paris: Gallimard, 1956.

Richelieu, Armand Jean Du Plessis, cardinal duc de. *Mémoires du cardinal de Richelieu sur le règne de Louis XIII.* Collection des mémoires relatifs à l'histoire de France. 2e sér. Vols. 21–30. Ed. C. B. Petitot. Paris: Foucault, 1823.

————. *Les Papiers de Richelieu.* Ed. Pierre Grillon. 4 vols. Paris: Pedone, 1975–80.

Saint-Simon, Louis de Rouvroy, duc de. *Mémoires de Saint Simon.* Nouv. éd. Ed. A. de Boislisle, L. Lecestre, J. de Boislisle. Paris: Hachette, 1879–1930. Vol. 28.

Tallemant des Réaux, Gédéon. *Historiettes.* Ed. G, Mongrédien. 8 vols. Paris: Garnier, 1932–34.

Talon, Omer. *Mémoires de feu M Omer Talon.* La Haye: Gosse et Neaulme, 1732, Vol. 3.

Tillières, Tanneguy Leveneur, comte de. *Mémoires inédites du comte Leveneur de Tillières, ambassadeur en Angleterre, sur la cour de Charles I, et son mariage avec Henriette de France.* Ed. M. C. Hippeau. Paris: Poulat-Malassis, 1862.

Varin, Jean Philippe. *Le Grand Jubilé de joye donné à la France pour le très-heureux mariage et arrivée de Louis XIII avec la serenissime princesse infante d'Espagne, Anne d'Autriche.* Paris: N. Alexandre, 1616.

———. *Le* Te Deum *de la France, pour le heureux mariage du roy avec la sérénissime infante d'Espagne.* Paris: N. Alexandre, 1615.

Vauquelin des Yveteaux, Nicolas. *Oeuvres complètes.* Ed. G. Mongrédien. Paris: A. Picard, 1921.

Vincent de Paul, Saint. *Correspondence, entretiens, documents.* Ed. Pierre Coste. Paris: J. Gabalda, 1920–70. Vol. 13.

SECONDARY WORKS

Adam, Antoine, *Histoire de la littérature française au XVIIe siècle.* 4 vols. Paris: Domat, 1948–54.

Allier, Raoul. *La Cabale des dévots, 1627–1666.* 1902; rpt. Genève: Slatkine Reprints, 1970.

Ariès, Philippe. *Centuries of Childhood: A Social History of Family Life.* Trans. Robert Baldick. New York: Vintage Books, 1965.

Aston, Trevor, ed. *Crisis in Europe, 1560–1660.* New York: Doubleday-Anchor, 1967.

Aulanier, Christiane. *Histoire du palais et du musée du Louvre.* Paris: Editions des Musées Nationaux 1947–71. Vols. 5, 8.

Aumale, Henri d'Orléans, duc d'. *Histoire des princes de Condé, pendant les XVIe XVIIe siècles.* Paris: C. Lévy, 1889–92. Vols. 5–6.

Bapst, Germain. *Histoire des joyaux de la couronne.* Paris: Hachette, 1889.

Baschet, Armand. *Histoire secrète du mariage de Louis XIII et d'Anne d'Austriche: le roi chez la reine.* Nouv. éd. Paris: Plon, 1933.

Batiffol, Louis. *La Duchesse de Chevreuse: une vie d'aventures et d'intrigues sous Louis XIII.* Paris: Hachette, 1913.

———. *Le Louvre sous Henri IV et Louis XIII: la vie de la cour en France au XVIIe siècle.* Paris: Calmann-Lévy, 1930.

———. *Richelieu et le roi Louis XIII: les véritables rapports du souverain et de son ministre.* Paris: Calmann-Lévy, 1934.

———. *Le Roi Louis XIII à vingt ans.* Paris: Calmann-Lévy, 1910.

———. *La Vie intime d'une reine de France au XVIIe siècle.* Paris: Calmann-Lévy, 1906.

Bibliothèque Nationale, *Mazarin: homme d'état et collectionneur, 1602–1661.* Exposition organisée pour le troisième centenaire de sa mort. Ed. M. Laurain-Portemer et R.-A. Weigert. Paris: n.p., 1961.

Bonney, Richard. *The King's Debts: Finance and Politics in France, 1589–1661.* Oxford: Clarendon Press, 1981.

———. *Political Change in France under Richelieu and Mazarin, 1624–1661.* Oxford: Oxford University Press, 1978.

Bremond, Henri. *Histoire littéraire du sentiment religieux en France depuis les guerres de religion jusqu'à nos jours.* 12 vols. Paris: Bloud et Gay, 1916–33.

Buchanan, Meriel. *Anne of Austria, the Infanta Queen.* 3d prtg. London: Hutchinson and Co., 1937.

Busson, Henri. *La Pensée religieuse française de Charron à Pascal.* Paris: Librairie Philosophique J. Vrin, 1933.

———. *La Religion des classiques, 1660–1685.* Paris: Presses Universitaires de France, 1948.

Capefigue, Jean Baptiste Honoré Raymond. *Anne d'Autriche, reine-régente, et la minorité de Louis XIV.* Paris: Amyot, 1861.

———. *Richelieu, Mazarin, la Fronde et le règne de Louis XIV.* 8 vols. in 4. Paris: Duféy, 1835–36.

Carmona, Michel. *Marie de Médicis.* Paris: Fayard, 1981.

Carré, Henri. *L'Enfance et la première jeunesse de Louis XIV.* Paris: A. Michel, 1944.

Champier, Victor, et G. R. Sandoz. *Le Palais-Royal d'après des documents inédits, 1629–1900.* 2 vols. Paris: Société de Propagation des Livres d'Art, 1900.

Chérot, Henri. *La Première Jeunesse de Louis XIV, 1649–1653, d'après la correspondance inédite du P. Charles Paulin, son premier confesseur.* Lille: Desclée, de Brouwer et Cie., 1892.

Chéruel, Pierre Adolphe. *Histoire de France pendant la minorité de Louis XIV.* 4 vols. Paris: Hachette, 1879–80.

———. *Histoire de France sous le ministère de Mazarin.* 3 vols. Paris: Hachette, 1882.

Chevallier, Pierre. *Louis XIII: le roi cornélien.* Paris: Fayard, 1979.

Cousin, Victor. *Madame de Chevreuse: nouvelles études sur les femmes illustres et la société du XVIIe siècle.* 7e éd. Paris: Perrin, 1886.

———. *Madame de Hautefort: nouvelles études sur les femmes illustres et la société du XVIIe siècle.* 5e éd. Paris: Perrin et Cie., 1886.

Dethan, Georges. *Gaston d'Orléans: conspirateur et prince charmant.* Paris: Librairie Arthème Fayard, 1959.

———. *Mazarin et ses amis.* Paris: Berger-Levrault, 1968.

———. *Mazarin: un homme de paix à l'âge baroque, 1602–1661.* Paris: Imprimerie Nationale, 1981.

Devèze, M. *L'Espagne de Philippe IV, 1621–1665.* Paris: Société d'Edition d'Enseignement Supérieur, 1970–71. Vol. I.

Dulong, Claude, *Anne d'Autriche, mère de Louis XIV.* Paris: Hachette, 1980.

Dumas, Alexandre (père). *Les Trois Mousquetaires.* 4 vols. Paris: Baudry, 1844.

———. *Vingt ans après: suite des "Trois mousquetaires."* 5 vols. Paris: Baudry, 1845.

Elliott, J. H. *Richelieu and Olivares.* Cambridge: Cambridge University Press, 1984.

Erlanger, Philippe. *The King's Minion: Richelieu, Louis XIII, and the Affair of Cinq-Mars.* Trans. G. and H. Cremonesi. Englewood Cliffs, N.J.: Prentice-Hall, 1972.

Fichtner, Paula Sutter. *Ferdinand I of Austria: The Politics of Dynasticism in the Age of the Reformation.* Boulder, Col.: East European Monographs, 1982.

Franklin, Alfred. *L'Enfant, la layette, la nourrice, la vie de famille, les jouets et les jeux.* La Vie privée d'autrefois. Vol. 19. Paris: Firmin Didot, 1896.

_____. *L'Enfant, la naissance, le baptême.* La Vie privée d'autrefois. Vol. 17. Paris: Firmin Didot, 1895.

Freer, Martha Walker. *The Regency of Anne of Austria.* London: Tinsley Bros., 1866.

Golden, Richard M. *The Godly Rebellion: Parisian Curés and the Religious Fronde, 1652–1662.* Chapel Hill: University of North Carolina Press, 1981.

Griffet, Henri. *Histoire du règne de Louis XIII, roi de France et de Navarre.* Histoire de France depuis l'établissement de la monarchie françoise dans les Gaules. Vols. 13–15. Nouv. éd. Ed. Gabriel Daniel, S.J. Paris: Librairies Associés, 1856.

Grouchy, vicomte de. *Inventaire après décès de la reine Anne d'Autriche, 1666.* Paris: privately published, 1892.

Guth, Paul. *Mazarin.* Paris: Flammarion, 1972.

Hanotaux, Gabriel, et Auguste de Caumont, duc de La Force. *Histoire du cardinal de Richelieu.* 6 vols. Paris: Société de l'Histoire Nationale, 1893–1947.

Henriot, Emile. *Courrier littéraire: XVIIe siècle.* Nouv. éd. augmentée. 2 vols. Paris: Albin Michel, 1958.

Herbillon, Emile Emmanuel. *Anne d'Autriche, reine, mère, régente.* Paris: J. Tallandier, 1939.

Hunt, David. *Parents and Children in History: The Psychology of Family Life in Early Modern France.* New York: Basic Books, 1970.

Kermina, Françoise. *Marie de Médicis: reine, régente et rebelle.* Paris: Perrin, 1979.

Knachel, Philip A. *England and the Fronde: The Impact of the English Civil War and Revolution on France.* Ithaca: Cornell University Press, 1967.

Kossmann, Ernst. *La Fronde.* Leiden: Universitaire Pers, 1954.

Lacour-Gayet, Georges. *L'Education politique de Louis XIV.* Paris: Hachette, 1898.

Laurain-Portemer, Madeleine. *Etudes mazarines.* Vol. I. Paris: Diffusion de Boccard, 1981.

La Varende, Jean de. *Anne d'Autriche, femme de Louis XIII, 1601–1666.* Paris: Les Editions de France, 1938.

Lavisse, Ernest. *Louis XIV, de 1643 à 1685.* Histoire de France depuis les origines jusqu'à la révolution française. Vol. 7. Ed. Ernest Lavisse. Paris: Hachette, 1905-7.

Lee, Maurice, Jr. *James I and Henri IV: An Essay in English Foreign Policy, 1603–1610.* Urbana: University of Illinois Press, 1970.

Lightman, Harriet L. "Sons and Mothers: Queens and Minor Kings in French Constitutional Law." University Microfilms International, (1981), 8220695 (Bryn Mawr).

Lintilhac, Eugène François Léon. *Histoire générale du théâtre en France.* Paris: Flammarion, 1904-9. Vol. 3.

Lockyer, Roger. *Buckingham: The Life and Political Career of George Villiers, First Duke of Buckingham, 1592–1628.* London: Longman, 1981.

Lorris, Pierre-Georges. *La Fronde.* Paris: Albin Michel, 1961.

Lougee, Carolyn C. *Le Paradis des femmes: Women, Salons, and Social Stratification in Seventeenth-Century France.* Princeton, N.J.: Princeton University Press, 1976.

Madelin, Louis. *Une Révolution manquée: la Fronde.* Paris: Plon, 1931.

Major, J. Russell. *Representative Government in Early Modern France.* Studies Presented to the International Commission for the History of Representative and Parliamentary Institutions. Vol. 63. New Haven, Conn.: Yale University Press, 1980.

Mariéjol, Jean-Hippolyte. *Henri IV et Louis XIII.* Histoire de France depuis les origines jusqu'à la révolution française. Ed. Ernest Lavisse. Vol. 6. Paris: Hachette 1905.

Marvick, Elizabeth Wirth. "Nature *versus* Nurture: Patterns and Trends in Seventeenth-Century French Child-Rearing." In *The History of Childhood*. Ed. Lloyd De Mause. New York: Psychohistory Press, 1974, pp. 259–301.

———. *The Young Richelieu: A Psychoanalytic Approach to Leadership*. Chicago: University of Chicago Press, 1983.

McGowan, Margaret M. *L'Art du ballet de cour en France, 1581–1643*. Paris: Editions du Centre National de la Recherche Scientifique, 1978.

Michelet, Jules. *Histoire de France*. Paris: Hachette, Chamerot, Lauvereyns, 1833–1867. Vol. 12.

Molinier, Victor. *Notice sur cette question historique: Anne d'Autriche et Mazarin étaient-ils mariés?*. Paris: A. Rousseau, 1887.

Mongrédien, Georges. *Etude sur la vie et l'oeuvre de Nicolas Vauquelin, seigneur des Yvetaux, précepteur de Louis XIII, 1567–1649*. 1921; rpt. Genève: Slatkine Reprints, 1967.

———. *La Journée des dupes: 10 novembre 1630*. Paris: Gallimard, 1961.

Moote, A. Lloyd. *The Revolt of the Judges: The Parlement of Paris and the Fronde, 1643–1652*. Princeton, N.J.: Princeton University Press, 1971.

Mousnier, Roland E. *L'Assassinat de Henri IV, 14 mai 1610*. Paris: Gallimard, 1964.

———. *Fureurs paysannes: les paysans dans les révoltes du XVIIe siècle, France, Russie, Chine*. Paris: Calmann-Lévy, 1967.

———. *The Institutions of France under the Absolute Monarchy, 1598–1789: Society and the State*. Trans. Brian Pearce. Chicago: University of Chicago Press, 1979.

———. ed. *Lettres et mémoires adressés au chancelier Séguier, 1633–1649*. 2 vols. Paris: Presses Universitaires de France, 1964.

Mousnier, Roland E., J. P. Labatut et Y. P. Durand éds. *Problèmes de stratification sociale: deux cahiers de la noblesse pour les états-généraux de 1649–1651*. Paris: Presses Universitaires de France, 1965.

Murat, Inès. *Colbert*, Paris: Arthème Fayard, 1980.

Pérez-Martin, Maria Jesús. *Margarita de Austria*. Madrid: Espasa-Calpe, 1961.

Perrens, François Tommy. *Les Mariages espagnols sous le règne de Henri IV et la régence de Marie de Médicis, 1602–1615*. Paris: Didier, 1869.

Porchnev, Boris F. *Les Soulèvements populaires en France de 1623 à 1648*. Trad. par un groupe d'historiens français. Paris: S.E.V.P.E.N., 1963.

Ranum, Orest. *Paris in the Age of Absolutism: An Essay*. New York: John Wiley and Sons, 1968.

———. *Richelieu and the Councillors of Louis XIII: A Study of the Secretaries of State and Superintendents of Finance in the Ministry of Richelieu, 1635–1642*. Oxford: Clarendon Press, 1963.

Robiquet, Paul. *Le Coeur d'une reine: Anne d'Autriche, Louis XIII et Mazarin*. Paris: Félix Alcan, 1912.

Roca, Emile. *Le Grand Siècle intime: le règne de Richelieu, 1617–1642*. Paris: Perrin, 1906.

———. *Le Grand Siècle intime: de Richelieu à Mazarin, 1642–1644*. Paris: Perrin, 1908.

Ruprich-Robert, Victor. *L'Eglise et le monastère du Val-de-Grâce, 1645–1665*. Paris: V. A. Morel et Cie., 1875.

Saint-Félix, Tomy. *La Reine stérile*. Paris: Del Duca, 1958.

Sainte-Aulaire, Louis Clair de Beaupoil, marquis de. *Histoire de la Fronde*. 3 vols. Paris: Baudoin Frères, 1827.

Salmon, J. H. M. *Cardinal de Retz: The Anatomy of a Conspirator*. New York: Macmillan, 1970.

Sauval, Henri. *Histoire et recherches des antiquités de la ville de Paris*. Paris: C. Moette et J. Chardon, 1724. Vol. 2.

Servier, Janvier J.-J. *Le Val-de-Grâce: histoire du monastère et de l'hôpital militaire.* Paris: G. Masson, 1888.

Snyders, Georges. *La Pédagogie en France aux XVIIe et XVIIIe siècles.* Paris: Presses Universitaires de France, 1965.

Société de l'Histoire de France. *Bibliographie des Mazarinades*. Ed. C. Moreau. Paris: Jules Renouard et Cie., 1850. Vol. 1.

Solomon, Howard M. *Public Welfare, Science, and Propaganda: The Innovations of Théophraste Renaudot*. Princeton, N.J.: Princeton University Press, 1972.

Stone, Lawrence. *The Family, Sex, and Marriage in England, 1500–1800*. New York: Harper and Row, 1977.

Taillandier, Madeleine Marie Louise Saint-René. *La Jeunesse du grand roi: Louis XIV et Anne d'Autriche*. Paris: Plon, 1945.

Tapié, Victor-L. *La France de Louis XIII et de Richelieu*. Paris: Flammarion, 1952.

––––––. *La Politique étrangère de la France et le début de la guerre de trente ans, 1616–1621*. Paris: Ernest Leroux, 1934.

Vaunois, Louis. *Vie de Louis XIII*. Nouv. éd. revue et augmentée. Paris: Del Duca, 1961.

Walckenaer, Charles Athanase, baron. *Mémoires touchant la vie et les écrits de Marie de Rabutin-Chantal, dame de Bourbilly, marquise de Sévigné, durant la régence et la Fronde*. Paris: Firmin Didot Frères, 1842–45. Vols. 1, 3.

Williamson, Hugh Ross. *George Villiers: First Duke of Buckingham*. London: Duckworth, 1940.

Wolf, John B. "The Formation of a King." In *Louis XIV and the Craft of Kingship*. Ed. John C. Rule. Columbus: Ohio State University Press, 1969. Pp. 102–31.

––––––. *Louis XIV*. New York: W. W. Norton and Co., 1968.

PERIODICAL ARTICLES

Alcouffe, Daniel. "Les Macé, ébénistes et peintres." *Bulletin de la Société de l'Histoire de l'Art Français*, 1971, pp. 61–82.

Batiffol, Louis. "Un Jeune Ménage royal." *La Revue de Paris* 16 (Nov.-Dec. 1909): 105–32.

Chéruel, Pierre Adolphe. "Les Carnets de Mazarin pendant la Fronde, Sept.-Oct. 1648." *Revue Historique* 20 (Mai-Août 1877): 103–38.

Cordey, Jean. "L'Inventaire après décès d'Anne d'Autriche et le mobilier du Louvre." *Bulletin de la Société de l'Histoire de l'Art Français*, 1930, pp. 209–75.

Cousin, Victor. "Des Carnets autographes du cardinal Mazarin, conservés à la Bibliothèque Impériale." *Journal des Savants* 1854, pp. 457–70, 521–47, 600–626, 687–719, 753–73; 1855, pp. 19–43, 84–103, 161–84, 217–42, 304–24, 430–47, 525–45, 622–37, 703–19; 1856, pp. 48–60, 105–19.

Darricau, Raymond, et Madeleine Laurain. "La Mort du cardinal Mazarin." *Annuaire-Bulletin de la Société de l'Histoire de France*, 1960, pp. 59–120.

Dethan, Georges. "Madame de Motteville et Mazarin, ou le complexe d'Oenone." Société d'Etude du XVIIe Siècle. *Actes et colloques*, No. 22. "Les Valeurs chez les mémorialistes français du XVIIe siécle avant la Fronde." Colloque de Strasbourg et Metz, 18–20 mai 1978. Paris: Klincksieck, 1979, pp. 103–10.

———. "Mazarin avant le ministère." *Revue Historique* 227 (Jan.-Mars 1962): 33–66.

———. "Retz juge de Mazarin." Accademia Nazionale dei Lincei. *Atti dei convegni Lincei*, No. 35. Colloquio italo-francese: "Il Cardinale Mazzarino in Francia." Roma, 16–17 maggio 1977. Roma: Accademia Nazionale dei Lincei, 1977, pp. 77–85.

Fichtner, Paula Sutter. "Dynastic Marriage in Sixteenth-Century Habsburg Diplomacy and Statecraft: An Interdisciplinary Approach." *American Historical Review* 81 (April 1976): 243–65.

Kleinman, Ruth. "Belated Crusaders: Religious Fears in Anglo-French Diplomacy, 1654–1655." *Church History* 44 (March 1975): 1–13.

———. "Changing Interpretations of the Edict of Nantes: The Administrative Aspect, 1643–1661." *French Historical Studies* 10 (Fall 1978): 541–71.

———. "Facing Cancer in the Seventeenth Century: The Last Illness of Anne of Austria, 1664–1666." *Advances in Thanatology*, vol. 4, No. 1 (1977), pp. 37–55.

———. "Gratitude Revisited: The Declaration of Saint-Germain, 1652." *French Historical Studies* 5 (Spring 1968): 249–62.

Laurain-Portemer, Madeleine. "La Politique artistique de Mazarin." Accademia Nazionale dei Lincei. *Atti dei convegni Lincei*, No. 35. Colloquio italo-francese. "Il Cardinale Mazzarino in Francia." Roma, 16–17 maggio 1977. Roma: Accademia Nazionale dei Lincei, 1977, pp. 41–76.

———. "Le Statut de Mazarin dans l'église: apercus sur le haut clergé de la contre-réforme." *Bibliothèque de l'Ecole des Chartes* 127 (1969): 355–419; 128 (1970): 5–80.

Marvick, Elizabeth Wirth. "The Character of Louis XIII: The Role of his Physician." *Journal of Interdisciplinary History* 4 (Winter 1974): 347–74.

———. "Childhood History and Decisions of State." *History of Childhood Quarterly: The Journal of Psychohistory* 2 (Fall 1974): 135–80.

———. "Favorites in Early Modern Europe: A Recurring Psychopolitical Role." *Journal of Psychohistory* 10 (Spring 1983): 463–89.

Pagès, Georges. "Autour du 'grand orage': Richelieu et Marillac, deux politiques." *Revue Historique* 179 (Jan.-Juin 1937): 63–97.

Ranum, Orest. "The French Ritual of Tyrannicide in the Late Sixteenth Century." *Sixteenth Century Journal*, vol. 11, No. 1 (1980), pp. 63–81.

Weigert, Jean-Armand. "Deux marchés passés par Simon Vouet pour les décorations de l'appartement d'Anne d'Autriche au Palais-Royal, 1645." *Bulletin de la Société de l'Histoire de l'Art Français*, 1951, pp. 101–5.

INDEX